REGULATORY STRATEGIES FOR ENERGY AND FINANCE

This open access book examines adaptive regulatory frameworks to tackle the emerging risks and opportunities of the digital transformation in the critical sectors of energy and finance.

With contributions from leading experts across Europe, the book reveals how digitalisation impacts public values, policy goals, and regulatory approaches, providing comparative insights on the benefits and risks of digital transformation. Through case studies on cybersecurity, data privacy, and regulatory sandboxes, it also explores the evolving role of non-state actors.

By advancing forward-looking solutions such as dynamic regulation and collaborative governance, the chapters are tailored to meet the unique regulatory needs of the critical sectors of energy and finance.

Ideal for academics, policymakers, and industry leaders, the book highlights strategies for achieving sustainability, stability, and resilience while fostering innovation. For those seeking actionable insights for policy adaptation or building industry resilience, it delivers indispensable tools to navigate the complexities of today's digital economy.

Regulatory Strategies for Energy and Finance

Sustainability in a Digitalised World

Edited by
Shanya Ruhela
Olga Hrynkiv
and
Saskia Lavrijssen

•HART•
OXFORD • LONDON • NEW YORK • NEW DELHI • SYDNEY

HART PUBLISHING

Bloomsbury Publishing Plc

Kemp House, Chawley Park, Cumnor Hill, Oxford, OX2 9PH, UK

1385 Broadway, New York, NY 10018, USA

Bloomsbury Publishing Ireland Limited, 29 Earlsfort Terrace, Dublin 2, D02 AY28, Ireland

HART PUBLISHING, the Hart/Stag logo, BLOOMSBURY and the Diana logo are trademarks of Bloomsbury Publishing Plc

First published in Great Britain 2026

A catalogue record for this book is available from the British Library.

A catalogue record for this book is available from the Library of Congress.

Library of Congress Control Number: 2025945688

ISBN:	HB:	978-1-50998-748-1
	ePDF:	978-1-50998-750-4
	ePub:	978-1-50998-749-8

Typeset by Compuscript Ltd, Shannon

For product safety related questions contact productsafety@bloomsbury.com

To find out more about our authors and books visit www.hartpublishing.co.uk. Here you will find extracts, author information, details of forthcoming events and the option to sign up for our newsletters.

This edited volume is dedicated to the power of collaboration – between energy and finance, between scholars and practitioners who work in different areas and between ideas and action. It is a testament to the synergies that emerge when diverse perspectives come together to address the complex challenges of our time.

FOREWORD

Academic literature studying how digitalisation accelerates efforts to promote sustainability has grown exponentially in modern times. It cannot be otherwise: the challenges of the 21st century – climate change, economic inequality, geopolitical uncertainty, and technological disruption – require an integrated response that harnesses the transformative potential of digitalisation without compromising the imperative of sustainability. Among the most pivotal domains in this pursuit are energy and finance. These two sectors not only undergird global economies and modern lifestyles but also act as powerful levers through which climate and sustainability objectives can either be achieved or undermined. Crucially, both sectors are prone to shocks in a polycrisis environment. In this setting, identifying adequate, smart and suitable regulatory responses remains a conundrum for regulators globally. Digital transformation and ever-increasing levels of cross-border investment (and economic activity, more generally) only complicates any regulatory effort, notably when made ex ante in order to address vulnerabilities. While both sectors have their own peculiarities and characteristics, systemic risk is a common theme transcending both sectors.

Digitalisation has become a defining feature of this dual transformation. As the introduction to this volume notes, digital technologies are reshaping not only business models and markets but also regulatory thinking and governance capacity. From blockchain-based peer-to-peer energy trading and AI-driven credit scoring to satellite-powered ESG (environmental, social, governance) monitoring and real-time regulatory oversight, data and algorithms radically alter the structure of both sectors. Yet, digitalisation also introduces systemic risks, amplifies asymmetries of power and information, and tests the limits of existing institutions.

This timely edited volume is a welcome addition in the relevant academic scholarship, not only because it underscores the importance of energy and finance for a sustainable future but also because it takes a hands-on approach to address both theoretical and practical issues surrounding the twin challenge of the green and digital transition. The contributors to this volume are well-versed into the pressing issues that regulators face, from addressing vulnerabilities in retail markets and critical infrastructures to boosting RegTech and SupTech to collaborating with innovators in energy and finance to jointly identify loopholes or reaching out to fellow regulators in Europe and beyond in order to promote sustainability without endangering consumer protection, data protection or innovation.

Decarbonising this sector through renewable energy deployment, smart grid development, and electrification is critical to achieving the goals set out in the Paris Agreement and the Sustainable Development Goals (SDGs). At the same time, the financial system – through capital allocation, investment decisions, and risk pricing – acts as a gatekeeper of economic transformation. The United Nations Environment Programme Financial Initiative (UNEP FI) estimates that we need $5–7 trillion of annual investment in sustainable infrastructure and clean technologies until 2030 to attain the SDGs worldwide. This unprecedented level of investment calls for cost-effective, smart solutions that fully deploy digital means and robust, well-functioning institutions, including financial institutions and energy firms that are equipped to support long-term, responsible decision-making for the common good over short-term returns.

This edited volume explores how regulation can evolve to keep pace with these developments. It positions regulatory strategy not as an obstacle to innovation, but as a critical enabler of sustainable, inclusive, and resilient socio-technical systems. Drawing on both sector-specific and cross-sectoral insights, contributors invariably demonstrate that digitalisation cannot be separated from the values it promotes or erodes. Justice, accountability, affordability, and non-discrimination must remain central to the development and deployment of technological solutions.

Importantly, the volume resists viewing regulation solely through the lens of law. Instead, it conceptualises regulatory strategy broadly, integrating formal legal norms with informal or experimental governance tools, inter-organisational coordination, and participatory mechanisms. Energy and financial regulators are increasingly operating in polycentric environments where non-state actors – platforms, data intermediaries, civic technologists – play growing roles in shaping outcomes. In this context, flexible, adaptive, and value-oriented regulatory approaches are necessary.

A noteworthy innovation in this regard is the emphasis on regulatory sandboxes, that is, controlled environments for testing new technologies and business models within regulatory oversight, as tools for experimentation and institutional learning. As highlighted in various contributions, sandboxes offer a middle ground between rigid adherence to outdated rules and a laissez-faire approach vulnerable to market excesses and consumer harm. Yet, as several contributors caution, Member States face limitations under EU law in fully leveraging sandbox approaches, raising important questions about the balance between national discretion and supranational coherence in sustainability governance.

The importance of collaborative regulation and governance as well as multi-stakeholder alignment also stands out in this volume. As the energy and finance sectors become increasingly interdependent – consider, for example, the role of green bonds in financing solar parks or the use of stablecoins in cross-border energy settlements – regulatory strategies must facilitate collaboration across silos. Only through such coordination can we meet the dual demands of digital transformation and environmental sustainability.

In summary, this volume does not merely document the pressures facing energy and financial regulators in an age of rapid technological change; it provides an ambitious and nuanced roadmap for embedding sustainability within regulatory design. It brings together diverse academic voices to chart the evolution of law and governance in critical infrastructures and lays the groundwork for forward-looking, normatively grounded policymaking. As societies confront an increasingly complex future, the ideas presented here remind us that regulation is not merely about containment but also about enabling managed transformation.

Panagiotis Delimatsis

ACKNOWLEDGEMENTS

This edited volume would not have been possible without the generous support of our funders: the TLS DLS Sectorplan, *the NWO/NGinfra funded VIA AUGUSTA project,* and the Tilburg University Library.

We are deeply grateful to the discussants, moderators, and participants of the *Governing the Giant: Workshop on Energy and Finance in the Era of Digitalization on May 31, 2024* for their insightful contributions, which enriched this volume in countless ways.

Finally, we thank the anonymous peer reviewers for their valuable comments and constructive feedback.

CONTENTS

CONTRIBUTORS

Tom AE Aben is an assistant professor at the University of Warwick, UK.

Max Baumgart is an associate professor of energy law and blockchain at the University of Lucerne's Institute for Blockchain Research (ZIBR), Switzerland.

Magdalena Brewczyńska is a postdoctoral researcher in AlgoSoc Project at Tilburg Institute for Law, Technology and Society (TILT), the Netherlands.

Din Buljević holds a Master's degree in Law & Technology from Tilburg University, the Netherlands.

Inge Graef is a vice dean of research and an associate professor of competition law at Tilburg University, the Netherlands. She is affiliated with the Tilburg Institute for Law, Technology and Society (TILT) and the Tilburg Law and Economics Center (TILEC).

Liebrich M Hiemstra is an assistant professor of climate change and financial regulation at the Vrije Universiteit in Amsterdam and senior legal counsel at Vattenfall, the Netherlands.

Olga Hrynkiv is a postdoctoral researcher and lecturer at Tilburg University, the Netherlands.

Eyup Kun is a doctoral researcher at KU Leuven Center for IT and IP Law, Belgium.

Shirley Kempeneer is an assistant professor at Tilburg University, the Netherlands.

Saskia Lavrijssen is the dean of the Nijmegen School of Management and professor of governance of responsible energy transitions at Radboud University in the Netherlands.

Shanya Ruhela is a postdoctoral researcher at Tilburg University, the Netherlands.

Kanerva Sunila works as counsel at Castrén & Snellman Attorneys Ltd, Finland.

Wendy van der Valk holds the Nevi chair in Purchasing & Supply Chain Management at Tilburg University, the Netherlands. Wendy is the main applicant of the *NWO/NGinfra funded VIA AUGUSTA project* (439.20.805; 2022–2026) and a co-applicant for the LONGA VIA project, also funded by NWO/NGinfra (439.16.807; 2018–2021).

Jasper van den Boom is an assistant professor at Leiden University, the Netherlands.

Emanuel van Praag is a professor of financial technology (FinTech) and law at Erasmus School of Law and a practicing lawyer with HVG Law LLP, the Netherlands.

Renske van 't Veer is a PhD candidate at the Faculty of Technology, Policy and Management at Delft University of Technology in collaboration with Tilburg University Institute for Law, Technology and Society (TILT), the Netherlands.

David Wodak is a PhD candidate at Tilburg University, the Netherlands, and is one of the primary researchers in the NWO and *NWO/NGinfra funded VIA AUGUSTA project*.

ABBREVIATIONS

ACER	Agency for the Cooperation of Energy Regulators
AFM	Authority for Financial Markets
AI	artificial intelligence
API	application programming interface
APP	authorised push payment
ASPSP	account servicing payment service provider
ATM	Automated Teller Machine
BMWi	German Federal Ministry of Economic Affairs and Energy
CBDC	Central Bank Digital Currency
CCPA	California Consumer Privacy Act
CEER	Council of European Energy Regulators
CGAP	Consultative Group to Assist the Poor
CI	critical infrastructure
CSDDD	Corporate Sustainability Due Diligence Directive
CSRD	Corporate Sustainability Reporting Directive
DNB	Dutch National Bank
DORA	Digital Operational Resilience Act (2022/2554)
DSO	Distribution System Operator
ECB	European Central Bank
EDSEP	Executive Order Decentral, Sustainable Electricity Production Experiments
EFDS	European Financial Data Space
EFT	Electronic Funds Transfer

EPI	European Payments Initiative
ESAP	European Single Access Point
ESG	Environmental, Social and Governance
ESMA	European Securities and Markets Authority
ESRB	European Systemic Risk Board
ETS	Emissions Trading System
EU	European Union
FCA	Financial Conduct Authority
FDSS	Financial Data Sharing Schemes
FEs	financial entities
FIDA	Financial Data Access
GDPR	General Data Protection Regulation
HTNO	Hydrogen Transmission Network Operators
IBAN	International Bank Account Number
ICT	Information and Communications Technology
MiCA	Markets in Crypto-Assets Regulation
MiFID II	Markets in Financial Instruments Directive
NAO	network administrative organisation
NFC	Near-Field Communication
NIS 2 Directive	Network and Information Security Directive (2)
NRA	National Regulatory Authority
NZIA	Net-Zero Industry Act
PED	Positive Energy District
PIN	personal identification number
PIS	payment initiation service
PISP	payment initiation service provider
POS	point of sale
PSD2	Second Payment Services Directive

PSP	payment service provider
PSR	Payment Services Regulation
RED	Renewable Energy Directive
SCA	strong customer authentication
SDGs	Sustainable Development Goals
SWIFT	Society for Worldwide Interbank Financial Telecommunication
UCPD	Unfair Commercial Practices Directive
UK	United Kingdom
US	United States of America

1

Introduction

OLGA HRYNKIV, SHANYA RUHELA AND SASKIA LAVRIJSSEN

Technological innovation requires legal innovation.

1. Introduction

'r/WallStreetBets' is a fully virtual platform where anonymous users often share sarcastic and comedic messages on the stock market and sometimes advise each other on trading. It's a location on Reddit, the Front Page of the Internet.[1] No one would have predicted the emergence and significance of this platform before the GameStop incident in 2021.[2] Users of this platform identified the stock of GameStop as undervalued and heavily shorted by large hedge funds. In a move that defied the expectations of the Wall Street gurus, these users, collectively, based on the discussion on the anonymous forum, began purchasing and hoarding the stocks of GameStop.[3] This unpredicted action led to a dramatic increase in the stock price, from USD 16 to USD 347 within a span of one month.[4] Many trading companies, such as Robinhood, could not handle the astronomical increase in trading traffic, which led to outages. Investigations into the activities of Robinhood revealed that, along with other alleged frauds, the trading platform had failed to add a simple computer code, leading to certain errors that the US financial regulator was incapable of identifying and correcting on time.[5]

Institutional structures and large trading companies sided with the wealthy players in the market and protected only their interests to the detriment of smaller

[1] P Singer and others, 'Evolution of Reddit: From the Front Page of the Internet to a Self-Referential Community?' (2014). Available at: https://arxiv.org/abs/1402.1386.

[2] D Bradley and others, 'Place your Bets? The Value of Investment Research on Reddit's Wallstreetbets' (2024) 37 *The Review of Financial Studies* 1409.

[3] S Long and others, '"I Just Like the Stock": The Role of Reddit Sentiment in the GameStop Share Rally' (2023) 58(1) *Financial Review* 19.

[4] Z Umar and others, 'A Tale of Company Fundamentals vs Sentiment Driven Pricing: The Case of GameStop' (2021) 30 *Journal of Behavioral and Experimental Finance* 100501.

[5] P Singer and others, 'Evolution of Reddit' (n 1).

traders.[6] Ultimately, this incident primarily affected smaller traders by not allowing them to execute transactions and, as a result, they lost their life savings. Policymakers and regulators scrambled to hold parliamentary hearings, fine the companies involved and gather experts to regain public trust.[7] This case is one among many where regulators around the globe neither anticipated the impact of the collective action enabled by digital means nor possessed adequate tools to scale back and correct the impact of market failure and digital disruption.

Could the regulator have anticipated this disruption? Could it have better protected the smaller traders and their investments? Could it have been better equipped with legal tools to identify and correct technological errors? While there are no easy or certain answers to these questions, the GameStop incident demonstrates the fundamental disconnect between the rapid and pervasive adaptation of technology and the existing regulatory oversight.

1.1. Bits, Watts and Beyond: Narratives of Digitalisation

The concept of *digitalisation* or *digital transformation* has come a long way from being understood as an enabler of post-industrial society to referring to an innovation in an invention-driven economy. It is a key driver that has led to the rise of a network society and an exponential growth of codified information (or Big Data).[8] It is a technological novelty that has impacted all facets of society, the economy and political systems. At the micro level, digital transformation refers to creating new or modifying existing business processes, organisational structures, or commercial relationships.[9] At the macro level, digitalisation encompasses the repercussions of digital technologies and the effect that digital transformation has on society.[10]

Despite its growing importance, the exact meaning and scope of the notion of digitalisation or digital transformation remain unclear and imprecise; there is no widely accepted definition of these terms among academics, industry pioneers and practitioners.[11] Definitions frequently highlight the key components of digitalisation, such as utilising digital technology and tools, developing a new business

[6] ibid.

[7] 'Game Stopped? Who Wins and Loses When Short Sellers, Social Media, and Retail Investors Collide. Part II' House Hearings, 117th Congress, 1st Session (2021); D Lawder and T Hunnicutt, 'Exclusive: Treasury's Yellen Calls Top Regulator Meeting on GameStop Volatility, Consults Ethics Lawyer' (*Reuters*, 3 February 2021).

[8] G Valenduc and P Vendramin, 'Digitalisation, Between Disruption and Evolution' (2017) 23 *Transfer: European Review of Labour and Research* 121. Available at: https://doi.org/10.1177/1024258917701379.

[9] G Vial, 'Understanding Digital Transformation: A Review and a Research Agenda' (2019) 28(2) *The Journal of Strategic Information Systems* 118. Available at: https://doi.org/10.1016/j.jsis.2019.01.003.

[10] D Spath and others, 'Digitalisation of Society', in *Handbook of Engineering Systems Design* (Springer 2022).

[11] EV Katrin, 'Approaches to the Definition of the Term "Digitalization"' (2021) 126 *European Proceedings of Social and Behavioural Sciences*.

model, optimising internal operations, refining the customer experience and contributing to the transformation of society.[12] This edited volume uses the terms digitalisation and digital transformation interchangeably, embracing their broad interpretation derived from the abovementioned components. This approach facilitates the discussion about different sectors under one framework while encompassing their diverse scales and nuances. It also acknowledges the evolving nature of these terms and the need for interdisciplinary perspectives in addressing the risks and challenges they pose.

1.2. Digitalisation: An Accelerator or a Threat?

The advent of digitalisation and digital technologies has enabled opportunities for addressing multiple societal issues and has aided in expanding the horizon of knowledge creation and accessibility. The crux of the challenge for regulators lies upon the need to mitigate not only *predictable* but also *potential risks* arising from digitalisation and foster an environment that can enable innovation for the benefit of the economy and society at large.[13]

By way of illustration, new technologies have catalysed a *paradigm shift* in the energy sector. From floating wind turbines to utilising hydrogen as energy storage, many innovations are emerging for the transition to a more sustainable energy future and automation of the management of energy systems.[14] The use of Information and Communication Technology (ICT), such as smart grids and smart metering, is essential for fostering a decentralised generation of energy and energy efficiency, as Kanerva Sunila discusses in this volume.[15] By instituting demand response programmes and making energy storage options like batteries accessible, the energy system gains flexibility.[16] This offers energy consumers the chance to become 'active' participants or 'prosumers', engaging in both energy consumption and production.[17]

At the same time, the integration of ICT networks into energy infrastructure creates more sophisticated channels for cyberattacks, bringing cybersecurity to

[12] Z Nazari and P Musilek, 'Impact of Digital Transformation on the Energy Sector: A Review' (2023) 16 *Algorithms* 211.

[13] M Amaral, 'Case 2. Digitalisation in Finance: Regulatory Challenges and Regulatory Approaches' in OECD/KDI, *Case Studies on the Regulatory Challenges Raised by Innovation and the Regulatory Responses* (OECD Publishing 2021). Available at: https://doi.org/10.1787/433f2a12-en.

[14] N Zhao and others, 'Emerging Information and Communication Technologies for Smart Energy Systems and Renewable Transition' (2023) 9 *Advances in Applied Energy* 100125; M Noorman, B Espinosa Apráez and S Lavrijssen, 'AI and Energy Justice' (2023) 16 *Energies* 2110.

[15] B Espinosa Apráez, 'The Challenges of Sharing Data at the Intersection of EU Data Protection and Electricity Market Legislation: Lessons from the Netherlands' (2023) 41 *Journal of Energy & Natural Resources Law* 403.

[16] S Lavrijssen, 'Power to the Energy Consumers' (2017) 26 *European Energy and Environmental Law Review* 172.

[17] S Lavrijssen and A Carrillo Parra, 'Radical Prosumer Innovations in the Electricity Sector and the Impact on Prosumer Regulation' (2017) 9 *Sustainability* 1207.

the forefront of governments' and companies' security concerns.[18] Cyberattacks targeting smart grids could disrupt power distribution, leading to widespread outages and economic damage. The risks are not merely hypothetical. In February 2022, a large number of windmills in Germany were rendered offline after an attack on Viasat's communication network, which was used by the windmills to send and receive data.[19] Later the same year, Enercity, one of the largest municipal energy suppliers in Germany, was targeted by a cyber-attack. Although the company's security systems 'reacted immediately' and averted 'greater damage' to the company, the attack limited the availability of customer services.[20] These incidents underscore the vulnerability of energy infrastructure in the context of increasing digitalisation and the need to enhance regulatory measures to ensure energy security.

Digital tools also provide opportunities for investors to directly engage in fulfilling *climate goals* and allow for expedited financial transactions while working with a more responsive regulator. Rapid digitalisation has improved the transparency of investments and environmental impact assessments, enabling the rapid and better monitoring of green projects. Liebrich Hiemstra argues in this volume that the use of digital means has boosted investments in green projects and, thus, contributed to the energy transition. In her chapter, Shanya Ruhela provides an example of digital technology's impact on improving a financial regulator's approach to identifying and monitoring threats and streamlining its internal processes, leading to a more efficient regulatory oversight. She further highlights the role of financial regulators as early adopters of technological innovation. Emanuel van Praag discusses in this volume additional examples of digital transformations and disruptions in the financial sector, such as peer-to-peer (P2P) lending platforms, instant and online payment systems, algorithmic-based financial advisers and more efficient trading strategies.

The landscape of digital technology is ever evolving, rendering the boundaries of traditional offences insufficient, hence, they are being redrawn, refined and, sometimes, inadvertently amplified. According to Emanuel van Praag, the digital shift has opened newer avenues for payment fraud that rely on sophisticated social engineering tactics and deepfake technology. Breaches of the financial data of half a million British Airways customers in 2018,[21] the Marriott/Starwood hack in 2018,[22] and the

[18] M Misra, 'Foreign Investment in Critical National Infrastructure (CNI) by State-Controlled Entities (SCEs) and Investment Screening Mechanisms (ISMs)', in P Delimatsis, G Dimitropoulos and A Gourgourinis, *State Capitalism and International Investment Law* (Hart 2023) 143.

[19] PH O'Neill, 'Russia Hacked an American Satellite Company One Hour Before the Ukraine Invasion' (*MIT Technology Review*, 10 May 2022).

[20] A Rekeraho and others, 'Cybersecurity Challenges in IoT-based Smart Renewable Energy' (2024) 23 *International Journal of Information Security* 101; A Martin, 'Major German Energy Supplier Hit by Cyberattack' (*The Record*, 27 October 2022).

[21] WG Voss, 'Airline Commercial Use of EU Personal Data in the Context of the GDPR, British Airways and Schrems II' (2021) 19 *Colorado Technology Law Journal* 377.

[22] RL Trope, 'To Secure, or Not Secure, Data Integrity – That Is the Question: Cybersecurity Developments' (2019) 75 *Business Law* 1655.

Capital One data breach in 2019[23] have demonstrated ways to steal and use the financial information of customers. Another example of the risks brought about by digitalisation includes the manifestation of biases that already exist in society, as evidenced in the gender discrimination case regarding issuing credit cards involving Apple, Inc and Goldman Sachs.[24] All these incidents shed light on the inherent vulnerabilities that come with increased digitalisation in the *financial sector* and the necessary role of the regulators as guardians of public values, consumer protection and financial stability.

1.3. Digitalisation and Critical Infrastructures

Commentators and scholars often have difficulties predicting the pace and ramifications of technological advancements in the absence of hindsight.[25] Crisis-level events, such as wars, global pandemics, economic depressions and recessions, political upheavals and the consequences of climate change, often reveal the limitations of traditional regulatory and governance approaches. These events also highlight systemic transformations that can accelerate the adoption of digitalisation. To illustrate, the financial crisis of 2007–08 brought to the forefront secondary risks like cybersecurity and liquidity, resulting in a global shift from traditional (static) regulatory approaches to (dynamic) regulatory approaches powered by digital tools.

Amara's law provides that new technology is overestimated in the short run while simultaneously being underestimated in the long run.[26] Digitalisation, thus, is often accompanied by unique and unforeseen opportunities and challenges, making regulators' work akin to running when the goalposts are constantly shifting. This becomes particularly evident when regulators are under pressure to adapt their regulatory approaches within critical infrastructures, given their vital importance and their susceptibility to constant changes.

Critical infrastructures include fundamental systems, networks and services that are essential to a nation's economic growth, security and social welfare.[27] This

[23] S Khan and others, 'A Systematic Analysis of the Capital One Data Breach: Critical Lessons Learned' (2022) 26 *ACM Transactions on Privacy and Security* 1.

[24] J Jablan, L Lakovic and A Micanovic, *Algorithmic Discrimination: Continuation of Human Bias or a Gateway to Equality?* (IEEE 2024).

[25] G Valenduc and P Vendramin, 'Digitalisation, Between Disruption and Evolution' (2017) 23 *Transfer: European Review of Labour and Research* 121; M Lee and others, 'How to Respond to the Fourth Industrial Revolution, or the Second Information Technology Revolution? Dynamic New Combinations Between Technology, Market, and Society through Open Innovation' (2018) 4 *Journal of Open Innovation: Technology, Market, and Complexity* 21.

[26] W Naudé, 'Artificial Intelligence: Neither Utopian nor Apocalyptic Impacts Soon' (2021) 30 *Economics of Innovation and New Technology* 1.

[27] JD Moteff, *Critical infrastructures: Background, policy, and implementation* (Congressional Research Service, Library of Congress 2007); JJ Chung, 'Critical Infrastructure, Cybersecurity, and Market Failure' (2017) 96 *Oregon Law Review* 441.

edited volume seizes the opportunity to unite the discussions on the diverse challenges and benefits posed by digitisation in two of these critical infrastructures: *energy* and *finance* thus maintaining a robust regulatory framework to mitigate the inherent risks and challenges of safeguarding these infrastructures is generally a governmental priority, as argued by Eyup Kun in this volume.

Despite having distinct characteristics, energy and finance share certain core similarities from which our edited volume draws comparative insights. For instance, both are highly regulated and interdependent sectors.[28] Digitalisation has further augmented these interdependencies. It has not only impacted the traditional markets and products in energy and finance but also created additional markets and products, necessitating a pervasive shift in regulatory scope and approach. P2P trading and the use of blockchain technologies to facilitate transactions and the rapid decentralisation of supply chains serve as compelling illustrations of these phenomena.

Highly regulated sectors have high entry barriers and are defined by significant setting-up, operational and compliance costs. For instance, traditional financial institutions like banks, building societies, wealth management and investment firms and insurance firms require considerable tangible and intangible assets and resources to establish and continue operations.[29] Similarly, large physical infrastructures, integrated energy systems and networks and energy services are prerequisites for firms entering and operating in the energy sector.[30]

Firms in energy and finance work together to increase their value, leading to a high degree of interdependencies. These interdependencies make them prone to certain inherent weaknesses, which renders the entire sector unstable and open to vulnerabilities, as discussed by Wendy van der Valk in this volume. The failure of one unit has the potential to have cascading effects which could lead to a large-scale collapse of related or dependent firms, a central characteristic of both energy and finance. As a result, regulators must particularly ensure that such sectors remain stable in silos while preserving the independent functioning of interdependent components. Conversely, regulators have to maintain a balance among interdependent units to preserve system stability as a whole. Thus, this edited volume combines the discussion over energy and finance, recognising that their shared vulnerabilities and regulatory challenges demand integrated analysis and cross-sectoral insights.

[28] C Hadjiemmanuil, 'A Heavily Regulated Industry: The Varied Objectives of Financial Regulation' (2015) 2015(4) *Eucrim: The European Criminal Law Associations Forum* 138; PS Krüger and J-P Brauchle, *The European Union, Cybersecurity, and the Financial Sector: A Primer* (Carnegie Endowment Int Peace Publications Dept 2021); T Hoppe, A Butenko and M Heldeweg, *Innovation in the European Energy Sector and Regulatory Responses to It: Guest Editorial Note* (MDPI 2018).

[29] S Du and CM Ellis, 'Multidimensional Barriers to Entry in the Insurance Industry' (2024) 18(1) *Asia-Pacific Journal of Risk and Insurance* 21; JA Bikker and L Spierdijk, 'Measuring and Explaining Competition in the Financial Sector' (2010) 11 *The Journal of Applied Business and Economics* 11.

[30] J Franc-Dąbrowska, M Mądra-Sawicka and A Milewska, 'Energy Sector Risk and Cost of Capital Assessment – Companies and Investors Perspective' (2021) 14 *Energies* 1613; B Steffen and P Waidelich, 'Determinants of Cost of Capital in the Electricity Sector' (2022) 4 *Progress in Energy* 033001.

2. Navigating Regulatory Strategies for the Future

Regulators can seize the new challenges brought by digitalisation as opportunities to revisit existing regulatory frameworks, reassess internal operations, collaborate effectively with non-state actors and realign their capabilities with evolving expectations. This involves implementing new regulatory frameworks for cybersecurity and data protection, investing in technology and innovation to fortify security measures, fostering collaborative efforts within and across industries and emphasising resilience planning and risk management.

Regulators may face challenges in understanding the impact of emerging technologies on both *markets* and *society* at large.[31] This edited volume argues that a common challenge that digitalisation brings to both energy and finance lies in designing and implementing regulatory strategies that make room for necessary flexibility while protecting public values. Further, these new strategies need to consider the evolving involvement of non-state actors and the complexities of collaboration within and among industries.

2.1. The Protection of Public Values

Public values encompass a wide range of realms, including social welfare and well-being, environmental sustainability, equality, affordability and freedom.[32] Although different market actors should try to address these public values in their decisions, there are instances when governments realise that the adequate protection of public values requires regulatory intervention. To illustrate, many governments have prioritised ensuring *availability*, *affordability* and *environmental sustainability* within their energy policies.[33] Similarly, the notion of *fairness* is fundamental to the obligations that many legal systems impose on suppliers when interacting with consumers, particularly in the financial sector.[34]

Effectively balancing the benefits of digitalisation with the need to mitigate the risks to public values arising from increased connectivity and dependence on digital systems poses significant challenges. For example, Inge Graef and Din Buljević argue in this volume that despite the increasing number of legislative initiatives in the area of data, balancing the need for data sharing against the need to protect

[31] OECD, 'The Impact of Emerging Technologies on Economic Regulators' in *Shaping the Future of Regulators* (OECD 2020). Available at: www.oecd-ilibrary.org/governance/shaping-the-future-of-regulators_acafa450-en.

[32] B Wang, L Xia and AM Wu, 'Social Development with Public Value: An International Comparison' (2022) 162 *Social Indicators Research* 909.

[33] MG Edens and S Lavrijssen, 'Balancing Public Values during the Energy Transition: How Can German and Dutch DSOs Safeguard Sustainability?' (2019) 128 *Energy Policy* 57.

[34] P Cartwright, 'Fairness, Financial Services and the Consumer in an Age of Principles-Based Regulation: Competing Visions for Competitive Markets' (FSRF). Available at: www.nottingham.ac.uk/business/who-we-are/centres-and-institutes/gcbfi/documents/researchreports/paper52.pdf.

personal data, intellectual property rights, and competition in specific situations remains difficult.

Digitalisation presents a multifaceted challenge involving various stakeholders, often necessitating the establishment of shared objectives and the delicate balancing of collective and individual interests. Strategising *trade-offs* among competing interests can enhance the effectiveness of governance frameworks. To this extent, each country attempts to determine how to reconcile potentially incompatible interests and public values in its respective national legislation.

The *concept of justice* can provide a normative framework for evaluating policy goals and shaping the policy objectives of different stakeholders and their decision-making processes that reflect the preferences and priorities of citizens.[35] It can also help critically evaluate governmental policies by considering societal implications often overlooked in favour of technological advancements. Additionally, it can promote cross-sectoral governance and provide a framework to balance competing interests and align the policy with public values. Shanya Ruhela argues that the regulatory adoption of artificial intelligence (AI) must be tempered with strong safeguards to protect public values such as fairness, accountability and transparency. Her chapter calls for algorithmic tools to remain subject to legal norms such as due process, non-discrimination and proportionality – principles that are equally vital in the regulation of energy or finance.

Ultimately, choosing which public values to prioritise in any given situation becomes a *political decision* rather than a purely technical one. This edited volume argues that, while making political decisions, policymakers and regulators should engage in transparent deliberation and incorporate ethical reasoning into their judgements. This can foster accountability and legitimacy in their decision-making processes, aiming to promote equitable outcomes and societal well-being.

2.2. The Need for Regulatory Flexibility

The chapters in this volume focus on ensuring the security of data and the resilience and security of critical infrastructures in the face of digitalisation. Governments can employ various tools and approaches to tackle the regulatory and governance challenges they encounter. For example, their regulatory strategies in the energy sector have varied from direct obligations and incentivising measures to non-regulation. The conventional regulatory strategies, which are typically tailored to address an issue in a specific sector or set of technologies, may not effectively meet the challenges presented by *data-driven interconnected markets*. For one, they might lack the flexibility to keep pace with rapid technological advancements, leading to outdated rules and inefficient regulatory approaches.

[35] RJ Heffron and D McCauley, 'The Concept of Energy Justice across the Disciplines' (2017) 105 *Energy Policy* 658.

One notable solution that could introduce the required flexibility in regulating energy and finance is *regulatory experimentation*. It stands out for its potential to foster regulatory learning and provide insights for regulatory design, delivery and adaptation.[36] The contributors to this volume reaffirm that the concept of regulatory experimentation encompasses a broad spectrum of institutional configurations involving public policy instruments, procedures and organisational frameworks aimed at the development, implementation, evaluation and adjustment of laws and regulations.[37]

Regulatory experimentation is now prevalent in the renewable energy sector and financial services, as well as with respect to decarbonisation technologies and data protection, often in the form of *regulatory sandboxes*. The chapter by Renske van't Veer, Max Baumgart and Saskia Lavrijssen in this volume explains common characteristics of regulatory sandboxes, including the focus on genuine innovations that are not yet available in the market, the need to benefit consumers and/or society, clearly defined boundaries in terms of time and scope and the implementation of appropriate safeguards to ensure their safety and effectiveness. Regulatory sandboxes allow market players to test innovations in a controlled environment under the supervision of a regulator. They are particularly suitable in situations of legal uncertainty where both market players and regulators are not yet knowledgeable enough to properly manage risks. Shanya Ruhela's contribution adds that regulatory sandboxes in the financial sector have not only supported market experimentation but also fostered collaborative supervision.

In this volume, Inge Graef and Din Buljević look at regulatory sandboxes as a form of experimental law-making and compare existing experiences with their implementation in finance and energy. The contributions by Max Baumgart and Jasper van den Boom and by Renske van't Veer, Max Baumgart and Saskia Lavrijssen discuss how regulatory experimentation can offer the necessary flexibility and temporality for the energy market while providing a learning opportunity for regulators.

The recurring theme throughout these chapters is that while regulatory experimentation is a valuable complementary strategy, it should not replace established legal and governance frameworks. These new approaches must also be tested in real-world scenarios before drawing any broad conclusions or making specific policy recommendations.

2.3. The Involvement of Non-State Actors

An implication of increasingly digitalised critical infrastructures is the broader involvement of various stakeholders, not only in regular business operations

[36] OECD, *Regulatory Experimentation: Moving Ahead on the Agile Regulatory Governance Agenda* (*OECD Public Governance Policy Papers 2024*). Available at: https://doi.org/10.1787/f193910c-en.
[37] See also ibid.

but also in developing suitable regulatory strategies and frameworks.[38] Digital transformation has created opportunities for non-state actors to become more involved and to contribute to regulatory solutions. These may be private actors, non-governmental functionaries, think tanks or other interested stakeholders. Integrating non-state actors is essential to bridging the *regulatory knowledge gap*.[39] At the same time, their involvement in the development of legal and regulatory frameworks gives rise to unique circumstances that are yet to be comprehensively addressed by scholars working on collective action and the theories of regulation.

Digital transition requires different *inter-organisational governance* mechanisms. In her chapter, Wendy van der Valk explains the need for good governance initiatives and collective action at different levels: individual firms and industries, as well as the entire sector and network. These initiatives and actions have the potential to contribute towards effective solutions to the many challenges of critical infrastructures, such as those pertaining to coordination, collaboration and participatory action

The contribution by Emanuel van Praag highlights the role of the private actors who help the development of policy and regulatory frameworks but do not derive any direct benefit from these frameworks. Regulatory solutions, while being open to the involvement of knowledgeable partners, need to take on board and thwart the risk of lobbying. Liebrich Hiemstra, in her chapter, investigates the potential improvement of accountability, transparency and supervision in green investments using digital tools. While this provides a real-time solution to enhancing trust and contributes to climate goals, Liebrich Hiemstra argues for the empowerment of regulators with the right tools that allow for cooperation with non-state actors, such as investors. In this volume, Shanya Ruhela probes the role and involvement of industry participants in regulatory sandboxes and digital innovations adopted by a financial regulator. She asserts the significance of involving private actors and technical experts early in the regulatory innovation process.

Thus, the contributors to this volume study the role of different state and non-state actors in providing or contributing to regulatory solutions in energy and finance, emphasising the need for balancing market competition and intervention while addressing the emerging risks and opportunities posed by digitalisation. This edited volume argues that regulatory frameworks should incorporate input from a wide range of actors to strengthen the stability and efficiency of digitalised critical infrastructures.

[38] F Brunetti and others, 'Digital Transformation Challenges: Strategies Emerging from a Multi-Stakeholder Approach' (2020) 32 *The Total Quality Management Journal* 697.

[39] C Abbot, 'Bridging the Gap: Non-State Actors and the Challenges of Regulating New Technology' (2012) 39 *Journal of Law and Society* 329.

2.4. The Complexities of Collaboration

A high degree of *interconnectedness* coupled with increasing digitalisation in various industries and firms of energy and finance has increased formal and informal collaborations.[40] This has also added to the risks and complexities in the mechanics of coordination and collaboration and the functioning of operations. For example, in his chapter, Eyup Kun asserts that the risk around cybersecurity in the financial sector is no longer a threat in silos. He provides evidence that cybersecurity in the financial sector goes beyond mere operational risk (which only affects the relevant network or set of firms) and concerns a systemic risk that is more complex in nature, hence requiring collaborative regulatory action and a response that is macro in nature. Building on this, Shanya Ruhela explains that algorithmic or AI systems used by regulators must be interoperable, explainable and subject to oversight. Without shared governance mechanisms, technical innovations risk further increasing institutional silos rather than enhancing coordination.

Firms and industries in critical infrastructures have always relied on collaboration and interdependent workings to benefit from networks and develop synergy from common positive gains. The need and opportunities for collaboration and coordination have increased due to pervasive changes like digital transformation, climate change initiatives and the growing emphasis on the incorporation of public values, such as sustainability, security, stability and resilience.[41] Emerging complexities necessitate re-evaluation of existing regulatory and governance frameworks to ensure they adequately address the heightened demands of modern interconnected critical infrastructures. This edited volume provides a holistic analysis of such infrastructures, proposes solutions to the challenges of collaboration within and among firms in these infrastructures and examines regulatory strategies to improve and streamline good governance.

In their chapter, Tom AE Aben and David Wodak highlight the increasing complexity of collaboration among firms and the impact of digitalisation in the highly scrutinised energy sector. They examine how digitalisation has contributed to effective data sharing and collaborations with various actors. According to them, *trust* constitutes the bedrock for these collaborations and coordination in critical infrastructures, necessitating various creative governance and regulatory solutions.

[40] FM Hoffart and others, 'Exploring the Interdependence of Climate, Finance, Energy and Geopolitics: A Conceptual Framework for Systemic Risks Amidst Multiple Crises' (2024) 361 *Applied Energy* 122885; M Hellström and others, 'Collaboration Mechanisms for Business Models in Distributed Energy Ecosystems' (2015) 102 *Journal of Cleaner Production* 226; TR Sonesson, J Johansson and A Cedergren, 'Governance and Interdependencies of Critical Infrastructures: Exploring Mechanisms for Cross-Sector Resilience' (2021) 142 *Safety Science* 105383.

[41] B Klievink, N Bharosa and Y-H Tan, 'The Collaborative Realization of Public Values and Business Goals: Governance and Infrastructure of Public–Private Information Platforms' (2016) 33 *Government Information Quarterly* 67.

Wendy van der Valk, in her chapter, explains the difficulties of collaboration in a network of firms and industries as a function of differences in levels of digitalisation. The increasing use of data leads to the demand for a network-based governance approach towards collaboration. Wendy van der Valk proposes the usage of *Systems of Systems*, a novel network governance approach, to tackle the increasing complexities and challenges to collaboration and coordination among firms and industries in critical infrastructures. This approach, a borrowed concept from various disciplines (systems engineering, design theory and organisational studies), views the sector as a Complex Adaptive System which requires constant evaluation and the re-evaluation of issues that it faces due to the high degree of uncertainty and time-specific constraints.

This volume explains the new face of collaboration and coordination that has only become possible through digital tools while simultaneously highlighting the resultant risks leading to increased complexity in energy and finance. Consequently, framing regulatory and governance solutions that consider these risks and complexities is essential for forward-looking regulatory strategies, as this edited volume aims to formulate.

3. Outline and Conclusion

Part I of this volume addresses the governance of digital transformation in critical infrastructures. Wendy van der Valk (Chapter 2) explores the principles of good governance using a network approach. Liebrich Hiemstra (Chapter 3) evaluates the role of digital finance in energy transition by aligning the goals of state and non-state actors. Shanya Ruhela (Chapter 4) examines how a financial regulator uses technological innovations to modernise its supervision and enforcement and the accompanying legal considerations.

Part II examines the integration of digital innovations and data management across the sectors of energy and finance. Inge Graef and Din Buljević (Chapter 5) discuss best practices for implementing European Data Spaces through regulatory sandboxes in finance and energy. Tom AE Aben and David Wodak (Chapter 6) analyse how actual and perceived regulatory barriers obstruct cross-sectoral data sharing from a management perspective. Shirley Kempeneer and Magdalena Brewczyńska (Chapter 7) focus on achieving a just distribution of burdens and benefits in digitalised data spaces. Eyup Kun (Chapter 8) investigates data-driven vulnerabilities that exist at the intersection of critical infrastructure and systemic risk in the financial sector.

Part III focuses on regulatory responses to digital transition in the energy and finance sectors. Emanuel van Praag (Chapter 9) considers how European payments can become faster, cheaper and more inclusive with the use of regulatory experimentation and the involvement of private actors. Max Baumgart and Jasper van den Boom (Chapter 10) examine strategies for introducing smart technologies in positive energy districts in the Netherlands. Renske van't Veer, Max Baumgart and Saskia Lavrijssen (Chapter 11) explore regulatory sandboxes for the green hydrogen sector in the Netherlands. Kanerva Sunila (Chapter 12) presents strategies to promote digitalisation in the Finnish electricity sector.

As digitalisation continues to reshape our world, the diverse perspectives and case studies presented in this edited volume serve as crucial resources for policymakers, regulators, industry professionals and academics. They highlight the ongoing need for adaptive and innovative regulatory frameworks that can effectively respond to the rapid evolution of technology and its implications. By fostering a deeper understanding of these dynamics, this volume aspires to contribute to the development of more resilient and balanced regulatory systems across energy and finance. It advances the proposals for framing regulations that incorporate learnings from enhancing multi-actor collaborations to address actual and perceived legal obstacles and leveraging regulatory sandboxes as a complementary strategy to fortify existing legal, regulatory and governance frameworks.

PART I

Governing Critical Infrastructures

2

Principles of Good Governance

A Network Approach

WENDY VAN DER VALK

1. Introduction

Principles of good governance – ie, governance that is effective and just – are imperative for organisations' success, yet difficult to develop and consistently apply. Governance furthermore is a multi-level phenomenon, meaning that principles of good governance are needed at various interconnected levels of organising. This is particularly the case for critical infrastructures, such as the energy and finance sectors, which require good governance at the level of individual organisations running business processes, at the level of inter-organisational exchange and collaboration in supply chains and networks, at the level of the sector or industry as a whole, and increasingly even across sectors, as the ongoing intertwinement and mutual dependence of critical infrastructures and the grand societal challenges they collectively face increasingly requires them to organise themselves in a more concerted fashion. Furthermore, these critical infrastructures are also increasingly digitalising, resulting in additional governance challenges pertaining to the IT infrastructure and processes that are largely fundamental for meaningful and effective organising in chains, networks and industries. Finally, our understanding of and view on the public values that infrastructures are required to adhere to and safeguard is changing, partly in response to the opportunities that digitalisation may bring. Taken together, these developments make the design and implementation of principles of good governance a highly complex endeavour.

This edited volume gives ample attention to the evolution of regulatory strategies in increasingly digitalised infrastructures. The contribution of this specific chapter therefore resides in its focus on network governance, a helpful paradigm for dealing with complex, uncertain and evaluative problems, such as those involved with the growing need for critical infrastructures to organise themselves in a concerted fashion with public and private partners within and across sectors, ie, in collaborative networks. As collaborative networks are infused with evolving challenges pertaining to coordination, cooperation and participatory action, an enhanced understanding of which network governance approaches (ie, governance form and contractual and relational mechanisms deployed) may be effective at which point in time is highly needed. Essentially, the question I intend to shed light on is who governs collaborative networks in the energy and finance sectors, and how? More formally: *What network governance approaches (ie, form and mechanisms) could be conducive for collaborative networks in energy and finance?*

Building on literature in systems engineering, complex adaptive systems, systems integration and organisational networks, I examine network governance approaches in the context of collaborative networks. I particularly focus on the Dutch energy sector, as I have engaged with this sector via various research projects for over eight years now. These experiences have helped me to familiarise myself with the sector and its challenges, and this enables me to put governance concepts discussed hereafter in context.

In the remainder of this chapter, I first elaborate on the concept of collaborative networks in the context of the Dutch energy sector. I conceptually investigate network membership and boundaries, as well as network objectives in relation to members' contributions to these objectives. The discussion of network objectives I link to literature on New Public Governance, which in my view provides a useful lens for considering network objectives in relation to public values, thereby relating to good governance being effective. Throughout, I contextualise discussions by providing examples in the context of the Dutch energy sector.

I then turn my attention to the governance of these collaborative networks in terms of selecting the governance form and mechanisms that should be set up and subsequently deployed to monitor the network's progress towards its network-level objectives. These topics are important as the co-existence of network-level and individual objectives raises questions with regard to organising in the collaborative network and of governance and control of the network, thereby relating to good governance being just. More generally, as prominent forms of economic organisation increasingly involve multiple firms as well as communities of noncontractually linked individuals, our traditional focus on intra-firm organisation design may be considered out of date, or at least incomplete. Thinking about organisational design for new organisational forms is highly needed.

The chapter will conclude with recommendations for good governance approaches (form and mechanisms) for collaborative networks in the Dutch energy sector, although I expect recommendations and their underlying argumentation to be equally applicable and insightful for the financial sector.

2. Collaborative Networks in the Dutch Energy Sector

Critical infrastructures – ie, systems that are critical to the security, economic prosperity and social well-being of a nation, such as road and rail, water, and energy and finance systems – are becoming more and more interconnected and intertwined, and mutually dependent in complex ways. Against the backdrop of major contemporary developments such as urbanisation, the energy transition, increased attention for climate change and sustainability, and digitalisation, their intertwinement and mutual dependence warrant a major transition in infrastructure management, in which critical infrastructures increasingly organise themselves in a more concerted fashion. In such a collaborative network approach, individual critical infrastructures as members depend on all other members, and typically form a group of loosely coupled entities (including governments, universities, industry associations, and (end) consumers) that share a common fate. Both the collaborative network and its members have reasons-for-being, and the former may or may not be at odds with the latter. As such, the notion of collaborative networks provides organisations with a view of cross-industry collaboration that goes beyond collaboration with directly linked partners.

Consider the Dutch energy sector, a sector in which collaborative networks are both increasingly emerging and also very much needed in light of the major transformation it is undergoing as a result of the energy transition. As such, the energy sector can be considered to be an appropriate context for studying critical infrastructures engaging in collaborative networks. Digitalisation is furthermore considered an important enabler for organisations to fundamentally revisit their operations. Think, for example, of the ambition to leverage detailed information gathered about local energy consumption and production (eg, through solar panels) for balancing demand and supply, enhancing grid management, and reducing operational costs. Given the complexity of such ambitions and the sector's grand challenge overall, and given the myriad of actors that are directly or indirectly involved, the energy collaborative network can truly be considered a giant.

The energy collaborative network involves the managers of the (regional) energy infrastructure, ie, the Distribution System Operators (DSOs), plus interconnected public and private supply chain partners, such as customers, contractors, suppliers, brokers, intermediaries, governmental organisations (eg, the national government, local municipalities) and non-governmental organisations of various kinds. For example, through the energy infrastructure, energy suppliers supply energy to households and to small, medium-sized and large organisations (both public and private). The energy suppliers, DSOs and energy consumers are physically interconnected. Geographical interconnections exist with local (ie, the municipality), regional (ie, a province or region) and national governments who are responsible for spatial planning of the infrastructure, thereby affecting, for example, whether the electricity net can be expanded. The infrastructure also needs to be constructed. The network includes various other organisations, such as knowledge institutes, consultants, and interest groups of various kinds (eg, a homeowners' association). The energy transition puts requirements on all these actors, each with their own place and role in the system, and each with their own challenges and opportunities. Furthermore, the transition requires all these actors to take part and contribute, each in their own unique way. This raises challenges with regard to the conditions under which concerted efforts among network members could bring benefits and for whom, and how these could be leveraged.

Theoretically speaking, the concept of collaborative networks bears resemblance to concepts coined in various different literature streams, including systems engineering, and operations and supply chain management. Here, the properties of self-organisation and emergence are considered features that warrant studying the coordination systems that lead to 'adaptive, flexible, and coherent collective behaviour in supply chains'.[1] In other words: the presence of interdependencies should give rise to concerted efforts from those that are interdependent.

By contrast, literature on inter-organisational networks draws attention to the coordinated mobilisation of resources and coordination of efforts by organisations that belong to the system or are part of the network. These concerted efforts are key for achieving network-level objectives and to sustain the network as a whole, with the result being more than the sum of the parts. Similarly, management science literature advances the so-called systems approach to problems, that is, an approach that is concerned with total-system performance[2] and that focuses on systems as a whole (ie, on the collective of agents) rather than on its separate parts (ie, on individual agents).

Studies on inter-organisational networks are typically concerned with questions pertaining to the structure or composition of the network, and how it may effectively be governed. These questions persist over time, as many challenges in the energy transition are affected by temporality, such as which actors are (to be) involved, decisions on governance form, and the interplay between governance mechanisms and their effects. Drawing on organisation design theory – which builds on the premise that design in the form of specifying and regulating how (in the present case) organisations work together in networks is a key determinant of performance – effectively positions the collaborative network as an organisation design problem, which fits with questions that organisations in the energy sector I engage with typically advance: What does the higher-level system of the collaborative network look like in terms of tasks, roles and responsibilities? Who is responsible for the functioning of the collaborative network? Who controls the network? What outcomes may be rightfully expected when collaborative networks are successful? Does this change over time and, if so, how?

These questions pertain to organisation design (ie, task division and task allocation, and reward and information provision) and effective network governance approaches in terms of who is governing and in what way, while acknowledging temporality. Regarding the 'who', various streams of literature feature the notion of a so-called systems integrator or network orchestrator, ie, usually a

[1] A Surana and others, 'Supply-chain Networks: A Complex Adaptive Systems Perspective' (2005) 17 *International Journal of Production Research* 4235. Available at: https://doi.org/10.1080/00207540500142274.

[2] R Ackoff, 'Toward a System of Systems Concepts' (1971) 17 *Management Science* 661. Available at; https://doi.org/10.1287/mnsc.17.11.661.

lead firm that sets up and leads the network. Regarding the 'what', researchers have extensively discussed formal and informal inter-organisational governance approaches. Discussing organisation design solutions for collaborative networks first, however, requires a better understanding of the concept of collaborative networks. The next sections therefore elaborate on network membership and boundaries (section 3), and on network-level objectives and expected member contributions (sections 4 and 5). Sections 6 and 7 then shed light on principles of good governance of the network and for monitoring its progress relative to the network-level objective, two stages in shaping the organisation of the network after its initiation. While section 6 draws attention to approaches to controlling the network, section 7 focuses on what mechanisms are most conducive in collaborative network settings. Connections to the empirical context of energy collaborative networks are made in both sections. The temporal component features to a larger or lesser extent in all the sections. The chapter concludes with an overview of good network governance principles, while also highlighting certain challenges in need of further study.

3. Collaborative Networks: Membership and Boundaries

Before elaborating on network membership and boundaries, it is important to conceptualise the collaborative network. An organisation can be defined as a purposeful concrete system that contains at least two interrelated purposeful elements with a shared objective regarding desired outcomes.[3] These elements can reside within organisations, but one could also consider individual organisations/agents as interrelated elements. Only purposeful elements have the ability to carry out the activity of organising a system. On the other hand, an aggregation of purposeful elements does not constitute an organisation unless they have at least one shared objective. As Ackoff notes 'an organisation is *always* organized around this common purpose'.[4] The relationships between what the purposeful elements

[3] Network and supply chain management researchers advance the triad as capturing the basic essence of a network as that allows for studying how nodes (here: elements) affect other nodes as well as how links (here: actions/activities between elements) affect other links (TY Choi and Z Wu, 'Triads in Supply Networks: Theorizing Buyer-Supplier-Supplier Relationships' (2009) 45 *Journal of Supply Chain Management* 8). Following this logic, an organisational network would refer to a collection of *at least three* organisations deliberately working together to achieve a common goal (Peeters R and others, 'So Happy Together: A Review of the Literature on the Determinants of Effectiveness of Purpose-Oriented Networks in Health Care' (2023) 80 *Medical Care Research and Review* 266). In this sense, the network is a concrete system, but the concrete system does not necessarily classify a network. Both, however, are forms of organisation which can be studied using an organisation theory perspective. For simplicity, I will adhere to networks consisting of at least two elements.

[4] R Ackoff, 'Toward a System of Systems Concepts' (1971) 17 *Management Science* 661, 669. Available at: https://doi.org/10.1287/mnsc.17.11.661.

do and the pursuit of their common purpose is what gives unity and identity to the organisation. Literature on organisational networks defines these to be

> *systems of coordinated action among organizations* but also groups and individuals who differ on multiple dimensions and where conflict is converted into cooperation and where the mobilization of resources and the coordination of effort is key for achieving the network goals and make the network sustainable.[5]

Organisational networks clearly possess the generally accepted elements of an organisation: ie, they are multi-agent systems with identifiable boundaries and with system-level goals that can only be achieved through contributions of the constituent agents. As such, like purposeful systems, organisational networks have agency and an objective, possibly an ideal that can be worked towards.

Consider again the empirical context of the energy collaborative network, which brings relevant elements or organisations together. In other words, we conceptualise the different actors who interrelate in relation to energy to be the elements that make up the larger network and that have specific objectives co-existing alongside the objectives of the collaborative network. I have already provided various suggestions for which actors could be considered, without intending to be exhaustive. A simple collaborative network, then, is made up of at least two organisations, one of which is from the energy sector, eg, the manager of electricity infrastructure in the example given earlier, while the other may come from outside (eg, the construction sector). The collaborative network furthermore requires coordinated action to achieve its network-level objectives, as these can only be achieved through the contributions of all elements that make up the collaborative network. For example, the manager of electricity infrastructure and construction organisations share the objective of ensuring access to electricity for, eg, newly constructed houses while managing net congestion. There should be sufficient net connections for newly constructed houses, and these houses should be as energy efficient as possible.

Who to consider as members of the collaborative network, then, is not easy, as interrelations or relevance may be more easily observable for some parties than for others. In other words, it is not always straightforward to see who the stakeholders are, especially when considering different levels of analysis. Miandar and others, for example, identify the firm, the dyad, the supply chain, and the supply chain-plus-stakeholder-level (which the authors refer to as 'network') as levels of analysis in supply chain management research, whereby the latter includes 'not only multiple levels of the supply chain but also other stakeholders, such as non-governmental organizations and public authorities'.[6] Another perspective which enhances understanding while also adding to complexity is that of direct and

[5] P Kenis and J Raab, 'Back to the Future: Using Organization Design Theory for Effective Organizational Networks' (2020) 3 *Perspectives on Public Management and Governance* 109, 111.

[6] T Miandar, TE Johnsen, and F Caniato, 'The Role of Purchasing and Supply Management in Diffusing Sustainability in Supply Networks: A Systematic Literature Review' (2024) 33 *Business Ethics, the Environment & Responsibility* 505, 509. Available at: https://doi.org/10.1111/beer.12622.

indirect interdependencies. Following this line of thinking, Tate and others use the natural ecosystem as an analogy for the business ecosystem, identifying scavengers (ie, actors that dismantle, sort and/or transport used materials) and decomposers (ie, actors that transform used materials and feed it back into the system) as typical business ecosystem roles besides traditional producers and consumers.[7] More generally, stakeholder theory draws attention to 'any group or individual who can affect or is affected by the achievement of the organisation's objectives', eg, employees, communities, customers, political groups, investors, governments, suppliers and trade associations, all of whom could be relevant collaborative network members.[8]

Clearly, these perspectives add to the level of complexity involved with overseeing the network; with higher numbers of stakeholders, network relationships become increasingly difficult to observe, a phenomenon known as network opacity. Furthermore, while networks and their environments are essentially objective things, they are at the same time also subjective because the particular configuration of elements that form both is usually dictated by the interests of the researcher. Hence, every network can be conceptualised as part of another and larger network, which also has objectives that co-exist alongside the objectives of its constituent elements. Finally, which members are included in the network may vary over time, depending on perspective as well as on the requirements at a specific point in time (eg, think of membership in the early versus more mature stages of the collaborative network). Taken together, these issues might explain why interdependencies among actors, and their power and influence, are not typically studied in dyadic or supply chain-focused analyses. On the other hand, change and transformation (ie, elements of temporality) are likely to be inhibited if individual organisations do not oversee their networks or understand the roles and influence of stakeholders of various natures. Consequently, (re)identifying meaningful boundaries is highly important when the aim is to understand the composition of the network.

The collaborative network and its environment thus are subjective things in the sense that the particular configuration of elements that form both is to be decided, so boundaries and objectives jointly identify the network in a unique way. Starting from the network-level objective more or less implies that the network can be intentionally designed, in the sense that all the relevant subsystems that are expected to contribute to achieving network-level objectives can be identified and included in the network. Alternatively, network identification may be more emergent when it is inferred from subsystems' efforts that appear to contribute to a shared objective: as argued if network-level objectives can be recognised at

[7] WL Tate and others, 'Seeing the Forest and not the Trees: Learning from Nature's Circular Economy' (2019) 149 *Resources, Conservation and Recycling* 115. Available at: https://doi.org/10.1016/j.resconrec.2019.05.023.

[8] J Kujala and others, 'CSR as Company Stakeholder Responsibility: Empirical Investigation of Managers' Attitudinal Changes' (2015) 2015(1) *Academy of Management Proceedings* 16793. Available at: https://doi.org/10.5465/AMBPP.2015.16793.

all, it must be because the constituent subsystems' efforts appear to contribute toward this goal. Root cause analysis is, then, a useful technique to identify interdependencies and causal linkages between network-level objectives and activities of individual actors, and may hence be used to verify which actors are relevant members of the network. The notion of the network as emergent is also helpful when considering the evolutionary character of networks: network identification is then an ongoing process with outcomes that change over time.

Specific focus is likely to come from the one who is observing the network, eg, a manager of a subsystem experiencing specific problems or challenges, or a researcher with a specific scholarly interest. In both cases, it is important to keep an open mind, as specific problems or challenges may quickly render the observer blind for subsystems whose linkages are less obvious, yet relevant. Furthermore, care must be taken that the network in focus does not become overly complex. It is therefore important that whoever conceptualises the network has a clear objective in mind when doing so, where this objective can help decide when to include an identified subsystem and when not. The next sections will elaborate more substantively on the notion of network-level objectives and expected network member contributions.

4. Network-Level Objectives

Network-level objectives can essentially be established in two main ways. The first is when considering interdependencies between interrelated systems, where the behaviour of system A affects the behaviour or outcomes of system B. In the case of energy, the behaviour of electricity suppliers in terms of tariff structures offered may affect the behaviour of electricity users, which is an important driver of the electricity network performance of the DSOs. In such cases, collaboration and coordination between actors aimed at levelling demand is necessary to balance the load on the grid, especially as investment in network capacity takes time to realise (and is not always feasible; this is indeed what is happening in this sector today). Another example is spatial planning by the municipality, which affects demand for electricity in terms of quantity and geography. Alternatively, limitations of the grid may actually be driving spatial planning decisions. In these examples, actors need to collaborate and coordinate to ensure timely and sufficient access to electricity for all current and new end users. The interdependencies point at the possibility of identifying a higher-level (network) objective (eg, availability to all) that each network member can contribute to.

The second way in which a network-level objective can be conceived is by starting from the main societal challenges that affect each network member, albeit to different effects. The energy transition is one such societal challenge that has implications for all involved: small and large business customers, consumers, semi-public organisations, municipalities and provinces, energy suppliers, etc. Here, one could start conceiving shared network-level objectives or what Mazzucato refers to as a 'mission',[9] namely, a bold idea about a certain desired outcome. A just transition, in which the inclusion and active participation of low-income, vulnerable and marginalised groups is ensured (ie, leaving no one behind), could be such a mission. Transitioning to renewable sources of energy could be another one. Subsequently, the relevant constituents that can play a role in achieving the mission need to be identified, though these constituents are likely to all belong not to one particular (ie, the energy) sector but to multiple sectors, hence engaging with diverse types of activities. For example, a cross-sectoral approach to the future of energy should also entail making existing houses and buildings more energy-efficient (eg, insulation, or new construction techniques) and helping farmers to reduce their energy consumption as well as their pollution levels and greenhouse gas emissions.

Network-level objectives are generally anchored to some kind of notion of *public value*, value than can be created through managerial work in the public sector, just as private value may result from managerial work in the private sector. Building on thinking from New Public Governance, Mills argues that public value (or social/societal value) relates to 'an attitude or judgement made by a person of some object at issue (whether this is a product, service, process or other person) against some resource'.[10] In the context of the public sector, it refers to a multitude of conceptualisations of procuring works, supplies or services in which societal expectations are met. Actors in the energy collaborative network, for example, may seek to shift towards renewable sources of energy (which is the public value that is being created), while safeguarding other public values such as safety, affordability, and accessibility of energy.

By contrast, public *values* refer to shared expectations about a collective benefit. They are 'abstract, humanly held notions and beliefs that provide a broad and relatively universal framing structure to understand particular choices in a wider context of concerns', and entail normative personal judgements about the social standards, principles and ideals to be pursued and upheld by government agents and officials.[11] As public organisations are accountable to many different stakeholders in society (eg, public and private, societal and market parties), public values provide consensus on the principles on which government activity should be based.

At the same time, public values are challenging to deal with in various ways. First of all, their subjective nature means there are differences in the interpretation of values. This adds to the complexity both of public procurement and of

[9] M Mazzucato, *Mission Economy: A Moonshot Guide to Changing Capitalism* (Allen Lane 2021).

[10] GR Mills, *Values and Value in Design* (University Institutional Repository 2013), p. 118, cited in L Kuitert, L Volker, and MH Hermans, 'Taking on a Wider View: Public Value Interests of Construction Clients in a Changing Construction Industry' (2019) 37 *Construction Management and Economics* 257, 260. Available at: https://doi.org/10.1080/01446193.2018.1515496.

[11] ibid.

the dynamic context in which governmental decision-making occurs. Second, values cannot always simultaneously be achieved. Value pluralism implies that the pursuit of certain values will limit the ability to pursue others, meaning that some form of coping behaviour is likely to be required. For example, investment in renewable energy is likely to be reflected in higher energy tariffs and hence less affordability, at least for some, and this trade-off should carefully be considered. Finally, incommensurability refers to the fact that there usually is no single currency or scale for evaluating conflicting values. This is also the reason that scholarly work is increasingly being conducted under the 'beyond GDP' umbrella, trying to include broader notions of value beyond costs and returns, such as contributions to societal welfare and well-being. This is more broadly referred to as a broad welfare approach, with broad welfare being the mission, or at least the network-level objective.

Related to subjectiveness and particularly pluralism, the network and its network-level objectives bring additional complexity in the form of interpretations varying between network members, as well as the fact that network members also have individual objectives. After all, members each have their own reasons-for-being, which could potentially be compromised as a result of pursuing shared objectives. For example, letting the network-level objective prevail may in certain cases be too damaging for individual members given their individual objectives or given the cost involved for compensating damages or for putting in additional effort. Also, for some objectives, members may not legally be allowed to compromise. To date, however, how to manage competing value objectives in collaborative network settings and implications for individual network members and their interrelations has hardly been addressed. This sets the stage for discussing the contributions of individual members in the next section.

5. Member Contributions

Attaining the system-level goal requires contributions from all system constituents, whereby the whole of the contributions is more than their sum. These constituents seek these contributions alongside the tasks and activities necessary to achieve their own individual objectives. Clearly, this requires a balance and sometimes even compromise, as achieving the system-level objective may sometimes be at odds with achieving individual objectives.

Regarding the energy transition, one such example occurs when, eg, energy suppliers carry part of the responsibility to help their customers manage and ultimately reduce their energy consumption. While this is in the interest of energy users and society as a whole, and hence for the energy collaborative network, it is not in the interest of individual energy suppliers that derive their income from energy volumes. A study on the rollout of the smart electricity meter by Aben and others shows that the opposite may also occur: in the Netherlands, the Dutch national government decided that DSOs could not develop any tools or services that would help energy users manage and reduce their energy consumption.[12] While developing such tools and services would have been in the interest of the DSOs as it would help them to better manage their electricity grids in terms of daily supply and demand and required investment, this task was specifically charged to the energy suppliers instead. The direct interest of energy suppliers, however, is not to reduce consumption.

This example clearly shows how individual objectives can be at odds with the network-level objective. Energy suppliers would only be inclined to really take on this task (beyond merely demonstrating some efforts in this direction) if they were able to compensate for the income loss as a result of decreasing volumes. One way to achieve this would be to allow the energy suppliers to generate income through the sales of tools and associated services, but this would subsequently put the investment with energy users who would have to increase their spend on energy by investing in tools to reduce their spend on energy. While it is generally commonly accepted that investment involves a payback period, this seems not to be so well accepted in the case of these tools, where energy users are not always very engaged with their energy consumption and do not see why they should be paying first to obtain savings later. This example shows that new methods of value creation and distribution are required for network members to overcome the barrier associated with decreasing their reliance on their incumbent business models. Appropriately incentivising the various members provides one way to achieve this, but more fundamental approaches, in which governments develop missions and invite all kinds of parties (which are then members) to help realise each mission and, as such, develop markets, could be equally or perhaps even more successful. We will return to this in the next section.

Another important issue to consider is that the existence of network-level objectives does not imply that the members actually share these objectives. In other words, the network's reason for being is not that the members have a shared purpose. While misalignment between network-level and individual objectives may be a reason for members not to share the former, members also may not even be (fully) aware of the fact that they are or should be part of a larger whole with a purpose. And again, this awareness or acknowledgement may be dependent on time. As Gulati and others point out,[13] networks that have legally autonomous firms as their constituents are not bound by authority based on employment relationships. It is this absence of formal authority that is a defining feature of

[12] T Aben and others, 'Making Smart Use of Smart Meters: How to Effectively Govern the Network of Actors Involved in the Dutch Energy Transition' (2023) *Proceedings of the 32nd IPSERA conference 'Systemic Change'*, Esade University, Barcelona, Spain.

[13] R Gulati, P Puranam and M Tushman, 'Meta-organization Design: Rethinking Design in Interorganizational and Community Contexts' (2012) 33 *Strategic Management Journal* 571. Available at: https://doi.org/10.1002/smj.1975.

such – what are referred to as – 'meta-organisations'. This raises questions regarding how to organise the relations between the legally autonomous entities, as authority that emerges through employment relationships plays a key part in shaping the organisation of the network. In other words, how can the network effectively organise member contributions to be in line with the network's objective? Even before that, network members should understand they are part of a network and what that network is for, but who is the architect that gets to decide?

For meta-organisations such as those surrounding P&G, Toyota or Apple, there may indeed be little doubt whose goals shape those of the larger whole. The architects in these examples also typically have bargaining power, as well as significant informal authority based on expertise, reputation, status and gatekeeping privileges. Missions-thinking, as advocated by Mazzucato, clearly puts this role of uniting public and private actors in the mission spearheaded by the government.[14] For example, in the energy collaborative network, the government has taken a leading role in local action to implement global (eg, the Paris Agreement) and regional (eg, the European Green Deal) agreements. For other networks, again, it may be less clear who is or should be the architect; eg, when considering the network of critical infrastructures, which critical infrastructure manager would best adopt the role of architect? Should that be one single infrastructure manager democratically selected by the other critical infrastructures, or one merely claiming the role of architect, for example because it has the highest stakes involved? And how does it depend on different conceptualisations of time and aspects of evolution such as network maturity? Should it be a decision-making body in which all infrastructures are (equally?) represented? Or should it preferably be the government, in this case the Ministry of Infrastructure and Water Management, which safeguards the shared interest? What would be the role of the ministry when the architect role is for one individual critical infrastructure or for a set of critical infrastructures? The next section elaborates on the question of who should be the architect or orchestrator that not only initiates but also oversees the network in operation. Meanwhile, it is important to note that in the context of energy collaborative networks, collaboration between members and mutual acknowledgement of and accounting for members' objectives are absolutely imperative because of the fundamental interdependencies between DSOs, the government (national, regional, local), consumers and energy suppliers. The energy collaborative network therefore is uniquely complex in comparison to the meta-organisations mentioned above. In the energy collaborative network, members cannot be exchanged: DSOs have a monopoly position and the government is obliged by European law to move towards the realisation of its climate goals, while consumers are in need of a sustainable and affordable energy supply. The objectives of each therefore need to adequately be taken into account if a gridlock is to be avoided.

[14] M Mazzucato, *Mission Economy: A Moonshot Guide to Changing Capitalism* (Allen Lane 2021).

6. Who Governs the Network: Principles Regarding Form

Authority that emerges through the employment relationship plays a key part in shaping an organisation's design, in terms of the fundamental choices about the division of labour and about the grouping and linking structures that promote integration of effort. The fact that the collaborative network lacks authority creates basic problems in terms of organising, giving rise to questions of who has authority to perform organisation design (ie, to conduct task division and allocation, and to design and implement reward and information distribution systems). These problems feature in organisation design theory, which starts from the premise that organisation design involves specifying and regulating how people, teams or organisations work together in organisations, or here, organisational networks. As with any form of organisation, the collaborative network must find solutions to these four universal problems of organising. The ways in which these problems are solved can vary considerably, which generates novelty in forms of organising. Foremost, though, it needs to find an answer to the question of who is doing the organising. In other words, who is the architect, orchestrator or integrator that – after creating initial connections, building legitimacy and establishing trust – designs and oversees the processes of *governing the network* and of *monitoring its progress* relative to network-level objectives. Key challenges reside in understanding how to effectively orchestrate the efforts of participants in networks to achieve common strategic objectives, ie, who should establish and constitute the governance structure, how governance should be executed, and what checks and balances are key.

Extant scholarly work has given ample attention to structural aspects of network governance. This literature advances three main forms of network governance along with four contingencies determining the effectiveness (ie, the extent to which network-level outcomes are achieved) of each form: (1) shared networks that are participant-governed and highly decentralised; (2) participant-governed networks that are more centralised and have one member organisation taking the lead in governing the network; and (3) the network administrative organisation (NAO) model, which involves the creation of a separate entity exclusively for the purpose of network governance. Essentially, this implies deciding whether choices on how to organise should be made in a decentralised manner or through a centralised designer. In collaborative networks, this would either be organising through self-organising groups (ie, shared) or more like the way in which traditional bureaucracies operate (ie, lead-organisation). The NAO model I consider to be similar to the lead-organisation model, with no single organisation being in the lead but rather a set of organisations who have intentionally been brought together for this purpose and who may or may not be representative of (a subset of) the network. Admittedly, there is likely to be one architect that brings this set of organisations together.

Effectiveness of these forms is subsequently contingent on four network characteristics: (1) the degree of goal consensus; (2) the degree to which network-level competences are required for the task at hand; (3) network size; and (4) trust within the network. As such, Provan and Kenis[15] argue that shared governance is effective when goal consensus is high, network-level competences are not really required for the task at hand, and the number of network participants and trust levels are high. By contrast, lead-organisation governance is effective for larger networks involving little trust, moderate goal consensus and a requirement for some network-level competences. Finally, the NAO model is effective for large networks with moderate trust levels, moderately high goal consensus and a high need for network-level competences. Hence, the most appropriate form of governance can only be determined after the network and its boundaries have properly been identified.

Finally, regardless of whether the governance form fits the network's characteristics, all three governance forms have their advantages and disadvantages. The shared governance form has the advantage that all members are heard. Usually, decision-making involves highly democratic processes. At the same time, hearing all members becomes difficult in contexts involving large numbers of actors. Also, democratic processes are usually less conducive when difficult decisions need to be made, that at the very least take a long time. The lead-organisation form is quite the opposite in the sense that there is one controlling party that makes decisions (including difficult ones). The lead-organisation form also brings some advantages in terms of coordination between actors. At the same time, this form is weaker when it comes to representing and safeguarding diverse interests. The NAO model has the advantage of forming or bringing in a third party that is (more) neutral and usually has a lot of expertise and experience. At the same time, establishing legitimacy can be highly challenging in this form.

I consider energy collaborative networks to suffer from varying degrees, or even a lack, of goal consensus. Although members of the network generally commit to the need for transition, I highlighted earlier that the interests of individual members do not always align well with the system-level objective. I consider the number of members to be generally high. Given the complexity associated with the transition, the need for network-level competencies is also considered to be high. Trust is an issue, with higher levels of trust *within* network subgroups but lower levels of trust *between* such subgroups. This would make the NAO the preferred model for organising the governance of this specific (yet approximate) conceptualisation of the network. The most suitable governance form may change over time and with the changing needs of the networks. Therefore, it is evident that no single governance structure can perfectly address the complex challenges posed by the energy transition. Also, as there may be different perceptions about

[15] KG Provan and P Kenis, 'Modes of Network Governance: Structure, Management, and Effectiveness' (2008) 18 *Journal of Public Administration Research and Theory* 229. Available at: https://doi.org/10.1093/jopart/mum015.

the network (eg as a result of differing perspectives among actors), different forms of governance may be in place. For example, citizens may be organised in energy communities that involve a shared governance model. At the same time, their voices are important for initiatives from, eg, local government, in which governance may take the lead-organisation form. As such, multiple governance forms may co-exist and interplay and these need to be managed appropriately.

As a central and leading actor during network initiation, the government should establish the separate and dedicated governance and monitoring of NAO and bring together representation of all or at least most relevant actors to ensure that those who govern have sufficient expertise and experience. Opting for an NAO, however, also implies that it can be hard to actually implement decisions, as the NAO has no formal power and is strongly reliant on the buy-in from network members for its success. This is something that needs to be considered when designing the governance *mechanisms*, ie, how the interrelations between network members will be governed.

7. How to Govern the Network: Principles Regarding Mechanisms

The question of how the network should be governed involves decisions regarding the governance mechanisms to adopt, ie, the formal and informal mechanisms that individual organisations usually draw on to manage their interrelations with direct exchange partners. Two streams of literature have offered important insights regarding these mechanisms.

First, the literature on inter-organisational relationships (eg, alliances in strategic management, and buyer–supplier dyads in operations and supply chain management) understands governance to comprise both formal and informal mechanisms, where formal is usually considered to mean contractual governance and informal refers to relational governance.[16] When it comes to contracts and trust in dyads, much of the scholarly debate has traditionally focused on whether the two are substitutes or complements. The substitute view argues that, in the presence of trust, contracts are not needed and could even harm trust. In other words, contracts or trust produce the desired outcomes. By contrast, according to the complementarity view, trust *and* contracts jointly produce desired outcomes. More recent contributions draw attention to the conditions under which contracts and trust may act as either substitutes or complements. Nevertheless, to date, little

[16] Note that more recent contributions in these fields have suggested that this dichotomy may be an oversimplification: relational governance can be more formal when considering *codified patterns of expected behaviour* that parties should adhere to (eg, meeting procedures), whereas contractual governance can be more informal when considering *uncodified enforceable promises* (eg, confidentiality agreements) (see, eg, A Keller and others, 'Alliance Governance Mechanisms in the Face of Disruption' (2021) 32 *Organization Science* 1542).

is known about how the two mechanisms may effectively be deployed over time and to what effects. This is especially true for collaborative network settings, which cannot be reduced to a set of inter-organisational alliances or dyadic relationships. In collaborative networks, members *may* or *may not* have alliances among themselves, but their alignment is key to achieving network-level objectives. This is also why collaborative networks cannot build hierarchical (ie, authority-based) relationships between members.

Second, literature on governing a plurality of actors in networks (eg, in organisation studies) advances so-called dominating versus consensus-based governance modes. In the dominating mode, a core actor (eg, in the case of lead-organisation governance) or a group of core actors (as is the case when an NAO is opted for) sets the collaborative agenda, recruits partners, and typically relies on *formal contracts as mechanisms* to steer relationships. By contrast, in the consensus-based mode, partners collectively negotiate the agenda, membership is often voluntary, and *trust predominantly governs* relations. These works demonstrate that there is a role for dyadic mechanisms such as contracts and trust as part of a larger set of network-focused governance mechanisms. Hybrid forms are also possible: in their study of a large innovation network involving 57 stakeholders, Reypens and others showed how the orchestrator (here, a consortium of public and private stakeholders, like an NAO) switched between dominating and consensus-based modes, and hence between formal contracts and trust, as a way of addressing network challenges emerging (and fading) over time.[17]

Whether to opt for contract-based or trust-based approaches is likely in part to be contingent on the earlier-discussed characteristics of the collaborative network. For example, in a network with high trust-density, a strong focus on contracts may be counter-intuitive and could even be counter-productive and undermine the network. More importantly, the mechanisms are supposed to address problems of organising, as well as addressing their monitoring and periodical review. First, establishing a functional division of labour in pursuit of the system-level objectives involves establishing a division of tasks (ie, translating and dividing the system-level objective into tasks, jobs or assignments) and subsequently allocating tasks (mapping the tasks resulting from the task division to network constituents). Task division and task allocation can be formalised in task descriptions for the various constituents; in the case of dyadic relationships, the specification of tasks is likely to be captured in a formal contract. Clauses related to this may be more behaviour-based, describing the actual tasks that need to be executed, or more performance-based, describing desired output or outcomes. Establishing corresponding key performance indicators allows for subsequent measurement, monitoring and management.

[17] C Reypens, A Lievens, and V Blazevic, 'Hybrid Orchestration in Multi-stakeholder Innovation Networks: Practices of Mobilizing Multiple, Diverse Stakeholders Across Organizational Boundaries' (2021) 42 *Organization Studies* 61. Available at: https://doi.org/10.1177/0170840619868268.

Subsequently, problems of cooperation and coordination need to be addressed. After all, organisations involved in an organisational network differ on multiple dimensions, and there will be conflict between them that needs to be turned into cooperation. Such problems of cooperation are usually addressed by putting incentives in place: for example, in dyadic relationships, incentives are specified in a (performance-based) contract in the form of good performance being tied to higher rewards, larger volumes and/or contract renewal. In the context of, eg, electricity, end users may be rewarded with reduced rates when they shift their electricity demand to times during the day when overall demand is low. At the same time, in section 5, I also showed that aligning the interests of, eg, energy suppliers and the government as the main stakeholders in the energy transition is not that straightforward, and, hence, coopetition (cooperation co-existing with competition) may just be a fact of life. Mazzucato, meanwhile, argues that incentives may indeed help to turn conflict into cooperation but that missions help to shape markets through the government selecting the *willing* as opposed to selecting winners.[18] Placing problem-solving at the heart of strategy brings the direction of innovation to the core of the discussion. In the context of energy transition, this includes providing appropriate conditionalities to steel companies willing to reduce their carbon content. This is not only in the interests of the government and its mission but also in the interests of individual markets and market players, as markets develop on their own and in directions that – without the mission – could not have been expected or foreseen. As a result, actors could be incentivised by intangibles, such as sharing risks and the prospect of innovation, which will enable them to identify and refine, eg, product-service offerings, processes, systems and technologies in support of new and existing markets alike.

Similarly, the provision of information needed to coordinate activities may be formalised in a contract (or an addendum to one). At the same time, the provision of information and (particularly the less tangible) rewards could be governed using relational mechanisms, particularly through cooperative norms regarding the exchange of information. Information exchange is critical in the context of, eg, energy cooperatives, as all members will need to coordinate demand within the boundaries of supply available from the grid. Whether information exchange should then be a norm, or something dictated through a contract, is highly context-specific, making the detailed design of effective network governance mechanisms a highly intricate undertaking. The design subsequently also has implications for how the network will function. Contracts provide opportunities for enforcement with regard to key performance indicators that are not being met, but enforcement may not always be effective in that it may still not bring desired performance improvements and also does not prevent performance problems from occurring in the future. A focus on relationships is likely to leave more room for parties to be vulnerable, to reflect and to learn, even though it may take a long time before

[18] M Mazzucato, *Mission Economy: A Moonshot Guide to Changing Capitalism* (Allen Lane 2021).

corresponding benefits may be reaped. On this point, a recent study by Fang and others showed that focusing on contractual governance may negatively impact communication and trust, allowing performance problems to persist, whereas a focus on trust allows for open communication, learning, revisiting contracts (if needed) and the closing of performance gaps.[19]

8. Conclusion

Organisational networks concern a complex playing field requiring a systems perspective for collective action towards a clear network-level objective, along with coordination and cooperation between network members in support of this shared objective. Principles of good governance of these giants therefore involve multiple decisions regarding, first of all, the preferred network governance form and, subsequently, effective governance mechanisms that support progress towards the network-level objective. This gives rise to abundant research opportunities, some of which will be highlighted hereafter.

First, regarding the governance form, networks can opt for either a shared or participative governance structure, in which all network members have equal input; a lead-organisation structure involving one central steering agent; or governance through a third 'neutral' party. Which governance structure is effective depends on various network contingencies – such as the degree of goal consensus, the degree to which network-level competences are required for the task at hand, the number of network constituents, and trust within the network – and is also likely to be time-dependent. As I show above, each governance structure has its own specific benefits as well as challenges that need to be carefully addressed once a specific structure has been selected. For example, a main challenge, particularly in the Dutch context, is ensuring that the democratic process that is a strength of the shared governance mode does not culminate in endless 'poldering', ie, continual discussions and procrastination slowing down the decision-making process. At some point decisions must be made and, hence, procedures need to be put in place to make clear when to escalate issues and more specifically to whom (eg, in the case of the energy transition, whether this kind of leadership should reside with the Ministry of Infrastructure and Water Management). Governance forms may co-exist and interplay and are likely to evolve over time in response to changing network composition and/or requirements. To date, however, our understanding of which governance form is effective (including for energy collaborative networks), and how this changes over time, remains limited and work of both a theoretical and an empirical nature is required.

[19] F Fang and others, 'Down the Drain: The Dynamic Interplay of Governance Adjustments Addressing Setbacks in Large Public–Private Projects' (2024) 70 *Journal of Operations Management* 80. Available at: https://doi.org/10.1002/joom.1277.

Second, navigating the collective subsequently involves coordination of tasks, roles and responsibilities, decision-making authority, and information sharing. It also involves managing cooperation (and competition) in the sense both of aligning goals, ideals, and investment and value appropriation between network members, and of continued mutual commitment and trust. While the former is mostly concerned with how network members operate on a day-to-day basis, the latter provides the foundation for collaboration in the network in the form of shared goals, a joint identity, and explication of how the individual interests of members will be balanced with those of the collective. Different mechanisms may be deployed, ranging from more directive or formal (eg, reliance on contracts, strict target setting, top-down focus) to more mutual or informal (eg, reliance on trust, more flexible target setting, bottom-up focus). While the detailed design of effective contractual and relational governance mechanisms and their interplay in general is an area in need of scholarly attention, there is a dearth of such work pertaining to collaborative network settings.

Finally, considerations involved with coordination and collaboration are many and sometimes even contradicting resulting in governance usually being messy and far from straightforward. Consequently, fit is required, depending on aspects of time, such as the phase the network collaboration is in (ie, start-up or more mature); or the nature and diversity of tasks involved. Important issues to consider here include how to select solutions that are helpful both in the short term and in the long term, or how to effectively consider both public value/societal goals and economic value/the business case. And whether it is really a matter of having either a positive business case or ensuring fair energy supply: such an 'either/or' mindset usually results in one-sided solutions that are not collectively pursued. Instead, actors should adopt a 'both/and' mindset, which promotes contradictions and hence adds to complexity but at the same time explicates the tensions that network members are experiencing and have to navigate; as such it may also provide opportunities for achieving synergetic effects. Different strategies can be deployed to deal with the complexity of collaboration in networks (ie, focusing on mindset, temporal approaches, breaking down activities), yet which approaches are most effective in what situations is another area in need of scholarly knowledge.

Hence, it is clear that governing the giant will not be easy and warrants both experimenting in practice as well as dedicated scholarly attention. By highlighting the challenges that organisations face when engaging in collaborative networks, this chapter provides an overview that may be used to think about how governance forms may facilitate or complicate the creation and distribution of different kinds of value, how legal perspectives may promote or inhibit 'good governance', or how digitalisation may be tied into the governance process. I conclude by calling upon scholars to pursue work in these areas and as such help develop the body of knowledge on network governance approaches conducive for effective collaboration that helps in tackling grand societal challenges.

3

Sustainable Digital Finance and its Role in the Energy Transition

Are Investors and Supervisors on the Same Team?

LIEBRICH M HIEMSTRA

1. Introduction

Since 2020, two main issues have driven the EU policy agenda: sustainability and digitalisation, in the form of the Sustainable Finance Action Plan and the Digital Finance Strategy.[1] The Sustainable Finance Action Plan sets out a roadmap to boost the role of finance in achieving a well-performing economy that delivers on environmental and social goals. It will be instrumental in helping to deliver on the Paris Climate Agreement and the Sustainable Development Goals and has a focus on reorienting capital flows towards a more sustainable economy.[2] The Sustainable Finance Action Plan includes the creation of a taxonomy of sustainable activities,[3] a European standard for green bonds,[4] and rules for corporates to report on their sustainable activities.[5] The Digital Finance Strategy on the other hand has a focus

[1] Regulation (EU) 2023/2631 of the European Parliament and of the Council of 22 November 2023 on European Green Bonds and optional disclosures for bonds marketed as environmentally sustainable and for sustainability-linked bonds [2023] OJ L2023/2631.

[2] Communication from the Commission to the European Parliament, the European Council, the Council, the European Central Bank, the European Economic and Social Committee and the Committee of the Regions, 'Action Plan: Financing Sustainable Growth' COM (2018) 97 final.

[3] Regulation (EU) 2020/852 of the European Parliament and of the Council of 18 June 2020 on the establishment of a framework to facilitate sustainable investment and amending Regulation (EU) 2019/2088 [2020] OJ L198.

[4] Regulation (EU) 2023/2631 of the European Parliament and of the Council of 22 November 2023 on European Green Bonds and optional disclosures for bonds marketed as environmentally sustainable and for sustainability-linked bonds OJ L2023/2631.

[5] Directive (EU) 2022/2464 of the European Parliament and of the Council of 14 December 2022 amending Regulation (EU) No 537/2014, Directive 2004/109/EC, Directive 2006/43/EC and Directive 2013/34/EU, as regards corporate sustainability reporting [2022] OJ L322.

on how Europe can support the digital transformation of finance in the coming years while regulating its risks.[6] According to the European Commission, the Digital Finance Strategy supports the EU's ambition for a recovery that embraces the digital transition and it seeks to promote innovation and competition in the financial sector.

Even though these two packages have different goals, they are interconnected in several ways. Digital technologies can facilitate investors in their choice of sustainable finance products, for example by improving data collection and analysis or by increasing transparency on why and how a financial product is identified as sustainable. Also, sustainable finance can benefit from digital technologies, such as online platforms that make it easier to connect climate-focused investors with sustainable projects. Hence, the Sustainable Finance Action Plan and the Digital Finance Strategy both play a role in obtaining the goals of the European Green Deal and can, therefore, contribute to a low-carbon transition in society. The intersection between sustainable finance and digitalisation leads to the question what exactly is meant by sustainable digital finance?[7] And what are the opportunities and challenges of digital finance in relation to the energy transition for both investors and regulators?

This chapter identifies a field of tension between the advantages of digital finance in supporting the transition to a low-carbon economy and the complexities it may impose, especially from a regulatory perspective. With an increased focus from both regulators and supervisory authorities on digital finance, the question that arises is which regulatory boundaries come into play in relation to effective supervision. In answering this question, it pinpoints practical advantages and disadvantages of 'sustainable digital finance' – to be further defined in section 3 – from the perspective of both investors and supervisory authorities. While not intending to offer a comprehensive review of the existing literature on governance and regulation in finance, this chapter offers suggestions for aligning investors and supervisory agencies to effectively contribute to the goals of the Paris Agreement. This chapter, therefore, aims to contribute to the discussion on regulatory strategies necessary for effective supervision in a continuously developing and increasingly digitalised world. Effective supervision is explained in this chapter as the effective monitoring of a market, its players, and the products traded in that market so as to provide a supervisory authority with the necessary information to identify market abuse and the ability to take enforcement measures.

[6] Communication from the Commission to the European Parliament, the Council, the European Economic and Social Committee and the Committee of the Regions on a Digital Finance Strategy for the EU, COM (2020) 591 final.

[7] M d. Carmen Sandoval Velasco, *The Digital Finance and Sustainability Nexus: In Search of a Conceptual Approach to 'Sustainable Digital Finance'* (EUI: Florence School of Banking and Finance 2022). Available at: https://fbf.eui.eu/the-digital-finance-and-sustainability-nexus-in-search-of-a-conceptual-approach-to-sustainable-digital-finance/.

2. Digital Finance as a Concept

Prior to diving into the concept of digitalisation in the financial sector, the next section first addresses the concept of sustainable finance.

2.1. What is Sustainable Finance?

Sustainable finance looks at how investing and lending interacts with economic, social and environmental issues.[8] Sustainable finance is seen as an accelerator of the energy transition: it plays a key role in delivering on the policy objectives of the Green Deal. And the trend is on the rise: the global demand for climate-focused fund assets increased by 16 per cent in 2023, reaching a total of USD 540 billion. Of this global growth, the European Union contributed 84 per cent.[9] Investors use their available capital to make sustainable investments that may have an impact on the health of our planet, mitigate climate risks and leverage climate investment opportunities. In this way, investors can exert influence on corporates in which they want to invest and steer corporates towards sustainable business practices.[10] In turn, the concept of profit will encompass more than just maximising shareholder returns, as sustainable finance can affect economic, social and natural capital. The outdated focus on maximising return for shareholders as reflected in the Friedmann doctrine – according to which the sole responsibility of a corporation is to ensure that shareholders receive maximised returns – is subject to discussion.[11] Society as a whole would benefit from reconsidering the ways (beyond financial wealth) in which humans and nature have value, in addition to the mere focus on profit maximisation for shareholders.[12] Also, the notion of sustainability covers the introduction of the environment and humans as stakeholders – rather than shareholders being the sole stakeholders of a corporation. The sustainability of a corporation is dependent on the sustainability of both its shareholders and key stakeholders, and corporations would therefore need a balance between stakeholderism and shareholderism.[13] These two views are therefore

[8] D Schoenmaker and W Schramade, *Principles of Sustainable Finance* (Oxford University Press 2019) 4.

[9] Morningstar, 'Investing in Times of Climate Change, 2023 in Review' (April 2024). Available at: https://assets.contentstack.io/v3/assets/blt4eb669caa7dc65b2/blt0dde375ee90f6ddd/66265ab3ca88748371ed23ae/Investing_in_Times_of_Climate_Change_2024_final.pdf.

[10] ibid.

[11] M Friedman, 'The Social Responsibility of Business Is to Increase Its Profits' *New York Times* (1970). Available at: www.nytimes.com/1970/09/13/archives/a-friedman-doctrine-the-social-responsibility-of-business-is-to.html.

[12] B Kramer, 'The Regenerative Economy: A New Approach to Capitalism' (*Next Billion*, 18 April 2017). Available at: https://nextbillion.net/the-regenerative-economy-a-new-approach-to-capitalism/.

[13] C Mayer, 'Shareholderism versus Stakeholderism: A Misconceived Contradiction. A Comment on "The Illusory Promise of Stakeholder Governance" by Lucian Bebchuk and Roberto Tallarita' (3 June 2020) European Corporate Governance Institute, Law Working Paper 522/2020. Available at: https://ssrn.com/abstract=3617847 or http://dx.doi.org/10.2139/ssrn.3617847.

not necessarily opposite to each other. Profitable sustainable finance is key in this discussion: combining a return for shareholders with maximising the additional value to environmental and human capital would meet the needs of each stakeholder. It is in the field of sustainable finance where the environment as a stakeholder on the one hand and the financial sector on the other overlap. Profitable sustainable finance involves balancing the shareholders' returns with the optimisation of environmental and human capital values, which ultimately satisfies the interests of all stakeholders. Sustainable finance is the intersection where the environment and the financial sector meet as two equally important stakeholders, making it a significant domain to consider in the road towards the Green Deal objectives. The Commission confirmed that sustainable finance is relevant for reaching the Paris Agreement targets as it may channel private investments into the transition to a climate-neutral, climate-resilient, environmentally sustainable, resource-efficient and fair economy as a complement to public money.[14] Simultaneously, the emphasis on digital finance extends beyond the boundaries of the European Union. With the adoption of the Sustainable Development Goals (SDGs) by the United Nations in 2015, a focus on digital and emerging technology emerged.[15] This was illustrated by the UN Task Force on Digital Financing of the SDG's, established in 2018. The focus of this UN Task Force was not just on how digital and emerging technologies could promote efficient and innovative solutions for the SDG's but also on the actual financing of those goals.

2.1.1. Environmental, Social and Governance (ESG) Criteria

Within the financial sector, the SDGs are primarily viewed through the lens of ESG criteria, which financial institutions and corporations use to report on climate and sustainability practices.[16] ESG criteria can influence a company's investment strategies, in addition to financial goals, to support the financing of the sustainability transition. Goldman Sachs, for example, aligned investments with its sustainability goals by funding projects related to renewable energy, sustainable transport, and accessible and innovative healthcare by allocating USD 750 billion to sustainable investments by 2030.[17] Also, Citigroup has made a significant push toward sustainability, committing to USD 1 trillion in sustainable finance by 2030. The firm has been integrating ESG factors into its business operations, investments, and lending practices.[18]

[14] European Commission, 'Overview of Digital Finance'. Available at: https://finance.ec.europa.eu/digital-finance/overview-digital-finance.en.

[15] K Foster, 'Fintech and Green Fintech: Digital Innovation for the SDG's and Climate Agenda' in T Beck, Lo Giani, and G Sciascia, *Digital Finance in the EU: Drivers, Risks, Opportunities*' (European University Institute 2023).

[16] ibid.

[17] See on sustainable finance Goldman Sachs. Available at: www.goldmansachs.com/our-firm/sustainable-finance.

[18] Citigroup Sustainable Progress Strategy. Available at: www.citigroup.com/global/our-impact/sustainability/our-commitment.

ESG criteria are used as guiding principles to disclose how a company's activities affect sustainability. The EU provides for two mandatory reporting schemes. Firstly, the Corporate Sustainability Reporting Directive (CSRD)[19] aims to ensure that stakeholders have access to the information they need to assess the impact of companies on people and the environment and ensure that investors can assess financial risks and opportunities arising from climate change and other sustainability issues. Such access to information is enabled by reporting and disclosure obligations placed on corporations regarding how their businesses impact the fields in scope. Secondly, the Corporate Sustainability Due Diligence Directive (CSDDD)[20] goes a step further by addressing sustainable and responsible corporate behaviour in companies' operations and across their global value chains. The new CSDDD rules will ensure that companies in scope identify and address adverse human rights and environmental impacts of their actions, both inside and outside Europe. One of the main goals of these reporting obligations and regulations to force corporations to disclose information about their businesses is to enable investors to make informed – and hopefully more sustainable – decisions.

2.2. What is Digital Finance?

Digital finance is a term used to describe the impact of new technologies on the financial services industry and includes a variety of products, applications, processes and business models that have transformed the traditional way of providing banking and financial services.[21] Payments, lending, insurance and wealth management are reshaped by digital technology and are also described as fintech: digital innovations in the financial sector.[22] Digital technologies in the financial sector are on the rise. One example can be found in digital banks – also known as virtual or online banks – which have emerged over the past decade as a new type.[23] These digital banks can contribute to sustainable finance as they may offer green financial products, providing digital tools to track the carbon footprint of financial products and may also promote awareness and education of sustainable finance

[19] Directive (EU) 2022/2464 of the European Parliament and of the Council of 14 December 2022 amending Regulation (EU) No 537/2014, Directive 2004/109/EC, Directive 2006/43/EC and Directive 2013/34/EU, as regards corporate sustainability reporting [2022] OJ L322.

[20] Directive (EU) 2024/1760 of the European Parliament and of the Council of 13 June 2024 on corporate sustainability due diligence and amending Directive (EU) 2019/1937 and Regulation (EU) 2023/2859 [2024] OJ L2024/1760.

[21] European Commission, 'Overview of Digital Finance'. Available at: https://finance.ec.europa.eu/digital-finance/overview-digital-finance_en.

[22] E Feyen and others, 'Fintech and the Digital Transformation of Financial Services: Implications for Market Structure and Public Policy' (July 2021) Bank of International Settlement Paper No 117. Available at: www.bis.org/publ/bppdf/bispap117.pdf.

[23] O Wyman and WeBank, *Global Digital Banking: Development and Innovation Trends* (2024). Available at: www.oliverwyman.com/content/dam/oliver-wyman/v2/publications/2024/sep/OliverWyman-WeBank_Global-Digital-Banking-Development-and-Innovation-Trends.pdf.

via digital platforms. Digitalisation has an increased impact on financial markets and it appears that both supervisory agencies and regulators have also increased their focus on digitalisation. For example, the Dutch national regulatory authority *Autoriteit Financiële Markten* (AFM) states that the digital transition affects the role and responsibilities of the AFM and that new skills, expertise and a certain nimbleness are required when adapting to these changes.[24] Another example of such increased supervisory focus on digitalisation is the EU Digital Finance Package, which – according to the Commission – supports the EU's ambition for a recovery that embraces the digital transition.[25] Digital financial services can help modernise the European economy across sectors and turn Europe into a global digital player. The Digital Finance Package states that boosting digital finance would support Europe's economic recovery strategy, as well as broader economic transformation, and that it would open up new channels to mobilise funding in support of the Green Deal for Europe.

3. Sustainable Digital Finance

Digitalisation and sustainable finance are connected in a number of ways. One of the main links is that digital technologies can facilitate investors in their choice of sustainable finance products, for example by improving data collection and analysis or by increasing transparency on why and how a financial product is identified as sustainable. Such increases in transparency allow investors to have access to more information on the sustainability performance of a financial product and more accurate real-time data on its actual performance. This leads to better decision-making opportunities for investors on the one hand and to clearer performance ratings related to sustainability for financial products on the other.[26] Also, sustainable finance can benefit from digital technologies, such as online platforms that make it easier to connect climate-focused investors with sustainable projects. Digital technologies are therefore a tool to increase access to capital for ESG projects. In this context, digital platforms – or new forms of finance, such as crowdfunding or peer-to-peer lending – can enhance shareholder engagement and activism, allowing a broader range of stakeholders to participate in ESG projects and related financial products. Another link between digitalisation and sustainable finance is that digital technologies can simplify risk management for sustainable investments. This, in turn, enables investors to make more informed decisions about where and how to invest their capital.

[24] Autoriteit Financiële Markten, *State of the Capital Markets 2023* (2023). Available at: www.afm.nl/en/sector/actueel/2023/oktober/europese-kapitaalmarktendata-socm.

[25] Beck, Giani, and Sciascia, *Digital Finance in the EU* (n 15).

[26] D Hariyani and others, 'Leveraging Digital Technologies for Advancing Circular Economy Practices and Enhancing Life Cycle Analysis: A Systematic Literature Review' (2024) 2(3) *Waste Management Bulletin* 69.

Beyond this list, one could think of numerous ways in which digitalisation and sustainable finance intersect. Such intersection can be defined as sustainable digital finance: the approach in which financial practices – supported by digital technologies – promote environmental sustainability and social responsibility, and the effective governance thereof.[27] Sustainable digital finance is broader than the concept of green digital finance, which has a focus on the environment and carbon neutrality as influencers of financial products.[28] The concept of sustainable digital finance seeks to address the entire range of SDGs, encompassing social and governance objectives alongside environmental ones. Examples of social objectives in sustainable digital finance may include affordable access to technology and social inclusion, with the aim of providing or increasing access to affordable digital financial services for underserved populations in society. Governance objectives in the field of sustainable digital finance may cover strong policies to protect data privacy and security and anti-corruption measures, such as promoting fair business practices and developing systems to prevent digital fraud, bribery and corruption.

With the emergence of sustainable digital finance, new market developments came ashore. Not only have new financial products like green securities, green bonds and green leasing emerged, but the number of venues and exchanges for trading digital financial products has also grown. Such growth has a positive impact on the energy sector, as more private capital can be attracted to finance the energy transition. The following sections will discuss the pros and cons of digital finance as an accelerator for the energy transition from the perspective of both investors and supervisory agencies.

3.1. Sustainable Digital Finance in the Energy Sector

There are several examples of how digital finance is used in the energy transition.

3.1.1. Crowdfunding Platforms

In the solar energy sector, numerous crowdfunding platforms are engaging private investors to support solar plants. Crowdfunding platforms are also seen in other fields of the energy transition, such as battery projects.[29] Investors in this sector come from around the globe, while the platforms operate in various countries,

[27] K Oertli, 'How Sustainable Digital Finance can unlock a Low-Carbon Economy' (World Economic Forum Green Horizon Sumit: The Pivotal Role of Finance, 2022). Available at: www.weforum.org/agenda/2020/11/sustainable-digital-finance-low-carbon-economy/.

[28] VK Singh, 'Regulatory and Legal Framework for Promoting Green Digital Finance, Economics, Law, and Institutions in Asia Pacific' in F Taghizadeh-Hesary and S Hyun (eds), *Green Digital Finance and Sustainable Development Goals* (Springer 2022) 3.

[29] Giga Storage, 'GIGA Rhino Battery Raises More Than €3,6 Million in Crowdfunding'. Available at: https://giga-storage.com/en/crowdfunding-successful/.

and the solar projects may be situated in yet another location.[30] This effectively connects international investors with local initiatives. At the same time, it might be a challenge to address such international trading activities with effective local regulations. An example can be found in local know-your-customer regulations, which may differ per country or EU Member State as national implementation of the EU directive leaves room for differences.[31] For example, if two crowdfunding platforms are owned by the same financial institution and are based in two different Member States, investors may encounter varying know-your-customer checks on each platform, even though the investing counterparty is the same company.

3.1.2. Blockchain for Energy Trading

There are trading platforms that use blockchain technology to link producers and consumers to each other. Such peer-to-peer trading is, for example, seen in a situation where homeowners with solar panels sell excess electricity directly to neighbours.[32] The increasing amount of distributed power generation from rooftop solar panels allows new electricity markets to emerge in which prosumers and consumers can trade locally produced energy. The use of blockchain technology has increasingly emerged in energy markets and shows great potential to facilitate peer-to-peer energy trading.[33] The use of blockchain technology in the energy trading sector enables secure and decentralised energy trading.[34]

3.1.3. Green Bonds

Institutions and companies are issuing green bonds through digital platforms to raise funds for renewable energy projects. Green bonds are fixed-income debt instruments that are designed to raise capital for climate and environmental projects.[35] For example, the World Bank has used digital marketplaces to issue several bonds, including sustainable development bonds and green bonds.[36] Since the first issuances of green bonds by the European Investment Bank and the

[30] Crowdspace, 'The Best Green Energy Crowdfunding Platforms'. Available at: https://thecrowdspace.com/directory/green-energy-crowdfunding-platforms/.

[31] Directive (EU) 2019/1153 of the European Parliament and of the Council of 20 June 2019 laying down rules facilitating the use of financial and other information for the prevention, detection, investigation or prosecution of certain criminal offences, and repealing Council Decision [2019] OJ L186.

[32] See for example projects by Dutch firm Powerpeers. Available at: https://powerpeers.nl/groene-energie/energie-delen/.

[33] P Wongthongtham and others, 'Blockchain-enabled Peer-to-Peer energy trading' (2021) 94 *Computers and Electrical Engineering* 1.

[34] A Shinde and others, 'Renewable Energy Trading Platform using Blockchain' (2024) 233 *Procedia Computer Science* 243.

[35] Investopedia, 'Green Bond: Types, How to Buy and FAQs'. Available at: www.investopedia.com/terms/g/green-bond.asp.

[36] World Bank, 'International Bank for Reconstruction and Development Funding Program'. Available at: https://treasury.worldbank.org/en/about/unit/treasury/ibrd/ibrd-issues.

World Bank, the market growth has been explosive and is increasingly attracting interest from investors.[37] This explosive growth of the green bonds market called for regulation and standardisation. That is why several market-based solutions for establishing the sustainability of a green bond have been introduced, as well as an EU-wide standard to open new opportunities for issuers and investors and to tackle greenwashing risks.[38]

3.1.4. Smart Contracts

Digital finance can use smart contracts to automate and enforce agreements related to the supply of energy projects and payments. The advantage of the use of smart contracts is that it may reduce transaction costs, increase trust between contracting parties and reduce the amount of time it takes to settle payments. An example of such smart contracts is the electronic bill of lading, a document of title used in the freight and transportation businesses.[39] The maritime industry plays a key role in the energy transition as the use of alternative fuels and sustainable logistics is used to reduce the dependence of the sector on traditional fossil fuels and to lower emissions. Also, the wholesale products used for the construction of (offshore) wind farms and solar plants cannot always be produced locally and need to be transported globally, in which the maritime sector plays a role. The electronic bills of lading play a role in the energy transition by facilitating the maritime shipping movements that could support the construction of sustainable energy facilities.

4. Investor's Perspective

This section distinguishes between several ways in which digital finance can play a role in the energy transition from an investor's point of view: (1) digital finance may increase the level of financing for green projects as investors can access a wider range of investment opportunities;[40] (2) monitoring of the environmental impact of green projects may increase as digitalisation enables investors to track the carbon footprint of their portfolios and receive information

[37] N Badenhoop, 'Green Bonds: An Assessment of the Proposed EU Green Bond Standard and Its Potential to Prevent Greenwashing' (European Parliament 2022). Available at: www.europarl.europa.eu/thinktank/en/document/IPOL_STU(2022)703359.

[38] Directive (EU) 2023/959 of the European Parliament and of the Council of 10 May 2023 amending Directive 2003/87/EC establishing a system for greenhouse gas emission allowance trading within the Union and Decision (EU) 2015/1814 concerning the establishment and operation of a market stability reserve for the Union greenhouse gas emission trading system [2023] OJ L130.

[39] The Baltic and International Maritime Council (BIMCO), E-Bills of Lading Standard. Available at: www.bimco.org/ships-ports-and-voyage-planning/maritime-digitalisation/ebl.

[40] Recently, the adoption of digital tools has begun to emerge in commodity markets, which may generate business opportunities for market participants, volatility and trading platforms: Commodity Trading, 'Digitalisation in Commodity Trading in 2021' (*Insider Blog*, 12 July 2021). Available at: www.commoditytradingweek.com/insider/digitalisation-in-commodity-trading-in-2021/.

on the environmental impact, risks and opportunities of their investment;[41] (3) transparency and accountability in the financial sector may be promoted as a result of investors being able to monitor their investments; and (4) liquidity may improve as electronic proof of ownership and payment documents reduce contract settlement times, which in turn accelerates the disbursement of funds. These developments enable investors to make better-informed decisions on how to invest their capital. At the same time, digital finance connects investors who have sustainability goals to investment opportunities that have a focus on developing or supporting sustainable projects. So, can we assume that the impact of digitalisation on sustainable finance is solely positive? Not necessarily.

4.1. All that Glitters is not Gold

It is essential to understand the downsides and challenges from an investor's perspective to ensure that digitalisation actually supports, rather than undermines, sustainable finance.

First off, with the expanded access that investors have to information regarding sustainable projects and amplified data generation, the potential for cyber-attacks, technical glitches and operational disruptions also increases, which might result in potential negative system impacts and risks for individuals if not adequately managed.[42] An increased dependency on technology can also create vulnerability in case of a technological failure or disruption.

Secondly, the excessive quantity of data has both a positive and a negative side. The rise in data flows and available information on the sustainability aspects of an investment enhances transparency, but at the same time it can also be challenging to find the needed information amid the overwhelming amount of data. The amount of information available may even deter new investors in sustainable finance. This could create inequality for both investors and organisations seeking funding: only those who are tech-savvy or able to effectively utilise digitalisation can keep pace with the sustainable finance trend. As a result, other organisations – potentially with projects that rank higher in sustainability – might be overlooked. This does not mean that the market itself is unwelcoming for smaller companies or organisations with limited resources; rather, it indicates that the technological requirements for participation are exceptionally stringent. Such inequality might impact the way digitalisation is perceived among investors and organisations. It appeared that the use of new digital technology in financial products eroded trust in both institutions

[41] McKinsey, 'Metals and Mining: Unleashing the Power of Technology in Commodities Trading' (11 January 2023). Available at: www.mckinsey.com/industries/metals-and-mining/our-insights/metals-and-mining-unleashing-the-power-of-technology-in-commodities-trading.

[42] K Foster, 'Fintech and Green Fintech: Digital Innovation for the SDGs and Climate Agenda' in Beck, Giani, and Sciascia (n 15).

and technology.[43] Such inequality only contributes to such a decrease in trust, which is one of the reasons why the link between digital technology usage and trust in financial markets is relevant. On the one hand, trust is vital for the functioning of financial markets.[44] On the other, forms of digital technology in finance such as bitcoin were actually designed as a system for making electronic transactions without relying on trust.[45] At the same time, Rijswijk and others mention that limited trust hinders digitalisation in several ways, inducing a vicious cycle whereby limited trust results in limited digitalisation, which in turn causes more distrust due to uncertainties around the digitalisation process, further increased by existing (technological) path dependencies.[46] The International Labour Organization recognises that maintaining public trust in payment systems and infrastructures is key for digitalisation to be sustainable in the finance sector.[47]

A third challenge of sustainable digital finance from an investor's perspective is the rapid evolution of technologies that enable sustainable digital finance to outpace regulatory frameworks. This may lead to compliance challenges from an investor perspective and difficulties for supervisors to keep track of market behaviour. This requires governments and regulatory authorities to step in and enforce robust data protection, cybersecurity regulations and regulatory frameworks that are fit to stand the pace at which digitalisation in the sustainable finance market develops. Such an increased role for governments in this field contributes to the trust in sustainable digital finance. But that is easier said than done and the next sections will address the challenges that supervisory authorities face in this field.

5. Supervisor's Perspective

When switching the scope from the opportunities for investors to the authorities who should supervise sustainable digital finance, it appears that both supervisory agencies and regulators face challenges with the increased digital tools available on financial markets, but they do see the digitalisation of the financial sector as

[43] T Tillemann and others, 'The Blueprint for Blockchain and Social Innovation' (*New America*, October 2019). Available at: www.newamerica.org/digital-impact-governance-initiative/blockchain-trust-accelerator/reports/blueprint-blockchain-and-social-innovation/.

[44] P Sapienza and L Zingales, 'A Trust Crisis' (2012) 12(2) *International Review of Finance* 123. For a more elaborate view on the role of trust in the financial sector see O Abdelsalam and others, 'Trust Matters: A Global Perspective on the Influence of Trust on Bank Market Risk (2024) 92 *Journal of International Markets, Institutions and Money* 1.

[45] S Nakamoto, 'Bitcoin: A Peer-to-Peer Electronic Cash System' (March 2014). Available at: https://bitcoin.org/bitcoin.pdf.

[46] K Rijswijk and others, 'The Enabling and Constraining Connections between Trust and Digitalisation in Incumbent Value Chains' (2023) 186 *Technological Forecasting and Social Change* pt A.

[47] International Labour Organization, 'The Impact of Digitalization in the Finance Sector. Technical Meeting on the Impact of Digitalization in the Finance Sector' (Note on the proceedings, Geneva, January 2022) www.ilo.org/meetings-and-events/sectorial/technical-meeting-impact-digitalization-finance-sector.

a key point of focus for the future.[48] For example, the increased transparency reporting obligations regarding financial products are closely connected to the lack of transparency of cross-border trading activities by market participants and the difficulties that regulators may have in detecting market abuse. Simply put, digitalisation may make it more difficult to track and monitor which trades are concluded by market participants and what their trading motives are. In addition, the complexity of data and the rapid technological advancements of trading platforms and products requires supervisory authorities and regulators not only to be closely connected to the market but also to have the knowledge, tools and budget to monitor the market in an effective way to be able to detect market abuse. Effective supervision can therefore be explained as the effective monitoring of a market, its players and the products traded in that market to provide a supervisory authority with the necessary information to identify market abuse. At the same time, effective supervision entails the ability of a supervisory authority to take enforcement measures based on the identified behaviour of market participants.

5.1. National Mandate with a Cross-Border Trading Activity

Supervisory agencies and their supervision and enforcement powers are based on national law and therefore limited to their national mandate. In the field of financial supervision, there is a correlation between the complexity of enforcement governance and the verticalisation of enforcement: as enforcement governance becomes more complex in terms of the number of actors and functions, verticalisation of enforcement increases.[49] The 'verticalisation' of enforcement in the EU implies upgrading (direct) enforcement powers, from the national to the supranational level, providing EU authorities with the competence to directly carry out enforcement actions.[50] In the financial sector, both the European Securities and Markets Authority (ESMA) and the European Central Bank (ECB) are equipped with direct enforcement powers, yet ESMA, the ECB and the Agency for the Cooperation of Energy Regulators (ACER) in the energy sector are highly dependent on the agenda and enforcement powers of national regulatory authorities. Such dependency requires further alignment and cooperation between regulatory authorities,

[48] Autoriteit Financiële Markten, 'State of the Capital Markets 2023' (2023) www.afm.nl/en/sector/actueel/2023/oktober/europese-kapitaalmarktendata-socm.

[49] F Cacciatore, 'Patterns of Networked Enforcement in the European System of Financial Supervision: What is the New Role for the National Competent Authorities?' (2019) 10(3) *European Journal of Risk Regulation* 502.

[50] M Scholten, 'Mind the Trend! Enforcement of EU Law Has Been Moving to Brussels' (2017) 24(9) *Journal of European Public Policy* 1348; M Scholten and others, 'The Proliferation of EU Enforcement Authorities: A New Development in Law Enforcement in the EU' in M Scholten and M Luchtman (eds), *Law Enforcement by EU Authorities. Implications for Political and Judicial Accountability* (Edward Elgar 2017) 1.

both at the vertical level and at the horizontal level.[51] Cooperation between EU authorities and national regulatory authorities (NRAs) is considered vertical, while cooperation between either EU authorities or NRAs is viewed as horizontal.

Such field of tension between national supervisory boundaries and international trading activities becomes clear in carbon markets. Carbon markets are trading systems in which greenhouse gas emission credits are traded. There are multiple carbon markets at international, national and even subnational level, such as the California Cap-and-Trade Program. To detect market abuse in these carbon markets, transparency is essential. The most effective way to achieve such transparency for investors and supervisory authorities is to provide reliable data on each transfer of a carbon emission certificate, such as reflected in the EU Emissions Trading System (ETS) data viewer from the European Environment Agency.[52] However, transparency provisions have often been overridden by arguing confidentiality concerns on cost information for new technologies or to protect buyers from liability after buying fraudulent allowances.[53] This has led to quite different provisions on transparency for market transactions in different countries. As a consequence, the rules on reporting real-time data for cross-border transactions may vary per jurisdiction and are confusing for market participants. At the same time, comparing different sets of data from the same cross-border carbon emission certificate trading transaction is like comparing apples to oranges, making it unsuitable for a supervisory authority to identify market abuse.

5.2. Knowledge of the Market

Understanding a market is essential for supervisory authorities to effectively fulfil their roles. A deep knowledge of market dynamics, behaviours and transaction patterns allows these authorities to identify irregularities and potential market abuse. By grasping the nuances of the market, supervisory authorities can identify and respond swiftly to suspicious market behaviour. Without it, supervisory authorities would struggle to detect market abuse, undermining overall trust in both the financial system and its supervisory framework. Digitalisation in the field of sustainable finance brings significant advantages for market analysis by supervisory authorities, but it also introduces several challenges and downsides that must be carefully considered. A key issue is data overload; vast amounts of reported data can overwhelm supervisory authorities, making it hard to identify relevant trading patterns or determine how sustainable a financial product truly

[51] LM Hiemstra, 'Energy Trading and the Exchange of Information Between Supervisors: Effectiveness of Fragmented Supervision and Information Sharing' (2021) 39(2) *Journal of Energy & Natural Resources Law* 159.

[52] European Environment Agency, 'EU Emissions Trading System (ETS) Data Viewer'. Available at: www.eea.europa.eu/en/analysis/maps-and-charts/emissions-trading-viewer-1-dashboards.

[53] R Betz and others, *The Carbon Market Challenge: Preventing Abuse Through Effective Governance of Elements in Earth System Governance* (Cambridge, Cambridge University Press 2022).

is. The complexity of technology presents another challenge. As financial markets advance technologically, supervisory authorities may struggle to keep pace with the evolving tools and techniques used by market participants, potentially leading to gaps in oversight. The use of digital technology, for example algorithms for data analysis, can create blind spots, as these automated systems might not fully capture the nuances of human behaviour or the complexities of market dynamics. This is an important downside of digitalisation in the scope of supervision and enforcement as the reasons for conducting certain trades are important qualifiers for market abuse. For example, hedging is a well-known trading strategy for mitigating future price risks, while speculation and arbitrage are based on taking risks in order to make profits instead of mitigating those risks.[54] This distinction is not always easy to make.[55] Yet, it is important for assessing to which extent the Markets in Financial Instruments Directive (MiFID II)[56] and the European Market Infrastructure Regulation[57] apply to the trading activity, as positions held by non-financial market participants for hedging purposes may be exempted from the scope of both regulations.

5.3. Complexity of Regulation

One of the challenges that sustainable digital finance imposes is to be found in the structure of the regulation. The regulatory framework of sustainable finance at EU level is much broader than the previously mentioned Sustainable Finance Action plan. It encompasses – among others – the Sustainable Finance Disclosure Regulation,[58] the EU Taxonomy Regulation,[59] and amendments to the MiFID II, the Alternative Investment Fund Managers Directive,[60] the Undertakings for the Collective Investment of Transferable Securities Directive,[61] the European green

[54] J Hull, *Options, Futures and Other Derivatives* (Pearson Education 2012).

[55] I-H Cheng and W Xiong, 'Why Do Hedgers Trade So Much' (2014) 43(52) *The Journal of Legal Studies* 183.

[56] Directive 2014/65/EU of the European Parliament and of the Council of 15 May 2014 on markets in financial instruments and amending Directive 2002/92/EC and Directive 2011/61/EU [2014] *OJ L173*.

[57] Regulation (EU) 648/2012 of the European Parliament and of the Council of 4 July 2012 on OTC derivatives, central counterparties and trade repositories [2012] *OJ L201*.

[58] Regulation (EU) 2019/2088 of the European Parliament and of the Council of 27 November 2019 on sustainability-related disclosures in the financial services sector [2019] *OJ L317*.

[59] Regulation (EU) 2020/852 of the European Parliament and of the Council of 18 June 2020 on the establishment of a framework to facilitate sustainable investment and amending Regulation (EU) 2019/2088 [2020] *OJ L198*.

[60] Directive 2011/61/EU of the European Parliament and of the Council of 8 June 2011 on Alternative Investment Fund Managers and amending Directives 2003/41/EC and 2009/65/EC and Regulations (EC) No 1060/2009 and (EU) No 1095/2010 [2011] *OJ L174*.

[61] Directive 2009/65/EC of the European Parliament and of the Council of 13 July 2009 on the coordination of laws, regulations and administrative provisions relating to undertakings for collective investment in transferable securities [2009] *OJ L302*.

bond standard,[62] the EU Climate Transition Benchmarks Regulation,[63] and the CSRD. The multitude of these reforms are sometimes seen as meticulously engineered laws and regulations that show features of complex rules, such as density, granularity, ethicality, cross-referencing, difficult determinations and functional dependence.[64] There may be very good reasons for such complexity in regulatory frameworks, such as sector-specific needs or multi-level governance. Regulators often struggle to keep up with the fast-paced changes brought about by digital technology in finance. This is due to the slow and bureaucratic processes involved in developing and implementing new rules. As a result, by the time these rules are put into place, they may already be outdated due to the continued evolution of digital finance innovation. Potential solutions to this problem are to shift towards principles-based regulations, which can be more adaptive to the market compared to the rigid framework of rules-based regulations, or to design regulations to be technology-neutral so that digital finance regulations do not need to be adapted as digital technology changes or when innovations emerge.[65] The focus on principles-based regulation as a potential solution is further explained below in section 6.3.

6. Finding the Balance: Regulatory Boundaries in the Equation

When trying to find a balance between the – both positive and negative – implications from an investor's perspective on the one hand and the supervisory challenges on the other, a field of tension can be identified. As the number of sustainable digital finance products in the market increases, so do the investment opportunities. At the same time, the increase in the diversity of these financial products also expands the scope for supervisory authorities to monitor, supervise and take enforcement measures in case of market abuse. In an ideal scenario, both investors and supervisory authorities leverage sustainable digital finance and its regulatory framework as a catalyst for the energy transition, instead of slowing the transition down by ineffective supervision. When reviewing this field of tension, several questions arise: How can supervisory agencies position themselves as valuable contributors to the energy transition, rather than obstacles, when supervising sustainable digital finance? What regulatory boundaries come into play regarding the effective

[62] Regulation (EU) 2023/2631 of the European Parliament and of the Council of 22 November 2023 on European Green Bonds and optional disclosures for bonds marketed as environmentally sustainable and for sustainability-linked bonds [2023] *OJ L2023/2631*.

[63] Regulation (EU) 2019/2089 of the European Parliament and of the Council of 27 November 2019 amending Regulation (EU) 2016/1011 as regards EU Climate Transition Benchmarks, EU Paris-aligned Benchmarks and sustainability-related disclosures for benchmarks [2019] *OJ L317*.

[64] FE Mezzanotte, 'EU Sustainable Finance: Complex Rules and Compliance Problems' (2023) 42 *Review of Banking & Financial Law* 845.

[65] PK Ozili, 'Digital Finance Research and Developments around the World: A Literature Overview (2023) 8(1) *International Journal of Business Forecasting and Marketing Intelligence* 35.

supervision of trading in sustainable digital finance? What are possible solutions for a more effective supervision of sustainable digital finance as a tool to support the transition to a sustainable economy and how would such effective supervision work in practice?

As highlighted before, effective supervision in the field of sustainable digital finance can be explained as the effective monitoring of a market to enable a supervisory authority to actually identify market abuse and – additionally – to enforce the regulatory framework in case of such behaviour. When applying this definition to the functioning of supervisory authority, two key points stand out: (1) the necessity of having a supervisory authority that understands the market well enough to identify behaviours that deviate from the status quo in the market; and (2) ensuring the supervisory authority is equipped with the necessary tools to effectively carry out its tasks. The sections below show and explain different ways to increase the effectiveness of supervision in the field of sustainable digital finance.

6.1. Increased Market Insights

A well-informed supervisor is able to be more effective in its supervisory work because it understands market dynamics and can spot abnormal market behaviour as a consequence thereof.[66] In order to provide tools for more effective supervision of sustainable digital finance – enabling a supervisor to detect market abuse and to act on it – a distinction needs to be made between providing a supervisory authority with insights and knowledge on market developments and, at the same time, providing it with the right tools to supervise and enforce.

There are several fields in which supervisory authorities can increase their insight into the markets where sustainable digital finance plays a role and connect with market participants to stay up to date with recent developments. These include both informal and formal ways. Informal consultations, industry round tables, public consultations and feedback sessions with market players can be organised without a specific mandate and are not mandatory for market participants to join. This informal nature may suggest that only market participants displaying legally compliant market behaviour would be willing to cooperate, resulting in only one facet of the diamond being visible. Formal tools, backed by a legal mandate, can encompass the full range of supervised market participants and include audits, inspections and thematic reviews. A tool that is mutually beneficial for both supervisory authorities and market participants alike is the concept of regulatory sandboxes; these offer market players the chance to try new products and services in a controlled environment, thus providing regulators with insights while fostering innovation.

[66] LM Hiemstra, 'Energy Trading and the Exchange of Information Between Supervisors: Effectiveness of Fragmented Supervision and Information Sharing' (2021) 39(2) *Journal of Energy & Natural Resources Law* 159.

6.1.1. *Regulatory Technology (RegTech)*

The role of RegTech when exploring how supervisory authorities can enhance their understanding of the market is worth highlighting. The use of RegTech could be considered the supervisory answer to fintech developments on the regulatory side.[67] Simply put, it is defined as the technological solution within financial supervision to digitalise supervisory reporting and implementation of supervisory processes like monitoring, predictive analysis and the use of robo advisers.[68] Technological innovations and the use of artificial intelligence can streamline research on market behaviour, detect fraud, provide a deeper insight into trends and market activities, and – last but not least – lead to cost-efficient supervision as it may improve and speed up automated market monitoring. Such advanced technology may therefore enable supervisory authorities to spot market abuse sooner than without the use of such technology. At the same time, RegTech is not the holy grail either as it may come with data privacy concerns and might be quickly outdated in a fast-evolving landscape of sustainable digital finance.

6.2. Sufficient Tools to Enforce

There are two straightforward options to expand the tools available to supervisory authorities to address suspected market abuse: (1) to expand the authority's mandate and broaden the range of tools at its disposal; or (2) to improve the use of existing tools by increasing budgets, hiring more staff and enhancing their capacity to carry out enforcement tasks. However, neither of these options is likely to be realised in the short term, as both would require either changes to the current regulatory framework or lengthy approval processes involving various EU legislative bodies. So, what options do supervisory authorities have to enhance the effectiveness of the current tools they have? Below, I further explore two possibilities: a more proactive and leading role of a supervisory authority in the market rather than an ex-post enforcement tool; and the concept of cooperation amongst supervisory authorities.

6.2.1. *Supervisor as a Proactive Player*

Supervisory authorities have a wide scope of tasks and powers, which may differ significantly per authority. For example, ESMA has a range of enforcement powers while ACER has a more coordinative role and is dependent on NRAs for the

[67] J Monkiewicz and M Monkiewicz, 'Financial Sector Supervision in Digital Age: Transformation in Progress' (2022) 14 *Foundations of Management* 1.

[68] J Prenio and D Broeders, 'Innovative Technology in Financial Supervision (Suptech): The Experience of Early Users' (Bank for International Settlements 2018). Available at: www.bis.org/fsi/publ/insights9.htm.

execution of enforcement tasks. Both authorities, however, may choose to issue guiding principles in the form of position papers, guidelines and recommendations to address recent market developments and issues. In new markets – such as the market for sustainable digital finance – market participants as well as supervisory authorities are redefining their role and strategies. A knowledgeable supervisory authority that offers clarity on current issues to market participants helps build their trust in the market itself. From that perspective, supervisory authorities are closer to the market and its participants and are able to detect atypical market behaviour at an earlier stage. Hence, the proactive role of a supervisory authority can increase the effectiveness of its supervisory task. The Financial Conduct Authority (FCA) confirmed that in order to meet challenges – like rapid technological change – it must continue to become a forward-looking, proactive regulator that is more proactive, meaning more innovative, more assertive and more adaptive.[69] In order to do this, supervisory authorities can provide more guidance and initiate meetings with stakeholders from the industry – market participants and industry groups – to provide clarity on their interpretation of the scope of enforcement. However, it would be beneficial to coordinate this approach with other NRAs at a horizontal level and with the EU supervisory authorities at a vertical level. That is where the concept of supervisory cooperation comes in.

6.2.2. Cooperation Among Supervisory Authorities

I believe that regulation can serve as a catalyst for change. An international approach with centralised or – at least – coordinated enforcement would better reflect a truly global financial system. Only in this way can regulation drive the transition to a greener future and guide private investments towards supporting sustainability. Hence, this chapter states that coordinated enforcement and cooperation between supervisory authorities is vital for the sustainability transition. Another reason mentioned in the literature for why cooperation between supervisory authorities is beneficial for the enforcement of a regulatory framework is that differences in the scope of application of the relevant regulatory framework, and methods of legal or administrative recourse, may affect the transparency of interstate supervision.[70] Such transparency is vital for investor trust in the market as is the way supervision is conducted. This need for cooperation is also recognised by De Nederlandsche Bank in the field of sustainable digital finance; it states that supervisory authorities with mandates in the areas of cybersecurity, data protection, competition and financial supervision should cooperate more closely.[71] There

[69] N Rathi, CEO FCA (speech, July 2021). Available at: www.fca.org.uk/news/speeches/transforming-forward-looking-proactive-regulator.

[70] M Luchtman, 'EU Influence on Law Enforcement and International Cooperation in the Field of Insider Dealing (2006) 2(1) *Utrecht Law Review* 136.

[71] De Nederlandsche Bank, 'Changing Landscape, Changing Supervision. Developments in the Relationship Between Bigtechs and Financial Institutions' (2023). Available at: www.dnb.nl/en/general-news/press-releases-2021/rise-of-bigtechs-requires-adjustments-in-financial-supervision/.

are many ways to shape such cooperation. Examples include the development of networks of national enforcers and coordinated enforcement measures including the transfer of power from one supervisory authority to the other, as well as transnational regulatory networks whereby NRAs cooperate directly with their counterparts to address common regulatory issues.[72] In addition, networked tasks such as the alignment of homogeneous interpretation of the EU regulatory framework may be coordinated.[73] The exchange of best practice and information on the supervised market and its participants takes many forms and may be based on soft-law instruments.[74] In the field of sustainable digital finance, it seems challenging to capture the terms of cooperation and coordination between supervisory authorities in a pre-established and fixed legal framework, because the supervised market and its products are by nature highly subject to change and adaptation. This requires an adaptive way of thinking of the interpretation of the law.

6.3. Looking Beyond the Existing Toolbox: Adaptive Regulatory Frameworks

Above, two options have been explored on how supervisory authorities can enhance the effectiveness of the current tools at hand, meaning that they can use the current set of tools to monitor the market, its players and products traded on the market to be able to obtain the necessary information to identify market abuse. Are there other options available to increase the effectiveness of supervision in the field of sustainable digital finance? Are more rules on – for example – reporting obligations on the trading details of sustainable digital finance products or a participant's market behaviour perhaps a solution? Not necessarily. Having more rules is not always better. As Baldwin states: rules do not work when those willing to comply do not know what compliance involves and when those less willing or able to comply are not informed or stimulated in the appropriate manner. Finding the right rule for the job does make a difference to regulation. Effective rule use

[72] PH Verdier, 'Transnational Regulatory Networks and their Limits' (2009) 34(1) *Yale Journal of International Law 113.*

[73] F Cacciatore, 'Patterns of Networked Enforcement in the European System of Financial Supervision: What is the New Role for the National Competent Authorities?' (2019) 10(3) *European Journal of Risk Regulation* 502.

[74] Examples of such soft-law instruments, on which cooperation between supervisory authorities is based, are the memorandum of understanding between ESMA and the CFTC regarding cooperation and the exchange of information with respect to certain registered derivatives clearing organisations that are recognised in both jurisdictions (ESMA, 'MoU USA – CFTC Supplemental Arrangement' (2021). Available at: www.esma.europa.eu/document/supplemental-arrangement-2016-memorandum-understanding-related-esma%E2%80%99s-assessment-compliance) and the memorandum of understanding between ESMA and ACER to strengthen their cooperation to further improve information exchange and avoid potential market abuse in Europe's spot and derivative markets (ESMA, 'ACER and ESMA Enhance Cooperation to Strengthen Oversight of Energy and Energy Derivative Markets' (2022) www.esma.europa.eu/press-news/esma-news/acer-and-esma-enhance-cooperation-strengthen-oversight-energy-and-energy).

demands that those who design rules take into account the enforcement strategies that will have to be used to achieve compliance.[75] That is a problem in the field of sustainable digital finance, as drafting regulations that effectively address a rapidly evolving market is almost impossible. Also, Mufarrige and Zywicki argue that simplicity in the regulatory framework is essential for financial institutions to manage risk and conduct their affairs efficiently and prudently and that complexity, by contrast, begets a variety of destabilising problems, including the likelihood of regulatory arbitrage and errors by regulators that increase risk. They argue that simple rules would create a more stable and efficient financial regulatory system.[76] At the same time, Scholten argues the contrary, by stating that the effectiveness of policies and regulation is better if promoted thanks to the rule of law, which needs to be strengthened at the level of primary law – meaning EU treaties.[77] One of the complexities of our time is the choice for a legislator between these two approaches. On the one hand, there is the industry- and investor-led approach to regulation, which advocates that over-regulation in an undeveloped market leads to poor incentives for investors to comply. On the other hand, the regulatory approach, underlines the importance of more comprehensive regulatory frameworks and considers sustainability risks and impacts, where more robust legislative intervention is required to set clear expectations that firms take action on sustainability.[78]

One solution is to draft clear, simple legislation that can be tailored to newly invested financial products or the newly developed digital use of those products. Such regulation would be adaptive to multiple products and situations in a fast-developing market. This requires not only a broad mandate for a supervisory authority interpreting the law but also the trust of market participants that such supervisory authority will handle such a broad mandate and policy freedom. An example can be found in the Initial Coin Offerings Guidelines of the Swiss Financial Market Supervisory Authority.[79] In this 11-page guideline, the authority provides a legal classification system for tokens, focusing on their characteristics, such as function and transferability, rather than imposing rigid technological criteria. This approach provides clarity while also allowing space for the development of new types of tokens. Such experimental legal regimes have been criticised in the past – highlighting the risks of frequent politicisation and the general absence of methodological preoccupations – yet they are acknowledgements that

[75] R Baldwin, 'Why Rules Don't Work' (1990) 53 *The Modern Law Review* 321.

[76] C Mufarrige and T Zywicki, 'Simple Rules for a Complex Regulatory World: The Case of Financial Regulation' (2021) 52 *European Journal of Law and Economics* 285.

[77] M Scholten, 'A "House of Cards" Construction for the Expanding Mandate of Supervision of Financial Markets in the EU' (2022) Jean Monnet Network on EU Law Enforcement Working Paper Series 35/22.

[78] S Eriksson 'The Centrality of Law for EU Sustainable Finance Markets: Outlining a Research Agenda' (2024) 33 *Review of European, Comparative & International Environmental Law* 57.

[79] Swiss Financial Market Supervisory Authority FINMA, 'FINMA Publishes ICO Guidelines' (16 February 2018). Available at: www.finma.ch/en/news/2018/02/20180216-mm-ico-wegleitung/.

law-making takes place in a complex environment that is inherently characterised by uncertainty and permanent changes.[80]

It is time that a discussion takes place on how legislators see the role of regulation and – as a result thereof – to further refine the role of supervision in the field of sustainable digital finance in order to provide both market participants and supervisory authorities with clarity on their role. Only then can supervisory authorities and market participants be positioned in the same team: one that advocates the use of sustainable digital finance to drive the transition to a greener future and to guide private investments towards supporting sustainability goals.

7. Conclusions

This chapter identifies a field of tension between, on the one hand, the implications of sustainable digital finance from an investor's perspective and, on the other hand, the implications from a supervisory perspective. Both perspectives provide upsides and downsides to the increased digitalisation of the finance sector in supporting the transition to a sustainable economy and the complexities in relation thereto. The advantages and disadvantages for both investors and supervisory authorities have been described, which – in conclusion – highlight the complex character of the fast-developing market of sustainable digital finance and its products. The increased focus of both the regulators and supervisory authorities on digital finance initiates the question of which regulatory boundaries come into play in relation to effective supervision. Digital finance, as well as the focus on sustainability, is not just a temporary trend; both developments are here to stay. Taking this as a starting point, the EU, NRAs and market participants need to focus on how they can use the current regulation to their benefit and in line with the underlying purpose: to create an investment climate which is fit for the future and with supervisory agencies well equipped for their purpose. A continuous dialogue between legislators, supervisory authorities and market participants to refine their role in the field of sustainable digital finance is vital to achieve this goal.

[80] S Ranchordás, 'Experimental Regulations and Regulatory Sandboxes – Law Without Order?' (2021) 2021 *Law and Method* 1.

4

Financial Conduct Authority's Approach Towards Supervision and Enforcement

Impact of RegTech on Digital Disruption

SHANYA RUHELA

1. Introduction

The relationship between the financial services industry and technological developments has long been distinctive and enduring. Financial institutions have historically and consistently embraced technological innovations and new digital tools, whether in products, infrastructure, or consumer interface and engagement, to expand market reach, improve efficiency and develop new services. Consequently, financial supervisors and regulators have been tasked with ensuring that such innovations are deployed within a regulatory framework that upholds market integrity, protects and safeguards the interests of consumers, mitigates systemic risks and ensures financial stability. As the pace and scale of digital innovation and technological advancements accelerate, driven by the proliferation of algorithmic trading, digital assets, artificial intelligence (AI) and Big Data, the role of regulators in overseeing this ever-changing landscape becomes increasingly challenging and important.

In the UK, this regulatory responsibility falls to the Financial Conduct Authority (FCA), a body created in 2013 following the dissolution of the erstwhile regulator.[1] The FCA's mandate includes consumer protection, market integrity and the promotion of effective competition within financial services, and it is rooted in the Financial Services and Markets Act 2000 (FSMA 2000) and the Financial Services Act 2012.[2] To fulfil these objectives in an increasingly data-intensive society and the financial services industry, the FCA has taken tangible steps to

[1] Financial Services and Markets Act 2000 (FSMA 2000) c 8.
[2] Financial Services Act 2012 c 21.

embrace digital transformation and disruption. The regulator has kept pace and found innovative ways to adopt regulatory technologies (RegTech) and supervisory technologies (SupTech) that make use of technological tools and techniques, including but not limited to machine learning (ML), natural language processing (NLP) and cloud-based analytics platforms.

The FCA's embrace of technological innovations has been in parallel with its developments in supervisory approach, which has evolved toward a forward-looking and judgement-based approach. This shift moves beyond retrospective assessments or rigid compliance checklists, focusing instead on proactive risk identification and early intervention. Digitalisation has enabled the FCA to enhance its monitoring capabilities, especially in areas such as market surveillance, conduct supervision and financial crime detection. Through various projects and initiatives like Digital Regulatory Reporting (DRR), Tech and other sprints, and the deployment of AI-driven enforcement tools, the FCA has sought to embed innovation within its regulatory apparatus.[3]

This chapter examines the evolving role of the FCA as a regulator that succeeded its predecessor in turbulent times. It begins by tracing the regulator's institutional transformation following the financial crisis and the LIBOR scandal. It then evaluates the FCA's current supervisory and enforcement strategies, with a particular focus on its use of RegTech and SupTech. Further, it examines the legal and procedural challenges posed by the incorporation of technological innovations into regulatory apparatus, especially in relation to data governance, transparency and algorithmic accountability. Ultimately, the chapter argues that while the FCA's embrace of AI and data-driven tools offers the potential for more responsive, predictive and scalable regulation, it also demands scrutiny to ensure that core principles of fairness, due process and public accountability are not compromised in the pursuit of technological efficiency.[4] The analysis conducted in this chapter is based on statutory and legislative documents, rules and regulations framed thereunder, policy papers, case studies, news reports and existing academic scholarship.

2. Inside the FCA: Origins, Purpose and Powers and Adaptation to the Digital Era

This section explores the inception and purpose of the UK's financial regulator, the FCA, following the Great Financial Crisis 2007–08 (GFC) and expounds on the

[3] FCA, 'Innovation, AI and the Future of Financial Regulation' (Speech by Jessica Rusu, 17 April 2023). Available at: www.fca.org.uk/news/speeches/innovation-ai-and-future-financial-regulation.

[4] K Yeung, 'Algorithmic Regulation: A Critical Interrogation' (2018) 12 *Regulation & Governance* 505; J Black, 'FinTech and Financial Regulation: New Developments and Challenges' (2019) LSE Law, Society and Economy Working Papers 2/2019. Available at: www.lse.ac.uk/law/people/academic-staff/julia-black.

recalibrated enforcement mandate, as well as examines how the FCA is responding to the era of digital transformation and disruption.

2.1. FCA: Inception and Purpose

A few days before the erstwhile financial regulator, the Financial Services Authority (FSA), was replaced by new regulators, a national daily summarised its legacy as 'the watchdog that didn't bark'.[5] Although harshly worded, both empirical evidence and the opinion developed henceforth have concluded that the newspaper was not mistaken in declaring the FSA to be a weak enforcer and regulator.[6]

Established in 1997,[7] the FSA took over banking supervision from the Bank of England.[8] It was responsible for the supervision of financial institutions under the *tripartite* system, whereby the HM Treasury, the Bank of England and the FSA were collectively responsible for maintaining financial stability.[9] This system laid down operational rules for dealing with financial failures and crises, which were tested during the Northern Rock debacle[10] and the GFC, at which it very publicly failed.[11]

The FSA is remembered as incompetent and dishonest, not an enforcement-driven regulator, and for its failure to modernise and become *smarter*.

Fines imposed by the FSA were usually relatively low and it had a history of not prosecuting individual executives. It shied away from pursuing lengthy and expensive legal battles and, considering the level of penalties imposed, the fines imposed by the FSA were increasingly being viewed as just another business expenditure, which did not cause any significant impact, leading to the FSA's enforcement regime achieving little in terms of deterrence. The FSA was more concerned with *box-ticking* or compliance. As a result, its inaction was often interpreted as a sign of acceptance,[12] as well as political pressure to pursue a light-touch approach while

[5] J Treanor, 'Farewell to the FSA – and the Bleak Legacy of the Light-Touch Regulator' *The Guardian* (24 March 2013).

[6] JC Coffee, 'Law and the Market: The Impact of Enforcement' (2007) 156 *University of Pennsylvania Law Review* 229; E Ferran, 'Capital Market Competitiveness and Enforcement' [2008] SSRN Electronic Journal.

[7] In 1997, the Securities and Investments Board was replaced by the Financial Services Authority. However, the legislative infrastructure of the FSA under the *tripartite* system was established by the FSMA 2000. It was only post-2004, that the FSA took over the regulation and supervision of the mortgage and insurance markets. It should also be noted that, previously, the Securities and Investments Board had taken over the responsibilities of the eight other former regulators.

[8] R Peston, *Brown's Britain* (Short Books 2006).

[9] Tripartite's Memorandum of Association, retrieved from National Web Archives. Available at: www.fsa.gov.uk/pubs/mou/fsa_hmt_boe.pdf.

[10] Treasury Committee, *The Run on the Rock* (HC 2007–08, 56–1). Available at: https://publications.parliament.uk/pa/cm200708/cmselect/cmtreasy/56/56i.pdf.

[11] S K Blei, 'The British Tripartite Financial Supervision System in the Face of the Northern Rock Run' (Federal Reserve Bank of St Louis 2008).

[12] JW Markham, 'Regulating the Too Big to Jail Financial Institutions' (2017) 83 *Brooklyn Law Review* 517.

discharging its duties.[13] This was particularly concerning given the FSA's mandate to preserve financial stability, maintain trust in the financial system and protect consumers.[14]

The lack of a strong enforcement approach led to broader concerns regarding the ethical responsibilities of the regulator, especially in cases where it prioritised market freedom over consumer protection.[15] The FSA trusted that the markets could self-correct and discipline firms that took excessive risks and implemented risky business models. It naively believed that the senior executives would act in the interests of the consumers. Therefore, it spent its resources and time on obvious outliers rather than looking at and investigating systemic problems, or holding to account those liable for the GFC.[16] Along with not being able to hold firms and individuals liable and deter undesirable activities, the FSA relied on outdated IT systems that led to oversights and contributed to the buildup of systemic risks in the financial sector.[17] Thus, FSA's short reign was marked by its failure to prevent the meltdown of the UK's banking system[18] and being an inept regulator.[19]

Prior to 2013, the FSA was responsible for both prudential and conduct regulation. This left the regulator with too many objectives to manage and an inability to keep up with market innovations and advancements.[20] FSA, the UK's principal regulator, focused too much on the supervision of individual institutions and insufficiently on wider sectoral and system-wide risks.[21]

One of the major institutional reforms that took place in 2013, *vide* the Financial Services Act 2012, was the adoption of the so-called *Twin Peaks* structure, whereby the FSA ceased to exist and was replaced by two new institutions, the FCA and the Prudential Regulatory Authority (PRA).[22] Splitting the FSA into two new regulators was one of the immediate and direct implications of its mishandling of the financial sector, which allowed for failures like the GFC and the LIBOR rate manipulation.[23] Many believed that the creation of specialised regultors would lead

[13] Tony Blair's speech in 2005 on how the FSA is hindering competition.

[14] C Russo, *The Ethics of Banking and Financial Regulatory Authorities: A Study of the Bank of England, the Prudential Regulation Authority, the Monetary Policy Committee and the Financial Conduct Authority, a report annexed to the CSPL Commanding report to the UK Parliament on 'Striking the Balance: Upholding the Seven Principles of Public Life in Regulation'* (2016).

[15] R Wardrop and T Ziegler, 'A Case of Regulatory Evolution: A Review of the UK Financial Conduct Authority's Approach to Crowdfunding' (2016) CESifo DICE Report 14/2, 23–32.

[16] *Financial Services Authority, A Regulatory Response to the Global Banking Crisis* (March 2009) (The Turner Review).

[17] GJ Croll, *Spreadsheets and the Financial Collapse* (European Spreadsheet Risks Interest Group 2009).

[18] Along with prevention of this meltdown, the FSA has also been criticised for letting the individuals who were responsible get away. *See* The Turner Review (n 16).

[19] O Hail, 'Why the FSA was Split into Two Bodies' (*FT Adviser*, 8 May 2013).

[20] R Hadley, P Morgan, N Robson, and R Stephens, *An Overview of Enforcement by the Financial Services Authority (K&L Gates LLP 2007).*

[21] The Turner Review (n 17).

[22] Financial Services Act 2012, which came into force in April 2013. HM Treasury, *A New Approach to Financial Regulation: Judgement, Focus and Stability* (2010).

[23] P Tannion and A Colclough, 'The New LIBOR Rules that Split Up the FSA' (29 April 2013); P Aldrick, 'Bank of England in the Spotlight over "Nod and Wink" to LIBOR Rigging' *The Telegraph* (4 July 2013).

to more effective supervision and enforcement.[24] Subsequently, on 1 April 2013, the FSA[25] ceased to exist and new regulatory institutions took its place.

The PRA functions as the prudential regulator in the UK. Its objectives are to promote and ensure the safety and soundness of banks, insurance companies, building societies and (some large) investment firms, thereby protecting customers.[26] By doing so, it aims to maintain the stability of the nation's financial system.

The FCA is responsible for regulating the conduct of business in the country, for protecting consumers, maintaining the stability and integrity of the financial system and promoting competition among service providers. Its strategic aim is to ensure that markets for financial services work smoothly.[27] In addition, the FCA has been given enhanced investigative and enforcement powers to address market abuses and systemic risks that may arise in the financial sector. The FCA is the primary regulator responsible for the investigation of financial misconduct.

The new twin regulators were set up to take strong enforcement action against individuals and firms, and they regularly cooperate on such matters.[28] When it was established, the FCA promised to be a more responsive regulator and to rectify its predecessor's mistakes.[29] However, these promises were met with some scepticism, as the statements of the former and the new regulators were very similar.[30] There were also concerns that enforcement might remain ineffective despite the regulatory overhaul, especially if the same regulatory culture persisted. In light of the legacy of the FSA and the reform that led to the formation of the FCA, it is pertinent to analyse how the new regulator has fared in terms of keeping up with the needs of the market.

2.2. RegTech and SupTech in Enforcement and Market Surveillance

RegTech and SupTech are beyond mere *buzzwords*. They refer to technologies, innovations and digital advancements that are used by regulators and firms to adapt to an increasingly digitalised financial landscape.

RegTech has provided firms with tools to drive efficiency and sustainability in regulatory compliance by addressing the need for standardisation, automation

[24] D Johnson, 'What Are the Merits of Taking a Hybrid Regulatory Approach toward the Enforcement of Corporate Financial Crime in the United Kingdom and United States of America?' (2022) 3(1) *Journal of White Collar and Corporate Crime* 23.

[25] Financial Services Act 2012, which came into force 1 April 2013.

[26] The business conducted by the firms authorised by PRA is regulated by the FCA, making these *dual regulated* firms.

[27] FSMA 2000, s 1B.

[28] FCA, *Annual Report and Accounts 2013–2014* (HC 349, 2014).; Bank of England, 'Policy' (2025). Available at: www.bankofengland.co.uk/pra/Pages/policy/handbook.

[29] FCA, 'Enforcement' (2024). Available at: www.fca.org.uk/about/how-we-regulate/enforcement.

[30] Both aim to use the enforcement tools available to attain credible deterrence. M Cole, 'Delivering Credible Deterrence' (Speech at the FSA Annual Financial Crime Conference, 27 April 2009).

and reduced compliance costs.[31] RegTech, a sub-set of fintech, is the application of technology to the regulation[32] or management of regulatory processes through technological innovations in the financial sector.[33] It is a tool for a top-down approach whereby regulators use RegTech to regulate and interact with their subjects for positive welfare outcomes for consumers, regulators and supervisors and to provide reputational benefits for the financial services sector.[34]

In contrast, SupTech describes the application of technology by regulators themselves to enhance supervision, market surveillance and enforcement.[35] The FCA has actively embraced both RegTech and SupTech. Further, the FCA has undertaken various activities that demonstrate that it recognises that traditional, manual oversight of the market is increasingly inadequate in an era that is marked by daily innovations, digital disruption and transformation.

The FCA's commitment to leveraging RegTech and SupTech aligns with its broader goals of fostering innovation, maintaining market integrity and adapting to technological disruption.[36] Since its establishment, the FCA has sought to 'see the functioning of the markets holistically'[37] and to adjust its supervision and surveillance structure accordingly. Over the past decade, the regulator's supervision and surveillance capabilities have adapted to the evolving data-driven and tech-enabled era and, hence, has been transformed from those of its predecessor.

RegTech has been prominently applied in areas of Anti-Money Laundering, Know Your Customer and combating financial crimes.[38] RegTech has demonstrated its ability to reduce manual and menial tasks, increase reporting accuracy and improve data quality through digital tools such as report automation, robotic process automation and visual analytics. Thus, their advantages include the ease of compliance and disclosure burdens, as well as ease of access to information for stakeholders.[39]

[31] EY, *Regulatory Technology (RegTech): Navigating the Right Technology to Manage the Evolving Regulatory Environment* (2019).

[32] DW Arner, J Barberis, and RP Buckley, 'The Evolution of Fintech: A New Post-Crisis Paradigm' (2015) 47 *Georgetown Journal of International Law* 1271.

[33] K Ghosh, 'RegTech: Bits and Bytes of Financial Regulation' (2021) 3(1–2) *Journal of Business Strategy Finance and Management* 103.

[34] I Anagnostopoulos, 'Fintech and Regtech: Impact on Regulators and Banks' (2018) 100 *Journal of Economics and Business* 7.

[35] PF Azuikpe and others, 'The Necessity of Artificial Intelligence in FinTech for SupTech and RegTech Supervisory in Banks and Financial Organizations' (2024) 12(2) *International Journal of Science and Research Archive* 2853.

[36] FCA, *Business Plan 2021/22* (July 2021. Available at: www.fca.org.uk/publications/business-plans/2021-22; FCA, *Data Strategy* (January 2020). Available at: www.fca.org.uk/publications/corporate-documents/data-strategy-2020.

[37] FCA, 'Effective Compliance with the Market Abuse Regulation: A State of Mind' (Speech by Julia Hoggett, 17 November 2017). Available at: www.fca.org.uk/news/speeches/effective-compliance-market-abuse-regulation-a-state-of-mind.

[38] T Butler and L O'Brien, 'Understanding RegTech for Digital Regulatory Compliance' in T Lynn, J G Mooney, P Rosati and M Cummins (eds), *Disrupting Finance: FinTech and Strategy in the 21st Century* (Palgrave Macmillan 2019).

[39] DW Arner, JN Barberis, and RP Buckley, 'FinTech, RegTech, and the Reconceptualization of Financial Regulation' (2017) 37 *Northwestern Journal of International Law and Business* 371.

Further, the COVID-19 pandemic in 2020 has accelerated the adoption of RegTech, as it highlighted the potential of technology in automating compliance, reducing costs and improving consistency in regulatory processes. However, RegTech implementation is not without challenges. These include the high cost of integration, concerns about data security, and the impact of market volatility on RegTech start-ups. These barriers may hinder equitable access and widespread deployment, especially among smaller financial institutions.[40]

The FCA has taken an active role in encouraging RegTech innovation through various internal and external initiatives. A prominent example of such an initiative is the RegTech Sprint, which involved collaboration with financial institutions and led to the development of the DRR[41] system. These efforts originated to demonstrate the FCA's commitment to automated, straight-through compliance and its advocacy for open-source technologies and semantic standards to improve data governance and interoperability.[42]

SupTech has also played a role in the transformation of the supervisory and enforcement approach of the FCA. The FCA has significantly invested in data-driven market surveillance systems that helps to detect market abuse, including insider dealing and manipulation.[43] Under the UK's market abuse regime, the FCA receives over 30 million transaction reports and 100 million order reports daily. These are processed through the market data processor, a cloud-based platform that applies algorithms to identify potential misconduct in near real time.[44] This level of automation enhances the FCA's surveillance reach and allows for continuous real-time monitoring that would otherwise not be practically feasible.

To improve its ability to detect irregularities, the FCA has adopted ML models that analyse massive transaction datasets and generate risk signals for review.[45] It uses ML to scan over millions of equity transactions daily and flag patterns potentially indicative of insider trading. These alerts are subsequently assessed by human analysts, illustrating a human–machine hybrid model of oversight.[46] The FCA has also experimented with network and graph analysis to uncover sophisticated misconduct schemes that traditional methods might miss, such as collusive

[40] European Banking Authority, 'EBA Analysis on RegTech in the EU Financial Sector' (2021). Available at: www.eba.europa.eu/sites/default/files/document_library/Publications/Reports/2021/1015484/EBA%20analysis%20of%20RegTech%20in%20the%20EU%20financial%20sector.pdf.

[41] FCA, 'Digital Regulatory Reporting' (10 February 2023) www.fca.org.uk/innovation/regtech/digital-regulatory-reporting.

[42] FCA and Bank of England, 'Digital Regulatory Reporting: Phase One Pilot Report' (October 2018) www.fca.org.uk/publication/discussion/digital-regulatory-reporting-pilot-phase-1-report.pdf.

[43] FCA, *Annual Report and Accounts 2021/22* (2022) 44, www.fca.org.uk/publication/annual-reports/2021-22.pdf; FCA, *Data Strategy Update 2022* (2022) www.fca.org.uk/publications/corporate-documents/data-strategy-update-2022.

[44] 'FCA's Work on Market Abuse and Manipulation – Update 17 June 2022' (17 June 2022) www.fca.org.uk/news/news-stories/market-abuse-manipulation-update.

[45] ESMA, 'Financial Innovation: RegTech and SupTech: Change for Markets and Authorities' (16 October 2018) www.esma.europa.eu/press-news/esma-news/regtech-and-suptech-%E2%80%93-change-markets-and-regulators.

[46] FCA, 'AI Update' (2023) 19–20, www.fca.org.uk/publication/corporate/ai-update.pdf.

behaviour or coordinated trading strategies. Such graph learning algorithms help detect hidden relationships in order and execution data that suggest manipulative behaviour,[47] such as cross-market spoofing or pump-and-dump schemes.

Beyond market abuse, the FCA has explored the usage of AI and ML techniques, such as random forest models, to support broader supervisory activities. In particular, these models have been investigated for their potential to identify patterns of firm behaviour associated with regulatory risk. While specific applications have not been publicly confirmed, the FCA has highlighted the promise of these approaches in supporting proactive supervision and enabling early interventions to reduce consumer harm.[48] The FCA has similarly used analytics to address financial crime, including fraud and money laundering, often in partnership with other agencies. It seeks to deploy AI tools to analyse, surveil and vet large volumes of suspicious activity reports and payment data to detect anomalous transactions or account networks.[49]

Another noteworthy initiative of the FCA embracing technological innovation includes an Authorised Push Payment (APP) Fraud TechSprint in 2022, whereby synthetic banking data was used to develop AI models that could detect payment scams. Several working prototypes emerged from the event, some of which were subsequently adopted by industry participants.[50] This demonstrates how collaborative experimentation has become a unique feature of the FCA's approach to technological innovation.

When misconduct is identified, the FCA's Enforcement Division relies on digital tools to manage and investigate cases efficiently.[51] Given its statutory powers under FSMA 2000 (including sections 165, 167 and 171), the FCA often obtains a large number of documents, emails and records per investigation.[52] This data is processed using e-discovery systems and NLP. These tools allow investigators to search for relevant communications, detect trading anomalies and reconstruct timelines to determine who had access to what information and when. NLP also assists in detecting cartel-like communication patterns or insider tips based on keyword clusters across emails or messages.[53] In internal trials, the FCA even tested chatbot technologies to help its staff navigate regulatory processes, although their role in enforcement remains limited.[54]

[47] FCA, 'Market Abuse Surveillance TechSprint' (9 October 2024) www.fca.org.uk/firms/techsprints/market-abuse-surveillance-techsprint.

[48] FCA, *From Maps to Apps: The Power of Machine Learning and Artificial Intelligence for the FCA* (2016). Available at: www.fca.org.uk/publication/documents/from-maps-to-apps.pdf.

[49] FCA, 'AI: Moving from Fear to Trust' (Speech, 23 February 2022). Available at: www.fca.org.uk/news/speeches/ai-moving-fear-trust.

[50] FCA, 'Authorised Push Payment (APP) Fraud TechSprint' (22–24 September 2022). Available at: www.fca.org.uk/events/authorised-push-payment-fraud-techsprint.

[51] FCA, *FCA to Improve Pace and Transparency Around Enforcement Cases* (2023). Available at: www.fca.org.uk/news/press-releases/fca-improve-pace-and-transparency-around-enforcement-cases.

[52] FSMA 2000, ss 165, 167 and 171.

[53] FCA, *Pilot Study: Bias in Natural Language Processing* (Research Note, 2022). Available at: www.fca.org.uk/publications/research-notes/pilot-study-bias-natural-language-processing.

[54] FCA, *AI Update* (2024), which integrates the UK government's five principles on the regulation of AI.

Despite these technological advances, regulatory decisions continue to rest with human officials. The FCA's Regulatory Decisions Committee retains ultimate authority to determine whether enforcement action is warranted, ensuring processes remain grounded in legal accountability and procedural fairness.[55] Thus, digital innovations have been increasingly common and have augmented rather than replaced the decision-making role of regulators.

These developments highlight the FCA's ongoing transformation into a regulator that keeps pace with technological and digital developments. Its investments in RegTech and SupTech enable it to monitor financial markets more effectively, enforce standards more rigorously and intervene earlier in cases of misconduct. However, the application of technology in supervision and enforcement is still at a nascent stage. It prompts further inquiry into how digitalisation is reconfiguring regulatory authority, reshaping institutional behaviour, and challenging approaches to supervision and enforcement. The FCA's *proactive* engagement with these tools not only positions it as a leader in regulatory innovation but also fuels its critics about the future role of regulators in an algorithmically governed financial landscape.

3. Becoming a Smart Regulator: The FCA in a Digital Age

A study of how the FCA adapts to technological disruption and digital transformation brought by AI that pervasively impacts all facets of consumer and market behaviour and redefines its regulatory approach is incomplete without exploring its internal transformation efforts and the accompanying challenges. The following sections examine the FCA's initiatives to harness data and AI as well as the ethical, legal and operational dilemmas that arise from such initiatives. Together, these sections demonstrate the FCA's approach to AI as a technology-agnostic, principles-based and outcomes-focused regulator while securing consumer protection, public trust and regulatory integrity in an era of algorithmic governance.[56]

3.1. From Digital Reporting to AI Labs

The use of AI by the FCA is not ad hoc or a one-time sporadic experiment but rather has been touted as a part of a strategic push to become a data-driven regulator.[57] The FCA has recognised that a better use of data and technology can lead to

[55] FCA, 'Regulatory Decisions Committee' (6 December 2024. Available at: www.fca.org.uk/about/who-we-are/committees/regulatory-decisions-committee.

[56] FCA, *AI Update* (2024). Available at: www.fca.org.uk/publication/corporate/ai-update.pdf.

[57] FCA, *Data Strategy 2020* (7 January 2020). Available at: www.fca.org.uk/publications/corporate-documents/data-strategy-2020.

better regulatory outcomes, and, hence, has launched several initiatives and pilot programmes. These include projects to transform regulatory data reporting and the creation of innovation hubs (like TechSprints, sandboxes and an AI lab).[58]

The DRR system is a flagship FCA initiative, launched in 2016–17 with the Bank of England. It aims at fundamentally altering how firms submit regulatory data to the FCA by making the process more efficient, accurate and machine-readable. Currently, the FCA receives over half a million scheduled regulatory reports from firms each year, which include multiple types of reports ranging from financial statements and capital adequacy returns to transaction reports. These reports are used for off-site supervision and identification of risks.[59] This system has historically been cumbersome, fragmented and expensive, and it has had multiple instances of data being inconsistent or delayed. The DRR project was established to address this issue by exploring machine-readable regulation and machine-executable regulation to develop standards and tools (such that regulatory rules and reporting instructions are written in a format that computers can interpret unambiguously) that allow for automated collection and compliance of data.[60]

To test the feasibility of DRR, the FCA and BoE organised TechSprints that tested these model-driven, machine-executable and -readable reporting systems.[61] Following the sprints, they partnered with seven major banks to pilot DRR.[62] These pilots and trials demonstrated the feasibility of linking firms' internal systems directly to regulatory requirements using a shared data model and code that reflects the FCA's rules. By January 2020, the FCA confirmed the model's viability, noting its potential to cut compliance costs and improve data quality.[63] It has since been embedded in its data strategy, a policy instrument. The DRR project shows

[58] FCA, *Fostering Innovation through Collaboration: The Evolution of the FCA TechSprint Approach* (March 2020). Available at: www.fca.org.uk/publication/research/fostering-innovation-through-collaboration-evolution-techsprint-approach.pdf; FCA, *FCA Celebrates 10 Years of Innovation and Launches AI Lab to Shape the Future of Financial Services* (17 October 2024). Available at: www.fca.org.uk/news/speeches/ten-years-fca-innovation-impact-and-opportunity; FCA, 'Financial Conduct Authority's Regulatory Sandbox Opens to Applications' (9 May 2016). Available at: www.fca.org.uk/news/press-releases/financial-conduct-authority%E2%80%99s-regulatory-sandbox-opens-applications.

[59] FCA and Bank of England, *Digital Regulatory Reporting: Pilot Phase 1 Report* (November 2018). Available at: www.fca.org.uk/publication/discussion/digital-regulatory-reporting-pilot-phase-1-report.pdf.

[60] ibid; FCA, *FCA launches Call for Input on the Use of Technology to Achieve Smarter Regulatory Reporting* (20 February 2018); Bank of England, *Digital Regulatory Reporting 2023 Update* (October 2023). Available at: www.bankofengland.co.uk/-/media/boe/files/prudential-regulation/transforming-data-collection/digital-regulatory-reporting-2023-updates.

[61] Financial Stability Board, *The Use of Supervisory and Regulatory Technology by Authorities and Regulated Institutions* (9 October 2020). Available at: www.fsb.org/2020/10/the-use-of-supervisory-and-regulatory-technology-by-authorities-and-regulated-institutions-market-developments-and-financial-stability-implications.

[62] FCA, *Regulation Round-up January 2020* (2020). Available at: https://content.govdelivery.com/accounts/UKFCA/bulletins/274ab23.

[63] Bank of England, *Digital Regulatory Reporting Pilot Phase 1* (13 March 2019). Available at: www.bankofengland.co.uk/research/fintech/proofs-of-concept/digital-regulatory-reporting-pilot-phase-1.

how the FCA is embracing technology not only to detect misconduct but also to reduce compliance burdens and resources for consumers. It further demonstrates the FCA's approach of more timely data for earlier support and more targeted supervisory interventions before escalation is needed.

It also showcases that the FCA is actively developing creative, forward-looking solutions to meet the needs of an ever-evolving market and economy. By engaging in rounds of experimentation and trials and innovations through pilots and TechSprints before rolling out full implementation, the FCA has adopted a cautious but iterative approach, aiming to reduce delays while ensuring regulatory soundness. In doing so, the FCA has positioned itself not merely as a regulator that plays catch-up with digital transformation but as an equal player in shaping and driving innovation.

In parallel with DRR, the FCA overhauled and modernised its own data collection infrastructure through a project called RegData. It was rolled out in phases between 2020 and 2021, and all regulated firms and users migrated to this new platform.[64] While RegData's user interface is faster, more stable and more intuitive, the real transformation lies in its back-end architecture. RegData is built to be flexible and scalable, allowing the FCA to adapt data requirements, fix system issues more efficiently, and integrate incoming data directly into its analytics infrastructure.[65] The FCA has embedded RegData into its broader data strategy, aiming to use advanced analytics to transform how regulation is delivered. This system allows the FCA to plug regulatory data directly into data warehouses and analytical tools, including cloud-based systems. This enables supervisors to query submissions, identify trends and combine regulatory returns with other datasets, such as complaints or market activity, to gain a more holistic view of firms and emerging risks.[66]

The successful deployment of RegData demonstrates the FCA's capacity to implement large-scale digital reform, signalling its capability to support future SupTech applications. While RegData did not change the scope of data collected, it lays the foundation for more real-time reporting in the future. In this way, RegData demonstrates how the FCA has become an enabler of data-driven supervision.

Another unique initiative by the FCA has been its use of TechSprints, AI sprints and PolicySprints, which are hackathon-style events bringing together policymakers, regulators, firms, and experts and academics to collaborate on RegTech/SupTech solutions in a time-bound competition to develop prototypes, which are often precursors to pilots. Such collaborative initiatives benefit the FCA by advancing its own surveillance technology, educating the regulator and the industry on what's possible with AI and other technological advancements, and aiding

[64] FCA, 'All Reporting Firms Moved to FCA's New Data Collection Platform RegData' (2021). Available at: www.fca.org.uk/news/news-stories/all-reporting-firms-moved-fcas-new-data-collection-platform-regdata.

[65] FCA, 'FCA Announces Benefits of New Data Collection Platform RegData' (2020). Available at: www.fca.org.uk/news/news-stories/fca-announces-benefits-new-data-collection-platform-regdata.

[66] FCA, *Data Strategy Update 2022* (2022). Available at: www.fca.org.uk/publications/corporate-documents/data-strategy-update-2022.

in generating tools the FCA may adopt later. TechSprints have addressed issues like money laundering (eg, the 2019 Global AML TechSprint), consumer scams, regulatory reporting and AI in finance (the 2025 AI Sprint).[67]

These sprints are complemented by the digital and regulatory sandbox initiatives, which allow firms and innovators to test new products with regulatory support and supervision in a controlled environment.[68] Through these efforts, the FCA continues to position itself as a leader in RegTech development and helps foster a public–private innovation space where regulators benefit from market-generated solutions.[69]

Furthermore, the FCA established dedicated internal structures for AI oversight to further its AI agenda. In late 2024, it launched an AI lab within its Innovation Division. The lab is a hub for AI experimentation, internal coordination and strategic development.[70] Its AI input zone is an online consultation portal inviting stakeholders to submit views on AI use cases, risks and regulatory challenges. Through this feedback loop, the FCA gains insight into emerging trends and identifies potential regulatory blind spots.[71]

The FCA has stated that it does not intend to write entirely new AI regulations,[72] and that would not be feasible to undertake in silos. Instead, it will apply and adapt existing rules, such as the Senior Managers & Certification Regime (SMCR) and Consumer Duty, to AI and digital settings. The FCA is integrating AI into its existing regulatory landscape, and its initiatives and projects, from the AI lab to testing sandboxes, reflect that. By building internal expertise (eg hiring data scientists, training supervisors) and engaging externally (eg forums, Global Financial Innovation Network),[73] the FCA is establishing itself as a smart regulator that can oversee AI in finance and use it for supervision.

3.2. Challenges of AI in Regulation

While the benefits of AI and data technologies for regulators are increasingly recognised – particularly in terms of enhanced efficiency, broader surveillance scope and capacity, and more real-time insights – their adoption also presents an

[67] FCA, *TechSprints* (2025). Available at: www.fca.org.uk/firms/innovation/techsprints.

[68] FCA, *Digital Sandbox* (2025). Available at: www.fca.org.uk/firms/innovation/digital-sandbox.

[69] FCA, *Innovation Hub* (2025). Available at: www.fca.org.uk/firms/innovation.

[70] Alina Khan, 'FCA Launches AI Lab to Help Firms with Implementation' (*FT Adviser*, 17 October 2024). Available at: www.ftadviser.com/regulation/2024/10/17/fca-launches-ai-lab-to-help-firms-with-implementation.

[71] FCA, *AI Update* (2023). Available at: www.fca.org.uk/publication/corporate/ai-update.pdf.

[72] Nikhil Rathi, 'Detailed AI Rules not on the Cards for Now, Says UK Financial Watchdog' (*Reuters*, 5 June 2024). Available at: www.reuters.com/technology/detailed-ai-rules-not-cards-now-says-uk-financial-watchdog-2024-06-05/.

[73] FCA, *Artificial Intelligence (AI) Update – Further to the Government's Response to the AI White Paper* (2024). Available at: www.fca.org.uk/publications/corporate-documents/artificial-intelligence-ai-update-further-governments-response-ai-white-paper.

array of ethical, legal and operational challenges. For the FCA, the adoption of AI tools requires careful navigation of risks, such as algorithmic bias, lack of explainability, governance gaps and infrastructure limitations, all while preserving public trust and staying within the bounds of the legal and regulatory landscape.[74]

One of the primary challenges and concerns is the risk of biased or unfair outcomes. ML systems trained on historical data may unintentionally perpetuate and reinforce existing biases and disparities. For instance, if algorithms rely heavily on past enforcement patterns, they could disproportionately target smaller firms or those with less developed compliance systems, not because they currently present higher risks but because they were historically overtly scrutinised. These feedback loops can entrench systemic inequalities.[75]

As a regulator, the FCA is subject to legal obligations of fairness and non-discrimination, including the public sector equality duty.[76] This imposes a proactive obligation to consider the impact of regulatory decisions on protected groups. Accordingly, the FCA must ensure that any AI systems it deploys do not produce discriminatory outcomes without a clear and proportionate justification. Similar concerns have been raised in other sectors. An investigation highlighted how opaque credit-scoring algorithms can embed racial or socioeconomic biases.[77] The FCA must mitigate these risks in financial regulation by carefully designing and testing AI systems.[78] This includes using representative datasets, conducting impact assessments and ensuring human oversight. The FCA is aware of these risks and concerns and has publicly acknowledged them. Its 2022–23 AI Public–Private Forum addressed fairness in financial markets, and recent governance principles affirm that AI must be designed and deployed to uphold legal rights and avoid unjust discrimination.[79] Translating these commitments into practice, such as in insider trading detection, requires both technical interventions and procedural safeguards.

Transparency poses another challenge to incorporating AI and other digital tools and techniques, especially given the need for public accountability and effective regulation. Deep learning models, while technically powerful, are often criticised for their opacity. If an AI system identifies a firm for investigation, both the FCA and the affected party must understand the rationale. Without

[74] FCA, *AI Update* (2023). Available at: www.fca.org.uk/publication/corporate/ai-update.pdf.

[75] FCA, *Research Note: A Literature Review on Bias in Supervised Machine Learning* (2024). Available at: www.fca.org.uk/publications/research-notes/research-note-literature-review-bias-supervised-machine-learning.

[76] Equality and Human Rights Commission, *Artificial Intelligence: Meeting the Public Sector Equality Duty*. Available at: www.equalityhumanrights.com/guidance/artificial-intelligence-meeting-public-sector-equality-duty-psed.

[77] Tom Simonite, 'How Algorithms Can Discriminate in Lending' (*Reuters*, 22 December 2020).

[78] FCA, *Research Note: A Literature Review on Bias in Supervised Machine Learning* (2024). Available at: www.fca.org.uk/publications/research-notes/research-note-literature-review-bias-supervised-machine-learning.

[79] Bank of England and FCA, *Artificial Intelligence Public-Private Forum: Final Report* (2022). Available at: www.bankofengland.co.uk/-/media/boe/files/fintech/ai-public-private-forum-final-report.pdf.

transparency, it becomes difficult to justify regulatory action or defend it through due process. Regulatory legitimacy depends on the capacity to explain and substantiate decisions.[80] This concern has led to calls for *glass-box approaches* to AI, where decision-making processes are transparent and open to scrutiny. The FCA must strike a balance between model complexity and interpretability. Simpler models like decision trees may offer more transparency but less predictive power on complex datasets. Conversely, more advanced models require complementary tools to generate meaningful explanations.[81]

A practical solution is to use AI for the initial stages, while ensuring that human investigators review and validate final decisions. However, if algorithmic outputs influence and shape enforcement priorities significantly, the FCA may be required to disclose how such systems operate, particularly in legal proceedings. This raises additional issues, including protection of intellectual property, concerns about system manipulation and compliance with the Freedom of Information Act 2000.

These tensions are not new. In *Bridges v South Wales Police*,[82] the Court of Appeal criticised the lack of regulatory safeguards surrounding live facial recognition technology. Drawing from this precedent, the FCA must adopt internal policies that clearly define how AI tools are designed, tested, used and audited. Some progress has been made through the Digital Regulation Cooperation Forum, a joint initiative with the ICO, Ofcom and the CMA.[83]

Accountability represents another major area of concern. The FCA remains responsible if an algorithm fails to detect serious misconduct or wrongly implicates an innocent party. Public law requires that regulatory decisions be attributable to human authorities.[84] While the FCA has established internal oversight mechanisms, increased reliance on AI may give rise to automation bias, where staff defer too readily to algorithmic outputs. This phenomenon occurs when individuals assume that automated systems are inherently accurate, thereby compromising their independent judgement. To prevent this, FCA staff must be trained to evaluate AI-generated insights and to intervene when necessary.

The FCA appears to have implemented model risk controls, including validation protocols and audit trails. It is likely that responsibilities for AI oversight fall within the scope of the SMCR, which ensures accountability within firms and, by extension, within regulatory bodies.[85] External oversight is equally important. The FCA is accountable to HM Treasury and Parliament and could be subject to review in the event of AI-related failures.[86] Where personal data is involved, the independent

[80] FCA, *AI Update* (2023). Available at: www.fca.org.uk/publication/corporate/ai-update.pdf.
[81] ibid.
[82] *R (Bridges) v Chief Constable of South Wales Police* [2020] EWCA Civ 1058.
[83] FCA, *Digital Regulation Cooperation Forum* (2024). Available at: www.fca.org.uk/about/how-we-operate/who-work-with/drcf.
[84] FCA, *AI Update* (2023). Available at: www.fca.org.uk/publication/corporate/ai-update.pdf.
[85] FCA, *Senior Managers and Certification Regime* (2025). Available at: www.fca.org.uk/firms/senior-managers-certification-regime.
[86] FCA, *AI Update* (2023). Available at: www.fca.org.uk/publication/corporate/ai-update.pdf.

authority may also investigate compliance with data protection laws. The challenge, therefore, is to preserve accountability even as regulatory decisions become more complex and data-driven. The FCA can address this by ensuring robust human oversight and governance frameworks at every stage of AI deployment.

Operational capacity is equally critical. Developing and maintaining SupTech tools requires sustained investment in personnel, infrastructure and technology.[87] The FCA is funded largely through industry levies and competes with the private sector to attract technical talent.[88] Recruiting skilled data scientists to the public sector is difficult, particularly given salary disparities. The FCA has responded by establishing dedicated data teams and promoting its public interest mission as a compelling value proposition.[89]

System integration also poses challenges. While the RegData platform demonstrates the FCA's ability to manage complex IT projects, AI systems require even more robust infrastructure.[90] This includes scalable cloud environments, secure data pipelines and continuous performance monitoring.[91] The FCA has adopted cloud computing to process large volumes of market data, which in turn requires high standards of cybersecurity and operational continuity. The UK is also developing rules to address risks associated with reliance on third-party technology providers.[92]

Data quality is a foundational issue. AI models depend on timely, accurate and well-structured data. The FCA's initiatives, such as DRR and RegData, aim to improve data inputs for regulatory use.[93] However, harmonising datasets from diverse sources, including transaction reports, consumer complaints and firm filings, remains a labour-intensive task and continues to pose major integration challenges.

Operational resilience must also be a priority. The FCA must ensure that core systems function effectively, especially during periods of market volatility.[94] Supervisory tools must be reliable, scalable and rigorously tested.[95] The FCA's data strategy emphasises continuous improvement in digital governance and

[87] FCA, *Regulatory Initiatives Grid – April 2025* (2025). Available at: www.fca.org.uk/publication/corporate/regulatory-initiatives-grid-apr-2025.pdf.

[88] FCA, *Annual Report and Accounts 2024/25* (2025). Available at: www.fca.org.uk/publication/annual-reports/annual-report-2023-24.pdf.

[89] FCA, *AI Update* (2023). Available at: www.fca.org.uk/publication/corporate/ai-update.pdf.

[90] FCA, *RegData* (2021). Available at: www.fca.org.uk/firms/regdata.

[91] FCA, *FG16/5: Guidance for Firms Outsourcing to the 'Cloud' and Other Third-Party IT Services* (2016). Available at: www.fca.org.uk/publication/finalised-guidance/fg16-5.pdf.

[92] Bank of England, *CP26/23: Operational Resilience: Critical Third Parties to the UK Financial Sector* (2023). Available at: www.bankofengland.co.uk/prudential-regulation/publication/2023/december/operational-resilience-critical-third-parties-to-the-uk-financial-sector.

[93] FCA, *Data Strategy Update 2022* (2022). Available at: www.fca.org.uk/publications/corporate-documents/data-strategy-update-2022.

[94] FCA, *PS21/3: Building Operational Resilience* (2021). Available at: www.fca.org.uk/publications/policy-statements/ps21-3-building-operational-resilience.

[95] FCA, *Data Strategy Update 2022* (2022). Available at: www.fca.org.uk/publications/corporate-documents/data-strategy-update-2022.

infrastructure. Establishing a dedicated executive role for data and information oversight reflects this institutional focus.

Thus, while AI offers transformative potential for financial regulation, its integration into the FCA's supervisory functions must be tempered by a clear commitment to legality, fairness and transparency. The challenges, ranging from algorithmic bias and explainability to infrastructure demands and accountability, underscore the need for robust governance frameworks. Human oversight, institutional safeguards and meaningful public accountability are not optional but essential for maintaining trust and legitimacy in data-driven regulation. As the FCA continues to innovate, ensuring that technological advancement aligns with core regulatory principles will remain paramount.

4. Legal Concerns Regarding FCA's Digital Transformation

As the FCA increasingly integrates AI and digital tools into its regulatory landscape, an inquiry into the legal concerns becomes essential. This section examines the regulatory constraints and boundaries that govern the FCA's digital transformation. While much of the focus on RegTech and SupTech tends to be centred around innovation and efficiency, it is equally important to scrutinise the legal safeguards, accountability structures and procedural guarantees that accompany this adaptation to digital transformations.

4.1. Existing Legal Framework

The integration of AI and digital tools and techniques into regulatory supervision by the FCA is shaped by a legal and regulatory landscape, which is outlined in this section.

4.1.1. Data Protection and Confidentiality

As a data controller, the FCA is bound by the UK General Data Protection Regulation (UK GDPR) and the Data Protection Act 2018 (DPA 2018). The vast amount of supervisory data it processes, such as transaction reports, communications, personal account details and other records, often contains personal data. Generally, the FCA processes this information on the lawful basis of 'public task', which is linked to its statutory mandate under the FSMA 2000.[96] This implies that the FCA is allowed to use personal data when necessary to carry out its official duties and fulfil its mandates.

[96] Data Protection Act 2018, ss 8–10; UK GDPR, Art 6(1)(e) (public task).

Data protection law sets specific obligations, including fairness, security, data minimisation and purpose limitation. Under this law, automated decision-making is dealt with very strictly. Individuals have the right not to be subject to decisions made solely by automated processing that significantly affect them.[97] This is done to ensure that human oversight is in place, that affected individuals have a right to understand and challenge decisions, and that the decision-making process remains fair and explainable. Although the FCA does not currently render decisions (on enforcement or otherwise) without human involvement, any future expansion of AI-based or algorithm-based decision-making must remain within these legal bounds.

In addition to the data protection law, FSMA imposes strict confidentiality rules on the FCA.[98] The FCA is prohibited from the disclosure of confidential information obtained from firms unless permitted by a statutory provision, or if consent is explicitly provided. When deploying AI or digital tools, the FCA must ensure safeguarding personal data under GDPR and firm data under FSMA.

Therefore, the deployment of AI and digital tools involves a dual compliance challenge for the FCA. It is obligated to protect personal data under the UK GDPR and firm-sensitive data under FSMA. In 2020, however, the FCA mistakenly disclosed the personal information of over 1,600 individuals in response to a Freedom of Information request, highlighting the real risks of mishandling sensitive data even within a regulatory body.[99] The FCA's approach to using pseudonymised or synthetic datasets in initiatives such as TechSprints suggests that, as an institution, the FCA is aware of these obligations and makes a proactive effort to manage them responsibly.

4.1.2. Administrative Law and Procedural Fairness

The FCA, as a public authority, is subject to judicial review on various grounds.[100] These include illegality, irrationality and procedural impropriety.[101] The adaptation of AI and digital tools does not lessen these obligations.[102] In fact, it necessitates the formulation of new procedural safeguards to uphold the principles of natural justice and administrative law.

Procedural fairness requires that affected individuals have the right to make representations and challenge decisions. If AI-generated or digitally generated outputs materially contribute to or influence enforcement decisions, the FCA must disclose the reasoning and methodology behind those outputs. Failure to do so may lead to a breach of its duty of fairness. Moreover, overt or excessive reliance

[97] UK GDPR, Arts 5(1)(a)–(e), 22.

[98] FSMA 2000, s 348.

[99] FCA, 'Statement on FCA Data Breach' (26 February 2020). Available at: www.fca.org.uk/news/statements/fca-data-breach.

[100] Colin D Campbell, 'The Nature of Power as Public in English Judicial Review' (2009) 68 *CLJ* 90.

[101] *Council of Civil Service Unions v Minister for the Civil Service* [1985] AC 374 (HL).

[102] Jenner & Block, 'Government Pressure on Regulators Could Prompt Premature AI Adoption and a Surge in Judicial Review' (2024). Available at: www.jenner.com/en/news-insights/news/government-pressure-on-regulators-could-prompt-premature-ai-adoption-and-a-surge-in-judicial-review.

on algorithmic tools may lead to unlawfully fettering discretion. The exercise of regulatory judgement must remain context sensitive and case specific. Further, it should not solely depend upon historical data patterns contained or embedded in AI and digital systems.[103]

The FSMA 2000 embeds procedural protections for those subject to FCA enforcement action. These protections include the Warning Notice and the Decision Notice, which set out the grounds for proposed regulatory action and the FCA's final decision, respectively.[104] Affected parties may challenge these notices before the Tribunal, which conducts a *de novo* hearing.[105] This includes evidentiary safeguards such as cross-examination and expert testimony, providing an important check on arbitrary or opaque decision-making, especially where AI-generated insights or outputs have influenced enforcement priorities.[106]

In instances or cases of criminal enforcement, for example, there is a guarantee of the right to a fair trial.[107] Where the FCA relies on AI-generated analytics or outputs in evidence, the defence must be given meaningful access to the underlying models, data inputs and decision logic. This reflects emerging disclosure expectations in cases involving algorithmic trading systems, source code and others.[108]

As the FCA integrates AI and digital tools and techniques into its supervisory and enforcement approaches and more tangibly into its various functions, it must ensure that there exists human accountability, procedural fairness and transparency. Existing legal and regulatory frameworks, such as FSMA and the Human Rights Act, provide a good set of ground rules to follow, but their application must evolve to address the distinct challenges posed by algorithmic or digital decision-making, inputs and outputs.

4.1.3. Surveillance and Powers of Investigation

If the FCA were to engage in real-time market monitoring or the covert collection of personal communications data, its actions could engage legal duties under the Regulation of Investigatory Powers Act 2000 (RIPA) and the Investigatory Powers Act 2016 (IPA 2016).[109] While these frameworks are more commonly associated with law enforcement and intelligence services, they remain relevant even in

[103] M Veale and L Edwards, 'Clarity, Surprises, and Further Questions in the Article 29 Working Party Draft Guidance on Automated Decision-Making and Profiling' (2018) 34 *Computer Law & Security Review* 398.

[104] FSMA 2000, ss 387–395.

[105] FSMA 2000, s 133; pt 2; *Banque Havilland SA v Financial Conduct Authority* [2024] UKUT 00115 (TCC).

[106] FSMA 2000, ss 387–394; Tribunal Procedure (Upper Tribunal) Rules 2008, SI 2008/2698.

[107] Human Rights Act 1998, s 6; Criminal Justice Act 1993, art 6; See also *R v Grant* [2005] UKHL 2, [2006] 1 AC 1.

[108] Francesca Palmiotto, 'Preserving Procedural Fairness in The AI Era' (*Verfassungsblog*, 5 January 2023). Available at: https://verfassungsblog.de/procedural-fairness-ai.

[109] RIPA 2000, ss 1–5, 27–29; IPA 2016, pts 2–7.

financial regulation, particularly in market abuse investigations involving personal data.[110] This means the FCA must follow strict laws if it starts using surveillance techniques similar to those used by police or security services.

In practice, the FCA typically relies on firm-reported data, such as transaction reports and suspicious activity notifications.[111] Nonetheless, scenarios may arise where personal communications data, such as emails, phone records or messaging metadata, is accessed under judicial warrant or via inter-agency cooperation with various bodies like the National Crime Agency or the Serious Fraud Office.[112] In such cases, any AI-based or digital-based analysis and outputs performed on this data must strictly comply with the conditions under which the data was lawfully obtained.[113] So, even when working with other agencies or using warrants, the FCA must be careful to only use data in ways the law allows.

Moreover, the FCA is bound by principles of necessity and proportionality when processing data derived from such surveillance, even if it is not the primary subject of RIPA or IPA oversight.[114] Where investigatory techniques touch upon private life or communications, the FCA must ensure that its tools and processes align with both statutory safeguards and the right to privacy.[115] This means the FCA must always balance its actions with people's right to privacy and only use intrusive tools when absolutely necessary.

Thus, as the FCA increasingly engages with advanced data-backed analytics, including AI and digital surveillance tools, it must remain vigilant in upholding rights, standards and the law. This includes ensuring that any intrusion into private communications or personal data is not only lawful but also justified by a legitimate regulatory objective and proportionate in its scope and effect. Respect for privacy, legal transparency and proper authorisation must be reflected in every step of such processes. In doing so, the FCA can safeguard both regulatory legitimacy and build public trust, even as it adopts more innovative forms of supervision and enforcement.

4.1.4. Freedom of Information

The FCA is subject to transparency obligations under the Freedom of Information Act 2000.[116] While many requests may be declined due to statutory exemptions,

[110] FCA, 'EG 19.5 Regulation of Investigatory Powers Act 2000 (RIPA)' (FCA Handbook). Available at: www.handbook.fca.org.uk/handbook/EG/19/5.html.

[111] *See*, eg, FCA, 'Market Watch 70' (2022). Available at: www.fca.org.uk/publications/newsletters/market-watch-70.

[112] FSMA 2000, ss 165–76; Home Office, 'Operational Case for the Use of Communications Data by Public Authorities' (2016). Available at: https://assets.publishing.service.gov.uk/media/5a80226aed915d74e622cabd/operational-case-for-the-use-of-communications-data-by-public-authorities.pdf.

[113] FCA, 'AI Update' (2023). Available at: www.fca.org.uk/publication/corporate/ai-update.pdf.

[114] RIPA 2000, s 28; IPA 2016, s 2; *R (on the application of Catt) v Association of Chief Police Officers* [2015] UKSC 9, [2015] AC 1065.

[115] Human Rights Act 1998, s 6; European Convention on Human Rights, Art 8.

[116] Freedom of Information Act 2000, s 1.

such as regulatory confidentiality or the risk of market manipulation, there is increasing public interest in algorithmic governance and the usage of AI and digital tools.

The UK government has introduced an Algorithmic Transparency Standard that, while not binding on the FCA, signals a broader trend toward its adoption of *openness*.[117] The FCA could adopt voluntary practices such as publishing summaries of its use of AI in its annual reports or via the Digital Regulation Cooperation Forum. Excessive opacity is generally unwelcome, especially where decisions based on opaque technologies that impact regulated firms and individuals lead to the risk of undermining institutional legitimacy.[118]

In an era of increasing reliance on data and digital tools, the FCA faces growing public demand for transparency in algorithmic decisions. While it can legally withhold certain information under the Freedom of Information Act 2000, excessive secrecy, particularly around AI-driven decisions that impact firms and individuals, may lead to the erosion of public confidence. Although not legally required to follow the UK government's Algorithmic Transparency Standard, the FCA could voluntarily adopt clearer reporting practices, such as publishing summaries of its AI use. Doing so would help demonstrate accountability and build trust. Transparency about the role of technology in regulatory processes is not just good practice, as it becomes essential for preserving the FCA's institutional legitimacy in the age of digital disruption and transformation.

4.1.5. Financial Regulation and Internal Governance

There are recent developments in financial services legislation which have the potential to further shape the legal context for the FCA's use of AI. The Financial Services and Markets Act 2023 introduced a new secondary objective for the FCA, which is to facilitate the growth and international competitiveness of the UK economy.[119] This objective has been interpreted as encouraging innovation in regulatory practices, including the deployment of AI, RegTech, SupTech and other digital tools.[120] This implies that the FCA is now also expected to support innovation and economic growth, which may push it to adopt more advanced technologies like AI.

[117] Central Digital and Data Office, 'Algorithmic Transparency Recording Standard Hub' (*gov.uk*, 5 January 2023). Available at: www.gov.uk/government/collections/algorithmic-transparency-recording-standard-hub.

[118] Public Law Project, 'Securing Meaningful Transparency of Public Sector Use of AI' (October 2024). Available at: https://publiclawproject.org.uk/content/uploads/2024/10/Securing-meaningful-transparency-of-public-sector-AI.pdf.

[119] Financial Services and Markets Act 2023, s 26.

[120] ibid, s 1(3); FCA, 'Secondary International Competitiveness and Growth Objective Report 2023/24' (2024). Available at: www.fca.org.uk/publication/corporate/sicgo-report-2023-24.pdf; HM Treasury, *Policy Paper: Building a Smarter Financial Services Framework* (2022). Available at: www.gov.uk/government/publications/building-a-smarter-financial-services-framework-for-the-uk.

Moreover, provisions in the FCA Handbook, particularly the Senior Management Arrangements, Systems and Controls (SYSC) sourcebook, impose obligations on regulated firms to manage the operational risks associated with algorithmic systems.[121] Although these provisions apply to market participants, they arguably reflect normative standards with which the FCA itself should comply. In the context of algorithmic trading, rules derived from the Markets in Financial Instruments Directive require firms to implement safeguards such as kill switches, stress testing and pre-deployment validation.[122] Thus, it follows that any AI or digital systems used by the FCA for surveillance or enforcement purposes should be subject to similar oversight and control mechanisms. In simple terms, if the FCA expects firms to handle algorithm risks responsibly, it should hold itself to the same standards when using AI.

In addition, international frameworks offer relevant guidance. The EU's proposed Artificial Intelligence Act, the OECD's Principles on Trustworthy AI, and the FCA and Bank of England's AI Public-Private Forum Final Report all emphasise principles such as accountability, transparency and human oversight.[123] While these instruments are not binding on the FCA, they inform regulatory best practices and are likely to shape future guidance or sector-specific codes of conduct. This means the FCA should pay attention to global best practices, even if they are not legally required, to ensure responsible and trustworthy use of AI.

Therefore, the FCA's use of AI in supervision must align with a range of overlapping legal requirements. Current practice, characterised by *human-in-the-loop* decision-making, pseudonymised datasets and public engagement, suggests a cautious but proactive approach. As regulatory tools evolve, so must the FCA's internal controls, legal justifications and accountability mechanisms to ensure continued compliance with its statutory and constitutional responsibilities.

4.2. Accountability, Due Process and Fairness

The increasing use of AI, digital and algorithmic tools in regulatory enforcement has attracted significant scrutiny.[124] While its advantages and efficiency gains

[121] FCA Handbook, SYSC 4.1.1R, SYSC 13.1.6R (Operational risk); FCA, *Algorithmic Trading Compliance in Wholesale Markets* (2018). Available at: www.fca.org.uk/publications/multi-firm-reviews/algorithmic-trading-compliance-wholesale-markets.

[122] Directive 2014/65/EU (MiFID II), Arts 17(1)–(3); Commission Delegated Regulation (EU) 2017/589, Arts 12–15.

[123] Commission, 'Proposal for a Regulation of the European Parliament and of the Council Laying Down Harmonised Rules on Artificial Intelligence (Artificial Intelligence Act)' COM (2021) 206 final; OECD, *Recommendation of the Council on Artificial Intelligence* (2019). Available at: https://legalinstruments.oecd.org/en/instruments/oecd-legal-0449; FCA and Bank of England, *AI Public-Private Forum Final Report* (2022). Available at: www.bankofengland.co.uk/-/media/boe/files/fintech/ai-public-private-forum-final-report.pdf.

[124] DF Engstrom and others, 'Government by Algorithm: Artificial Intelligence in Federal Administrative Agencies' (2020) NYU School of Law, Public Law Research Paper No 20–54.

are patent and are being widely acknowledged, there are concerns regarding the potential erosion of principles of administrative justice, particularly in the context of financial regulation.[125] These principles include accountability, due process and fairness, each of which has profound implications for the legitimacy and legality of regulatory enforcement and the regulator itself.[126] While AI can help regulators work faster and smarter, it may also risk undermining the fairness and transparency that are essential in any legal process.

A primary concern where algorithmic tools influence enforcement action is whether persons or actors, such as authorised firms or their representatives, subject to regulatory scrutiny, are able to exercise all the procedural rights that are owed to them.[127] Due process in this context entails the right to notice, the right to be heard and the right to have decisions taken by an impartial adjudicator.[128] These protections are embedded in domestic administrative law as well as the Human Rights Act 1998.[129] Algorithmic opacity or hiding behind decisions taken using a digital tool may hinder these rights by obscuring the rationale behind decisions. For example, if the FCA were to prioritise investigations based on algorithmically derived 'risk scores', it must be capable of providing specific, intelligible reasons for that prioritisation, supported by identifiable data points rather than abstract references to a model.[130] This means people and firms affected by regulatory decisions should be able to understand and challenge them, even if AI tools are involved in the process.

Algorithmic outputs should not be treated as determinate conclusions but rather as components in a decision-making process that require human oversight and contextual understanding.[131] Enforcement decisions must ultimately rest on independently verifiable evidence and must remain subject to disclosure. These must be allowed to be challenged. While there has not yet been a reported case in which a decision by the FCA was overturned or upheld solely based on an AI tool, it is foreseeable that such litigation may arise as the usage and application of SupTech or digital tools expands. As a result, the FCA needs to maintain proper records of algorithmic design, limitations and audit trails that can withstand legal scrutiny.[132] AI tools should support decisions, not replace human judgement, and

[125] F Pasquale, *The Black Box Society: The Secret Algorithms that Control Money and Information* (Harvard University Press 2015).

[126] Mireille Hildebrandt, 'Algorithmic Regulation and the Rule of Law' (2018) 376 *Philosophical Transactions of the Royal Society A* 20170355.

[127] Danielle Keats Citron and Frank Pasquale, 'The Scored Society: Due Process for Automated Predictions' (2014) 89 *Washington Law Review* 1.

[128] European Convention on Human Rights, Art 6; Human Rights Act 1998, sch 1, pt I, art 6.

[129] Human Rights Act 1998, sch 1, pt I, art 6.

[130] Sandra Wachter, Brent Mittelstadt, and Chris Russell, 'Counterfactual Explanations Without Opening the Black Box: Automated Decisions and the GDPR' (2018) 31 *Harvard Journal of Law & Technology* 841.

[131] Michael Veale and Lilian Edwards, 'Slave to the Algorithm? Why a Right to an Explanation Is Probably Not the Remedy You Are Looking For' (2018) 16 *Duke Law & Technology Review* 18.

[132] OECD, 'Principles on Artificial Intelligence' (2019). Available at: www.oecd.org/en/topics/sub-issues/ai-principles.html.

the FCA must be ready to explain and defend how these tools were used if challenged in court.

Concerns about regulatory overreach are also prominent. The scalability of AI tools means regulators may be tempted to expand surveillance and enforcement capabilities without a proportionate increase in procedural safeguards.[133] Public law requires that powers be exercised proportionately and in accordance with legitimate goals and objectives. The use of algorithmic systems must therefore be targeted at serious misconduct, with mechanisms in place to avoid the over-penalisation of technical or low-risk breaches that harm no one. Oversight mechanisms, including judicial review, statutory panels and stakeholder consultations, are essential to prevent regulatory excess.[134] Just because AI can monitor more, it doesn't mean it should, and regulators must use it carefully and fairly, with proper checks in place.

There is scope for the FCA to institutionalise internal safeguards, such as forming an AI governance board or ethics committee tasked with reviewing algorithmic tools for bias, reliability and fairness. Doing so would enhance transparency and internal accountability, reflecting emerging best practices across the public and private sectors.[135] Furthermore, engagement with external experts and the publication of guidelines regarding AI use in supervision and enforcement would promote legitimacy and public confidence.[136] Setting up internal checks and sharing clear rules about AI use can help the FCA build trust, avoid misuse of technology and gain further legitimacy.

Beyond legal compliance, the wider normative concern is whether algorithmic enforcement transforms the nature of regulatory justice. Financial supervision should not be reduced to a mechanistic process devoid of human engagement. Supervisors are expected to detect non-compliances and breaches, foster good conduct, encourage compliance and maintain trust in regulatory institutions. Excessive reliance on automated tools may weaken these relational aspects of regulation.[137] The FCA has repeatedly described its supervisory approach as outcomes-focused and judgement-led.[138] These descriptors suggest a regulatory philosophy that values dialogue and discretion. AI should support, not replace, this model, and, as mentioned earlier, AI and digital tools should be helpers in supervision and not a replacement for existing processes.

Used prudently, AI can free supervisors from repetitive data processing tasks and allow them to focus on more complex, value-sensitive aspects of

[133] Frank Pasquale, *The Black Box Society: The Secret Algorithms That Control Money and Information* (Harvard University Press 2015).

[134] UK Government, 'AI Regulation: A Pro-Innovation Approach' (White Paper, 2023). Available at: www.gov.uk/government/publications/ai-regulation-a-pro-innovation-approach/white-paper.

[135] Reid Blackman, 'Why You Need an AI Ethics Committee' (*Harvard Business Review*, 2022).

[136] FCA, 'AI Update' (2024). Available at: www.fca.org.uk/publication/corporate/ai-update.pdf.

[137] Iyad Rahwan, 'Society-in-the-Loop: Programming the Algorithmic Social Contract' (2017).

[138] FCA, 'Our Approach to Supervision' (2024). Available at: www.fca.org.uk/publications/corporate-documents/our-approach-to-supervision.

enforcement.[139] However, resource constraints may incentivise over-reliance on automation, which could undermine the quality and legitimacy of decisions.[140] If AI tools are not carefully designed to distinguish between material misconduct and insignificant anomalies, enforcement may become overly rigid. Without careful design, ML tools risk treating all anomalies uniformly, potentially leading to rigid or inappropriate enforcement responses that fail to account for the contextual differences between trivial irregularities and serious misconduct.[141] Therefore, any AI system deployed by the FCA must incorporate thresholds, contextual filters and human oversight to ensure proportional responses. In short, AI can help, but, without proper design and human checks, it could lead to unfair or overly harsh enforcement.

While the UK currently lacks case law directly addressing the use of AI by financial regulators, judicial review principles are increasingly being tested by analogous developments in administrative decision-making, where courts are beginning to grapple with the opacity, accountability and procedural fairness challenges posed by algorithmic tools.[142] In *R (Bridges) v South Wales Police*, the Court of Appeal held that the use of automated facial recognition technology violated rights under Articles 8 and 14 of the ECHR due to inadequate and insufficient safeguards.[143] Similarly, in the Dutch *SyRI* case, the courts found that an algorithmic system for fraud detection was incompatible with the right to privacy and the principle of non-discrimination.[144] These cases demonstrate that public authorities must apply rigorous legal standards when adopting novel technologies. These examples show that courts are willing to step in when automated systems threaten privacy, fairness or equality, something the FCA must keep in mind.

In the financial regulatory context, the use of algorithmic classifications, such as placing firms on high-risk internal watchlists without affording them procedural safeguards, could prompt legal challenges. Such practices may amount to de facto adverse decisions and thus attract the full range of administrative law protections.[145] The FCA has thus far avoided such practices, and recent consultations have shown a reluctance to introduce measures that could unduly harm firms' reputations. The principle of fairness requires regulators not only to act lawfully but also to treat regulated entities equitably throughout all stages of the enforcement process. This means the FCA must

[139] FCA, 'AI Update' (2024). Available at: www.fca.org.uk/publication/corporate/ai-update.pdf.

[140] Mirishli Shahmar Sakit, 'Regulating AI in Financial Services: Legal Frameworks and Compliance Challenges' (2024) 358 *Qanun* 29.

[141] Cary Coglianese and David Lehr, 'Regulating by Robot: Administrative Decision Making in the Machine-Learning Era' (2017) 105 *Georgetown Law Journal* 1147.

[142] Philip Sales, 'Judicial Review Methodology in the Automated State' (Speech at the Conference on Automation in Public Governance: Theory, Practice and Problems, Prato, September 2024) 1–2.

[143] *R (Bridges) v Chief Constable of South Wales Police* [2020] EWCA Civ 1058.

[144] *Rechtbank Den Haag*, 5 February 2020, ECLI:NL:RBDHA:2020:865.

[145] UK Government, 'Implementing the UK's AI Regulatory Principles: Initial Guidance for Regulators' (2023). Available at: www.gov.uk/government/publications/implementing-the-uks-ai-regulatory-principles-initial-guidance-for-regulators.

ensure firms are treated fairly and not penalised or flagged by AI tools without due process.

AI tools must also be capable of triage. A risk-based approach to enforcement requires that resource allocation and regulatory scrutiny be proportionate to the severity and likelihood of harm.[146] Human supervisors must retain discretion to assess whether an alert warrants escalation. Over-enforcement based on algorithmic flagging risks undermining both procedural fairness and operational efficiency. In simpler terms, AI should help focus attention where it's most needed and not flood or overwhelm the system with alerts that waste resources or cause unfair actions.

Thus, the integration of AI into FCA enforcement activity must be guided by principles of legality, transparency and accountability. The regulator has publicly committed to deploying technology in a responsible manner, and it must ensure that it is equipped and capable of meeting the challenges that might follow the usage of such technology. Continued transparency, external engagement and a willingness to adapt supervisory models are essential for sustaining public trust and legal defensibility. In a digital regulatory environment, justice must not only be done but also be demonstrably governed, reviewed and understood by human decision-makers. The goal is to use AI or digital tools in a way that improves regulation without sacrificing fairness or legality or eroding public trust in the system.

5. Conclusion

The FCA has undergone a significant transformation since its inception in 2013, evolving from the ashes of the FSA while trying to shed off the legacy of the erstwhile regulators. This shift reflects a more proactive, judgement-based regulatory approach focused on anticipating risks and safeguarding market integrity. As digitalisation accelerates in the financial sector, the ability of the FCA to effectively supervise, regulate and enforce depends on continued internal reform and the need to foster closer collaboration with the actors in the market. Further, the complexities introduced by innovations and new technologies require a regulatory approach that is anchored on adaptability, quick response and shared responsibility.

The cultural shift propagated by the FCA towards innovation and the adaptation of digital and AI tools has prepared it to lead in a world where technology plays a pivotal role in regulatory compliance and supervision. This includes the FCA's strategic use of SupTech solutions for market surveillance, enforcement automation and predictive supervision. However, the increasing reliance on digital tools also necessitates a conducive and collaborative regulatory landscape. The private sector, especially financial institutions and technology providers, will need to be actively

[146] FCA, 'Our Approach to Supervision' (2024). Available at: www.fca.org.uk/publications/corporate-documents/our-approach-to-supervision.

involved in shaping these landscapes. Close collaboration between regulators and other actors will be essential to ensure that technological innovations are implemented effectively while maintaining market integrity and ensuring the protection of consumers and vulnerable groups. This collaborative approach will be important in navigating the complexities of a digitalised financial world. As technologies such as AI, ML and blockchain reshape market operations, the FCA must continue engaging with non-state actors, private firms, academics and industry experts to refine regulatory frameworks that are flexible enough to accommodate innovation and competent to manage emerging risks. By doing so, the FCA can leverage industry expertise to better understand the risks posed by new technologies and create regulatory environments that encourage innovation without compromising market integrity and consumer safety.

The growing importance of public-private partnerships is evident in initiatives like the FCA's RegTech Sprint, which brings together financial institutions and technology providers to test and develop solutions for regulatory challenges. These partnerships will ensure that the FCA can effectively monitor market behaviour and enforce on a real-time basis. Events such as the APP Fraud TechSprint and initiatives like DRR and RegData demonstrate how digital tools are reshaping the FCA's operational capacity. The private sector's involvement is not merely about compliance; it must also bridge the regulatory knowledge gap, as needed to adapt to the rapidly evolving financial landscape.

Furthermore, the FCA's focus on cultural change extends beyond its internal reforms and aims to influence the behaviours and governance structures of the firms it regulates. Initiatives like the SMCR promote accountability at all levels, ensuring that firms align their operations with public interest goals. This cultural shift is equally important in creating a regulatory environment that encourages ethical business practices and transparency, fostering a stronger partnership between regulators and the financial services sector. As algorithmic supervision becomes more prevalent, instilling a culture of responsibility, auditability and transparency within the FCA and across regulated firms will be indispensable to ensuring procedural fairness and trust.

Therefore, the FCA's transformation and growing reliance on technology highlight the need for closer collaboration with the private sector to navigate the challenges of digital disruption. The regulator's success in the digital era will depend on its ability to foster a regulatory culture that is not only adaptable but also collaborative in nature. The FCA can create regulatory frameworks that promote innovation, ensure consumer protection and maintain market integrity by working closely with industry leaders, tech innovators and non-state actors. The increasing digitalisation of financial services demands this collaborative approach, where both the public and private sectors share the responsibility of shaping the future of regulation in an interconnected world.

PART II

Digitalisation and Data

5

Regulatory Sandboxes in Finance and Energy

Best Practices for Implementing the European Data Spaces

INGE GRAEF AND DIN BULJEVIĆ

1. Introduction

One of the policy dilemmas that the EU is facing in regulating data is how to facilitate data sharing to foster data-driven innovation, while also ensuring safe and secure data processing in line with European values. Data-driven innovation is expected to boost economic growth and bring societal benefits, for example through personalised healthcare and improved energy efficiency.[1] But European values may sometimes require restrictions in data processing – for instance to protect personal data, to uphold intellectual property rights and to prevent collusion through the exchange of commercially sensitive information.[2] How to balance these values against the interest in data sharing is a dilemma at the heart of the 'European data spaces'.

In strategic economic sectors, such as health, mobility and agriculture as well as finance and energy, the EU is setting up European data spaces as secure and privacy-preserving infrastructures combining legal and technical measures to facilitate data sharing.[3] According to the European Commission, the key features of a European data space include not only an infrastructure 'to pool, access, share, process and use data' but also full respect for 'European rules and values, in particular personal data protection, consumer protection legislation and competition

[1] Commission, 'A European Strategy for Data' (Communication) COM (2020) 66 final, 1–2.

[2] W Kerber, 'Governance of IoT Data: Why the EU Data Act Will not Fulfill Its Objectives' (2023) 72 *GRUR International* 120.

[3] Commission, 'Commission Staff Working Document on Common European Data Spaces' SWD (2022) 45 final, 2–3, and Commission, 'Commission Staff Working Document on Common European Data Spaces' SWD (2024) 21 final, 4.

law'.[4] How to balance the need for data sharing against the need for protecting personal data, intellectual property rights and competition in specific situations remains unclear.[5] The Data Act, for example, contains provisions that attempt to reconcile the right to access IoT data with data protection and intellectual property interests in the same data,[6] but they leave room for interpretation by market players and regulators. Until this legal uncertainty is resolved by the courts, businesses and regulators may feel disincentivised to invest in data sharing – potentially undermining the EU's data strategy.

The premise of the chapter is that the use of regulatory sandboxes may help overcome the dilemma between the need for data sharing and the need to protect data. Regulatory sandboxes allow businesses to test innovations in a controlled environment under a regulator's supervision. With legal safeguards in place to protect consumers, regulatory sandboxes both incentivise businesses to introduce innovations by letting them experiment with new services and allow regulators to build expertise to balance the tension between promoting regulatory goals and enabling innovation.[7] While the European data spaces combine different strategies, from introducing new legal rules to setting up infrastructures and adopting technical measures, the use of regulatory sandboxes has so far not been considered. The Artificial Intelligence (AI) Act, however, does require Member States to ensure that there is at least one AI regulatory sandbox at the national level by August 2026.[8] Several of the objectives to which the AI regulatory sandboxes aim to contribute according to the EU legislator are also relevant for the European data spaces. Among others, the AI Act refers to: improving legal certainty, fostering innovation and competitiveness, and facilitating and accelerating access to the EU market, in particular for SMEs and start-ups.[9] This confirms the potential of regulatory sandboxes also in the context of the European data spaces.

Against this background, the chapter discusses to what extent regulatory sandboxes can indeed help overcome the dilemma between the need for data sharing and the need for protecting data in European data spaces. The context of European

[4] Commission, SWD (2022) ibid, 2–3, and Commission, SWD (2024) ibid, 4.

[5] For an earlier discussion, see T Tombal, *Imposing Data Sharing among Private Actors: A Tale of Evolving Balances* (Kluwer Law International 2022).

[6] See Regulation (EU) 2023/2854 of the European Parliament and of the Council of 13 December 2023 on harmonised rules on fair access to and use of data and amending Regulation (EU) 2017/2394 and Directive (EU) 2020/1828 (Data Act) [2023] OJ L2023/2854 (the Data Act), arts 4 (6–8 and 12) and 5 (7–11).

[7] A Attrey, M Lesher, and C Lomax, 'The Role of Sandboxes in Promoting Flexibility and Innovation in the Digital Age' (Going Digital Toolkit Note No 2, OECD 2020) 9–10. Available at: https://goingdigital.oecd.org/data/notes/No2_ToolkitNote_Sandboxes.pdf; S Ranchordás, 'Experimental Regulations and Regulatory Sandboxes – Law Without Order?' (2021) *Law and Method* 1, 5–6.

[8] Regulation (EU) 2024/1689 of the European Parliament and of the Council of 13 June 2024 laying down harmonised rules on artificial intelligence and amending Regulations (EC) No 300/2008, (EU) No 167/2013, (EU) No 168/2013, (EU) 2018/858, (EU) 2018/1139 and (EU) 2019/2144 and Directives 2014/90/EU, (EU) 2016/797 and (EU) 2020/1828 [2024] OJ L2024/1689 (Artificial Intelligence Act), art 57(1).

[9] AI Act, art 57(9).

data spaces is more complicated than earlier applications of regulatory sandboxes, which mainly focused on innovations triggering only one domain-specific regime. Data-driven innovations are peculiar in this regard because they trigger several regimes at the same time and require the involvement of domain-specific as well as general regulators in areas such as data protection and competition. By analysing existing experiences with regulatory sandboxes in finance and energy, this chapter provides insights into how regulatory sandboxes can be effectively implemented in a more complex environment such as the European data spaces. After discussing the main features of regulatory sandboxes as a form of experimental law-making in section 2, section 3 analyses the experiences of their application in the financial and energy sectors – aligning the chapter with the focus of this book. Based on this analysis, section 4 draws lessons in the form of three best practices for the possible implementation of regulatory sandboxes in the context of the European data spaces. Section 5 concludes and reflects on the question of whether the use of regulatory sandboxes can be an appropriate law-making strategy for governing data.

2. Regulatory Sandboxes as a Form of Experimental Law-Making

Experimental law-making concerns different forms of experimentation with laws and regulations, typically with the objective of establishing a temporary legal framework with a limited scope of application to test new policies that would be too risky to implement otherwise. More specifically, selected activities or actors are exempted from certain rules or made subject to new rules for a limited period to see what effect this has. The insights gained from the experiment can then inform subsequent law-making on a larger and more permanent scale.[10]

Regulatory sandboxes are a specific type of experimental law-making in which market players and regulators work together to test the implementation of an innovation. They are particularly suitable in situations of legal uncertainty where both market players and regulators are not yet knowledgeable enough to properly manage risks.[11] Interest in regulatory sandboxes has grown over the past decade at the Member State and EU level. In 2020, the Council of Europe called on the European Commission to strengthen its approach towards designing experimental regulation including regulatory sandboxes.[12] To provide a basis for comparing their implementation in the financial and energy sectors, this section discusses the main features and challenges of regulatory sandboxes.

[10] Ranchordás, 'Experimental Regulations and Regulatory Sandboxes' (2021) (n 7) 1, 8.

[11] HJ Allen, 'Regulatory Sandboxes' (2019) 87 *The George Washington Law Review* 579, 591–92.

[12] Council, 'Council Conclusions on Regulatory sandboxes and experimentation clauses as tools for an innovation-friendly, future-proof and resilient regulatory framework that masters disruptive challenges in the digital age' (16 September 2020) 12683/1/20 REV 1. Available at: www.consilium.europa.eu/media/46822/st13026-en20.pdf.

2.1. Main Features of Regulatory Sandboxes

Regulatory sandboxes have been defined in the literature as a 'decreed state of exception within a regulatory regime that allows market players to offer products or services for a limited time to a limited number of customers in a modified regulatory environment for the purpose of allowing the market player to test a product or service before it is offered more broadly'.[13] Such modifications usually either involve the application of temporary regulatory waivers and exemptions to experiment with selected technologies or services without certain legal rules applying for a period, or involve targeted guidance from regulators to provide clarity to market players about what certain legal rules entail or whether a planned activity would constitute a breach of said rules.[14] On the one hand, the collaboration with regulators within regulatory sandboxes provides market players with more insight into the legality of their conduct and therefore allows them to focus more of their resources on innovation. On the other hand, regulatory sandboxes enable regulators to learn from innovative market players to improve their supervision activities.

Regulatory sandboxes were first introduced in the financial sector by the UK Financial Conduct Authority (FCA).[15] The objective of the first sandbox was to promote 'disruptive innovation' in the sector by letting market players experiment with innovative business models based on new financial technologies (fintech). The FCA was concerned that certain regulatory burdens might need to be lifted to allow for genuine innovation, as the existing regulatory framework was not created with these technologies in mind. However, as innovation also brings risks, it was necessary to guide its application in order to continue to protect consumers. For this reason, the FCA relied on a regulatory sandbox to promote the development of innovation in the financial sector.[16]

Regulatory sandboxes not only benefit market players and regulators by allowing them to learn about the impact of new business models and technologies in a safe testing environment but can also bring innovations to the market more quickly, to benefit consumers and attract investment. For example, a study looking at nine countries that introduced regulatory sandboxes in the financial sector found a remarkable increase in the amount of investment received by participating market players.[17]

[13] B Knight and T Mitchell, 'The Sandbox Paradox: Balancing the Need to Facilitate Innovation with the Risk of Regulatory Privilege' (2020) 72 *South Carolina Law Review* 445, 446 fn 1.

[14] Ranchordás (n 7) 1, 2–3.

[15] UK Financial Conduct Authority, 'Regulatory Sandbox' (2015). Available at: www.fca.org.uk/publication/research/regulatory-sandbox.pdf.

[16] ibid, paras 2.2–2.6.

[17] JJ Goo and J-Y Heo, 'The Impact of the Regulatory Sandbox on the Fintech Industry, with a Discussion on the Relation between Regulatory Sandboxes and Open Innovation' (2020) 6 *Journal of Open Innovation: Technology, Market, and Complexity* 43, 58.

While regulatory sandboxes differ in their design, the OECD has outlined some characteristics common to most of them:

- *Genuine innovation*: market players must have a truly novel business idea.
- *Need and readiness*: market players must demonstrate the need for regulatory waivers or guidance and be ready to test the novel business idea.
- *Defined limits*: regulatory sandboxes apply for a limited period of time and can also be limited sectorally or geographically.
- *Safeguard mechanisms*: safeguards are put in place to avoid negative consequences for consumers or the market more broadly.[18]

2.2. Challenges of Regulatory Sandboxes

While regulatory sandboxes offer benefits to both market players and regulators, there are also risks and challenges to their implementation that regulators need to consider. By testing innovations, regulatory sandboxes may create unknown and unpredictable risks for consumers or for the market. For instance, the implementation of regulatory sandboxes in the financial sector can give rise to negative impacts on financial stability.[19] Some have gone as far as to denounce regulatory sandboxes (or at least those in fintech) as 'riskwashing', namely making products or processes appear less risky than they are by mimicking genuine attempts to reduce risk.[20] The concern is that regulators are engaging in a 'race-to-the-bottom' in terms of the applicable legal rules to attract investment in a sector.[21]

Beyond this, regulatory sandboxes may impact competition by providing advantages to selected market players who participate in a sandbox and receive personalised treatment from the regulator. As long as the differentiation is temporary and based on objective criteria, such risks can be mitigated.[22] Another way to address the risk of an uneven playing field is to share the learning from regulatory sandboxes with the wider community, so that everyone can benefit from the experience gained.[23]

However, to what extent the experience from a regulatory sandbox has a wider relevance beyond the experiment. Unlike a scientific experiment conducted under

[18] Attrey, Lesher, and Lomax, 'The Role of Sandboxes in Promoting Flexibility and Innovation in the Digital Age' (n 7) 8–11.

[19] R Parenti, 'Regulatory Sandboxes and Innovation Hubs for FinTech' (2020) Study for the Committee on Economic and Monetary Affairs, Policy Department for Economic, Scientific and Quality of Life Policies, European Parliament, 25. Available at: www.europarl.europa.eu/RegData/etudes/STUD/2020/652752/IPOL_STU(2020)652752_EN.pdf.

[20] E Brown and D Piroska, 'Governing Fintech and Fintech as Governance: The Regulatory Sandbox, Riskwashing, and Disruptive Social Classification' (2022) 27 *New Political Economy* 19, 20.

[21] Parenti, 'Regulatory Sandboxes and Innovation Hubs for FinTech' (n 19) 24.

[22] Ranchordás (n 7) 1, 7.

[23] Parenti (n 19), 38.

controlled laboratory conditions, regulatory experimentation is much less capable of establishing reliable causal relationships. If a market player participating in a regulatory sandbox is exempt from a certain rule and ends up achieving a desired outcome, there is no guarantee that this happened because of the exemption. There is therefore a need for caution when interpreting results for future policymaking.

Finally, operating a regulatory sandbox uses the regulator's resources to design the sandbox, assess the eligibility of market players that wish to participate, monitor the implementation and potentially also give personalised advice. Because regulatory sandboxes often do not scale well, market-wide benefits can be limited so that regulators lose out on resources they could spend on more generally applicable forms of supervision and enforcement.[24]

This discussion shows that regulatory sandboxes can be a useful tool to let market players and regulators experiment to test the impact of certain innovations in a safe and controlled environment. Based on the analysis in this section, two main measures can be taken to maximise the potential and minimise the risks of regulatory sandboxes. First, adequate selection criteria and safeguards should be put in place to avoid harm for consumers or for the market. Second, the learnings should be shared with the entire community to level the playing field and make the most out of the scarce public resources that the regulator devotes to operating a regulatory sandbox.

3. Analysing Regulatory Sandboxes in Finance and Energy

Beyond finance and energy, regulatory sandboxes have been implemented in other sectors like health and aviation.[25] The decision to focus on finance and energy in this chapter stems from the theme of this book as well as from the fact that these two sectors are important targets as European data spaces.[26] This section analyses and compares the implementation of regulatory sandboxes in finance and energy, so that the next section can draw lessons on how they could advance the development of the European data spaces.

After a brief introduction to the existing experience with regulatory sandboxes in both sectors, this section discusses three main aspects by way of

[24] Attrey, Lesher, and Lomax (n 7) 12.

[25] Regarding the health sector, see for instance: E Leckenby and others, 'The Sandbox Approach and Its Potential for Use in Health Technology Assessment: A Literature Review' (2021) 19 *Applied Health Economics and Health Policy* 857. Regarding the aviation sector, see for instance the sandbox of the UK Civil Aviation Authority. Available at: www.caa.co.uk/our-work/publications/documents/content/cap-2616/.

[26] Commission, 'Commission Staff Working Document on Common European Data Spaces' SWD (2022) 45 final, 23–26.

comparison: eligibility criteria, type of regulatory waivers and risk mitigation measures.

3.1. Regulatory Sandboxes in Finance

As noted in the previous section, regulatory sandboxes were first conceived as a tool to encourage innovation in finance. The UK FCA believed that a regulatory sandbox could reduce the time and cost of getting innovative ideas to market and enable greater access to finance for innovators.[27] It admitted its first cohort of participants in June 2016 and has, to date, included over 150 market players in its sandbox test.[28] Apart from the UK, the regulatory sandbox has found its way into the financial sectors of numerous other countries, including the US, China and Japan, as well EU Member States such as Poland, Denmark and the Netherlands.[29]

The appeal of regulatory sandboxes in finance seems closely linked to fintech's perceived potential to create economic growth. Many policymakers and researchers alike see great opportunities in technologies such as AI, blockchain and Big Data analytics.[30] What regulatory sandboxes promise is to enable market players to deploy these technologies in controlled environments, allowing both market players and regulators to learn from these experiences without putting the entirety of the financial system at risk. Nevertheless, because of the interconnectedness of financial institutions, the conduct of one or several market actors can have very far-reaching, potentially systemic, consequences. It is for this reason that risk mitigation is one of the key concerns held by regulators when operating a fintech regulatory sandbox.[31]

The precise characteristics of each sandbox vary. However, many are modelled after the FCA sandbox as the pioneer in the field.[32] For example, eligibility criteria for participation in most sandboxes are based on demonstrating innovation and a potential benefit to consumers, which were first established by the FCA in 2015.[33] The duration of the testing periods differs. While testing in the FCA

[27] UK Financial Conduct Authority, 'Regulatory Sandbox' (2015) para 1.3.

[28] UK Financial Conduct Authority, 'Regulatory Sandbox Accepted Firms' (24 May 2024). Available at: www.fca.org.uk/firms/innovation/regulatory-sandbox/accepted-firms.

[29] World Bank, 'Key Data from Regulatory Sandboxes across the Globe' (1 November 2020). Available at: www.worldbank.org/en/topic/fintech/brief/key-data-from-regulatory-sandboxes-across-the-globe.

[30] D Ahern, 'Regulatory Lag, Regulatory Friction and Regulatory Transition as FinTech Disenablers: Calibrating an EU Response to the Regulatory Sandbox Phenomenon' (2021) 22 *European Business Organization Law Review* 395, 396.

[31] ibid 412.

[32] Goo and Heo, 'The Impact of the Regulatory Sandbox on the Fintech Industry, with a Discussion on the Relation between Regulatory Sandboxes and Open Innovation' (n 17), Table 2; Brown and Piroska, 'Governing Fintech and Fintech as Governance'(n 20) 20.

[33] D Ahern, 'Regulatory Lag, Regulatory Friction and Regulatory Transition as FinTech Disenablers'(n 30) 409; UK Financial Conduct Authority, 'Regulatory Sandbox' (n 27) para 3.4.

sandbox lasts for three to six months, most sandboxes last between six months and two years.[34]

3.2. Regulatory Sandboxes in Energy

Like the financial sector, the energy industries of EU Member States require constant innovation in order to flourish. While stimulating innovation in finance generally stems from a desire to attract investment, innovation in energy production and distribution is needed to meet the EU's ambitious environmental objectives.[35] For the most part, this means moving to renewable energy sources and away from fossil fuels, as well as increasing the overall efficiency of production and distribution.[36] This need for innovation has led regulators in this sector to adopt forms of experimental regulation, including regulatory sandboxes.

The first regulatory sandbox for energy was introduced in the Netherlands in 2015, the same year as the UK's sandbox for finance. It was introduced in response to the growing number of Dutch households producing their own renewable energy.[37] The regulator wanted to encourage this behaviour, but it was unclear what the impact would be on the wider energy system.[38] The sandbox therefore provided the regulator with the opportunity to learn.

Despite being the first sandbox in energy, the Dutch sandbox was suspended in 2018 in favour of potentially more permanent changes to the country's energy regulations.[39] Nonetheless, regulatory sandboxes for energy have been introduced in a number of EU Member States since then, including in France, Spain and Italy.[40] The UK, the finance sandbox pioneer, has also launched a number of sandboxes in its energy sector.[41]

Many of the challenges associated with operating a regulatory sandbox in the financial sector, such as risk management, market distortions and lack of resources, are common to both energy and financial sandboxes. However, there

[34] World Bank, 'Key Data from Regulatory Sandboxes across the Globe' (1 November 2020). Available at: www.worldbank.org/en/topic/fintech/brief/key-data-from-regulatory-sandboxes-across-the-globe.

[35] F Gangale and others, 'Making Energy Regulation Fit for Purpose. State of Play of Regulatory Experimentation in the EU' (JRC Publications Repository, 20 March 2023) 5. Available at: https://publications.jrc.ec.europa.eu/repository/handle/JRC132259.

[36] ibid.

[37] A Schneiders, 'Regulatory Sandboxes in the Energy Sector: Are They Key to the Transition to a Net Zero Future?' (University College London (UCL) Energy Institute, 2021) 5. Available at: www.biee.org/resources/regulatory-sandboxes-in-the-energy-sector-are-they-key-to-the-transition-to-a-net-zero-future/.

[38] ibid.

[39] J Gorenstein Dedecca and others, 'Regulatory Sandboxes in the Energy Sector – Final report' (European Commission 2023) 13. Available at: https://data.europa.eu/doi/10.2833/848065.

[40] E Beckstedde and others, 'Regulatory Sandboxes: Do They Speed up Innovation in Energy?' (2023) 180 *Energy Policy* 113656.

[41] ibid.

is no single approach to designing a sandbox and there are differences not only between the two sectors but also within them. Nevertheless, by looking at the relatively short history of regulatory sandboxes in both sectors, some comparisons can be made and some lessons can be drawn.

3.3. Eligibility Criteria

An important aspect of a regulatory sandbox is its eligibility criteria, because these determine which market players can participate. As such, the eligibility criteria define the scope of the sandbox, in particular which technologies and business models will be subject to experimentation. Clear and pre-defined eligibility criteria are also essential to avoid discrimination. By limiting the discretion of regulators in deciding which companies to include in the sandbox, eligibility criteria can reduce the potential for arbitrary decisions.

Eligibility can be based on a number of different criteria, depending on the objectives and concerns of the regulator. For example, access to a fintech sandbox may be limited to authorised financial institutions or to those under the jurisdiction of a particular regulator.[42] Access may also be restricted to a particular segment of the financial sector, such as banking or insurance, or to a particular technology, such as cryptocurrency.[43] Meanwhile, eligibility for energy sandboxes often targets non-business entities such as energy communities and homeowners associations.[44]

In setting the eligibility criteria, regulators must decide on the scope of the sandbox. These decisions can be very consequential, as setting the scope too narrowly can limit the potential of a sandbox to stimulate innovation. If too few market players are eligible to participate, the sandbox experiment may be too small to generate useful learnings for the regulator. However, if too many participants are eligible, the risks associated with sandboxes are likely to be exacerbated.[45]

The eligibility criteria for most regulatory sandboxes in both the financial and energy sectors allow for a broad scope of application.[46] It therefore appears that most regulators are concerned about under-excluding market players and missing out on the knowledge and innovation that regulatory sandboxes can generate.

[42] B Lim and C Low, 'Regulatory Sandboxes' in Jelena Madir (ed), *FinTech: Law and Regulation* (Edward Elgar Publishing 2021) para 14.006.

[43] Ahern (n 30) 408.

[44] Gorenstein Dedecca and others, 'Regulatory Sandboxes in the Energy Sector – Final report' (n 39) 21.

[45] Ahern (n 30) 408.

[46] ibid; Beckstedde and others, 'Regulatory Sandboxes: Do They Speed up Innovation in Energy?' (n 40) 5.

3.4. Regulatory Waivers

The impact of a regulatory sandbox is determined not only by its participants but also, and crucially, by the rules from which they are exempted. Although regulatory waivers are usually not the only feature of a sandbox, they are perhaps the most influential. The derogations that regulators grant to sandbox participants define both the risks and the potential rewards of that sandbox.

These exemptions will vary from sandbox to sandbox. For example, financial sandboxes may exempt participants from meeting certain licensing requirements or having certain credit ratings.[47] Energy sandboxes may include exemptions from metering and billing rules or technical documentation requirements.[48] Both in financial and energy sandboxes, there is generally no specific list of exemptions that the regulator can adopt.[49] This means that, in most cases, regulators have a relatively high degree of discretion to operate the sandbox in the way they consider most conducive to its objectives.

Nevertheless, regulators do not have complete freedom to grant exemptions. First and foremost, they may be constrained by their own obligations to comply with certain rules.[50] And they may simply not have the power to waive certain rules. This can be the result of national legislation, but in the case of EU Member States, regulators often find that Union-level rules are a limiting factor for their sandboxes. For example, when the FCA launched its sandbox in 2015, it highlighted that it 'is limited in what it can waive by EU legislative requirements'.[51] This is also the case for energy sandboxes.[52] In the energy sector in particular, sandboxes may be constrained by environmental regulations, which energy regulators generally do not have the power to waive. For this reason, governments may wish to include several regulators in a sandbox to avoid such obstacles.[53]

It should also be noted that scholars have called for the establishment of a cross-border and possibly EU-wide sandbox. This could have a number of advantages, including the potential to waive EU rules and thus allow greater freedom for regulatory experimentation.[54] The European data spaces would require such involvement of different regulators, taking into account the different legal domains and levels of competence in regulating data.

[47] Monetary Authority of Singapore, 'Frequently Asked Questions on MAS Fintech Regulatory Sandbox Framework' (9 November 2021) 3. Available at: www.mas.gov.sg/-/media/MAS-Media-Library/development/Regulatory-Sandbox/FAQsNov2021.pdf?la=en&hash=075D18DC2B19BD6BCB5A98D1B974666736F87553.

[48] Beckstedde and others, '(n 40).

[49] Lim and Low, 'Regulatory Sandboxes' in Jelena Madir (ed.) *FinTech: Law and Regulation* (Edward Elgar Publishing 2021) para 14.009; Beckstedde and others (n 40) 7.

[50] Lim and Low (n 42) para 14.009.

[51] UK Financial Conduct Authority, 'Regulatory Sandbox' (2015) para 3.13.

[52] Beckstedde and others (n 40) 7.

[53] ibid 8.

[54] Ahern (n 30) 424.

3.5. Risk Mitigation Measures

There are, of course, risks in exempting issues from regulatory obligations, even in a controlled sandbox environment. Some of these are common to both financial and energy sandboxes, such as the risk of consumer harm and distortions of competition in the market.[55] The latter is a direct consequence of the discriminatory nature of sandboxes, as they offer exemptions to a limited number of regulated entities and inherently exclude others. This need not necessarily lead to distortions of competition, but the risk is present in almost all sandboxes.[56] Risks may also be specific to the sector in which the sandbox is used, or to a particular sandbox. For example, an energy sandbox may give rise to environmental risks, while a fintech sandbox may need to mitigate risks posed to the financial system.[57]

The extent to which regulators can successfully mitigate these risks is a matter of debate.[58] The ability of regulators to mitigate risks may depend on their experience in the sector. More experienced regulators will be better able to balance the risks and benefits of innovation when designing and operating a regulatory sandbox, and they are thus better positioned to mitigate risks.[59] It is important to note that regulators can never completely neutralise the risks of a sandbox but, by limiting the scope and impact of a sandbox product, they can mitigate the risks to an acceptable level. Regulators have developed and used a number of approaches to managing risk in practice. For example, the FCA takes a 'risk and proportionality-based approach', meaning that the risks that customers are exposed to for a particular fintech product must be proportionate to the innovation that the product hopes to bring to the market.[60] Safeguards put in place to mitigate risk typically focus on limiting the scale at which the product is rolled out, by restricting the customers it can reach or the capital that can be invested.[61]

What can be concluded from this comparison is that the overall objectives and eligibility criteria differ across the financial and energy sectors, because of their different features and needs in terms of experimentation and learning. At the same time, there are similarities in terms of the limited scope of regulatory exemptions that a regulator can grant within its own competences and the need for proportionality in addressing risks. These aspects will also play a role in possible regulatory sandboxes in the context of the European data spaces.

[55] Gorenstein Dedecca and others (n 39) 27; Knight and Mitchell, 'The Sandbox Paradox (n 13) 445.
[56] Knight and Mitchell ibid 445.
[57] Ahern (n 30) 412.
[58] Brown and Piroska (n 20).
[59] Dirk A Zetzsche and others, 'Regulating a Revolution: From Regulatory Sandboxes to Smart Regulation' (2017) 23 *Fordham Journal of Corporate & Financial Law* 31, 39.
[60] Lim and Low, (n 42) para 14.008.
[61] Ahern (n 30) 412.

4. Best Practices for European Data Spaces

As environments in which the European Commission wants innovation to flourish, the European data spaces could arguably use regulatory sandboxes as a tool to allow market players and regulators to experiment with new technologies or business models in a controlled way. The approach underlying the European data spaces is to stimulate innovation by enabling the sharing and reuse of data. How to reconcile this push to open up datasets with restrictions on data protection, intellectual property rights and the risk of collusion under competition law has not been fully explored. It follows from the discussion in the previous section that in such situations of both high demand for innovation and considerable legal uncertainty as to the interpretation of the applicable rules, market players and regulators may benefit from experimenting with applying selected innovations in a regulatory sandbox, while putting in place appropriate safeguards to manage risks.

While the Commission published a proposal for a Regulation on Financial Data Access in June 2023 to stimulate the sharing of data for the development of financial services,[62] the Energy Data Space is still in the earlier stages of development, with a 'Smart Energy Expert Group' and a 'Data for Energy' working group in the process of being established.[63] As no legislation has yet been proposed, the scope for introducing regulatory sandboxes in the context of the energy data space may be greater than in the financial data space. Another possibility would be for the EU legislator to provide a general competence to regulators to introduce regulatory sandboxes as a tool to implement the European data spaces – irrespective of the sector. Similarly, the AI regulatory sandbox mandated by the AI Act can cover a wide range of industries. While regulatory sandboxes have not yet been considered in the context of the European data spaces, there is room to provide for their implementation. This section discusses three best practices based on existing experience of regulatory sandboxes in the financial and energy sectors, as analysed in the previous section.

4.1. Align Eligibility Criteria with the Overall Objective and the Potential for Wider Learning

The eligibility criteria determine the scope of a regulatory sandbox and should therefore be carefully defined.[64] In setting these criteria, a balance needs to be

[62] Commission, 'Proposal for a Regulation of the European Parliament and of the Council on a framework for Financial Data Access and amending Regulations (EU) No 1093/2010, (EU) No 1094/2010, (EU) No 1095/2010 and (EU) 2022/2554' COM (2023) 360 final.

[63] Commission, SWD (2024) (n 4), 22–23.

[64] As an illustration, the AI Act states that the eligibility and selection criteria of AI regulatory sandboxes need to be transparent and fair. See AI Act, art 58(2)(a).

struck between making the sandbox broad enough to stimulate innovation, but not so broad that it becomes unworkable or too unfocused to deliver its outcome. Achieving this balance is particularly challenging when the regulator does not have extensive knowledge of what kind of innovation to expect and from whom. It is therefore advisable to consult with market participants in advance so that the regulatory sandbox can be designed to meet demand and support the learning that the regulator is seeking. Arguably, the more certain a regulator is about its own needs and those of the market, the narrower the regulatory sandbox can be. Where the regulator's insight is less clear, a broader scope may be justified to avoid the sandbox being under-inclusive and missing out on the knowledge and innovation that could otherwise be gained. Regulators will also learn over time, so that the scope of regulatory sandboxes can become narrower as experience grows.

The overall objective forms a key factor in setting the eligibility criteria. For the European data spaces, the ambition to facilitate data sharing as a means for data-driven innovation in line with 'European rules and values, in particular personal data protection, consumer protection legislation and competition law'[65] can be seen as the overall objective of a possible regulatory sandbox. Depending on the sector, this can be made more specific. For example, the financial data space aims to develop better and more innovative financial products for consumers and businesses, while the energy data space focuses on achieving energy security and sustainability.[66] Given the tension between the need for access to data and the protection of personal data, intellectual property and competition, a regulatory sandbox to test the sharing of data covered by data protection or intellectual property rights or commercial sensitivity can be valuable to learn how these interests can be reconciled in practice for innovative services requiring such data. While the circumstances will vary from sector to sector, there are broader lessons to be learned from such an experiment – especially considering that this is a cross-cutting dilemma for many data-intensive industries. Aligning the eligibility criteria with the overall objective and the potential for wider learning is therefore a first best practice for implementing regulatory sandboxes in the European data spaces.

4.2. Rely on Proportionality to Tailor the Implementation to the Relevant Needs and Risks

Testing an innovation in a regulatory sandbox comes with certain risks for the market and for consumers. However, such risks may be necessary to stimulate regulatory learning. For example, if certain risks to the protection of individuals' personal

[65] Commission, 'Commission Staff Working Document on Common European Data Spaces' SWD (2022) 45 (n 3) 2–3 and Commission, 'SWD (2024) (n 4) 1, 4.

[66] Commission, SWD (2024) ibid, 22 and 24.

data are unavoidable when testing a particular innovation of high public interest, it should nevertheless be possible to conduct such an experiment on the condition that appropriate risk mitigation measures are taken. The 'risk and proportionality-based approach' of the UK's FCA can serve as a guiding principle, where higher risks in terms of detrimental impact on the market or on consumers are only desirable when the innovation is particularly promising for promoting the public interest.[67] Inspiration can also be drawn from how the AI Act addresses possible data protection risks resulting from regulatory sandboxes. The AI Act lays down a range of conditions applicable to the processing of personal data, lawfully collected for other purposes, to develop, train and test AI systems in a sandbox. These conditions include that the sandbox pursues a 'substantial public interest', such as public safety or public health, environmental protection, energy sustainability, critical infrastructure resilience; that the processing of anonymised, synthetic or non-personal data is not effective to achieve the purpose of the sandbox; and that there are effective monitoring and mitigation mechanisms in place to identify and address data protection risks.[68]

As a best practice to minimise risks and maximise learning, the implementation of the regulatory sandbox can be tailored to the features of an innovation, the needs of market players and the risks. The relationship between these three aspects could be thought of as a kind of matrix. Where the risks are low, there is more flexibility to include complex or less predictable innovations and more demanding needs of market players in terms of regulatory exemptions. Where the risks are high, the innovations part of a regulatory sandbox should be more predictable or less complex or at least be subject to appropriate safeguards and mitigation measures. This may mean that market participants only benefit from narrower regulatory exemptions and less lenient regulatory guidance in the sandbox. More generally, proportionality requires that a regulatory sandbox be limited in time to what is necessary given the complexity and scale of the experiment.[69]

4.3. Put in Place Appropriate Safeguards and Develop Mechanisms for Coordination between Regulators

A third best practice is to put in place appropriate safeguards. These can have a legal, technical or institutional nature. For example, from a data protection perspective market players involved in a regulatory sandbox should make sure that the data protection rules are complied with as much as possible. In this regard, the AI Act states that originally collected personal data can only be shared further in line with EU data protection law and that any personal data created in the sandbox cannot be shared outside of it.[70] Technical or organisational measures can also be

[67] Lim and Low (n 42) para 14.008.
[68] AI Act, art 59(1)(a)–(c). Art 59(1)(d)–(j) lays down further conditions.
[69] This wording is derived from the condition laid down in AI Act, art 58(2)(h).
[70] AI Act, art 59(1)(e).

taken to make sure that any personal data is processed securely, for instance by anonymising or encrypting personal data where possible.

What makes regulatory sandboxes in the context of the European data spaces different from earlier applications in sectors like finance and energy is that several types of interests come together that fall under the competences of different regulators. Whereas the regulatory sandboxes in the financial and energy sectors discussed in the previous section mainly involved exemptions and guidance regarding sector-specific rules monitored by either financial or energy regulators, the mix of different interests and legal frameworks is much more prominent in the European data spaces. The sharing of data cannot only be assessed from the perspective of financial or energy law but requires equal attention for data protection, intellectual property and competition concerns. Whereas regulatory sandboxes have so far been mainly applied to innovations triggering only one domain-specific regime, data-driven innovations trigger several regimes at the same time. From an institutional perspective, the operation of regulatory sandboxes in European data spaces will therefore be more complex. Some jurisdictions already appear to be more advanced in dealing with cross-sectoral regulatory sandboxes because they have a broader, overarching strategy for regulatory sandboxes in place at the national level. In this regard, the OECD refers to the Regulatory Sandbox in Korea programme that involves several ministries and Germany's Regulatory Sandboxes Strategy.[71] However, such coordination needs to be further facilitated for the European data spaces – in particular as cross-border cooperation between regulators may also be necessary given the involvement of EU and national authorities in the European data spaces.

While AI regulatory sandboxes also require coordination among regulators, the AI Act only lays down more general requirements for sandboxes to be designed and implemented in such a way that 'they facilitate cross-border cooperation between national competent authorities', for national competent authorities to 'coordinate their activities and cooperate within the framework of the [European Artificial Intelligence] Board', and for national competent authorities to submit annual reports to 'provide information on the progress and results of the implementation of those sandboxes, including best practices, incidents, lessons learnt and recommendations on their setup'.[72] In the context of the European data spaces, the European Data Innovation Board – established in the Data Governance Act – could coordinate the implementation of regulatory sandboxes for the European data spaces across Member States. The European Data Innovation Board is an expert group consisting of representatives of the competent national authorities enforcing the Data Governance Act as well as the European Data Protection Board,

[71] Attrey, Lesher, and Lomax (n 7) 13. Regarding Germany, see Federal Ministry for Economic Affairs and Energy, 'The Handbook for Regulatory Sandboxes: Making Space for Innovation' (2019) www.bmwk.de/Redaktion/EN/Publikationen/Digitale-Welt/handbook-regulatory-sandboxes.pdf?__blob=publicationFile&v=2 2 September 2024.

[72] See respectively, AI Act, art 57(13)–(16).

the European Data Protection Supervisor, ENISA (the European Union Agency for Cybersecurity) and the European Commission.[73] It is also worth mentioning the networks that a number of Member States have set up to coordinate across regulators and legal domains, including the Digital Regulation Cooperation Forum in the Netherlands, the Irish Digital Regulators Group and the Digital Cluster Bonn in Germany.[74] Beyond establishing these more general networks for coordination across domains and across Member States, more specific mechanisms for cooperation are also required. This may, for instance, include the development of cooperation protocols to ensure that regulators can exchange the necessary information and consult with each other.

5. Conclusion

The chapter discussed regulatory sandboxes as a form of experimental law-making to implement the European data spaces. As an area in need of innovation and subject to legal uncertainty on how to facilitate data sharing in line with European values, regulatory sandboxes would allow market players and regulators to engage in a learning process. Based on the experience with regulatory sandboxes in the financial and energy sectors, three best practices have been identified to implement regulatory sandboxes in the European data spaces. First, aligning eligibility criteria with the overall objectives and promoting wider learning from experiments is essential. Second, relying on proportionality to tailor the scope of a sandbox to the features of an innovation, the needs of market players and the risks helps minimise potential harm. Lastly, establishing appropriate safeguards and developing coordination mechanisms between regulators ensures that the range of concerns can be addressed effectively.

While the complexity of European data spaces, which bring together a range of interests that fall under the remit of different regulators pose additional challenges, the experience with regulatory sandboxes in finance and energy shows that measures can be taken to maximise their potential and minimise their risks. Based on the lessons learned from possible regulatory sandboxes in European data spaces, regulators and policymakers can develop more general guidelines on how to reconcile the need for data sharing with the protection of personal data, competition and intellectual property. If properly designed and implemented, regulatory sandboxes can therefore be an important additional tool to develop governance mechanisms for data in line with European values in the evolving European data spaces.

[73] Regulation (EU) 2022/868 of the European Parliament and of the Council of 30 May 2022 on European data governance and amending Regulation (EU) 2018/1724 [2022] OJ L152/1 (Data Governance Act), art 29(1).

[74] See www.acm.nl/en/about-acm/cooperation/national-cooperation/digital-regulation-cooperation-platform-sdt, www.ccpc.ie/business/wp-content/uploads/sites/3/2023/08/2023.06.29_CCPC_Annual-Report-2022.pdf and www.digitalclusterbonn.de/DCB/start.html. Outside of the EU, the UK pioneered such a cooperation network for the first time in 2021. See www.gov.uk/government/collections/the-digital-regulation-cooperation-forum.

6

Taking the Management Perspective

How Perceived Regulatory Barriers Hinder Cross-Sectoral Data-Sharing Initiatives

DAVID WODAK AND TOM AE ABEN

1. Introduction

The electricity grids in the energy sector, together with other public services such as transportation systems, public water systems and emergency services, are seen as a critical infrastructure (CI) that provides an essential service, typically benefitting a whole country.[1] CI networks play a crucial role in the functioning of our modern societies.[2] If one (or more) of these networks were to fail, the dependent society would experience significant nuisances and can even 'crumble'.[3] For example, a large-scale power outage due to a failing energy grid can potentially leave millions of people and businesses without electricity. A power outage also heavily affects other critical public services such as railway services (electric trains will come to a standstill), road services (traffic management systems will fail making it impossible to manage vehicles on roads) and emergency services (most communication channels will be disabled and hospitals will need to switch to back-up generators that have limited capacity). As such, it is no surprise that the energy sector and other CI networks are closely scrutinised by both the public and the governmental authorities; these networks should be effectively managed and maintained by their managers.[4] To support CI managers, the recent digital transformation of the world around us has provided them with numerous technologies

[1] MJ Egan, 'Anticipating Future Vulnerability: Defining Characteristics of Increasingly Critical Infrastructure-like Systems' (2007) 15 *Journal of Contingencies and Crisis Management* 4.

[2] G Pescaroli and I Kelman, 'How Critical Infrastructure Orients International Relief in Cascading Disasters' (2017) 25 *Journal of Contingencies and Crisis Management* 56.

[3] W Veeneman, W Dicke, and M De Bruijne, 'From Clouds to Hailstorms: A Policy and Administrative Science Perspective on Safeguarding Public Values in Networked Infrastructures' (2009) 4 *International Journal of Public Policy* 414.

[4] A Boin and M Lodge, 'Designing Resilient Institutions for Transboundary Crisis Management: A Time for Public Administration' (2016) 94 *Public Administration* 289.

with which they can more effectively manage and maintain their networks,[5] including electricity grids in the energy sector.

Although the digital transformation of CIs brings numerous advantages, it also comes with its challenges. The (semi-)public organisations that are responsible for CIs are confronted with rapidly changing market conditions (eg the rapid introduction of new technologies) and requests from the public (eg more transparency about the availability of infrastructure), which requires them to become more agile, reliable and efficient.[6] Moreover, they need to collaborate more extensively to effectively implement and use new digital technologies. This is not only because the implementation of new technologies is a costly endeavour (making it, at times, necessary to investigate the possibilities of joint investments) but also because organisations need to ensure their systems can communicate to facilitate efficient data sharing among the CI managers' organisations. However, the management of CIs is typically decentralised and divided among different organisations. For example, in the Netherlands six different distribution system operators (DSOs) manage and maintain a specific part of the Dutch electricity grid. Moreover, each DSO has its own local stakeholders. As such, the data regarding the electricity grids is dispersed over various organisations, each with its own objectives and (external) pressures.

Organisations in the energy sector also face increased pressure to take more integral decisions in conjunction with organisations active in their own sector, as well as in other CI sectors. For example, the energy transition requires joint decisions regarding the expansion of the current electricity grids to avoid blackouts and delays with other CI projects. The electricity grids in various parts of the Netherlands are already operating (near) capacity, making it impossible to connect new large industrial customers (and in a few areas even new residential properties) to local grids immediately.[7] New construction projects by other infrastructure organisations will also experience issues with getting access in the near future.[8] Moreover, expanding the electricity grids might also temporarily lower the availability of other infrastructure networks, forcing DSOs to carefully plan their

[5] HA Akkermans and others, 'All Along the Asset Life Cycle: Research Opportunities for Operations and Supply Chain Management' (2024) 70 *Journal of Operations Management* 864.

[6] M Poláková-Kersten and others, 'Digital Transformation in High-Reliability Organizations: A Longitudinal Study of the Micro-Foundations of Failure' (2023) 32 *The Journal of Strategic Information Systems* 101756.

[7] E Rooijers, 'Nog jarenlang wachtlijsten voor aansluiting op het stroomnet' '[Waiting lists for connection to the power grid for years to come'] *Financieel Dagblad* (Amsterdam, 28 February 2023). Available at: https://fd.nl/bedrijfsleven/1468954/nog-jarenlang-wachtlijsten-voor-aansluiting-op-het-stroomnet; C Grol and C De Horde, 'TenneT en Stedin gaan bedrijven soms verplichten om minder stroom te verbruiken' ['TenneT and Stedin will sometimes require companies to consume less electricity'] *Financieel Dagblad* (Amsterdam, 14 November 2024). Available at: https://fd.nl/bedrijfsleven/1537008/tennet-en-stedin-gaan-bedrijven-soms-verplichten-om-minder-stroom-te-verbruiken#:~:text=Het%20gaat%20dan%20om%20bedrijven,krijgen%20de%20bedrijven%20een%20vergoeding.

[8] E Rooijers, 'Uitbreiding van stroomnet in propvol Amsterdam is een "monsterklus"' ['Expanding the power grid in a congested Amsterdam is a "mammoth task"'] *Financieel Dagblad* (Amsterdam,

expansions in collaboration with the affected infrastructures. In short, managers of CIs are required to take a network perspective and invest in horizontal collaborations by connecting to organisations from other sectors in cross-sectoral collaborations.[9]

The challenges brought along by the implementation of new digital technologies and the increasing need to collaborate with other organisations (both within and across sectors) have a profound impact on 'cross-sectoral data-sharing initiatives'. In such initiatives, groups that consist of multiple organisations, active in different sectors, aim to efficiently share data to achieve a higher-level and joint goal. When taking a closer look at the management literature, multiple challenges and barriers have already been identified, and these can have an economic, organisational, technological and/or legislative nature.[10] While these challenges are significant, management scholars are already able to address (most of) them using existing theories and models. Similarly, practitioners in management positions often indicate that these challenges can be assessed (and potentially offset) by themselves or their departments or organisations.

Challenges and barriers of a legislative nature, however, are often more difficult to grasp for managers in organisations. For example, many managers indicate that they try to stay away from data or digital technologies that might have an impact on private data, as they are afraid to breach recent privacy regulation such as the General Data Protection Regulation (GDPR) or the California Consumer Privacy Act (CCPA). Moreover, many discussions about sharing data between managers and between collaborating organisations abruptly stop when privacy concerns arise, even if there is no legal basis for this. As such, managers and their organisations are hindered not only by actual legal barriers (eg GDPR that dictates that personal data cannot be shared without explicit consent from the individual who is the subject of that data) but at times also by 'perceived' legal barriers (eg wrongly classifying specific data as 'personal' under existing regulations). In this chapter, we aim to better understand how these (perceived) legal barriers impact collaborations between multiple data-sharing parties. Therefore, the main question posed by this chapter is: *How do these legal barriers hinder cross-sectoral data-sharing initiatives between critical infrastructure organisations?*

By investigating a single case study around a cross-sectoral data-sharing initiative involving six Dutch CI managers (each active in a different sector), we aim to uncover how (perceived) legal barriers impact data-sharing activities. In our specific case, the six CI managers aimed to set up a data-sharing platform, together with a knowledge institution (concerned with CIs) and a large international software company, which

5 March 2023). Available at: https://fd.nl/bedrijfsleven/1469092/uitbreiding-van-stroomnet-in-propvol-amsterdam-is-een-monsterklus?continue.

[9] W van Donge, N Bharosa, and MFWHA Janssen, 'Data-Driven Government: Cross-Case Comparison of Data Stewardship in Data Ecosystems' (2022) 39 *Government Information Quarterly* 101642.

[10] HS Birkel and E Hartmann, 'Impact of IoT Challenges and Risks for SCM' (2019) 24 *Supply Chain Management: An International Journal* 39.

would enable each CI manager to access (specific) parts of the data held by the others to achieve more effective decision-making regarding the maintenance and management of CIs in the Netherlands. For example, by accessing data from the manager of roads in the Netherlands, the DSOs could directly see which streets would be opened, making it easier for them to access the cables running underneath these roads. While the eight organisations in our case started with a lot of optimism about their project, several events occurred that eventually led to its dissolution as several (perceived) legal barriers emerged that hindered not only the discussions about data sharing but also the actual sharing of data between organisations.

2. Theoretical Background

2.1. Digital Transformation

The rapid digital transformation of the world around us includes smart meters, smart sensors, Internet-of-Things (IoT) devices and (Big) Data analytics, which have been developed and introduced in the past decade.[11] These technologies are a disruptive force in many organisations[12] and have had a profound impact on the 'fabric' of how they organise their activities.[13] For example, the rollout of smart meters among households and small business owners in many countries around the world have provided the organisations active in the energy sector, such as the DSOs and energy companies, with a wealth of data at the household level. Connecting smart meters with IoT devices ensures that data is quickly sent to consumers and small business owners as well as other actors in the energy sector who can access this data. Lastly, with (Big) Data analytics, actors in the energy sector are able to analyse this data on a large scale and obtain useful information and insights. However, this requires a new skill set for many employees of the organisations active in the energy sector and has initiated a significant shift in their operations.[14]

An important characteristic of digital technologies is their ability to generate massive amounts of (raw) data.[15] For this data to become useful, the right actors need to be able to effectively 'gather' and 'transform' it into information. The

[11] J Holmström and others, 'The Digitalization of Operations and Supply Chain Management: Theoretical and Methodological Implications' (2019) 65 *Journal of Operations Management* 728; G Vial, 'Understanding Digital Transformation: A Review and a Research Agenda' (2019) 28 *The Journal of Strategic Information Systems* 118.

[12] Vial ibid.

[13] BT Pentland and others, 'From Lock-in to Transformation: A Path-Centric Theory of Emerging Technology and Organizing' (2022) 33 *Organization Science* 194.

[14] J Bokrantz and others, 'Smart Maintenance: An Empirically Grounded Conceptualization' (2020) 223 *International Journal of Production Economics* 107534; V Delke and others, 'Implementing Industry 4.0 Technologies: Future Roles in Purchasing and Supply Management' (2023) 196 *Technological Forecasting and Social Change* 122847.

[15] B Søgaard and others, 'Facing Disruptive Technologies: Aligning Purchasing Maturity to Contingencies' (2019) 24 *Supply Chain Management: An International Journal* 147.

gathering activity entails the ability to access the 'right' data, which can either come from internal sources (eg sensors placed in important assets of organisations) or external sources (eg smart meters placed with consumers). Raw data in itself, however, is not highly informative. It needs to be collected from various sources, analysed and transformed into information. Often, individual organisations do not have sufficient capacity and/or knowledge to gather and transform data by themselves. Therefore, they need to collaborate with partners to effectively perform both data-processing activities,[16] otherwise the potential of the technologies may not be achieved. In other words, data-sharing initiatives are becoming increasingly important.

2.2. Opportunities and Barriers

Implementing new digital technologies and setting up data-sharing initiatives, either individually or in collaboration with partners, comes with both opportunities and challenges. When looking at the opportunities, the implementation of technologies helps organisations achieve higher levels of visibility and transparency, both internally and in their collaborations with other organisations.[17] The higher levels of visibility and transparency are the result of the large amounts of data that digital technologies can generate. At the same time, analytical tools are being developed that help manage large pools of data and extract useful information from these pools, while many tools are also equipped with various options that increase their connectivity (eg Wi-Fi, Bluetooth). The large amounts of data, increased availability of information and enhanced means (ie software, digital connections between systems, guidelines) of sharing this data not only help organisations to know more precisely what happens in their own organisations but also in those of their partners. This in turn enhances (joint) decision-making. Another opportunity that digital technologies may bring are efficiency gains and the ability to improve management and maintenance activities.[18] Technologies such as smart sensors provide organisations with (near) real-time information about the health of assets, enabling them to introduce smart maintenance;[19] a concept that focuses on using data to determine the optimal time and moment to maintain or replace (parts of) assets, thereby minimising down-time as much as possible.

[16] TAE Aben and others, 'Managing Information Asymmetry in Public–Private Relationships Undergoing a Digital Transformation: The Role of Contractual and Relational Governance' (2021) 41 *International Journal of Operations & Production Management* 1145.

[17] Z Seyedghorban and others, 'Supply Chain Digitalization: Past, Present and Future' (2020) 31 *Production Planning & Control* 96.

[18] F Kache and S Seuring, 'Challenges and Opportunities of Digital Information at the Intersection of Big Data Analytics and Supply Chain Management' (2017) 37 *International Journal of Operations & Production Management* 10.

[19] J Bokrantz and others, 'Smart Maintenance: Instrument Development, Content Validation and an Empirical Pilot' (2020) 40 *International Journal of Operations & Production Management* 481.

There are also various challenges that can potentially hinder the implementation of technologies and supporting data-sharing initiatives. First, organisations may experience technological challenges, preventing them from making a digital technology work within or across organisational boundaries.[20] Examples of technological challenges include security issues (ensuring that the technology itself cannot be breached by unwanted persons or organisations) or interoperability issues (ie a lack of a unified set of standards that enables communication and/or connections between different systems). Interoperability issues especially are quite common and disagreements between collaborating organisations about the content of these guidelines makes the creation of guidelines impossible. Organisations may also experience economic challenges as the implementation of new technologies often costs a lot of money and the economic potential (ie the ability of the technology to generate enough cost savings or profits to offset the initial cost) is often unknown or uncertain.[21] The same applies to the creation of data-sharing initiatives: it is costly to set up the guidelines and the connections to enable the data exchange. Even if there is enough capital to implement a new digital technology, economic issues may still prevent the actual implementation, as discussions about (the extent of) monetary contributions can be detrimental to implementation efforts. Related to the economic challenges are challenges of an organisational nature.[22] Digital technologies are not only costly but also require significant changes to an organisation's value creation process, structure and (work) culture.[23] It can also be the case that the organisation and its employees and environment are simply not yet ready to adopt new digital technologies.[24]

The three types of challenges listed above are often managed by individual organisations, or jointly managed by a network of collaborating organisations. Put differently, these challenges typically originate, and are managed, at the micro (ie an individual organisation) or meso (ie within a network or sector) level. However, there is also a macro level that consists of governmental institutions and regulatory frameworks,[25] which shape the environment within which organisations operate and implement new technologies. These regulatory frameworks originate from outside the micro or meso level and organisations need to find a way to act upon them. While they might bring new opportunities, they also create challenges for organisations that have a regulatory nature.[26]

[20] Birkel and Hartmann 'Impact of IoT Challenges and Risks for SCM' (n 10).

[21] O Maghazei, MA Lewis, and TH Netland, 'Emerging Technologies and the Use Case: A Multi-Year Study of Drone Adoption' (2022) 68 *Journal of Operations Management* 560.

[22] Birkel and Hartmann (n 10).

[23] Vial (n 11).

[24] S Lokuge and others, 'Organizational Readiness for Digital Innovation: Development and Empirical Calibration of a Construct' (2019) 56 *Information & Management* 445.

[25] SL Vargo and RF Lusch, 'Institutions and Axioms: An Extension and Update of Service-Dominant Logic' (2016) 44 *Journal of the Academy of Marketing Science* 5.

[26] Birkel and Hartmann (n 10).

Existing literature shows that regulatory frameworks often lag behind the rapid introduction of new digital technologies, which leads to lacking, unclear and inconsistent legal provisions that hinder organisations in their development of effective data-sharing policies.[27] Moreover, the slow response of regulatory institutions creates uncertainties among organisations regarding the actions to be taken. In the energy sector, for example, the digital transformation provides organisations in this sector with new opportunities, but due to uncertainty about how policymakers will react and change the regulatory framework prevents them from capitalising on these new opportunities.[28] A 'regulatory disconnection' is present between static legislation (introduced before the digital transformation of the sector) and the new dynamics of everyday practice nowadays.[29] Moreover, the regulatory domain is also concerned with ethical considerations regarding the introduction and use of new technologies. The sharing of data from, for example, smart meters, raise privacy concerns. On the one hand, this leads to new regulations (such as the GDPR and CCPA), but it also requires organisations to consider concerns from the public about what happens to their personal data, influencing the nature and degree of inter-organisational data flows.[30]

Regulatory challenges often cannot be addressed by individual managers or organisations alone. As such, organisations (and their managers) should collaborate not only with each other but also with governmental institutions to reshape existing policies and develop new policies to take new developments into account.[31] Also on the organisational level, managers within organisations should seek to collaborate with others, in this case the legal experts. This is needed to ensure that managers are not breaching any laws or policies. Also, legal experts can help managers to translate (inter)national or regional laws into company rules to ensure that employees work within the boundaries of the legal framework.[32] When managers and legal experts stay in their respective organisational silos, however, issues can arise in which legal barriers are not effectively taken away or, even worse, might be experienced by managers who might not actually be present in the first place.

[27] I Susha and others, 'Achieving Voluntary Data Sharing in Cross Sector Partnerships: Three Partnership Models' (2023) 33 *Information and Organization* 100448.

[28] GG Parker, B Tan, and O Kazan, 'Electric Power Industry: Operational and Public Policy Challenges and Opportunities' (2019) 28 *Production and Operations Management* 2738.

[29] MG Edens and SACM Lavrijssen, 'Balancing Public Values during the Energy Transition – How Can German and Dutch DSOs Safeguard Sustainability?' (2019) 128 *Energy Policy* 57.

[30] A Pietrix Seepma, C de Blok, and DP Van Donk, 'Designing Digital Public Service Supply Chains: Four Country-based Cases in Criminal Justice' (2021) 26 *Supply Chain Management: An International Journal* 418.

[31] T Tokar and M Swink, 'Public Policy and Supply Chain Management: Using Shared Foundational Principles to Improve Formulation, Implementation, and Evaluation' (2019) 55 *Journal of Supply Chain Management* 68.

[32] F-X De Vaujany and others, 'Rules, Practices, and Information Technology: A Trifecta of Organizational Regulation' (2018) 29 *Information Systems Research* 755.

2.3. Legal Considerations for CI Managers

The introduction of two landmark laws regarding the protection of consumer privacy – the GDPR and the CCPA, which came into effect in 2018 and 2020 respectively – highlights the need for effective management collaboration.[33] These two laws have an impact not only on an individual level, by prescribing how to manage and protect data that is deemed private, but also at an organisational level, as these influence the degree to which this type of data can be shared among organisations. Both laws have similar objectives: ensuring the regulation and protection of personal data collection and giving individuals greater control over their personal information.[34] The GDPR was created by the European Union and was eventually widely enforced as law throughout all its Member States. The CCPA, on the other hand, was created by the state of California; companies in other American states followed suit to ensure they were already in compliance with potential future laws.

Unfortunately, organisations (specifically employees with an organisational or a technical background) typically do not (fully) understand these laws.[35] Nevertheless, organisations soon installed guidelines and protocols to adequately protect and avoid misuse of personal data that falls under the GDPR and CCPA, so that this would be in line with the aforementioned laws. However, in reality, many of these guidelines aimed at the protection of personal information, were not installed to protect personal information.[36] In addition, many of these protocols constrain organisations in their search for best practices and innovation.[37] In other words, the many rules and guidelines in place seem to be installed because of 'perceived' legal barriers rather than 'actual' legal requirements. While literature has addressed several issues regarding data usage and the impact of laws like the GDPR,[38] to our knowledge there has not been any study yet that investigates the impact of these perceived legal barriers on the implementation of data-sharing initiatives.

[33] A Hovav, I Gnizy, and J Han, 'The Effects of Cyber Regulations and Security Policies on Organizational Outcomes: A Knowledge Management Perspective' (2023) 32 *European Journal of Information Systems* 154.

[34] P Cichy, TO Salge, and R Kohli, 'Privacy Concerns and Data Sharing in the Internet of Things: Mixed Methods Evidence from Connected Cars' (2021) 45 *MIS Quarterly* 1863.

[35] E Van den Broek, A Sergeeva, and M Huysman, 'When the Machine Meets the Expert: An Ethnography of Developing AI for Hiring' (2021) 45 *MIS Quarterly* 1557.

[36] Cichy, Salge, and Kohli 'Privacy Concerns and Data Sharing in the Internet of Things (n 34).

[37] A Asatiani, O Copeland, and E Penttinen, 'Deciding on the Robotic Process Automation Operating Model: A Checklist for RPA Managers' (2023) 66 *Business Horizons* 109; M Niemimaa and E Niemimaa, 'Abductive Innovations in Information Security Policy Development: An Ethnographic Study' (2019) 28 *European Journal of Information Systems* 566.

[38] B Carsten Stahl and M Lynne Markus, 'Let's Claim the Authority to Speak out on the Ethics of Smart Information Systems' (2021) 45 *MIS Quarterly* 485.

3. Research Method

To better understand the influence of (perceived) regulatory barriers on cross-sectoral data-sharing initiatives, we conducted an in-depth case study that involved six (semi-)public organisations that jointly aimed to set up a data-sharing platform to enable effective data sharing among their employees. Our case study approach enabled us to study the phenomenon and its context in detail,[39] thereby uncovering the relationship dynamics between the collaborating organisations and how (perceived) regulatory barriers affected these dynamics. The selection of our single case was guided by the theoretical sampling strategy,[40] enabling us to select an 'unusually revelatory' case with unique characteristics that warranted further investigation. First of all, our case was focused on a project that involved the first attempt (in the Netherlands) to bring together multiple (semi-)public organisations that manage CIs and need an effective means to share data with each other. Secondly, we specifically selected a case that involved (semi-)public organisations to ensure that (perceived) regulatory barriers were present. Even though there is a strong governmental influence present in many (semi-)public organisations, they also need to manage the inherent complexity and evolving nature of public procurement regulations and require employees with specialised skills and capabilities within public sector organisations,[41] making it more likely that (perceived) regulatory barriers indeed occur. Lastly, we had unique access to this case as we were able to interview representatives of all involved organisations and obtain rich archival data.

3.1. Data Collection and Analysis

To collect data for our study, we conducted nine semi-structured, in-depth interviews (515 minutes in total) with relevant project members. At least one representative of each of the six CI organisations was interviewed. Moreover, we also interviewed a representative of the private software company that developed the actual digital platform and two representatives of a Dutch knowledge institution that aims to bring managers of CIs together to prepare their respective organisations for the future. Table 6.1 shows a detailed overview of the interviews. The interviews focused on discussing the main purpose of the cross-sectoral data-sharing project, the development of the collaboration between the involved

[39] M Barratt, TY Choi, and M Li, 'Qualitative Case Studies in Operations Management: Trends, Research Outcomes, and Future Research Implications' (2011) 29 *Journal of Operations Management* 329.

[40] KM Eisenhardt and Melissa E Graebner, 'Theory Building from Cases: Opportunities and Challenges' (2007) 50 *Academy of Management Journal* 25.

[41] AS Patrucco and others, 'Enhancing Strategic Public Procurement: A Public Service Logic Perspective' [2024] *Public Management Review* 1.

organisations, and the shared or differing visions, issues and opinions regarding cross-sectoral data sharing. By employing a semi-structured nature during the interviews, we ensured that we had enough flexibility and time to capture the full opinions and experiences of our interviewees.[42] In addition to the interview data, we also collected archival data that included 14 relevant documents (89 pages in total), ranging from internal email communications to formal vision documents.

Table 6.1 Overview of interviews

Affiliation	Position	Expertise	Length
Energy	Data Manager	Data management	60 minutes
KnowInfra	Project Manager	Vision creation	65 minutes
KnowInfra	Director	Vision creation	55 minutes
Rail	IT Manager	IT systems	55 minutes
Rail	CIO	Data management & vision creation	35 minutes
Road	Programme Manager	Data management & IT systems	50 minutes
Sea	Asset Owner	Vision creation	75 minutes
Soft	Regional Director	IT systems	55 minutes
Water	Project Manager	Vision creation	65 minutes

All the interviews and the documents collected for this study were analysed separately by the two authors. During the analysis, we used a coding scheme that was informed by concepts coming from existing theory.[43] After the coding was done, we identified seven major events in our case that significantly changed the dynamics in the collaboration under investigation and revealed legal barriers that (potentially) hindered the progress of the project. The lead author subsequently wrote an extensive case description, which included each of the seven events that are shown in section 4. Both authors repeatedly discussed these events, including the dynamics and barriers at play, and assessed their impact on the overall project. The evaluation was based on how many different interviewees mentioned specific events, which interviewees mentioned them, and whether a clear connection to a subsequent event was established. The goal was to capture the full story of our case and highlight the dynamics at play. While some events were more visible, others required a more in-depth analysis, connecting and reviewing different statements in light of additional context obtained from further conversations with CI-organisation employees.

[42] M Alvesson, 'Beyond Neopositivists, Romantics, and Localists: A Reflexive Approach to Interviews in Organizational Research' (2003) 28 *Academy of Management Review* 13.

[43] S Sarker, X Xiao, and T Beaulieu, 'Qualitative Studies in Information Systems: A Critical Review and Some Guiding Principles' (2013) 37 *MIS Quarterly* iii.

3.2. Case Description

Six Dutch infrastructure organisations, which are active in different sectors and responsible for a specific type of (critical) infrastructure network, set up a knowledge institution (denoted as 'KnowInfra') to jointly investigate opportunities to manage and maintain the main CIs in the Netherlands in a coordinated manner. The organisations are responsible for a wide range of CIs, including a semi-public organisation managing a large seaport (denoted as 'Sea'), a semi-public organisation managing a large airport (denoted as 'Air'), an executive agency of the Dutch government managing all the major roads and waterways in the Netherlands (denoted as 'Road'), a public organisation managing of all major railways in the Netherlands (denoted as 'Rail'), a semi-public organisation managing a regional public water system (denoted as 'Water') and a semi-public organisation managing a regional electricity grid (denoted as 'Energy'). At the end of 2019, triggered by an opportunity provided by an international software developer (denoted as 'Soft'), and an urge to develop a data-driven approach, the infrastructure organisations initiated a large project to investigate how they could operate jointly as one infrastructure organisation for all CIs that fell under their responsibility.

The project consisted of three separate streams. The first stream focused on the collection and analysis of use cases in which two or more infrastructure organisations needed to collaborate closely with each other and, among other things, share (maintenance) data. For example, they identified a use case around a Dutch municipality where Road, Energy and Water had a part of their respective networks co-located in the main city of this municipality. Without collaboration and transparency between them, a specific street typically needed to be closed to the public three times within a two-year period as they independently maintained their assets around this street. However, by collaborating and actively sharing maintenance data (thereby increasing transparency), coordination between the three organisations could take place and they could potentially perform their maintenance activities in the same period (ensuring the street would be closed down only once).

The second stream focused on the development of a shared vision between the involved infrastructure organisations. With this vision, the organisations wanted to give direction to their idea to 'act as one' in the future, to define what this idea entailed, and to highlight why it was necessary. The vision entailed high-level ideas and did not look at either the underlying systems or the data necessary to achieve it. Rather, it encouraged the organisations to philosophise about how the collaboration should look and what decisions could (potentially) be jointly made. Moreover, this vision was intended to provide input for future (company) policies and more concrete plans regarding underlying systems and/or data streams.

The third and final stream focused on the development of a digital (data) platform that could enable the swift exchange of maintenance data between the infrastructure organisations. In this stream, Soft was involved as they had the expertise and resources to develop a so-called 'Identity Federation': a central system that digitally connected the individual systems of each of the partner organisations and oversaw the access rights of each employee to the data of each partner. Through this set-up, the individual infrastructure organisations would keep their own systems and databases, while at the same time enabling easy access to the systems and databases of their partners.

4. Findings

The cross-sectoral collaboration around the data-sharing platform (more specifically an Identity Federation platform that organised data access and data sharing among participants) commenced at the end of 2019 and was dissolved at the end of 2023. By analysing the interviews and archival data we collected retrospectively regarding the collaboration, we identified seven major events that changed its course and, at times, even the composition of the network of partners that were involved. A detailed description of each of the seven events can be found in the subsections below and are summarised in Figure 6.1. Each of the seven major events are denoted by a number in Figure 6.1 (eg event 3 is denoted as E3) and referred to accordingly in the text below.

Figure 6.1 Timeline and summary of events of the cross-sectoral data-sharing case

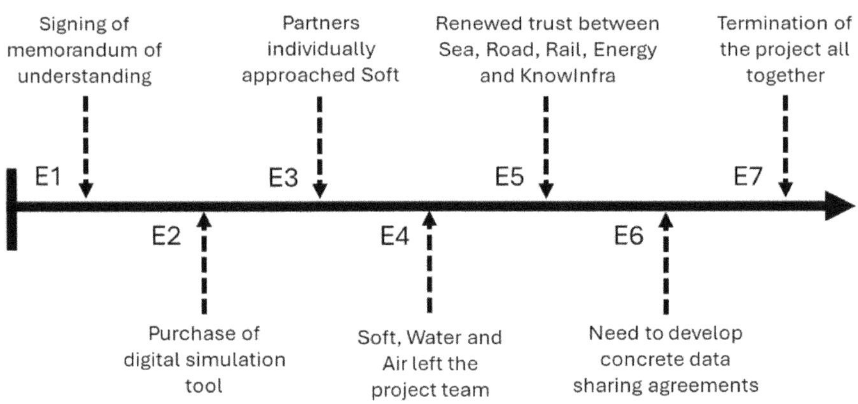

4.1. Event 1: Signing the Memorandum of Understanding

After initial talks between KnowInfra, Soft and the six infrastructure organisations, all partners were eager to work on the joint project. As such, they set the ambitious goal to build a federated platform to share (maintenance) data with each other in a first attempt to truly collaborate on a cross-sectoral basis. An asset owner from Sea stated that 'this [plan] has been presented to the board and the CIOs of all organisations, and there you more or less got the same responses, such as "Wow, this is amazing, innovative"'. Since there were no formal contracts involved, the relationship between the collaborating partners relied entirely on relational mechanisms. At the beginning all partners clearly trusted each other, with a regional director from Soft stating '[we signed] a memorandum of understanding, a gentleman's agreement … this does not hold in a court of law, but you will adhere to it because it is important for the relationship and your reputation'. This memorandum of understanding (MoU) was signed with the lawyers of each of the involved parties present. However, it was not a formal contract but a non-binding multilateral agreement indicating what each partner could expect from the others (E1). A formal, legally binding, contract was not signed between the partners as this would have made the project overly complex, something all partners tried to avoid as much as possible. Moreover, all partners regarded this as a simple formality, part of setting up the collaboration.

Trust in each other, each other's competencies and the institutions surrounding them was high in E1. This ensured that the core project members (consisting of representatives from each of the eight involved organisations) regularly met up and shared ideas and knowledge with each other. During this period, most of the collaboration consisted of theorising on how to proceed further with the project and its three streams. Ambitious and impactful ideas were shared, and the partners were optimistic about what was yet to come. None of the discussions resulted in any significant actions or changes to the composition of the network of partners. Eventually, as time progressed, several other events occurred that changed the dynamics in the project group.

E1 highlights both opportunities and barriers in the early stages of collaboration. The high levels of trust and a shared vision among the partners fostered openness, innovation and optimism, laying a strong foundation for the joint project. However, the reliance on an informal MoU, while simplifying initial collaboration, introduced risks of ambiguity regarding accountability and dispute resolution, opening the collaboration up to potential regulatory issues or even barriers. These dynamics underscore the importance of balancing relational trust with structured governance to ensure long-term success and resilience in multi-stakeholder initiatives. The high level of trust that was present at the start of the collaboration provided a good basis for the project, providing ample organisational opportunities.

4.2. Event 2: Purchase of a Digital Simulation Tool

After a couple of months, the positive atmosphere within the collaboration started to diminish as it became increasingly apparent that the relative interests of the infrastructure organisations (which were all [semi-]public organisations) and

Soft (a privately owned organisation) were too divergent. While Soft is primarily focused on maximising its own profits to satisfy its shareholders, the six infrastructure organisations and KnowInfra are primarily focused on maximising value for society as a whole to satisfy all users of the CIs they manage and maintain. Additionally, KnowInfra had noticed potential challenges that resulted from the different activities and data needs of the project members. Air and Sea, for example, operate at an international level and they are both an important hub in international transportation networks for freight and passengers. KnowInfra is primarily focused on facilitating enhanced collaborations between infrastructure organisations in the Netherlands and also seeks to build meaningful connections with other (Western-)European countries. Road and Rail operate at a national level as their networks span the whole of the Netherlands (but not beyond). Energy and Water, in the end, operate at a regional level, as their networks only span a limited number of Dutch provinces and municipalities. Since the seven infrastructure organisations operate at different levels, the data in their databases, and the data they required, differed tremendously. In short, organisational challenges arose due to the different levels at which the partners operate and the requirements that were placed on the organisation of data collection, storage and sharing.

Another factor which diminished the relationship between the eight partners was the purchase of a simulation tool by KnowInfra in addition to the platform being developed by Soft (E2). Even though the simulation tool was by no means a replacement for Soft's platform, Soft felt overlooked by the infrastructure organisations and KnowInfra as it was not informed about this decision. This created more tension between Soft and the infrastructure organisations. The purchase of the digital simulation tool also brought along economic challenges. To develop and maintain the digital simulation tool, KnowInfra required millions of euros. Unfortunately, both the infrastructure organisations and the Dutch government were unwilling to invest this amount of money in a system that had not yet proven itself, and KnowInfra did not have sufficient financial resources. The purchase of the simulation tool was also partially guided by the infrastructure organisations who feared that they were entering a lock-in situation with Soft. As a result, they started to doubt whether Soft could be trusted with their data and whether storing their data on Soft's servers was still in line with the GDPR. Therefore, Rail's servers were used to store data (as a temporary solution). These tensions led to a growing distance between Soft and the infrastructure organisations.

Collaborating with organisations from different sectors does not just have an effect on data needs. Organisations from different sectors also have to deal with different regulations that affect how they can and should treat their data. For example, Water was not allowed to share any data regarding their infrastructure due to a law from the early 1900s. The activities of Road, on the other hand, were not restricted by any such laws, so it had freely shared data with Rail for many years. Because of this, over time, questions arose regarding which data should be delivered, as well as what data could be accessed by employees from the respective infrastructure organisations, leading to the emergence of several barriers. Some of these were legal in nature, such as the law that was in place for Water, but others were purely organisational, such as how data should be delivered. Eventually, the six infrastructure organisations and KnowInfra decided to shift the scope of their project, as they had become increasingly worried about sharing their data, not only with each other but also with Soft. One of their primary concerns was determining who would be (legally) responsible for potential mistakes in the data: the provider, the user or the owner of the platform on which all the data was to be stored. These concerns became a bigger issue every time the project team met, with an IT manager from Rail stating in relation to data sharing:

> [T]here are potentially a number of legal aspects and privacy aspects … Ultimately, I can make data available, but if it is read in the wrong context, I will just be in the newspaper and they will say, well, you know Rail is neglecting the system or network.

E2 underscores the significant impact of (perceived) legal barriers on collaboration efforts. Diverging regulations, such as the outdated law restricting Water from sharing data, created discrepancies in how partners could engage in data exchange. Concerns over GDPR compliance and uncertainty about data responsibility, whether it lay with the provider, user or platform owner, amplified hesitation and distrust among the partners. These legal ambiguities not only strained relationships but also stalled progress, highlighting the critical need for clear legal guidelines and shared agreements to address regulatory and compliance challenges.

4.3. Event 3: Partners Individually Approached Soft

Despite the increasing difficulties in the collaboration with Soft, several infrastructure organisations still approached Soft individually (E3). Soft reported the following: 'individual project members started to approach us and told us "I want you to make that, because 'I' need it" … After a while you saw that the project slowly scattered.' In other words, the infrastructure organisations contacted Soft individually to express their own needs and to emphasise how their needs were more important for the collaboration than those of the others. This behaviour indicates that although there was a growing level of distrust towards Soft, and its role within the project became increasingly uncertain, the infrastructure organisations were determined to prioritise their own requirements over those of the project team as a whole. This highlighted that the friction and uncertainties between the parties were slowly becoming too difficult to manage within the project. Each of the six infrastructure organisations was more focused on advocating for their individual interests than working collaboratively towards a unified goal. This divergence of priorities not only strained the relationships between Soft, KnowInfra and the six infrastructure organisations but also hindered the overall progress of the project. As a result, the collective efforts to achieve the project's objectives were compromised, leading to a gradual breakdown in communication and cooperation among the eight partners.

The fact that several infrastructure organisations individually contacted Soft reflected the underlying tensions and disagreements that had been simmering beneath the surface all along. Instead of fostering a collaborative environment where all partners worked together towards a common purpose, the atmosphere within the project team became tense. This shift in dynamics made it increasingly challenging for the partners to find common ground and make decisions that would benefit everyone involved. Ultimately, the increasing difficulties in collaboration and the lack of a unified approach contributed to a growing sense of frustration and dissatisfaction among the partners. This, in turn, led to a breakdown in trust and communication, making it even more difficult to manage the project effectively.

E3 highlights how growing legal and organisational tensions fuelled by individual priorities contributed to a breakdown in collaboration. The infrastructure organisations' decision to approach Soft individually, each emphasising their own needs over the collective project goals, illustrates the shift from cooperative to more self-interested behaviour. This fragmentation, coupled with increasing distrust, exacerbated difficulties in managing the project and reaching agreements. The lack of a unified approach to both organisational and legal matters further hindered effective decision-making and deepened the communication rift, ultimately undermining the project's progress and collaboration. During this event, the cracks in the collaboration started to emerge, which eventually led to further distrust between the different partners.

4.4. Event 4: Soft, Water and Air Left the Project Team

After a series of additional issues emerged, Water, Air and Soft decided to leave the project altogether (E4). Water withdrew from the project because one of its key representatives moved to a new company, and they were unable to find a suitable replacement. Meanwhile, Air was severely impacted by the COVID-19 pandemic, which left it without the necessary funds or available personnel to contribute to the project. In the case of Soft, it became increasingly evident that its goals no longer aligned with those of the infrastructure organisations and KnowInfra. Their commercial objectives conflicted with those of the semi-public infrastructure organisations, which were focused on achieving a societal impact rather than purely financial gains. Additionally, since Soft had ceased the internal development of the tool that would be the basis of the federated platform, its role within the project had become unclear. As a response, the project team invited multiple software providers to propose other digital tools that could replace the original. Interestingly, Soft was not only part of the committee that evaluated these other tools but also had a representative who responded to the invitation and offered a new tool itself. This dual role raised concerns among the other partners, as it appeared to create a conflict of interest, for example an asset owner from Sea stated, 'I felt like I was in a kind of grip by [Soft]. We were doing this for society and then there is a market party among us taking advantage of us'.

The situation described in the previous paragraph highlighted the growing discomfort among the KnowInfra and the six infrastructure organisations regarding Soft's continued involvement in the project. The fact that Soft was both a participant in the decision-making process and a contender for providing a solution blurred the lines between their roles as a collaborator and a competitor. This ambiguity contributed to the perception that Soft was no longer a neutral partner, which further strained the relationship between them and the other partners. Ultimately, the departure of Soft, Water and Air from the project team signalled a significant shift in the dynamics of the project. With the exit of these key organisations, the remaining partners were left to navigate the challenges and uncertainties on their own. This turn of events underscored the importance of aligning goals and maintaining clear roles and responsibilities within a collaborative project, especially when multiple parties with differing objectives are involved.

E4 highlights how a lack of alignment in goals, roles and expectations, compounded by legal and organisational challenges, led to the departure of key partners. Soft's commercial focus clashed with the societal objectives of the infrastructure organisations, and their dual role in evaluating potential replacements for the digital tool created a conflict of interest that further eroded trust. Water and Air also withdrew due to internal issues, further destabilising the project. This departure of crucial partners underscored the need for clear, mutually understood roles and aligned objectives to maintain trust and collaboration in complex, multi-party projects.

4.5. Event 5: Renewed Collaboration Consisting of the Remaining Parties

After the departure of Soft, Air and Water, the remaining infrastructure organisations and KnowInfra convened to discuss their next steps. Initially, the remaining partners considered quitting the project altogether. The inability to reach a shared understanding or pursue a common goal had left them feeling uncertain about the project's future. However, after several discussions, they decided to give the collaboration one last chance (E5). With Soft no longer part of the team, the remaining partners were free from the complexities of its involvement in the project. Energy, Sea, Road, Rail and KnowInfra all shared the same vision and were willing to invest the necessary resources to ensure the project's success. As indicated by Sea, 'with those five we said at some point, okay, it seems to be a dead end. Why do we not just pull the plug? However, we decided to give it one last try'. This common ground allowed them to create a new plan for the project, outlining how to proceed and what the potential goals should be for the cross-sectoral data-sharing initiative. With this smaller, more focused group consisting of only motivated members, the team was able to get to work more efficiently. The smaller group dynamic fostered a more collaborative and cohesive environment, which enabled the remaining representatives to streamline their efforts and focus on the project's key objectives. The renewed goals and direction allowed the project team to make significant progress. By aligning their goals and working together effectively, the remaining partners were able to overcome the initial hurdles and move forward with a clear plan and shared commitment. This new plan included both the development of a roadmap for the cross-sectoral data-sharing initiative, which aimed to enhance the collaboration, and the expansion of the use cases. The development of a tool or platform to actually share data was shelved.

E5 illustrates how, after the departure of Soft, Air and Water, the remaining partners were able to overcome earlier legal and organisational barriers by realigning their goals and refocusing on a common vision rather than on detailed discussions about what data to share and how. The absence of Soft, whose involvement had previously created a conflict of interest, allowed for clearer roles and more efficient collaboration. With a smaller, more cohesive group, the partners could streamline their efforts and move forward with a clear plan, including a roadmap for the data-sharing initiative. This event underscores the importance of alignment of clear roles in overcoming obstacles and advancing a complex project like this.

4.6. Event 6: Need to Develop Concrete Data-sharing Agreements

As the development of the data-sharing platform and the simulation tool that was purchased by KnowInfra was no longer the primary focus of the project, the main emphasis for the project members shifted towards further developing their joint vision and strategy. They aimed to convince the top management of their respective organisations, as well as other Dutch organisations involved in the management and maintenance of CI assets, that this joint vision and strategy was both necessary and feasible. A key component of this shared vision was to establish more concrete agreements between the five core partners to actively share (maintenance) data with each other, which could then (in the future) be extrapolated to other organisations involved with managing and maintaining CIs. However, when Energy, Rail, Road and Sea approached their own organisations to seek support for these agreements, they encountered resistance.

The organisations of Energy, Rail, Road and Sea became defensive when their representatives introduced the plans of the project team and they began questioning the intentions behind the data-sharing agreements. As the asset owner from Sea explained,

> our organisations started to ask themselves: '"Are you [the other partner organisations] going to use the data for this?" And of course, that is scary. And then you also get a retreating behaviour, as this data can be used incorrectly.

This reaction highlighted the inherent fear and uncertainty within the organisations about how the shared (maintenance) data might be used or even misused. The concerns raised by the organisations were rooted in the potential risks associated with data sharing, such as data breaches, misuse of sensitive information and, most importantly, the possibility of legal repercussions when something went wrong. These fears led to a retreating behaviour, where the organisations became hesitant to commit to the data-sharing agreements, despite recognising the potential benefits of cross-sectoral collaboration.

The project members realised that, to gain the trust and support of their respective organisations, they needed to address these concerns and provide assurances about the security and proper use of the shared data (E6). This would require the development of clear guidelines and protocols for data handling, as well as implementing robust measures to protect the (maintenance) data from unauthorised access or misuse, which were in line with the law. In addition, the project members emphasised the importance of transparency and communication in addressing the concerns of their organisations. By openly discussing the objectives and benefits of the data-sharing initiative, as well as discussing the measures in place to safeguard the data, they aimed to alleviate fears and build confidence in the project's viability. However, it became apparent that the project team was not able to overcome the barriers they faced this time. The management of each organisation kept bringing up their fear of the potential legal repercussions in case of mistakes or data breaches. In doing so, they overlooked the fact that most of the data being shared was already publicly available. These fears, which were not actual legal barriers per se but rather perceived legal barriers, ensured that the project group eventually did not get the support from their respective managements to pursue the project further.

E6 highlights how perceived legal barriers, rooted in fears of data misuse and legal repercussions, hampered the development of concrete data-sharing agreements among the project partners. Despite recognising the benefits of cross-sectoral collaboration, concerns about the security and proper use of shared data led to hesitation and defensive behaviours from the participating organisations. The need for clear guidelines, legal assurances and transparency became evident, but the project team struggled to overcome these perceived legal barriers. This event underscores the significant impact of perceived risks, even when no formal legal barriers exist, on collaborative initiatives in sensitive areas like data sharing.

4.7. Event 7: Termination of the Project Altogether

After a period of intense discussions in which the representatives of Energy, Rail, Road and Sea tried to convince their respective organisations, they were forced to conclude that their organisations were not yet ready for this level of cross-sectoral collaboration. As the programme manager from Road stated, 'maybe it is [working together in this way] all too early in the sense that, yes, we are not that advanced with each other yet'. Although the will to collaborate was still present, setting up contractual agreements seemed to be a bridge too far for the top managers of each of the four infrastructure organisations; a service officer from Rail commented 'so we really want to work with each other and apparently cannot come to an agreement'. Ultimately, the project team decided to terminate the project altogether (event E7).

Despite the lack of explicit, written contracts, the five organisations (Energy, KnowInfra, Rail, Road and Sea) collaborated in a project-like manner with each other. They actively worked together and contributed resources, including 'man-hours', and organised recurring meetings, much as a project manager would do. Each organisation had representatives who formally worked on the project, ensuring that they were committed to its success. Trust and willingness among the partners were high, forming the foundation for their long-term, project-like collaboration. Even when some partners discontinued their membership, the remaining partners stayed committed to the joint goal of achieving cross-sectoral data sharing. However, the challenges became apparent when the vision and strategy documents, developed by the representatives, had to be translated into operational action points. As explicit agreements were made, requiring the partners to start sharing (maintenance) data, the top management of each infrastructure organisation began to get cold feet. The trust and support that had been built up over the course of the project started to waver when it came time to establish actual digital connections. The partners became increasingly concerned about how others might use their data and for what purposes. A significant worry was that each partner feared that the others might use their own data against them. As these concerns grew, perceived legal barriers emerged, ultimately stopping management from supporting the project further. This fear and lack of trust among the partners ultimately hindered the progress of the project, leading to its termination.

Their inability to reach concrete (operational) agreements, compounded by growing concerns about data usage, played a pivotal role in the termination of the cross-sectoral data-sharing initiative. Despite the initial high levels of trust and commitment among the five infrastructure organisations, the reality of formalising agreements exposed the limitations of their collaboration. The lack of explicit, written contracts ultimately led to significant hesitation when the time came to solidify the project into actionable steps. As the partners were asked to start sharing sensitive data, fears about potential misuse – fuelled by perceived legal risks – became overwhelming. These concerns, despite not being grounded in actual legal barriers, created insurmountable obstacles for the management teams of the reapective organisations. The result was a breakdown in the willingness to move forward with the project, leading to its eventual cancellation. E7, along with the preceding events, highlights the fragility of cross-sectoral collaborations, especially when it comes to sharing sensitive data. While initial trust and informal collaboration can provide a strong foundation, the introduction of formal agreements, especially in contexts involving legal and regulatory concerns, can quickly erode that trust. The overarching takeaway from these events is that perceived legal risks can significantly hinder progress in collaborative efforts. Even with strong initial cooperation, these perceived barriers can lead to a breakdown in communication and a reluctance to commit to actions that would require greater transparency, security and shared responsibility. The eventual failure of this project underscores the critical need for a thorough understanding of existing legal frameworks by (CI) organisations, robust data-protection mechanisms and the alignment of goals among partners before embarking on complex cross-sector collaborations.

5. Discussion and Conclusion

Navigating the complexities of cross-sectoral collaborations and data sharing presents a significant challenge for CI organisations, particularly when managing and maintaining their networks. The seven events in our case study provide an illustration of the inherent difficulties in these collaborative efforts. Despite initial enthusiasm and trust among the involved parties, the project ultimately failed due to a combination of legal, financial and organisational barriers. Some of these legal barriers were not even actual barriers but rather perceived barriers which emerged due to a lack of effective communication between managers and legal professionals. Only at the very beginning, in E1, when the MoU was signed, were legal experts present and actively engaged with the multi-party collaboration. Even though this was not a document that would stand up in court, the collaborating partners did seek legal advice. However, in subsequent events (ie E4 and E6) when legal issues were discussed, no legal experts were involved, only IT experts and managers. Legal experts would have been able to shed light on questions related to the sharing of maintenance data, but they were not consulted. Instead, all the managers and IT experts were so focused on trying to avoid dealings with the GDPR that they erected perceived legal barriers themselves. This eventually led to the termination of the project in E7.

Currently, there are no laws explicitly prohibiting CI organisations from sharing the majority of their maintenance data in a cross-sectoral setting, since the majority of this data is not (directly) related to individual people or national security concerns (and hence it is not regulated). The only exception is an outdated regulation affecting water suppliers dating back to the early 1900s, preventing water organisations from sharing any data with organisations outside their sector. A small portion of the maintenance data held by the CI organisations can directly be related to individual people or organisations and can only be shared if it is anonymised and in line with the existing GDPR and CCPA. An even smaller amount of maintenance data contains crucial information that can be used to threaten national security; this is is deemed as classified, which means it can only be shared under specific circumstances. Interestingly enough, the absence of clear regulations for the majority of the maintenance data (ie data that has no implications for individuals or national security) has actually discouraged organisations from engaging in data sharing altogether. Many partners cited the need to comply with the GDPR as the reason for their reluctance to share data in the first place, even though the majority of their maintenance data did not fall inside the GDPR's scope. As such, the 'legal barriers' that managers often refer to are not actual legal barriers but rather misconceptions they are unsure about how to address. This misunderstanding of regulatory frameworks can have significant consequences, including the termination of promising cross-sectoral data-sharing initiatives.

As our case demonstrates, although CI organisations increasingly rely on their managers to work with data, they do not adequately train them to communicate with legal professionals. Conversely, the lawyers within these organisations are not sufficiently engaged with management personnel, leading to a disconnect between the two groups. For example, when in E1 the MoU was signed there were lawyers present, but thereafter (from E2 to E7) they were not consulted at all. This lack of interaction usually stems from their differing perspectives on problem-solving and goal achievement, often resulting in differing opinions and, at times, even in conflict. In our case study, this gap became particularly evident as concerns about data sharing, legal repercussions and GDPR compliance surfaced. The CI organisations were reluctant to commit to data-sharing agreements due to perceived legal barriers, as could be seen in E6, even though most of the data involved was publicly available and not subject to GDPR constraints. The current gap in knowledge between managers and lawyers necessitates finding common ground and collaborating at a level that not only ensures the organisation operates within legal boundaries but also fosters innovation where possible. Spring and others highlight how the integration of information systems and innovative technology can enhance collaboration between legal professionals and managers, improving the execution of service delivery processes and expanding professional service offerings.[44] Our findings contribute to this literature by showing that, in the context of CI organisations, this integration could help bridge the gap between managers and legal departments, facilitating more effective communication and collaboration. Such improvements could have potentially mitigated the challenges faced in the project in our case study, enabling the involved organisations to better navigate the complexities of cross-sectoral collaboration.

Moreover, the reluctance to engage in cross-sectoral data-sharing activities, as observed in our case study, and more closely observed in E3 where CI organisations individually approached Soft, is further fuelled by CI organisations' inherent preference for stability and continuity over change and innovation. As predicted in previous research, these organisations prioritise protecting vulnerabilities, a core element of their operations, over the technological innovations and organisational changes associated with digital transformations.[45] This resistance to change further

[44] M Spring, J Faulconbridge, and A Sarwar, 'How Information Technology Automates and Augments Processes: Insights from Artificial-Intelligence-Based Systems in Professional Service Operations' (2022) 68 *Journal of Operations Management* 592.

[45] Poláková-Kersten and others 'Digital Transformation in High-Reliability Organizations' (n 6).

compounds the perceived complexity and risk associated with cross-sectoral data-sharing, ultimately hindering the progress of projects similar to the project in our case, which led to its termination in E7. Additionally, Davidson and others highlight that data-governance mechanisms, such as formal reporting structures, standardised data-processing procedures and employee training, are implemented to enhance data quality, security and regulatory compliance.[46] These mechanisms are crucial for optimising data management within organisations, but they can also contribute to the perceived complexity and risk associated with cross-sectoral data sharing. Our case study underscores the importance of aligning legal and managerial perspectives to facilitate effective cross-sectoral collaboration. By improving communication and collaboration between managers and legal professionals, CI organisations can ensure that they comply with legal requirements while also leveraging IT to drive innovation within those constraints. This approach could help them navigate the complexities of operating as networks, staying within the law and maximising opportunities for shared innovation. The findings of this case study suggest that addressing the communication gap between managers and lawyers could be critical to the success of similar collaborative efforts in the future.

The findings of this chapter make a case for more intensive collaboration between managers and lawyers or regulators, which connects to a recent line of increased calls in literature that management scholars should close the gap with law and policy scholars.[47] Management scholars are typically not equipped to fully analyse and understand the content and magnitude of existing and new regulations and policies;[48] assistance from law and policy scholars helps management scholars to better understand the exact implications of regulations such as the GDPR or CCPA. At the same time, management scholars can inform law and policy scholars about the current workings of organisations under existing regulatory and policy frameworks and pinpoint the areas in which these frameworks are missing.[49] Management scholars are especially well equipped to do this as they already have experience by investigating on multiple levels (eg individual, company or supply chain level). Especially in the realm of CIs, such as the energy sector, there is a dire need for closer collaborations between management and legal scholars as, for example, digital technologies have drastically changed the demands from end users, while other innovations such as solar panels, electrical vehicles and large batteries are rapidly changing the supply side for various organisations in the energy sector.[50] Also, our case study shows the drastic

[46] E Davidson and others, 'Future Directions for Scholarship on Data Governance, Digital Innovation, and Grand Challenges' (2023) 33 *Information and Organization* 100454.

[47] S Helper and others, 'Public Policy and Operations Management' (2021) 67 *Journal of Operations Management* 780.

[48] B Fugate, M Pagell, and B Flynn, 'Introduction to the Emerging Discourse Incubator on the Topic of Research at the Intersection of Supply Chain Management and Public Policy and Government Regulation' (2019) 55 *Journal of Supply Chain Management* 3.

[49] Tokar and Swink (n 31).

[50] Parker, Tan, and Kazan (n 28).

changes that CI organisations are faced with in these times of large-scale digital transformations. While management scholars are well equipped to investigate and 'handle' economic, organisational and technological barriers, the legal barriers should not be neglected and collaboration with legal scholars is much needed.

This chapter also reveals two important practical implications. First of all, we observed a disconnect in all our case study organisations between those working in the operations and management levels, on the one hand, and the lawyers (and other employees of the legal departments), on the other. This leads to missed opportunities as both 'sides' can learn much from each other. Where managers and other employees in the operations often lack (extensive) knowledge of regulatory frameworks, and especially the opportunities which these frameworks provide, the lawyers can sort this out and pre-emptively spot potential opportunities or issues. Lawyers (and other employees in legal departments), on the other hand, often do not know how their organisations work in detail and how the operations of these organisations are hindered by current regulatory frameworks. Managers can help lawyers understand the specifics of the organisation's processes. As such, we wholeheartedly encourage managers, lawyers and other practitioners to actively pursue closer collaborations. The second managerial implication is related to the conservative approach that is typically used in many (semi-)public organisations. Historically, many (semi-)public organisations have been heavily scrutinised by the public and tend to avoid taking significant risks. If a (risky) experiment fails, these organisations typically experience extensive public backlash. However, this also limits the willingness to innovate digitally. As such, we encourage the (semi-)public organisations (both their managers and their lawyers) and policy-makers to create safe spaces where experiments can be performed without risking damaging ongoing operations.

7

Regulating Digitalised Financial Spaces

The Way Towards Just Distribution of Burdens and Benefits

SHIRLEY KEMPENEER AND MAGDALENA BREWCZYŃSKA

1. Introduction

The rapid advancement of digitalisation has revolutionised various aspects of contemporary society, profoundly impacting the way individuals, businesses and governments interact and operate. In this chapter, we focus on the regulation of finance, a key infrastructure that has undergone vast digitalisation. Central to this discourse is the exploration of one of the latest EU regulatory initiatives, namely the Digital Finance Strategy and, more precisely, the European Financial Data Space (EFDS). The European single data spaces policy, of which the EFDS is a part, represents a pivotal attempt to harness the potential of data-driven innovation within the EU. The data spaces epitomise a concerted effort to create common ground where diverse stakeholders, including businesses, public administrations and individuals, can securely access and exchange data in a trusted environment. By fostering collaboration and data sharing while safeguarding privacy, security and other crucial values, this policy initiative aspires to unlock new avenues for economic growth and societal progress. The creation and maintenance of fair relationships among actors of the data economy is one of the key regulatory objectives.

However, the data spaces and, in the case of the present chapter in particular, the EFDS might not benefit everyone equally and might not impose an equal burden on everyone. Such a perspective on fair relationships brings to mind what is probably one of the most common understandings of justice, namely justice as fairness.[1] As such, this chapter adopts fairness as a lens to evaluate whether the EFDS succeeds in creating a more level playing field within the financial ecosystem. In accordance with such an account of justice, the policymaker should provide

[1] J Rawls and E Kelly, *Justice as Fairness: A Restatement* (Harvard University Press 2001).

fair (ie equal) liberties and opportunities for everyone.[2] This, in turn, invites two essential questions, which this chapter intends to address. Firstly, what are the current regulatory approaches? Do they come with a promise of a just distribution of the burdens and benefits for the actors involved? Secondly, Who will carry the burdens? Who will be the greatest beneficiaries of the EFDS?

In examining how digitalisation impacts regulation, this chapter discusses the evolution of regulatory strategies in increasingly digitalised financial infrastructures. It provides a preliminary reflection on the risks to values, such as the protection of privacy, personal data and justice, which data spaces may entail and proposes to advance the debate on just regulation of digitalised spaces. The EFDS attempts to foster a level playing field, where diverse actors, from large financial institutions to individual consumers, can operate within a system that ensures equitable opportunities. While it is true that banks and customers differ significantly in their resources and influence, fairness in this context does not imply treating them as equals in their capacities. Instead, it seeks to mitigate structural disparities by ensuring that customers have meaningful control over their financial data, access to transparent information, and protection against discriminatory practices. The focus on fairness as equal opportunities in our analysis is thus aimed at unpacking whether the EFDS successfully addresses these disparities and creates an environment where all actors (despite their differences) are empowered to engage in a fairer and more inclusive financial ecosystem.

The chapter begins by elucidating the most crucial developments of the digitalisation of finance and its regulation. To that end, section 2 discusses the historical milestones and sets the stage for the debate on the promises and problems the discussed developments entail. Then, section 3 focuses on the financial data space and sheds some light on its three building components. Section 4 briefly reflects on how this new regulatory initiative may (or may not) shape the 'just' distribution of burdens and benefits and explores what such justice means in the context of the most recent regulatory approaches to the digitalisation processes in the area of finance. Finally, section 5 summarises all findings and provides answers to the research questions.

2. Digitalisation of Finance and its Regulation: A History of Promises and Problems

The digitalisation and datafication of finance has been spurred by promises of efficiency and security along with improved customer service and increased access to financial products and services. Historically, these promises were always in tension with problems such as the protection of privacy, personal data and data security.

[2] B Barry and M Matravers, 'Justice', *Routledge Encyclopedia of Philosophy* (Routledge 2016). Available at: www.rep.routledge.com/articles/thematic/justice/v-1.

If we want to understand the just distribution of the burdens and benefits in the datafication of finance now, it is wise to first reflect on the history of the digitalisation of finance, its regulation (predominantly with a European focus) and its impact on justice so far.

2.1. Datafication and New Regulation

The roots of financial digitalisation can be traced back to the 1970s and 1980s with the introduction of technologies such as the Automated Teller Machine (ATM) and the Electronic Funds Transfer (EFT) system. ATMs provided customers with 24/7 access to cash and basic banking services, automating away (often undesirable[3]) retail jobs.[4] A more controversial technology was the EFT system. The EFT systems recorded detailed information about each transaction, including the amount, date, time, account numbers, and transaction type. This data was crucial for processing transactions accurately and quickly but held many more responsibilities and risks. Many of these were compiled in a book edited by Colton and Kraemer in 1980, with chapters warning for the potential impacts of EFT on stratification and inequality, as well as alterations in the prospects for invasion of personal privacy.[5] On EFTs, the editors write 'Such alterations foretell important impacts on people and society. Benefits are forthcoming, but the costs will also be real.'[6]

Banks used EFT transaction data to monitor for unusual patterns or anomalies that could indicate fraudulent activity. For instance, sudden large transfers or multiple transactions in a short period could trigger alerts for further investigation. However, early EFT systems were developed before the advent of advanced encryption and security protocols. As a result, they were more vulnerable to hacking, interception and unauthorised access. Moreover, systems often produced a high number of false positives, flagging legitimate transactions as potentially fraudulent.[7] This already speaks to the question of just distribution of burdens and benefits, where banks enjoy much of the (efficiency) benefits, while customers bear the brunt of the burden.

However, with new technologies came new regulations, in part to protect the customer and in particular the consumer. For instance, in 1975, the European Council issued a preliminary programme for a consumer protection and

[3] For instance, the increasingly unionised work force was demanding the end of Saturday morning opening of retail branches.

[4] *B Bátiz-Lazo, 'Emergence and Evolution of ATM Networks in the UK, 1967–2000' (2009) 51 Business History* 1, 7.

[5] KW Colton and KL Kraemer (eds), *Computers and Banking: Electronic Funds Transfer Systems and Public Policy* (Plenum Press 1980).

[6] ibid viii.

[7] PD Louderback, 'Status of EFT: An Assessment of Services and a Review of EFT in the Fifty States' in KW Colton and KL Kraemer (eds), *Computers and Banking: Electronic Funds Transfer Systems and Public Policy* (Springer US 1980) 46–47.

information policy, covering several areas, including the right to protection of economic interests. At the time, there were concerns, especially from Member States, that the purpose of protecting consumers might interfere with free market dynamics. As such, consumer protection remained quite superficial, with the focus remaining on competition laws and economic competitiveness in general.[8]

Aside from this, the emergence and spread of Information and Communication Technologies (ICTs) like EFT systems radically expanded the volume and speed of information handling, spurring the debate about the need for data protection. This debate was influenced by experiences of totalitarianism (such as data use by the Nazi regime) and fictional dystopias (such as Orwell's *1984*).[9] During the 1970s we saw several countries in Western Europe (such as Austria, Denmark and France) enact data protection laws while others (such as Belgium, the Netherlands and Spain)drafted reports contemplating legislation. In 1978 the European Parliament also passed recommendations for harmonising data protection at the EEC level. However, the European regulations were perceived as 'impractical, bureaucratic, and detrimental to the free flow of information, especially with the impact these regulations would have on transborder data flow'.[10]

Overall in this era, traditional structures of regulation were challenged under the pressure of powerful technological, economic and ideological forces. The 1970s and 1980s were decades of complicated societal challenge, often exacerbated or further complicated by technology and a kind of 'first wave' of digitalisation. This is often referred to, rather misleadingly, as 'deregulation': reducing state intervention in the economy and promoting competition and efficiency. However, some astutely observed that what was happening was not simply a dismantling of regulation but a combination of deregulation and re-regulation, in which Member States at the European level attempted to address the new concerns brought by ICTs and grapple with important tensions.[11] Notable examples include the deregulation of financial markets in the United States, such as the repeal of the fixed commission rates on stock exchanges in 1975 (via the Securities Acts Amendments) and the deregulation of savings and loan institutions, culminating in the Depository Institutions Deregulation and Monetary Control Act of 1980.[12] In Europe, similar trends were observed, such as the liberalisation of cross-border financial

[8] F Cafaggi and A Nicita, 'The Evolution of Consumer Protection in the EU' in *Research Handbook on the Economics of European Union Law* (Edward Elgar Publishing 2012) 276.

[9] K Yeung and LA Bygrave, 'Demystifying the Modernized European Data Protection Regime: Cross-Disciplinary Insights from Legal and Regulatory Governance Scholarship' (2022) 16 *Regulation & Governance* 137, 144.

[10] H Burkert, 'Institutions of Data Protection – An Attempt at a Functional Explanation of European National Data Protection Laws' (1981) 3 *Computer Law Journal* 166, 169.

[11] G Majone (ed), *Regulating Europe* (Routledge 1996) 2, 3.

[12] GA Jarrell, 'Change at the Exchange: Causes and Effects of Deregulation' (1984) 2 *Journal of Law and economics* 27.

transactions and the gradual removal of capital controls in many Member States of the European Community.[13]

2.2. Transborder Dataflows and Regulatory Coordination

The 1990s saw further advancements with the proliferation of personal computers and the introduction of the first online banking services, allowing customers to access their accounts and perform transactions remotely.[14] A key technological development to discuss here is the Society for Worldwide Interbank Financial Telecommunication (SWIFT) standardised international payment system. As large multinational banks turned their attention to establishing global operations and developing international business, cross-border transactions proliferated. However, as there was no worldwide standard for international financial transactions, there were many errors and delays. At first, the major banks developed competing proprietary networks that they tried to impose on others. This led to frustration, duplicated effort, wasted resources and errors in international transactions. Eventually, banks showed their willingness to engage in the cooperative effort needed and SWIFT, founded as a cooperative non-profit organisation, was widely adopted as an industry standard by the 1980s.[15] At a time of strong competition between financial institutions, large banks were able to put their own interests aside for the greater good, and a more just distribution of burdens and benefits through a smoother and standardised data exchange system emerged.

To be sure, this was not without risk. The widespread adoption of the internet in the 1990s further transformed the financial landscape. Online banking became more sophisticated, offering a broader range of services such as bill payment, fund transfers and account management. The increase in online transactions and digital interactions began to generate vast amounts of digital data – much of which was transferred through SWIFT. SWIFT messages contained sensitive financial information, and ensuring the privacy and protection of this data was a key concern. SWIFT laid bare the tension between the EU's desire for privacy and the United States' need for security from terrorists, particularly in the wake of the 9/11 attacks, which intensified the global focus on combating terrorism financing. The SWIFT scandal of 2006 highlighted this issue when it was revealed that the US Treasury Department accessed SWIFT data through the Terrorist Finance Tracking Program to trace financial transactions potentially linked to terrorist activities.[16]

[13] AFP Bakker, *The Liberalization of Capital Movements in Europe: The Monetary Committee and Financial Integration 1958–1994 (Springer Science & Business Media 2012).*

[14] B Bátiz-Lazo and D Wood, 'An Historical Appraisal of Information Technology in Commercial Banking' (2002) 12 *Electronic Markets* 192, 196.

[15] SV Scott and M Zachariadis, 'Origins and Development of SWIFT, 1973–2009' (2012) 54 *Business History* 462, 4–6.

[16] In 2006, it was revealed that, following the 9/11 terrorist attacks, the US Treasury Department had secretly been accessing SWIFT transaction data. This was part of the Terrorist Finance Tracking

The US argued that tracking these transactions was a vital counter-terrorism tool, helping identify and disrupt terrorist networks. This, however, raised concerns in the EU about unauthorised access to personal data, creating a fundamental conflict between privacy rights and security measures.

Importantly, combating terrorism financing was not solely a US concern. For instance, the German government employed Raster-Fahndung (dragnet profiling) to identify members of the Rote Armee Fraktion by cross-referencing financial and other data sources.[17] These examples underscore the international scope of counter-terrorism efforts and the shared challenge of balancing privacy with security. Overall, the establishment of SWIFT and the complications ensuing from it highlighted the need for robust international legal frameworks to manage the fundamental tension between privacy and security, and to safeguard a just distribution of burdens and benefits, in an increasingly international and datafied financial area.

The newly established EU heeded this call for regulatory coordination. A key regulatory event was the 1992 Maastricht Treaty.[18] In terms of consumer rights, the Treaty provided a legal basis for more comprehensive and harmonised consumer protection measures across Member States. This came alongside the Treaty's objective of creating an internal market characterised by the free movement of goods, persons, services and capital. This economic integration would provide a larger, more cohesive market for businesses and innovators. The Treaty also emphasised the importance of research and technological development as essential components of the EU's competitiveness. It led to the establishment of programmes and initiatives to support innovation, research and development across Member States.

Meanwhile, as transborder dataflows increased, data protection regulation did too. In an effort to harmonise the expanding member state legislation, the EU Data Protection Directive was adopted in 1995.[19] However, it required transposition into national laws by each member state, leading to variations in implementation. Moreover, the scope of regulatory enforcement was seen as questionable.[20] Adding to this, the increasing complexity of regulation governing international data flows created difficulties for individuals. Although many transborder data flows are conducted based on the consent of the individual, individuals may not understand what they are consenting to, and that they may not have a meaningful opportunity

Program, which aimed to track and disrupt terrorist financing. The data was obtained without the knowledge or consent of European authorities or the public, raising significant privacy concerns.

[17] U Schellinger, 'Clairvoyance for the Security of the Republic. Gerard Croiset and the Search for Hanns Martin Schleyer (1977)' in E Voss (ed), *Mediality on Trial: Testing and Contesting Trance and other Media Techniques* (De Gruyter Oldenbourg 2020) 284.

[18] Treaty on European Union [1992] OJ C191/1.

[19] Directive 95/46/EC of the European Parliament and of the Council of 24 October 1995 on the protection of individuals with regard to the processing of personal data and on the free movement of such data [1995] OJ L281/31.

[20] C Kuner, 'Regulation of Transborder Data Flows under Data Protection and Privacy Law: Past, Present and Future' (OECD 2011) 16.

to refuse consent.[21] While the EU thus addressed data and consumer protection in a more coordinated fashion, the key focus as of the 1990s was boosting the struggling economy and fostering innovation. These priorities were reiterated in the 2000 Lisbon strategy, which aimed to make the EU the most competitive and dynamic knowledge-based economy by 2010.[22] It emphasised innovation, research and development, calling for new regulatory approaches to foster technological advancements.

2.3. Fintech and New Forms of Risk Regulation

A next key moment to discuss in the digitalisation and datafication of finance is the 2008 financial crisis. Firstly, this led to massive changes for traditional banks, their regulators and their relationship to data.[23] Secondly, the crisis accelerated the fintech (financial technology) boom as consumers and businesses sought alternative financial services that were more efficient and transparent; this also led to intensified use of Big Data for real-time analysis and decision-making.[24] Regarding the first point, for traditional banks and regulators, the 2008 financial crisis was a crisis of theory. Regulators, banks and financial markets all had encompassing theoretical models about how the economy worked, but they all failed to predict the looming crisis.[25] The theoretical models had lost touch with the actual economic reality. In the words of Colander and others:

> Economists not only failed to anticipate the financial crisis; they may have contributed to it – with risk and derivatives models that, through spurious precision and untested theoretical assumptions, encouraged policy makers and market participants to see more stability and risk sharing than was actually present.[26]

Supervisors and banks alike turned to a wider collection of data and to the increased use of algorithms to distil meaning from this data and detect risk. Unfortunately, this did not always have the desired results as both banks and supervisors acknowledged they were uncertain about the validity of the knowledge claims drawn from the algorithms.[27] Datafication does not necessarily lead to a better understanding

[21] FH Cate, 'The Failure of Fair Information Practice Principles' in JK Winn (ed), *Consumer Protection in the Age of the 'Information Economy'* (Routledge 2006) 343.

[22] See Lisbon European Council 23–24 March 2000 Presidency Conclusions, points 11–23. Available at: www.europarl.europa.eu/summits/lis1_en.htm.

[23] S Kempeneer, 'A Big Data State of Mind: Epistemological Challenges to Accountability and Transparency in Data-Driven Regulation' (2021) 38 *Government Information Quarterly* 101578, 2.

[24] RP Buckley and others, 'The Dark Side of Digital Financial Transformation: The New Risks of FinTech and the Rise of TechRisk' [2019] *SSRN Electronic Journal* 11. Available at: www.ssrn.com/abstract=3478640.

[25] ibid.

[26] DColander and others, 'The Financial Crisis and the Systemic Failure of the Economics Profession' (2009) 21 *Critical Review* 249, 249.

[27] Kempeneer 'A Big Data State of Mind' (n 23) 5–6.

of financial risk. Moreover, it is important to keep a close eye on supervisors relying on Big Data to regulate banks, as this challenges our current understanding of accountability and transparency in the regulatory process.[28]

A second key shift was the fintech boom.[29] Fintech innovations, driven by advancements in mobile technology, cloud computing and data analytics, allowed for an array of new services such as peer-to-peer lending platforms and payment apps, crowdfunding platforms, digital wallets, personal finance management tools, robo-advisers, cryptocurrency exchanges and blockchain solutions. While these innovations can facilitate consumer access to financial products and services, for instance making it easier to lend or invest money, they also carry important risks. Given the vast amounts of data being processed, there are exacerbated risks of data security and data privacy. Moreover, the shift towards fintech exacerbates certain cybersecurity threats that are unique to the financial system, and subsequently to financial stability and systemic risk. The growing transition to cloud infrastructure creates more concentrated data nodes, with less software diversity, requiring higher security measures. Cybersecurity risk can thus be seen as a new source of traditional risk as well as an entirely new form of risk and one with potentially catastrophic consequences.[30] Beyond cybersecurity and data protection, the involvement of new financial participants such as fintech firms raises potential concerns. These firms often benefit from regulatory gaps and/or disparities in treatment with traditional financial institutions. A tricky situation arises where fintech companies might have better data than traditional financial institutions and may provide the financial intermediary function more effectively. However, fintechs still often operate in a (partially) unregulated environment. For instance, many fintechs are not subject to client/customer/investor protection rules, nor to measures that ensure the functioning of financial markets and prevent the build-up of systemic risk.[31] Fintech has thus introduced (i) new sources of traditional risk; (ii) new forms of risk; and (iii) entirely new markets and systems to be regulated. This has contributed to a revised distribution of burdens and benefits.

In the aftermath of the financial crisis, there was still a strong emphasis on encouraging innovation within the EU, but with a heightened sense of caution. This period saw the rise of new technological developments such as fintech and blockchain, which began to transform the financial sector. The 2010s also marked the era where 'Big Data' became a significant focus. As a result, European regulators started to place greater importance on cybersecurity, consumer protection and data privacy concerns. These advancements necessitated a more robust regulatory

[28] ibid 6.

[29] Buckley and others 'The Dark Side of Digital Financial Transformation' (n 24) 11.

[30] ibid 15.

[31] DA Zetzsche, 'Investment Law as Financial Law: From Fund Governance over Market Governance to Stakeholder Governance?' in H Søndergaard Birkmose, MNeville, and K Engsig Sørensen (eds), *The European Financial Market in Transition* (Kluwer Law International 2012) 348.

framework to ensure that the benefits of innovation could be harnessed without compromising the security and privacy of consumers.

For instance, in response to the new risks and markets brought about by fintech, in 2020 the EU introduced the Markets in Crypto-Assets Regulation (MiCA)[32] to create a comprehensive regulatory framework for cryptocurrencies and related services. MiCA also aims to strike a balance between fostering innovation in the financial sector, while enhancing consumer protection and ensuring market integrity. Though MiCa is also widely criticised, it is a clear first step in taking new risks and actors in the digital financial space seriously. More broadly in the domain of consumer protection, financial services regulation was tightened to protect consumers from misleading products and unfair practices. This included measures to ensure clearer information about financial products (such as the Consumer Credit Directive[33]), the introduction of caps on fees and charges (such as the Interchange Fee Regulation[34]), and the establishment of mechanisms for dispute resolution (such as the Alternative Dispute Resolution[35]). These efforts show clear steps in the direction of a more just distribution of benefits and burdens. Moreover, the Unfair Commercial Practices Directive (UCPD),[36] which had been adopted in 2005, was updated in 2019 to better deal with business practices in the digital economy, including better protection of consumer data.[37] For instance, the Italian Competition Authority fined Facebook on UCPD grounds for undisclosed data sharing with third parties. This proved that not just data protection but also the manipulation of consumer behaviour in commercial transactions can be sanctionable activities on the digital internal market.

The introduction of the General Data Protection Regulation (GDPR) in 2016 marked a pivotal moment in remedying data protection harms arising in the data economy.[38] This comprehensive Regulation, enforceable since 2018, was

[32] Regulation (EU) 2023/1114 of the European Parliament and of the Council of 31 May 2023 on markets in crypto-assets, and amending Regulations (EU) No 1093/2010 and (EU) No 1095/2010 and Directives 2013/36/EU and (EU) 2019/1937 (Text with EEA relevance) [2023] OJ L150/40.

[33] Directive 2008/48/EC of the European Parliament and of the Council of 23 April 2008 on credit agreements for consumers and repealing Council Directive 87/102/EEC [2008] OJ L133/66.

[34] Regulation (EU) 2015/751 of the European Parliament and of the Council of 29 April 2015 on interchange fees for card-based payment transactions (Text with EEA relevance) [2015] OJ L123/1.

[35] Directive 2013/11/EU of the European Parliament and of the Council of 21 May 2013 on alternative dispute resolution for consumer disputes and amending Regulation (EC) No 2006/2004 and Directive 2009/22/EC (Directive on consumer ADR) [2013] OJ L165/63.

[36] Directive 2005/29/EC of the European Parliament and of the Council of 11 May 2005 concerning unfair business-to-consumer commercial practices in the internal market and amending Council Directive 84/450/EEC, Directives 97/7/EC, 98/27/EC and 2002/65/EC of the European Parliament and of the Council and Regulation (EC) No 2006/2004 of the European Parliament and of the Council [2005] OJ L149/22 (Unfair Commercial Practices Directive).

[37] C Goanta, 'Regulatory Siblings: The Unfair Commercial Practices Directive Roots of the AI Act' in I Graef and B van der Sloot (eds), *The Legal Consistency of Technology Regulation in Europe* (Hart Publishing 2024) 71.

[38] Regulation (EU) 2016/679 of the European Parliament and of the Council of 27 April 2016 on the protection of natural persons with regard to the processing of personal data and on the free movement of such data, and repealing Directive 95/46/EC [2016] OJ L119/1 (General Data Protection Regulation).

designed to fully harmonise data protection laws across all EU Member States. The Regulation set a global benchmark for data protection standards, influencing similar legislation in other parts of the world. However, the enforcement of GDPR still varies across Member States, and it has been criticised for its complexity and ambiguity. It also received a backlash for potentially hindering technological innovation and putting European businesses at a competitive disadvantage; though many argue this is not the case in practice.

In this phase, we see an expansion of what Yeung and Ranchordás call the 'risk object', from conventional understandings of risk, like harm to human health or safety, to more normative interpretations of risk, including 'privacy risks' and wider 'risks to fundamental rights'.[39] The groundwork for this is visible in the Maastricht Treaty, which explicitly committed the EU to respecting fundamental rights as guaranteed by the European Convention on Human Rights, and the 1997 Treaty of Amsterdam,[40] which gave the EU a more explicit role in combating discrimination and promoting equality.[41] The 2007 Treaty of Lisbon made the Charter of Fundamental Rights legally binding,[42] which played a crucial role in shaping the human rights focus of the GDPR.[43] This era marks a pivotal moment where the EU seems to be searching for a new balance between promises of innovation and protection against the problems this may bring.

2.4. Navigating Promise and Problem

Over the past six decades, finance has undergone a digital transformation. Today, finance is not only the most globalised segment of the world's economy but also among the most digitised and datafied. This digital transformation has affected the just distribution of burdens and benefits and thus called for renewed regulation to address old and new risks.

Regulations spurred by technological changes call for legislative processes that have two objectives: (i) ensuring actors can take advantage of the merits of technological change; and (ii) ensuring actors are protected from the demerits of technological change. These can also be characterised as (i) regulating promises and (ii) regulating problems. This tension that technology regulation has to deal with is, in many ways, not completely new. In fact, these tensions reflect 'old'

[39] K Yeung and S Ranchordás, *An Introduction to Law and Regulation: Text and Materials* (2nd edn, Cambridge University Press 2024) 47.

[40] Treaty of Amsterdam amending the Treaty on European Union, the Treaties establishing the European Communities and certain related acts [1997] OJ C340/1.

[41] E Defeis, 'Human Rights, the European Union, and the Treaty Route: From Maastricht to Lisbon' (2012) 35 *Fordham International Law Journal* 1207.

[42] Treaty of Lisbon amending the Treaty on European Union and the Treaty establishing the European Community of 13 December 2007 [2007] OJ C306/1.

[43] G Di Federico, 'Fundamental Rights in the EU: Legal Pluralism and Multi-Level Protection After the Lisbon Treaty' in G Di Federico (ed), *The EU Charter of Fundamental Rights*, vol 8 (Springer Netherlands 2011) 15.

societal conflicts, mainly over the distribution of power between, for example, the individual (or groups of individuals) and the state, or between consumer and provider. However, the 'new' technological element in these classic dualisms seems to pose problems of a kind that can no longer be dealt with sufficiently by existing regulation. The reason for this, according to Burkert,[44] is that technology has introduced a 'new language of power'. The traditional conflicts now are put in terms of information handling, or data processing, namely access to information, distribution of information, and the capability to process information. Regulations thus have to adapt to this new language. Central to technology regulation is thus the handling of data and regulations pertaining to this. Tensions can thus be rephrased as tensions pertaining to data, meaning regulation has to strike a balance between encouraging digitalised and datafied spaces (promises) and regulating the risks that accompany these datafied spaces (problems).

As recounted in the sections above, the EU has tried to find a balance between safeguarding the promises and mitigating the problems that technology, digitalisation and datafication bring. So far, in the financial space but also beyond, it seems that regulation has favoured the promises over the problems.[45] For instance, the emphasis on fostering innovation and market competitiveness has sometimes led to gaps in consumer protection. The rapid expansion of fintech services, driven by promises of accessibility and innovation, has often outpaced regulatory frameworks, leaving certain risks – such as data breaches, cybersecurity vulnerabilities and systemic risks – unaddressed or insufficiently mitigated.

The GDPR, while a landmark for data privacy, has faced criticism for its complexity and uneven enforcement across Member States, which can disadvantage smaller enterprises and leave consumers vulnerable in some jurisdictions.[46] Additionally, the transition to 'open banking' under the Second Payment Services Directive (PSD2) has raised concerns about data misuse and privacy risks,[47] as these frameworks focus heavily on fostering innovation while struggling to ensure consistent consumer safeguards.

Importantly, a regulatory patchwork is forming around the digital financial space, where similar or even identical legal rules are used across different legal instruments that may sound the same but have very different interpretations and thereby create risks for legal consistency and justice.[48] Given this regulatory history and context, the establishment of European data spaces is a critical case in which

[44] Herbert Burkert, 'Institutions of Data Protection – An Attempt at a Functional Explanation of European National Data Protection Laws' (1981) 3 *Computer Law Journal* 166, 170.

[45] To be sure, we might have reached a turning point as fundamental rights are gaining more regulatory attention as legitimate 'risk objects'.

[46] G Gentile and O Lynskey, 'Deficient by Design? The Transnational Enforcement of the GDPR' (2022) 4 *International & Comparative Law Quarterly* 71, 79.

[47] M Gounari and others, 'Harmonizing Open Banking in the European Union: An Analysis of PSD2 Compliance and Interrelation with Cybersecurity Frameworks and Standards' [2024] *International Cybersecurity Law Review* 79, 80.

[48] Goanta 'Regulatory Siblings' (n 37) 71.

to unpack the tension between promise and problem, and the just distribution of burdens and benefits.

3. European Financial Data Space: A New Chapter in the History of Digitalisation of Finance and its Regulation

3.1. Towards the Single Common European Data Space in the Area of Finance

In September 2020, the European Commission announced a new 'Digital Finance Strategy for the EU'.[49] The document, being a part of the bigger initiative of the 'European Strategy for Data',[50] outlines how Europe can assist the digital revolution of finance while mitigating its hazards through regulatory means. The Digital Finance Strategy is based on four priorities: reducing fragmentation in the Digital Single Market, adjusting the EU regulatory framework to support digital innovation, boosting data-driven finance, and addressing the challenges and risks associated with digital transformation, including increasing the financial system's digital operational resilience. The third priority is intended to be achieved through the creation of the aforementioned EFDS, the main goal of which should be 'to stimulate, through enhanced data sharing, innovation, market transparency, sustainable finance, as well as access to finance for European businesses and a more integrated market'.[51]

The EFDS was initially designated as one of nine proposed common European data spaces, the other eight being: industrial (manufacturing) data space, Green Deal data space, mobility data space, health data space, energy data space, agriculture data space, skills data space, and data space for public administration.[52] Generally speaking, the rationale behind founding the European common data spaces is the fostering of a genuine single market for data.[53] This means that the EU wishes to establish a global data market that is open to data from all sources (both from the EU and outside the EU), where businesses can easily access virtually limitless amounts of high-quality data, spurring growth and creating value while reducing the carbon footprint of the industry and that of humans.

The ultimate goal of the EU initiative on data spaces should be realised by bringing together data infrastructures and governance frameworks to facilitate

[49] Commission, 'Digital Finance Strategy for the EU' (Communication) COM (2020) 591 final.
[50] Commission, 'A European Strategy for Data' (Communication) COM (2020) 66 final.
[51] ibid, 22.
[52] Later, the Commission added five new areas in which data spaces should be created, namely: cultural heritage, language, media, research and innovation, and tourism data space (see, eg, Commission, 'Commission Staff Working Document on Common European Data Spaces' SWD (2024) 21 final (SWD 2024)).
[53] Commission, 'A European Strategy for Data' (Communication) COM (2020) 66 final, 4.

trusted and secure data pooling and sharing in key economic sectors and domains of public interest.[54] Then, the sectoral and domain-specific data spaces are intended to be gradually interconnected to ultimately form a 'pillar of the single market for data'.[55]

Yet, on several occasions, the Commission has emphasised that the European data spaces should be designed in a way that respects EU rules and values and complies with legal frameworks on fundamental rights, including the right to the protection of personal data, data security, environmental protection and competition. The respect for the EU rules and values is also a prerequisite for any actors, be they organisations or individuals, to participate in common European data spaces.[56]

As regards specifically the EFDS, the first Staff Working Document on Common European Data Spaces, published in 2022, identified three components of the EFDS, namely a component concerning digital access to publicly disclosed financial information, a component focused on improving the reporting and sharing of supervisory information among EU and national financial supervisory authorities, and a component regarding data sharing and reuse of data in the EU financial sector, known as the 'open finance' initiative.[57] The following sections will briefly discuss the developments of the EFDS so far.

3.2. European Single Access Point: Free, User-Friendly, Centralised and Digital Access to Information on European Companies

The most advanced component of the EFDS appears to be the one that realises the goal of providing a digital, easily accessible source of free public financial and non-financial (including sustainability-related) information about EU companies and EU investment products through the so-called European Single Access Point (ESAP). The history of ESAP goes back to 2016 and the adoption of the Commission Delegated Regulation supplementing Directive 2004/109/EC of the European Parliament and of the Council with regard to regulatory technical standards on access to regulated information at the Union level.[58] In the Preamble to this legal act, it was explicitly acknowledged that:

> In order to ensure fast access to regulated information on a non-discriminatory basis and make that information available to end users, the European Securities and Markets

[54] Commission, 'Commission Staff Working Document on Common European Data Spaces' SWD (2022) 45 final, 2 (SWD 2022) and SWD (2024) 21 final, 3.
[55] SWD (2024) ibid.
[56] SWD (2022) 45 final, 4.
[57] ibid 23–24.
[58] [2016] OJ L234/1.

> Authority (ESMA) has an obligation to develop and operate a European Electronic Access Point (EEAP).[59]

This obligation will now be fulfilled by establishing and making the ESAP operational. This will happen based on the principal instrument of the ESAP legislative package proposed by the Commission in November 2021, as a part of the Capital Markets Union Action Plan, namely Regulation (EU) 2023/2859 establishing a European single access point providing centralised access to publicly available information of relevance to financial services, capital markets and sustainability.[60]

The ESAP does not require the collection of any additional information than already required by relevant legal frameworks; it is, however, expected to provide easy access to all already publicly available information released by regulated institutions in line with these frameworks (ie with the 35 European regulations and directives enumerated in the Annex to the ESAP Regulation). The Annex can be reviewed and the scope of information material at issue expanded.

The main goal of the ESAP is to increase the visibility of information and facilitate searches irrespective of the type and size of the regulated organisation it concerns or the EU language in which the information was submitted. The primary expected users of the ESAP are investors, financial analysts and market intermediaries including asset managers, financial counsellors, etc. On the one hand, the ESAP will allow them to access and compare information on a wider range of organisations across all EU Member States and make informed decisions. On the other hand, such organisations – especially start-ups and small and medium-sized enterprises – will be given a much more equal chance than ever before to encourage investors to support their growth. Consequently, the ESAP is expected to open up new funding opportunities and better allocate capital creating a more just environment, where every market participant can enjoy equal and indiscriminate visibility.

3.3. Data-Driven Financial Sector Supervision

In December 2021, the European Commission announced its 'Strategy on supervisory data in EU financial services',[61] the key objective of which is 'to modernise EU supervisory reporting and put in place a system that delivers accurate, consistent, and timely data to supervisory authorities at EU and national level, while minimising the aggregate reporting burden for all relevant parties'.[62] This is expected to result in a more efficient and agile supervision that will safeguard stability of the financial system, market integrity, and protection of the investor, from which

[59] ibid, point 1 of the Preamble.

[60] [2023] OJ L2859/1.

[61] Commission, 'Strategy on supervisory data in EU financial services' (Communication) COM (2021) 798 final.

[62] ibid 3.

ultimately all EU citizens, and in particular consumers using financial services, will benefit.

Through relevant legislative initiatives and implementation of technical solutions, the Commission wishes to take advantage of technological developments and data-driven opportunities to improve EU-level supervisory reporting, enable data sharing between EU and national financial supervisory authorities and make more data accessible to the industry. To achieve this goal, it is crucial to increase consistency and standardise the reporting, among other things, by creating the so-called 'common data dictionary', ie a clear common and thereby comparable terminology, as well as by introducing standards, machine-readable data formats and common rules of reporting. To that end, in 2023, the Commission tabled a proposal for a Regulation amending several legislative instruments governing EU financial sector supervision as regards certain reporting requirements in the fields of financial services and investment support.[63] This is not an entirely new sentiment. Ever since the financial crisis, EU regulators have recognised the interconnectedness of the banking system and have had a desire to harmonise banking processes and make their operations commensurable. However, these efforts have already proved to be challenging.[64] In parallel, several other workstreams at the sectoral and cross-sectoral levels are being carried out to implement the discussed strategy. The European supervisory authorities, specifically the European Banking Authority, the already mentioned ESMA, the European Insurance and Occupational Pensions Authority, and other authorities in charge of the technical matters have already started to collaborate to define and implement reporting requirements.[65] The results of this collaboration remain to be seen.

3.4. From Open Banking to Open Finance

Finally, the last component of the EFDS concerns the business-to-business and business-to-consumer data sharing and reuse of financial data, known as the open finance initiative. In response to the accelerating structural transformation in the financial sector caused by the unprecedented growth of digital technology, the emergence of new players in the financial market, ever-more innovative business models and, adapting to these novelties, consumer behaviours, the Commission decided to create a regulatory and technical environment that can foster financial

[63] Commission, 'Proposal for a Regulation of the European Parliament and of the Council amending Regulations (EU) No 1092/2010, (EU) No 1093/2010, (EU) No 1094/2010, (EU) No 1095/2010 and (EU) 2021/523 as regards certain reporting requirements in the fields of financial services and investment support' COM (2023) 593 final.

[64] See e.g. S Kempeneer and W Van Dooren, 'The Incommensurables: The Arduous Art of Making a Regulatory Indicator' (2020) 14 *Critical Policy Studies* 285, 297.

[65] For more about progress on the implementation of the supervision strategy, see SWD (2024) 45 final.

data sharing and support the financial industry to fully embrace data-driven finance.

The first step towards the realisation of that goal was taken in 2015 when PSD2[66] was adopted. The overarching objective of PSD2 was to optimise the European payment ecosystem in line with the needs emerging from the proliferation of data-centric technologies.[67] Thus, PSD2 introduced so-called 'open banking', ie an environment which enables and promotes the sharing of financial data between banks and other non-bank payment service providers through the use of application programming interfaces (APIs). Insofar as permitted by the customers (including both consumers and companies) of a payment service, banks had to open their data resources and provide API access for other market players (especially fintech companies) offering new types of payment services. In this way, PSD2 was intended to foster innovation and competition in the financial sector by reducing barriers for non-bank payment service providers and allowing them to access all EU payment systems. The customers of payment services could therefore be given a wider choice of payment instruments and, hence, as aptly noted by, for instance, Chomczyk Penedo and Trigo Kramcsák, the customers could more easily 'move their data across different service providers, … [and] benefit from better economic conditions as there would be competition between firms to both attract and retain customers'.[68]

Now, with the EFDS initiative, the EU legislator wishes to expand the 'open banking' framework to include not only payment services but a much broader array of financial services, including loans, investments, savings accounts or certain types of insurance and, thus, to create the environment of 'open finance'. According to the Commission, the embracing of data-driven digital finance 'will unleash innovation and create opportunities to develop better and more innovative financial products for consumers, including for people currently unable to access financial services'.[69] This argument mirrors the claims made during the 2008 fintech boom, described in section 2.3, that similarly promised innovative products and improved consumer accessibility; all of which were expected to be realised through the extensive use of Big Data.

To achieve the main objectives of the open finance initiative, on 28 June 2023, the European Commission issued a proposal for a Regulation on a framework

[66] Directive (EU) 2015/2366 of the European Parliament and of the Council of 25 November 2015 on payment services in the internal market, amending Directives 2002/65/EC, 2009/110/EC and 2013/36/EU and Regulation (EU) No 1093/2010, and repealing Directive 2007/64/EC (Text with EEA relevance) [2015] OJ L337.

[67] M Gounari and others, 'Harmonizing Open Banking in the European Union: An Analysis of PSD2 Compliance and Interrelation with Cybersecurity Frameworks and Standards' [2024] *International Cybersecurity Law Review* 79, 80.

[68] AC Penedo and PT Kramcsák, 'Can the European Financial Data Space Remove Bias in Financial AI Development? Opportunities and Regulatory Challenges' (2023) 31 *International Journal of Law and Information Technology* 253, 254.

[69] SWD (2024) 21 final, 24.

for Financial Data Access (FIDA Regulation).[70] The FIDA Regulation builds upon and complements the open banking regime established by PSD2 but as mentioned earlier, it enables the sharing, accessing and reusing of a considerably broader set of financial services data and lays down the rules according to which the goals are going to be achieved. Therefore, the proposal constitutes yet another building block of the European digital markets strategy and a piece of the complex regulatory puzzle. It fits into the broader context of the cross-sectoral initiatives, such as those concerning trust building in data sharing that is foundational in the Data Governance Act,[71] or limiting the powers of the 'gatekeeper' platforms, which is the primary goal of the Digital Markets Act.[72]

The underlying rationale behind the proposed FIDA Regulation (and the single European data space as a whole) is to maximise data availability and thereby allow for the realignment of market power in relation to data access, reuse and sharing.[73] At the same time, financial services customers should have effective control – in particular by the means of authorisation – over their financial data and the ability to decide for themselves how this data can be used, including who has access to it and for what purposes. The data under FIDA will encompass data supplied by the customer and data deriving from customer interactions, as well as data concerning terms and conditions for specific financial services or products. This, in practice, means both personal and non-personal data. According to the proposal, data holders (ie companies that provide financial services covered by FIDA) will need to supply data to data users (ie authorised financial information service providers), as well as making the data available directly to their customers. In both instances, the data must be provided 'without undue delay, continuously and in real-time'.[74] While the provision of data to the customers must be free of charge, compensation can be claimed from a data user. The maximum compensation can be determined in the so-called financial data sharing schemes (FDSS), jointly developed and mandatorily joined by data holders and users. The FDSS will have to establish rules and common standards for data access and sharing in compliance with the FIDA provisions and other applicable EU legal frameworks, including those on the protection of personal data. The proposal for FIDA Regulation, however, neither tasks any specific regulator or industry body with setting up the FDSS nor specifies much detail on how these schemes should govern the relationships between

[70] Commission, 'Proposal for a Regulation of the European Parliament and of the Council on a framework for Financial Data Access and amending Regulations (EU) No 1093/2010, (EU) No 1094/2010, (EU) No 1095/2010 and (EU) 2022/2554' COM (2023) 360 final (Proposal for FIDA Regulation).

[71] Regulation (EU) 2022/868 of the European Parliament and of the Council of 30 May 2022 on European data governance and amending Regulation (EU) 2018/1724 (Data Governance Act) (Text with EEA relevance) [2022] OJ L152, see eg Recital 5.

[72] Regulation (EU) 2022/1925 of the European Parliament and of the Council of 14 September 2022 on contestable and fair markets in the digital sector and amending Directives (EU) 2019/1937 and (EU) 2020/1828 (Digital Markets Act) (Text with EEA relevance) [2022] OJ L265.

[73] V Ferrari, 'The Platformisation of Digital Payments: The Fabrication of Consumer Interest in the EU FinTech Agenda' (2022) 45 *Computer Law & Security Review* 105687, 179.

[74] Proposal for FIDA Regulation, arts 4 and 5(1).

different stakeholders, leaving the question of the just distribution of burdens and benefits open.

On that point, it is noteworthy that the legislator has recognised some customers – in this case, consumers – as potentially vulnerable stakeholders and acknowledged the risk of financial exclusion that the open finance initiative may entail for them. Without going into too much detail here, financial exclusion is a term used to describe processes that result in preventing certain individuals and groups from gaining access to the financial system.[75] What the proposal for FIDA Regulation explicitly excludes from its scope is data that could directly increase the customer's risk of financial exclusion and – more precisely – data on consumers' sickness and health insurance, life insurance products or data collected in the context of creditworthiness assessment.[76] The next section will further address this problem.

4. Justice in the Context of Digitalisation and the Modernisation of Finance Regulation

As shown in sections 2 and 3, technological advancements have considerably impacted the area of finance, enhancing its digitalisation and thereby bringing both opportunities and challenges. Consequently, all these developments have been reflected in the latest regulatory agendas, most notably in the works on the EFDS. What is characteristic of the recent regulatory discourse is the recognition of the multiplicity of financial market stakeholders and the acknowledgement of the need to create an environment for their 'just' development and 'just' contribution to economic growth.

Yet, the classic account of justice (such as put forward by Rawls) understands this notion as an obligation to provide fair (ie equal) liberties and opportunities for everyone.[77] When scrutinising the proposed regulatory components of the EFDS through such a lens, one needs to observe the legislator's attempt to achieve justice between several participants of the financial market. The ESAP is designed with a view to enabling a wider range of entities to offer innovative services in the area of finance. When it comes to data-driven financial sector supervision, the newly proposed strategy postulates a rather gradual and pragmatic approach. It seeks to find 'the right balance between delivering improvements in terms of burden reduction, quality and availability of supervisory data and being mindful of the

[75] See M De La Cuesta González, C Ruzay Paz-Curbera, and B Fernández Olit, 'Banking System and Financial Exclusion: Towards a More Comprehensive Approach' in SC Valverde, PJ Cuadros Solas, and FR Fernández (eds), *Liquidity Risk, Efficiency and New Bank Business Models* (Springer International Publishing 2016) 128ff and the literature cited therein.

[76] Proposal for FIDA Regulation, Recital 9 and art 2(1)(e).

[77] Barry and Matravers, 'Justice' (n 2).

costs of transition'.[78] This is envisaged to result in more equality among banks, insurance and pension providers, funds and other relevant market players.

The most interesting development from the perspective of justice appears to be the open finance initiative. On the one hand, under the proposed FIDA Regulation, financial institutions (data holders) will have to share a wide set of customer data with authorised third parties (data users), which will give the latter a fair equality of opportunity and, therefore, mitigate the problem of the current economic inequalities between the financial market players. On the other hand, it is noticeable that, although the proposed framework mentions on several occasions the empowerment of the customers of financial services, the question of practical implementation of this postulate remains rather open. The proposal for FIDA Regulation seems to complement the narrative, according to which customer technological empowerment needs to be prioritised and considered to be a value that outweighs any risks the data-intensive financial technologies may bring. As argued by Ferrari, the objective of maximisation of data production and valorisation that has dominated recent policy discourse in fact primarily represents the interests of the industry.[79] In her words, 'while financial innovation is widely discussed from advantaging business perspectives, it is rarely scrutinized in terms of information control-related risks, power asymmetries and negative externalities'.[80] One of the practical examples of the relevance of such consideration in the context of the EFDS is the aforementioned risk of financial exclusion that can materialise when the open finance environment allows for combining customer and – most importantly – consumer data to create consumer profiles for credit scoring and other types of financial risk assessments.[81] The proposal for FIDA Regulation reveals that the EU legislator is well aware of this threat. Recital 18, for instance, admits that:

> Practices that lead to a more sophisticated or comprehensive analysis of certain vulnerable segments of consumers, such as persons with a low income, may increase the risk of unfair conditions or differential pricing practices like the charging of differential premiums.

Further, this recital explains that:

> The potential for exclusion is increased in the provision of products and services that are priced according to the profile of a consumer, notably in credit scoring and the assessment of creditworthiness of natural persons as well for products and services related to the risk assessment and pricing of natural persons in the case of life and health insurance.[82]

[78] SWD (2024) 45 final, 1.

[79] Ferrari 'The Platformisation of Digital Payments' (n 73).

[80] ibid 2.

[81] For more on this problem, especially in the context of the use of AI, see Penedo and Kramcsák 'Can the European Financial Data Space Remove Bias in Financial AI Development? (n 68).

[82] Proposal for FIDA Regulation, Recital 18.

This is striking given the fact that, as was explained in section 3.4, in view of the protection of certain vulnerable individuals, several types of data (such as those that endanger human rights and justice, understood as equal access to certain goods and services) should be excluded from the scope of the FIDA Regulation.

Yet, the processes of digitalisation encroaching upon the modern financial sector, together with the ever more popular trends of data sharing such as those inherently underlying European data space initiatives, create new risks. They increase the chances of discrimination and exploitation of vulnerable customers, despite the legislator's attempts to mitigate that problem by excluding certain types of data from the promoted data sharing schemes. Technology appears to be one step ahead of the regulator, as several observations concerning individuals can be indirectly inferred from other data sources and analytical tools. The situation is exacerbated by the complex and obscure decision-making processes and insufficient levels of digital and financial literacy among customers, which may further expose susceptible customers to privacy and security risks due to the opaque nature of algorithm-driven conclusions.[83]

Given this, the fact that the policy documents discussed in this chapter attribute so considerable a role to the private sector in shaping the new digital financial ecosystem may be somewhat worrisome and so calls for reflection about those whose fundamental rights can potentially be negatively impacted by the modernised regulation of finance. From the justice point of view, the fact that the technological infrastructures critical for a number of financial services' functionalities will largely be the responsibility of the private entities calls into doubt whether they will contribute to the equal allocation of burdens and benefits.

5. Conclusions: The Way Towards Just Distribution of Burdens and Benefits in Regulating Digitalised Spaces

The digitalisation of finance, marked by the advent of data-driven innovations and evolving regulatory frameworks, presents both opportunities and challenges. The EFDS, as part of the broader European data spaces initiative, exemplifies the EU's ambition to harness digitalisation for economic growth while attempting to ensure fairness across a diverse range of stakeholders. However, as this chapter has explored, the path to achieving a just distribution of burdens and benefits remains fraught with complexities.

Historically, the regulation of finance has been a balancing act between promoting innovation and safeguarding against the risks posed by technological advancements. The promises of improved access, efficiency and security have often been juxtaposed against the challenges of protecting privacy and personal

[83] See the discussion in, eg, G Colangelo, 'Open Banking Goes to Washington: Lessons from the EU on Regulatory-Driven Data Sharing Regimes' (2024) 54 *Computer Law & Security Review* 106018, 2.

data, ensuring data security and maintaining regulatory consistency. The EFDS and its components, such as the ESAP, the Strategy on Supervisory Data, and the open finance initiative, represent the EU's latest efforts to navigate these tensions.

Despite these efforts, the chapter highlights that the realisation of justice in the digital financial space is far from guaranteed. The proposed regulatory frameworks, while ambitious, may inadvertently favour certain stakeholders over others, particularly when private entities are entrusted with significant responsibilities in shaping the digital infrastructure. Moreover, the risks associated with the commodification of data, potential financial exclusion, and the reinforcement of existing power asymmetries underscore the need for vigilant and adaptive regulatory strategies.

In conclusion, the pursuit of a just distribution of burdens and benefits in the regulation of digitalised financial spaces requires continuous reflection and recalibration. Policymakers must remain cognisant of the evolving dynamics of the digital economy and strive to create a regulatory environment that not only fosters innovation but also protects the rights and interests of all stakeholders. The success of initiatives like the EFDS will ultimately depend on their ability to address these challenges and deliver on the promise of a fairer, more inclusive, digital financial ecosystem.

8

The Intersection of Regulating Systemic Cyber Risk within Financial Sector Digitalisation and Data Protection

Mind the Gap between Rights to Data Protection and Systemic Cyber Risk

EYUP KUN

1. Introduction

As financial entities (FEs) increasingly rely on digital technologies, their exposure to cyber incidents grows, with vulnerabilities that can escalate quickly and produce widespread effects across industries and regions. The Digital Operational Resilience Act (2022/2554) (DORA)[1] represents a key regulatory effort to strengthen the resilience of FEs by adopting an 'assume breach' approach, ensuring they are equipped to endure and recover from cyber-attacks. The Information and Communication Technology (ICT) risk management measures stipulated by DORA and its Delegated Regulation 2024/1774 can lead the FEs to process personal data.[2] This chapter investigates the intersection of DORA's ICT risk management requirements with the General Data Protection Regulation (2016/679) (GDPR).[3] Specifically, it evaluates whether DORA and the related

[1] Regulation (EU) 2022/2554 of the European Parliament and of the Council of 14 December 2022 on digital operational resilience for the financial sector and amending Regulations (EC) No 1060/2009, (EU) No 648/2012, (EU) No 600/2014, (EU) No 909/2014 and (EU) 2016/1011 (Text with EEA relevance). Available at: https://eur-lex.europa.eu/eli/reg/2022/2554/oj/eng (DORA).

[2] Commission Delegated Regulation (EU) 2024/1774 of 13 March 2024 supplementing Regulation (EU) 2022/2554 of the European Parliament and of the Council with regard to regulatory technical standards specifying ICT risk management tools, methods, processes, and policies and the simplified ICT risk management framework. Available at: https://eur-lex.europa.eu/eli/reg_del/2024/1774/oj/eng.

[3] Regulation (EU) 2016/679 of the European Parliament and of the Council of 27 April 2016 on the protection of natural persons with regard to the processing of personal data and on the free movement

Delegated Regulation 2024/1774 on ICT risk management can establish a legal obligation as a legal basis for the processing of personal data.

1.1. Overview of Digitalisation and Cyber Risk as Systemic Risk in the Financial Sector

The finance industry is widely acknowledged as one of the most digitised sectors within the global economy. Digitisation involves transforming analogue information into digital formats, which has significantly influenced the financial sector. The integration of emerging technologies like artificial intelligence and blockchain has deepened the connection between finance and data.[4]

As a result of the digital transformation, cyber risk stands out as a unique category of risk, differing considerably from traditional risks such as credit, market, liquidity or operational risk.[5] While cyber risk can be categorised under operational risk, it possesses distinct characteristics that set it apart.[6] One key distinction is the speed of dissemination. Cyber incidents can emerge and spread across systems much faster than other types of risks. For instance, during the 2017 NotPetya attack, the Ukrainian banks' systems were almost instantaneously compromised, underscoring the rapid nature of such events due to the interconnectivity of their automated information systems.[7] Additionally, the scale of dissemination makes cyber risk particularly significant, as a major cyber incident can have far-reaching consequences, often crossing geographical boundaries. Second, the interconnectedness of information systems within the financial sector further facilitates the widespread impact of cyber incidents across different sectors and regions, affecting entities that were not the initial targets.[8] A pertinent example is the IT outage in the payment industry in July 2024, which

of such data, and repealing Directive 95/46/EC (Text with EEA relevance). Available at: https://eur-lex.europa.eu/eli/reg/2016/679/oj/eng (General Data Protection Regulation).

[4] DW Arner, GG Castellano, and E Selga, 'Financial Data Governance: The Datafication of Finance, the Rise of Open Banking and the End of the Data Centralization Paradigm' (1 February 2022). Available at: https://papers.ssrn.com/abstract=4040604.

[5] See, for the definition of cyber risk, M Peihani, 'Regulation of Cyber Risk in the Banking System: A Canadian Case Study' (2022) 8(2) *Journal of Financial Regulation* 1, fjac006; I Aldasoro and others, 'Operational and Cyber Risks in the Financial Sector' (BIS 2020). Available at: www.bis.org/publ/work840.htm.

[6] See, for more comprehensive discussion in the context of the use of cloud service providers, E Kun, 'Challenges in Regulating Cloud Service Providers in EU Financial Regulation: From Operational to Systemic Risks, and Examining Challenges of the New Oversight Regime for Critical Cloud Service Providers under the Digital Operational Resilience Act' (2024) 52 *Computer Law & Security Review* 105931.

[7] A Greenberg, 'The Untold Story of NotPetya, the Most Devastating Cyberattack in History' (*Wired*, 22 August 2018). Available at: www.wired.com/story/notpetya-cyberattack-ukraine-russia-code-crashed-the-world.

[8] C Calliess and ABaumgarten, 'Cybersecurity in the EU the Example of the Financial Sector: A Legal Perspective' (2020) 21 *German Law Journal* 1149.

disrupted credit card transactions across multiple regions and industries, illustrating the pervasive nature of cyber risk.[9]

Considering the factors previously discussed, cyber risks are considered as systemic risk within the financial sector.[10] Systemic risk refers to the possibility that an economic shock, such as the failure of a market or an institution, triggers a cascade of events leading to the collapse of multiple markets or institutions, substantial losses for FEs, or an increase in the cost of capital alongside reduced availability. These scenarios are often accompanied by significant volatility in financial markets. Traditionally, systemic risk in the financial system has been associated with inherent financial risks like credit and liquidity.[11] Nevertheless, cyber risks are increasingly recognised for their potential to induce systemic disruptions. For instance, a cyber-attack can disrupt the operations of financial services on a global scale, affecting critical systems such as payment infrastructures. In a 2020 report addressing systemic cyber risk, the European Systemic Risk Board (ESRB) highlighted the extensive interconnectedness among FEs, markets and infrastructures.[12] The interdependencies of their ICT systems present significant systemic vulnerabilities. Cyber incidents have the potential to rapidly propagate across the approximately 22,000 FEs within the European Union, transmitting vulnerabilities through financial transmission channels. This could lead to liquidity shortages, cause a loss of confidence in financial markets, and ultimately threaten the stability of the entire financial system. An attack targeting a systemically important financial institution, or even multiple non-critical institutions that are closely linked, can give rise to systemic risk. Similarly, cyber-attacks on entities that are not deemed systemically important might initially appear isolated. However, the interconnected nature of the financial system can lead to cascading effects, particularly when critical infrastructures are compromised.[13] The ESRB provided a notable example of the ION Group ransomware attack in January 2023, which would have caused a systemic risk if appropriate measures had not been taken.[14] The LockBit ransomware gang targeted ION Group, which provides

[9] L Winchester, 'Global IT Outage Takes Banking Services Offline as Card Payments Hit with Issues' *The Mirror* (19 July 2024). Available at: www.mirror.co.uk/money/breaking-global-outage-takes-banking-33278652.

[10] The concept of systemic cyber risk is developed in the EU by the European Systemic Risk Board, which is responsible for dealing with systemic risk issues at the EU level. See European Systemic Risk Board, *Systemic Cyber Risk* (Publications Office of the EU 2020). Available at: https://data.europa.eu/doi/10.2849/566567.

[11] VV Acharya, 'A Theory of Systemic Risk and Design of Prudential Bank Regulation' (2009) 5 *Journal of Financial Stability* 224.

[12] European Systemic Risk Board, *Systemic Cyber Risk* (n 10).

[13] See, for different examples, ibid; see, for another example of a systemic cyber risk scenario, SJ Ruffle and others, 'Sybil Logic Bomb Cyber Catastrophe Stress Test Scenario' (Centre for Risk Studies, University of Cambridge 2014). Available at: www.jbs.cam.ac.uk/faculty-research/centres/risk/publications/technology-and-space/sybil-logic-bomb-cyber-catastrophe-stress-test-scenario/.

[14] European Systemic Risk Board, *Advancing Macroprudential Tools for Cyber Resilience: Operational Policy Tools* (Publications Office of the EU 2024). Available at: https://data.europa.eu/doi/10.2849/05420.

automation software for derivatives trading and clearing.[15] The attack disabled ION Group's derivatives services, forcing over 40 banks, hedge funds and brokerages to process trades manually and submit estimated reports. The lack of timely information from ION Group heightened concerns among regulators and clients, raising fears of systemic risk. However, contingency measures, including deadline extensions by exchanges and clearinghouses, helped mitigate the impact and prevent a broader loss of confidence. Although the incident did not escalate into a systemic event, it highlights how disruptions at a third-party service provider can significantly affect the financial system.

1.2. DORA as Micro-prudential Regulatory Response to Cyber Risk as Systemic Risk

Considering the systemic cyber risk aspect of digital transformation, the European Commission proposed DORA on 24 September 2020. Adopted on 28 November 2022, DORA took effect on 17 January 2025. DORA, as understood from its title, is fundamentally centred around the concept of an 'assume breach' mentality, which is closely tied to the broader notion of resilience.[16] This approach acknowledges that, despite the best preventive measures, breaches and cyber incidents are inevitable in a highly interconnected and digitised financial ecosystem.

DORA primarily functions as a micro-prudential tool, targeting individual FEs to strengthen their cybersecurity resilience.[17] DORA's application, according to Article 2, extends beyond just credit and payment institutions; it also applies to a wide range of financial sector participants, including investment firms, electronic money institutions, insurance and reinsurance entities, and ICT third-party service providers. DORA's scope, as outlined in Article 1, is divided into four key pillars. The first pillar addresses cybersecurity requirements, including ICT risk management, reporting of ICT-related incidents, digital operational resilience testing, and the sharing of information among FEs. The second pillar pertains to the contractual provision between ICT third-party service providers and FEs to mitigate the third-party risk in particular cloud services.[18] The third pillar establishes oversight rules for critical

[15] H Robertson, 'ION Brings Clients Back Online after Ransomware Attack – Source' *Reuters* (8 February 2023). Available at: www.reuters.com/technology/ion-starts-bring-clients-back-online-after-ransomware-attack-source-2023-02-07/.

[16] See, for analysis of the use of the concept of resilience in critical infrastructure protection in the EU, C Pursiainen and E Kytömaa, 'From European Critical Infrastructure Protection to the Resilience of European Critical Entities: What Does It Mean?' (2023) 8 *Sustainable and Resilient Infrastructure* 85; see, for another critical analysis of the concept of cyber resilience as a legal aspiration, LA Bygrave, 'Cyber Resilience versus Cybersecurity as Legal Aspiration' (10 October 2022). Available at: https://papers.ssrn.com/abstract=4243195.

[17] See European Systemic Risk Board, *Mitigating Systemic Cyber Risk* (January 2022). Available at: www.esrb.europa.eu/pub/pdf/reports/esrb.SystemiCyberRisk.220127~b6655fa027.en.pdf.

[18] See, for the overall analysis of DORA in the literature, M Schellemans and E Kun, 'Cyberresilience in the Financial Sector: Overall Analysis of the Digital Operational Resilience Act' (2024) 2023(92–93) *Revue du Droit des Technologies de l'Information* 100; Kun 'Challenges in Regulating Cloud Service

ICT third-party service providers that offer services to FEs.[19] Finally, the fourth pillar focuses on the rules governing cooperation between relevant authorities.

By imposing stringent cybersecurity requirements, DORA aims to enhance the operational resilience of FEs in three key areas: it delineates clear risk management responsibilities, improves coordination in handling cybersecurity risks and incidents, and establishes an oversight management framework for critical ICT third-party providers, thereby regulating third-party risks. The uniform application of these requirements across all FEs is intended to reduce systemic cybersecurity risks by improving the security posture of individual FEs.

1.3. Processing of Personal Data for Dealing with Systemic Risk under DORA and its Compatibility with the GDPR

The cybersecurity measures at micro-prudential levels (DORA and Delegated Regulation 2024/1774) for addressing systemic cyber risk can be a reason for the processing of personal data. For instance, at the micro-prudential level, anomaly detection technologies,[20] which rely on processing various types of personal data, are anticipated to be deployed to enhance cybersecurity. Thus, pursuing cybersecurity objectives to mitigate systemic risk under DORA would constitute an interference with the right to personal data protection, particularly when personal data is processed as part of risk management.

Personal data, as defined by Article 4(1) of the GDPR, includes any information[21] that is related[22] to an identified or identifiable natural person.[23] Any such processing must adhere to EU law, particularly the Charter of Fundamental Rights of the

Providers in EU Financial Regulation' (n 6); K Parchimowicz, 'Do Not Get Lost in the Cloud: How EU Financial Institutions Could Avoid Legal and Practical Problems with Cloud Services Arising Under DORA' (20 June 2023). Available at: https://papers.ssrn.com/abstract=4486264; HS Scott, 'The E.U.'s Digital Operational Resilience Act: Cloud Services & Financial Companies' (Social Science Research Network 2021) SSRN Scholarly Paper 3904113 Available at: https://papers.ssrn.com/abstract=3904113.

[19] See the discussion on the problems of the supervisory framework, Schellemans and Kun 'Cyberresilience in the Financial Sector' (n 6); CP Buttigieg and B Brunelli Zimmermann, 'The Digital Operational Resilience Act: Challenges and Some Reflections on the Adequacy of Europe's Architecture for Financial Supervision' (17 May 2024). Available at: https://papers.ssrn.com/abstract=4831717.

[20] VP Janeja (ed), 'Anomaly Detection for Cybersecurity' in *Data Analytics for Cybersecurity* (Cambridge University Press 2022). Available at: www.cambridge.org/core/books/data-analytics-for-cybersecurity/anomaly-detection-for-cybersecurity/D87EB27F10019F15BDE6FEE1F9CB6BCC.

[21] See, for how the element of information is broadly constructed in the GDPR, Case C-604/22 *IAB Europe v Gegevensbeschermingsautoriteit* [2024] ECLI:EU:C:2024:214, para 36; see, for a critique on the effectiveness of this approach, O Lynskey, 'Complete and Effective Data Protection' (2023) 76(1) *Current Legal Problems* 297. Available at: https://doi.org/10.1093/clp/cuad009.

[22] See, for the role of relatability in a risk-based approach towards the definition of personal data, V Rupp and M von Grafenstein, 'Clarifying "Personal Data" and the Role of Anonymisation in Data Protection Law: Including and Excluding Data from the Scope of the GDPR (More Clearly) through Refining the Concept of Data Protection' (2024) 52 *Computer Law & Security Review* 105932. See Case C-434/16 *Peter Nowak v Data Protection* Commissioner [2017] ECLI: EU:C:2017:994.

[23] N Purtova, 'The Law of Everything. Broad Concept of Personal Data and Future of EU Data Protection Law' (2018) 10 *Law, Innovation and Technology* 40.

European Union (the Charter), which protects privacy (Article 7)[24] and data protection (Article 8).[25] Furthermore, any legal framework that requires personal data processing must meet the standards of Article 52(1) of the Charter, ensuring that any limitations on rights are legally justified, necessary and proportionate. The Court of Justice of the European Union (CJEU) has affirmed that data processing impacts both privacy and data protection rights, and any limitations must be clearly justified with a precise legal basis that is foreseeable to those affected.[26] For such an obligation to constitute a valid legal basis, it must meet certain requirements as laid out in Articles 6(1)(c) and 6(3) of the GDPR.[27] Article 6(1)(c) of the GDPR allows personal data processing when it is necessary for compliance with a legal obligation. Specifically, the obligation must be grounded in Union law or the law of a Member State to which the data controller is subject. The legal basis must also clearly define the objective and purpose of the data processing,[28] ensuring that it is specified, necessary and proportionate.[29] In addition, it should delineate more specifically the conditions of data processing, categories of data that need to be processed, purpose limitation and data retention periods to respect the right to data protection.

1.4. The Gap in the Literature and Research Question: DORA and Delegated Regulation 2024/1774 as a Source of Legal Obligation for Personal Data Processing

The critical question that arises is whether and to what extent the cybersecurity requirements under DORA and Delegated Regulation 2024/1774 constitute a

[24] M Brkan, 'The Essence of the Fundamental Rights to Privacy and Data Protection: Finding the Way through the Maze of the CJEU's Constitutional Reasoning' (2019) 20 *German Law Journal* 864; G González Fuster, 'Study on the Essence of the Fundamental Rights to Privacy and to Protection of Personal Data (EDPS 2021/0932)'. Available at: https://edps.europa.eu/system/files/2023-11/edps-vub-study_on_the_essence_of_fundamental_rights_to_privacy_and_to_protection_of_personal_data_en.pdf.

[25] G González Fuster, *The Emergence of Personal Data Protection as a Fundamental Right of the EU*, vol 16 (Springer International Publishing 2014). Available at: https://link.springer.com/10.1007/978-3-319-05023-2; González Fuster 'Study on the Essence of the Fundamental Rights to Privacy' (n 24); Brkan 'The Essence of the Fundamental Rights to Privacy and Data Protection' (n 24); Dara Hallinan, 'The Essence of Data Protection: Essence as a Normative Pivot' (2021) 12 *European Journal of Law and Technology 1*. Available at: https://ejlt.org/index.php/ejlt/article/view/767.

[26] See, for comprehensive case law analysis of right to private life and data protection, EDPS, 'Guidance for Co-Legislators on Key Elements of Legislative Proposals', Draft for Public Consultation (2024). Available at: www.edps.europa.eu/data-protection/our-work/publications/guidelines/2024-01-16-guidance-co-legislators-key-elements-legislative-proposals_en.

[27] Case C-319/22 *Gesamtverband Autoteile-Handel eV v Scania CV AB* [2023] ECLI:EU:C:2023:837, paras 46–49. See W Kotschy, 'Article 6 Lawfulness of Processing' in C Kuner and others (eds), *The EU General Data Protection Regulation (GDPR): A Commentary* (Oxford University Press 2020). Available at: https://doi.org/10.1093/oso/9780198826491.003.0035.

[28] See, for the importance of the purpose definition for the legal basis, R Becker and others, 'Purpose Definition as a Crucial Step for Determining the Legal Basis under the GDPR: Implications for Scientific Research' (2024) 11(1) *Journal of Law and the Biosciences* lsae001.

[29] Case C-319/22 *Gesamtverband Autoteile-Handel eV v Scania CV AB* [2023] ECLI:EU:C:2023:837, paras 57–59.

legal obligation as provides a basis under Article 6(1)(c) of the GDPR for the processing of personal data. While the legal basis for personal data processing for cybersecurity purposes is discussed in the context of the Network and Information Security Directive (2) (NIS 2 Directive) by scholars,[30] the specific context of DORA and its relevant provisions are not discussed in the literature. This chapter aims to fill this gap in the literature by providing a response to the question of there being a legal basis for personal data processing by FEs in the cybersecurity context under DORA. By showing that DORA does not provide a legal obligation for personal data processing under Article 6(1)(c) of the GDPR, this chapter suggests legitimate interest may be used as a legal basis under Article 6(1)(f).

To answer the research question, this chapter will first provide a description of ICT risk-management measures and how these can contain personal data processing (section 2). In section 3, the focus will shift to evaluating whether DORA and Delegated Regulation 2024/1774 create a legal obligation that can be used as a legal basis for personal data processing. The discussion will be grounded in one concrete example: the use of anomaly detection technologies in DORA. Through this example, the chapter will explore how a legal basis for personal data processing might be established within the framework of these regulatory responses, offering a nuanced understanding of the interplay between cybersecurity measures and data protection requirements in the context of DORA.

The choice of anomaly detection technologies is justified by two reasons. First, it highlights the practical challenges of implementing cybersecurity. For instance, anomaly detection technologies often require the collection and analysis of user behaviour data, such as login patterns, transaction histories or access logs. These activities raise critical questions about the lawful basis for processing personal data under the GDPR, the proportionality of such processing, and the safeguards necessary to balance operational resilience with individual rights. Second, anomaly detection technologies are directly linked to DORA's objective of enhancing the digital operational resilience of FEs by ensuring they can promptly detect and mitigate cyber risks. By focusing on a widely used cybersecurity tool, the case provides a tangible context to evaluate whether DORA and its associated Delegated Regulation effectively addresses systemic risks without undermining data protection principles.

[30] See, for the discussion in the context of the NIS Directive, A Cormack, 'Processing Data to Protect Data: Resolving the Breach Detection Paradox' (2020) 17(2) *SCRIPTed* 197. Available at: https://script-ed.org/?p=3883; see C Sullivan and E Burger, '"In the Public Interest": The Privacy Implications of International Business-to-Business Sharing of Cyber-Threat Intelligence' (2017) 33 *Computer Law & Security Review* 14; P Rataj, 'Botnet Defense Under EU Data Protection Law' (2025) 56 *Computer Law & Security Review* 106080. Available at: https://doi.org/10.1016/j.clsr.2024.106080; E Kun, 'Searching for the Appropriate Legal Basis for Personal Data Processing for Cybersecurity Purposes under the NIS 2 Directive: Legal Obligation and/or Legitimate Interest?' (2025) 56 *Computer Law & Security Review* 106098. Available at: www.sciencedirect.com/science/article/pii/S0267364924001638#cit_73.

2. Overview of Personal Data Processing for ICT Risk Management in DORA and Delegated Regulation 2024/1774

This section aims to show how personal data processing is embedded in ICT risk management as stipulated by DORA and its Delegated Regulation 2024/1774. It briefly describes ICT risk-management requirements and possible personal data processing while implementing these requirements.

As part of ICT risk management, DORA requires the management body to be ultimately responsible for overseeing and controlling ICT risk management under Article 5 of DORA. This body is tasked with defining, approving and managing the implementation of the ICT risk management framework. Members of this body are required to undergo regular training to maintain the necessary expertise and understanding of ICT risks and their impact on the financial sector.[31]

In addition, FEs need to create a robust ICT risk management framework. This framework, guided by the management body, should be thoroughly documented and designed to address and mitigate ICT risks, ensuring strong digital operational resilience.[32] Article 3 of Delegated Regulation 2024/1774 outlines comprehensive requirements for FEs to manage ICT risks effectively, emphasising risk tolerance, treatment and acceptance. The framework requires a structured risk assessment procedure, identifying vulnerabilities and threats affecting ICT systems and business functions, and employing indicators to measure their impact and likelihood. FEs must implement risk treatment measures to mitigate identified ICT risks, ensuring alignment with defined risk-tolerance levels, while monitoring and evaluating the effectiveness of these measures. For residual risks that remain after treatment, entities must document and justify their acceptance, assigning roles for managing risks that exceed tolerance levels. Monitoring processes in ICT risk management must enable prompt detection of changes in the ICT risk landscape, internal vulnerabilities and threats. Additionally, the risk management strategy must adapt to changes in business and digital resilience strategies. This approach ensures ongoing alignment with strategic objectives while addressing evolving ICT risks comprehensively.

Personal data processing for ICT risk management under Article 6(1) of DORA and Article 3(1) of Delegated Regulation 2024/1774 would involve maintaining a database of employee roles and access privileges to enforce role-based access controls.[33] Under Article 3 of Delegated Regulation 2024/1774, such

[31] DORA, art 5(4). Managerial board responsibility is a new requirement in cybersecurity requirements; see, for the problems regarding the involvement of managerial boards in cybersecurity issues in the financial sector, E Kiesow Cortez and M Dekker, 'A Corporate Governance Approach to Cybersecurity Risk Disclosure' (2022) 13(3) *European Journal of Risk Regulation* 443.

[32] DORA, art 6(1).

[33] RS Sandhu, 'Role-Based Access Control' in MV Zelkowitz (ed), *Advances in Computers*, vol 46 (Elsevier 1998).

a system aligns with the requirement to mitigate ICT risks through structured risk-treatment measures and ensure that access to sensitive ICT systems is limited to authorised individuals based on their roles. In this case, personal data such as employee names, job titles, departments and associated access rights is processed to manage and enforce access control policies. This database allows FEs to ensure that only employees with a legitimate business need can access specific ICT systems or sensitive information, reducing the risk of accidental or malicious breaches.

FEs must identify, classify and document all critical ICT-related business functions, risk sources and physical equipment, as well as processes reliant on ICT third-party service providers.[34] Annual reviews of potential risk scenarios are required to assess their impact on FEs.[35] According to Article 4(1) of Delegated Regulation 2024/1774, the ICT asset management policy, as mandated by Article 9(2) of DORA, requires FEs to develop, document and implement a comprehensive framework for managing ICT assets. This policy must oversee the lifecycle of ICT assets, as classified under Article 8(1) of DORA, and maintain detailed records, including unique identifiers, physical or logical locations, ownership, classification, supported business functions, and continuity requirements such as recovery time and point objectives.[36]

To comply with Article 4(1) of Delegated Regulation 2024/1774 and to ensure the comprehensive lifecycle management of ICT assets as per Article 8(1) of DORA, FEs may need to process personal data. The ICT asset management could involve tracking user interaction data,[37] which can be considered as personal data, with critical ICT systems to identify and classify business functions and risk sources. For instance, FEs could analyse personal data such as user IDs, system login timestamps, and specific system access logs to determine which processes or business functions are most reliant on a particular ICT asset. For example, if multiple users access a core trading platform during peak hours, the system's criticality can be inferred from this usage pattern.

As part of protection and prevention measures within the ICT risk management framework, FEs must design and implement robust security policies, procedures and tools to maintain the availability, authenticity, integrity and confidentiality of data, especially in critical systems.[38] Appropriate ICT solutions must be used to secure data transfer, prevent data loss or unauthorised access, and protect against risks from poor management or human error.[39] Additionally, entities should

[34] DORA, art 8(1)–(5). See, for asset criticality and risk prediction for cybersecurity, HI Kure and others, 'Asset Criticality and Risk Prediction for an Effective Cybersecurity Risk Management of Cyber-Physical System' (2022) 34(1) *Neural Computing and Applications* 493.

[35] DORA, art 8(6).

[36] Delegated Regulation 2024/1774, art 4.

[37] A Adebayo, MS Sharif, and W Elmedany, 'The Role of Artificial Intelligence in Asset Management of Enterprise Systems' (International Conference on Innovation and Intelligence for Informatics, Computing, and Technologies (3ICT), Sakheer, Bahrain, 2022) 214–20, doi:10.1109/3ICT56508.2022.9990666.

[38] DORA, art 9(1)–(2).

[39] ibid art 9(3).

establish a sound network management structure, with mechanisms for isolating affected systems during cyber-attacks.

An example of personal data processing within this context involves monitoring user activity logs to prevent unauthorised access and mitigate risks arising from human error in critical systems. FEs can implement logging tools that collect and analyse personal data such as user IDs, timestamps of activities, access permissions, and detailed records of actions performed within critical systems (eg, file access, data transfers or system configuration changes). For instance, if a user attempts to access restricted data or transfer sensitive files without proper authorisation, this activity can be flagged and stopped in real time, preventing potential data breaches. Such monitoring also aids in maintaining data integrity and authenticity by identifying and reversing erroneous or malicious changes caused by human error.

FEs are required to implement mechanisms for the prompt detection of anomalous activities, such as ICT network performance issues and ICT-related incidents, while also identifying potential critical failure points.[40] These detection mechanisms must be regularly tested and should include multiple layers of control, with defined alert thresholds that trigger ICT incident response processes. Anomaly detection technologies in cybersecurity refer to the process of identifying observations or groups of observations within a dataset that exhibits substantial deviation from the normally expected patterns.[41] The anomaly in a dataset refers to a unique and contradictory observation that deviates from the established norm. In comparison to other clusters, this anomaly arises from its relatively larger size and greater distance from the others. Excessive network traffic on an FE application may suggest an abnormal period of network traffic in comparison to other locations. These technologies can be used to ensure a prompt response to ICT-related incidents. Furthermore, anomaly detection with respect to ICT network performance can involve using real-time sentiment analysis of IT helpdesk interactions to detect early signs of ICT network performance issues or incidents. FEs could monitor personal data, such as employee-submitted support tickets, chat transcripts or voice recordings from IT helpdesk interactions, to identify recurring complaints about system slowdowns, connectivity issues or unresponsive applications. By applying natural language-processing techniques to analyse the sentiment and frequency of these communications, the system can detect patterns suggesting potential critical failure points. For instance, a surge in frustrated or urgent language in helpdesk tickets might indicate widespread network latency or an emerging system outage, prompting immediate investigation and action.

[40] ibid art 10. The anomaly detection technologies are further discussed in section 3.

[41] VP Janeja (ed), 'Anomaly Detection Methods' in *Data Analytics for Cybersecurity* (Cambridge University Press 2022). Available at: www.cambridge.org/core/books/data-analytics-for-cybersecurity/anomaly-detection-methods/560540A339A8F145EED1C061CFB05632. See, for a comprehensive assessment of the risks of using insider threat detection technologies as part of anomalous detection technologies, W Christl, 'Employees as Risks' (Cracked Labs 2024). Available at: https://crackedlabs.org/dl/CrackedLabs_Christl_SecurityRiskProfiling.pdf.

This detection mechanism adds a human-centric layer of anomaly detection, complementing technical monitoring tools.

FEs must develop comprehensive ICT business continuity[42] and backup policies as part of their overall ICT risk management strategy.[43] This policy should ensure that critical functions continue to operate, that ICT incidents are responded to effectively, and that recovery occurs quickly. The policy must include written plans, procedures and mechanisms for limiting damage, communicating with others and managing crises. To ensure secure backups of critical systems and data, FEs could implement a backup solution where encryption keys are generated and managed dynamically based on personal data such as user IDs, authentication credentials, and role-based permissions. For instance, when a user initiates a system backup, their unique ID and access level determine the encryption key used to secure the data. This ensures that only authorised users can decrypt and restore the backup, adding a personalised layer of security. Additionally, metadata from backup logs may include personal data, such as user activity timestamps and file ownership details, to track who initiated or accessed a backup. This data helps in auditing and accountability, ensuring compliance with policies and identifying unauthorised attempts to access backup files.

3. Cybersecurity and Data Protection Objectives: Is there a Clear Alignment with Data Protection Rules?

This section discusses one case study where personal data processing is at stake to mitigate systemic cyber risk in the financial sector, that is, the requirement for FEs to use anomaly detection systems to detect cybersecurity incidents. The following subsections evaluate to what extent these requirements could constitute a legal obligation to process personal data for the purpose of cybersecurity.

3.1. Anomalous Detection Technologies as ICT Risk Management: Right to Data Protection and Right to Privacy at Stake

The cybersecurity measures outlined in DORA and Delegated Regulation 2024/1774 at the micro-prudential level aim to address systemic cyber risks, often

[42] For the comprehensive requirements of business continuity plans, see DORA, art 11. See, for the role of business continuity management from a cybersecurity perspective, T Savolainen and others, 'Business Continuity Management of Critical Infrastructures from the Cybersecurity Perspective' (IEEE Global Engineering Education Conference (EDUCON), Kos Island, Greece, 2024) 1–6, doi:10.1109/EDUCON60312.2024.10578811.

[43] For the backup policies, see DORA, art 12.

necessitating the processing of personal data, as discussed in section 2 of this chapter. For instance, anomaly detection technologies, which analyse various types of personal data, are expected to play a critical role in cybersecurity. However, such processing must align with the GDPR, particularly regarding the requirement for a legal basis under Article 6.[44] Under the GDPR, Article 6(1)(c) permits personal data processing when it is necessary to comply with a legal obligation established by Union or Member State law. This legal basis must articulate the objective and purpose of the processing, ensuring it is specified, necessary and proportionate. Furthermore, it must define the conditions for processing, including the data categories, purpose limitations, and retention periods, to safeguard the right to data protection. These requirements aim to balance cybersecurity objectives with fundamental rights, ensuring lawful and transparent personal data processing.

3.1.1. Logging Information in Detection of Anomalous Activities: Assessment of Logging Information as Personal Data

Article 10(1) of DORA requires that FEs must have mechanisms to promptly detect anomalous activities, including ICT network performance issues and incidents. Detection mechanisms, according to Article 10(2), must support multiple layers of control, define alert thresholds and criteria for triggering and initiating ICT-related incident response processes, and include automatic alert mechanisms. For further specification, Article 23 of Delegated Regulation 2024/1774 explicitly sets out the criteria for these mechanisms in anomaly detection systems. These mechanisms should allow the FEs to collect and analyse various internal and external factors, including logs, information from business and ICT functions, user reports, potential cyber threats, and notifications from third-party ICT service providers.

Logging information constitutes an essential part of anomalous detection activities. Article 12 of Delegated Regulation 2024/1774 establishes a relation between logging and anomalous detection activities and specifically sets the scope of logging. According to Article 12(2), FEs shall implement logging measures (which includes logging information); identify the specific events to be logged; determine the retention period for these logs; and establish measures to secure and manage the data based on the purpose of the logs. Article 12(2)(c) delineates the scope of logging information, including logical and physical access control, ICT operations and network traffic activities.

It is crucial to assess whether logging information constitutes personal data. This involves a consideration of each element of personal data as defined by Article 4(1) of the GDPR: 'any information'; 'relating to'; 'identifiability'; and 'natural person'. The first element, 'any information', refers to the broad notion of any

[44] See, for the appropriate legal basis for personal data processing to take cybersecurity measures stipulated by the NIS 2 Directive, Kun 'Searching for the Appropriate Legal Basis for Personal Data Processing' (n 30).

types of information. In the context of anomaly detection, data being analysed can encompass a wide range of types, from objective facts to subjective assessments of a user. For instance, logs of network traffic or user activities could include both quantifiable metrics (eg, time and volume of data transfer) and qualitative data (eg, user behaviour patterns). For this reason, the condition of 'any information' is met.

The 'relating to' or relatability element has three aspects: content (information about a person, like financial status), purpose (the objective of detecting the anomalous activity of an FE employee) and result (information used in a disciplinary procedure).[45] The CJEU upheld this concept in the *Nowak* case, where exam papers and evaluations were deemed personal data of the individual who took the exam.[46] This analysis suggests that relating to a person goes beyond mere content. As logging information is aimed at detecting the anomalous activities of an individual on the ICT systems, it meets the requirement of relatability.

Identifiability in personal data concerns whether an individual can be directly or indirectly identified. This concept is crucial in distinguishing between personal and anonymised data.[47] The assessment of identifiability must consider 'all reasonably likely means' that could identify a person, based on factors such as technology, cost and time.[48] In the *Breyer* case, a website user's dynamic IP address was deemed personal data because the website provider, though lacking direct access to additional data, could potentially identify the user through legal means with the internet service provider's assistance.[49] Furthermore, the General Court's decision in *SRB v EDPS* highlights the line between anonymity and pseudonymity, emphasising that identifiability hinges on the ability to associate data with an individual through additional information.[50] Overall, identifiability is a dynamic, context-dependent criterion, influenced by a risk-based approach under the GDPR. Data should be treated as personal when there is a realistic risk of identification, but if the risk is minimal, it can be considered non-personal or anonymised data, outside the scope of personal data protection. When it comes to the logging information that is used in anomalous detection technologies, it meets the requirement of identifiability as the logging information aims to identify malicious activities within the ICT systems of FEs; by using additional information such as IP addresses, the FEs can identify who initiated the anomalous activity within its ICT systems, in particular posing an insider threat within their organisation.[51]

[45] Article 29 Working Party, 'Opinion 4/2007 on the Concept of Personal Data' (20 June 2007) WP 136.

[46] Case C-434/16 *Peter Nowak v Data Protection Commissioner* [2017] ECLI: EU:C:2017:994.

[47] M Finck and F Pallas, 'They Who Must Not Be Identified: Distinguishing Personal from Non-Personal Data under the GDPR' (2020) 10 *International Data Privacy Law* 11.

[48] Recital 26 of the GDPR.

[49] Case C-582/16 *Patrick Breyer v Bundesrepublic Deutschland* [2016] ECLI: EU:C:2016:779.

[50] Case T-557/20 *SRB v EDPS* [2023] ECLI:EU:T:2023:219. See, for a similar interpretation by the CJEU, Case C-319/22 *Gesamtverband Autoteile-Handel eV v Scania CV AB* [2023] ECLI:EU:C:2023:837, paras 46–49.

[51] Christl 'Employees as Risks' (n 41).

The fourth element, 'natural person', specifies that personal data must relate to living individuals, excluding legal entities and deceased persons.[52] In the context of anomaly detection, this means that the focus must be on data that can be linked to individuals, such as employees, customers or users. As the anomaly detection technologies monitor the activities of employees or customers, logging information contains the fourth element of personal data definition.

In conclusion, the processing of logging information within anomaly detection technologies to mitigate systemic cyber risk in FEs constitutes personal data processing. The following subsection examines whether DORA and Delegated Regulation 2024/1774 could provide a legal basis, via a legal obligation, to process personal data.

3.1.2. Do DORA and Delegated Regulation 2024/1774 Constitute a Legal Obligation to Process Logging Information as Part of Anomalous Detection Technologies?

DORA, in Article 45 and legally non-binding Recital 34, refers to the GDPR for personal data processing in relation to information sharing for cybersecurity purposes, but it remains silent regarding the processing of personal data for ICT risk management measures, including anomaly detection technologies.[53]

It can be argued that Article 10 of DORA and Delegated Regulation 2024/1774 – which mandates the use of anomaly detection technologies and the logging of data for such purposes – would constitute a legal obligation that provides a legal basis for personal data processing under the GDPR, particularly Articles 6(1)(c) and 6(3), which allow for personal data processing when it is necessary for compliance with a legal obligation to which the data controller is subject.

DORA does specifically mention the use of anomalous detection activities, but it leaves the scope of these activities to Delegated Regulation 2024/1774; Article 15(1)(c) establishes a framework requiring FEs to employ anomaly detection technologies and log data as part of their cybersecurity and ICT risk management strategies. It is clear that the objectives of these provisions are to enhance the resilience of FEs against ICT-related incidents, including cyber-attacks, by promptly

[52] See for the analysis of the assessment of exclusion of legal and deceased persons from the scope of the right to data protection, D Erdos, 'Dead Ringers? Legal Persons and the Deceased in European Data Protection Law' (Social Science Research Network 2020) SSRN Scholarly Paper 3599852. Available at: https://papers.ssrn.com/abstract=3599852; B van der Sloot, 'Data Protection Rights for Legal Persons' (2023) 9 *European Data Protection Law Review* 264; B van der Sloot, 'Do Privacy and Data Protection Rules Apply to Legal Persons and Should They? A Proposal for a Two-Tiered System' (2015) 31 *Computer Law and Security Review* 26.

[53] In comparison to DORA, the NIS 2 Directive has a reference to the GDPR for personal data processing by essential and important entities while taking cybersecurity measures, see art 2(14) of the NIS 2 Directive as well as Recital 121 of the NIS 2 Directive. However, for the critical analysis of this provision and potential legal basis for personal data processing under the NIS 2 Directive, see Kun (n 30).

detecting and responding to anomalies that could threaten the stability of the financial system. These objectives align with broader public interest,[54] such as ensuring the security and integrity of financial services, which are explicitly stated in the operative text of DORA and the Delegated Regulation. This explicitness satisfies the GDPR requirement that the purpose of processing be clearly outlined in the law.

Delegated Regulation 2024/1774 explicitly define the roles and responsibilities of implementing anomalous detection activities, thereby fulfilling the GDPR's requirement that laws imposing data processing obligations must define the roles of data controllers and processors. This ensures that entities involved in processing personal data are fully aware of their responsibilities, including the obligation to secure data and set the retention period of logging data under Article 12(2) of Delegated Regulation 2024/1774. The processing of personal data under DORA and Delegated Regulation 2024/1774 is designed to benefit the general public by maintaining the security and stability of the financial system, a critical infrastructure within the EU. Thus, it justifies the process of personal data.

Personal data processing shall also be necessary and proportionate to the objective pursued. DORA's requirements for logging and anomaly detection would be considered as proportionate and necessary to achieve the intended public interest objectives – namely, the prevention of and response to ICT-related incidents that could have significant financial and societal impacts. Logging measures are essential to identify and mitigate potential threats, with no less intrusive means available to achieve the same level of protection and resilience. Moreover, Delegated Regulation 2024/1774 is designed to protect the data processed within these systems by setting out clear guidelines for data retention and access controls. These safeguards help ensure that the processing is not only lawful and necessary but also proportionate to the risks involved.

While the line of reasoning discussed until now reaches the conclusion that Article 10 of DORA and the relevant provisions of Delegated Regulation 2024/1774 provide a sufficient legal basis for the processing of personal data under the GDPR, this conclusion can be challenged by the following counter-argument. This counter-argument hinges on the fact that Article 10 of DORA does not explicitly mention logging or the necessity of processing personal data at this Regulation level (Basic Act), instead deferring significant details to be addressed in a Delegated Regulation. This raises concerns about whether such provisions can establish a sufficient legal obligation under the GDPR for data processing. Article 10 of DORA primarily addresses the resilience of FEs' digital operations, focusing on detecting, managing and mitigating ICT-related risks. However, it omits specific references to logging systems or the processing of personal data as part of these mechanisms.

[54] For the notion of public interest and its relation with cybersecurity in general in the GDPR, see S Bu-Pasha, 'Legal Aspects, Public Interest, and Legitimate Interest in Processing Personal Data to Operate Autonomous Buses in the Regular Transportation System' (2022) 5(5) *Security and Privacy* 1. Available at: https://doi.org/10.1002/spy2.247; Sullivan and Burger 'In the Public Interest' (n 30).

While Recital 41 of the GDPR, considering its legally non-binding nature, states that 'legal basis' does not necessarily mean that a legislative act (ie Basic Act at the EU level) shall be adopted to establish a legal obligation, the distinction between interference with fundamental rights by Basic Acts (eg DORA) and by Implementing or Delegated Acts (eg Delegated Regulation 2024/1774) in the case law of the CJEU needs to be clarified. According to Article 290 of the Treaty on the Functioning of the European Union, essential elements of legislation, which involve significant political decisions, must be reserved for the Basic Act.[55] The CJEU has emphasised that such essential elements cannot be delegated to the Commission through implementing or delegated powers.[56] As such, critical decisions impact fundamental rights (data protection in this example) to 'such an the extent that involvement of EU legislature is required'.[57] The question is then to what extent the processing of personal data as part of processing of logging information can be considered an interference to such an extent that involvement of EU legislature is required. The seriousness of interference with the right to data protection is critical here.[58] Detection of anomalous activities involves processing the logging information of all individuals' access to an FE's ICT systems and automated processing of data to determine the anomalous activity, as well as monitoring individuals' behaviours.[59] For this reason, the involvement of the EU legislature is necessary to establish a legal obligation to process personal data for the detection of anomalous activities within FEs to mitigate systemic cyber risk.

This lack of specificity and clarity under DORA may undermine there being a standalone legal basis under Article 10 of DORA and the relevant Delegated Regulation 2024/1774 for personal data processing. Recitals 19 and 30 of the Delegated Regulation 2024/1774 refer to the GDPR. However, these recitals do not establish personal data processing as a legal obligation. Recitals can aid in interpreting legislation but do not carry the same legal weight as the operative provisions and cannot substitute for the clear legal basis required by the GDPR. Therefore, in this case, decisions that significantly affect privacy and data protection should be made at the Basic Act level in DORA, ensuring they undergo the full legislative procedure with appropriate democratic oversight.

In conclusion, while Delegated Regulation 2024/1774 attempts to address the practicalities of logging and personal data processing, the lack of explicit

[55] Case C-355/10 *European Parliament v Council of the European Union* [2012] ECLI:EU:C:2012:516, paras 64–65; see also LA Campo, 'Delegated versus Implementing Acts: How to Make the Right Choice?' (2021) 22 ERA Forum 193.

[56] Case C-355/10 *European Parliament v Council of the European Union* [2012] ECLI:EU:C:2012:516, paras 64–65.

[57] ibid, para 77.

[58] See, for similar argument here, EDPS, 'Guidance for Co-Legislators on Key Elements of Legislative Proposals', Draft for Public Consultation (2024). Available at: www.edps.europa.eu/data-protection/our-work/publications/guidelines/2024-01-16-guidance-co-legislators-key-elements-legislative-proposals_en.

[59] Case C-311/18 *Maximilian Schrems v Facebook Ireland Limited* [2020] ECLI:EU:C:2020:559, para 176 and case law cited.

mention in the primary text of DORA at Basic Act level creates a gap in the legal framework. Without clear and direct provisions in DORA itself, there is a stringent argument that the legal obligation for personal data processing under the GDPR is not sufficiently established. The reliance on Delegated Regulation 2024/1774 and general references in recitals may not fulfil the requirements of the GDPR, potentially rendering Article 10 of DORA inadequate as a legal basis for personal data processing. However, it does not mean that personal data cannot be processed at all to detect anomalous activities. It only means that FEs should not rely on legal obligation as a legal basis while processing personal data.

3.2. Possibility of Legitimate Interest as a Legal Basis for Personal Data Processing under DORA in the Absence of Legal Obligation?

This subsection briefly discusses the possibility of legitimate interest as a legal basis for personal data processing without providing a comprehensive assessment, which is beyond the scope of this chapter.[60] Article 6(1)(f) of the GDPR establishes three essential conditions for the lawful processing of personal data.[61] First, the data controller or a third party must have a legitimate interest in the processing. Second, the processing must be necessary to achieve the legitimate interest being pursued. Third, the processing must not override the interests, fundamental rights or freedoms of the individual whose personal data is involved.

The use of anomaly detection technologies by FEs under DORA and its Delegated Regulation can be assessed against the three conditions set forth in Article 6(1)(f) of the GDPR to determine the lawfulness of personal data processing.[62] FEs have a clear and compelling legitimate interest in deploying anomaly detection technologies. Considering the broad interpretation of legitimate interest by the CJE in the *KNLTB* case,[63] these systems are essential for identifying and mitigating cybersecurity risks, ensuring the operational continuity of critical ICT functions and safeguarding financial stability. Given the systemic implications of cybersecurity breaches within the financial sector, the use of such technologies aligns with DORA's objective of enhancing digital operational resilience and protecting the broader financial ecosystem. The legitimate interest in

[60] See, for a comprehensive assessment of appropriateness of the legitimate interest for personal data processing under the NIS 2 Directive, Kun (n 30). The analysis of the author in this article can be applied in this context.

[61] See, for the guidelines on the legitimate interest, EDPB, 'Guidelines 1/2024 on Processing of Personal Data based on Article 6(1)(f) of the GDPR' (Version 1.0, adopted on 8 October 2024). Available at: www.edpb.europa.eu/system/files/2024-10/edpb_guidelines_202401_legitimateinterest_en.pdf.

[62] See, for a comprehensive assessment of appropriateness of the legitimate interest for personal data processing under the NIS 2 Directive, Kun (n 30).

[63] Case C-621/22 *KNLTB v Autoriteit Persoonsgegevens* [2024] ECLI:EU:C:2024:857, para 49.

this context extends beyond the FE itself to include its customers, stakeholders and the stability of the financial market as a whole.

For anomaly detection technologies to function effectively, the processing of personal data is often indispensable.[64] These systems analyse data such as login records, access patterns or transaction metadata to identify irregularities that may indicate potential security breaches or unauthorised activity. This processing is necessary to enable real-time detection and response to cybersecurity threats, since alternative methods, such as manual monitoring, would be significantly less effective and impractical given the volume and complexity of modern ICT operations. The necessity criterion is satisfied when the processing is directly linked to achieving the cybersecurity objectives outlined in DORA and when the data is used solely for this purpose.

The third condition requires a balancing test to ensure that the legitimate interests of the FE do not override the fundamental rights and freedoms of individuals whose data is processed. Anomaly detection technologies must be designed and implemented in a manner that minimises data processing activities.

4. Conclusion

The digital transformation of the financial sector has brought about significant advancements, but it has also introduced new challenges, particularly in the realm of cybersecurity. As FEs increasingly depend on interconnected digital systems, the risks associated with cyber threats have evolved from being merely operational concerns to becoming potential sources of systemic risk. Cyber risk's ability to propagate quickly across borders and sectors, facilitated by the interconnectedness of financial systems, has positioned it as a significant threat to financial stability.

Traditional systemic risks, such as credit and liquidity risks, are now joined by cyber risks. This recognition has led to the development of both micro-prudential and macro-prudential regulatory and policy responses, aimed at increasing the resilience of FEs and the financial system as a whole. As discussed in section 2, DORA represents a critical step in addressing these challenges by mandating that FEs adopt an 'assume breach' mentality. This approach emphasises resilience, ensuring that FEs can resist and recover from cyber incidents while maintaining critical functions.

Implementing cybersecurity measures required by DORA and Delegated Regulation 2024/1774 would require the processing of personal data. Anomaly detection systems, as discussed in section 3, which are anticipated to play a crucial role in enhancing cybersecurity, rely on processing various types of personal data. The primary question in this chapter, discussed in section 3, is whether the cybersecurity requirements under DORA can serve as a legal obligation to provide a

[64] Christl (n 41).

legal basis for processing personal data in accordance with Article 6(1)(c) of the GDPR. While Delegated Regulation 2024/1774 attempts to address the practicalities of logging and personal data processing, the lack of explicit provisions in DORA allowing for personal data processing itself creates uncertainty and a gap within the newly developed legal framework on cybersecurity. Without clear and direct provisions in the operative text of DORA, the necessary conditions for the legal obligation for personal data processing under the GDPR may not be sufficiently established. This gap means that FEs should be cautious in relying on the legal obligation as a basis for personal data processing in the context of DORA when implementing anomalous detection technologies, which is only one example of personal data processing for cybersecurity. Instead, alternative legal bases, such as legitimate interest, should be considered, as discussed in section 3.

In conclusion, while DORA represents a significant advancement in addressing the cybersecurity challenges facing the financial sector, its current framework may fall short in providing a clear legal basis for personal data processing under the GDPR. FEs must ensure that their cybersecurity measures not only enhance operational resilience to comply with DORA but also comply with data protection requirements. The discussion on the plausibility of these legal grounds for processing activities remains an important area for further exploration, as the financial sector continues to adapt to the evolving landscape of digital transformation and cybersecurity.

PART III

Transforming Regulations and Regulatory Strategies

9

European Payments

How New Trends Drive Far-Reaching Regulatory Intervention in the EU Payment Markets

EMANUEL VAN PRAAG

1. Introduction

This chapter deals with new legal developments on the European payments markets.[1] Some of the developments discussed are the introduction of the digital euro, the requirement for merchants to continue accepting cash alongside card payments, the efforts by the European lawmakers to stimulate homegrown payments systems as an alternative to VISA and MasterCard, and the more stringent liability laws for banks when their clients are being defrauded. This chapter aims to show the overarching policy perspective behind these various legal measures. It also evaluates these legislative developments, revealing a shift in the regulation of parties active within payment ecosystems from managing risk caused by their activities towards enlisting these actors in solving societal problems that are neither caused nor enlarged by them.

In my view, new legal trends are typically driven by changes in the real world. These changes most often stem from new technological possibilities and/or new perceived risks and values in society. The logical sequence is set out in Table 9.1.

[1] Parts of this chapter have been published previously in EJ van Praag, 'The Future of European Payments: Faster, Cheaper, More Digital and More European; with No One Left Behind' (2024) 18(4) *Journal of Payments Strategy & Systems 327*.

Table 9.1 Logical sequence of new legal trends

	Logical sequence	Example
(i)	New technological possibilities are introduced on the (payments) markets.	Possibility of use of the near-field communication (NFC) chip in telephones to make payments.
(ii)	These technological possibilities change the way that the payments market is organised and that products are offered.	Phones are increasingly used to make payments, leading to a further reduction in cash usage.
(iii)	With these changes, new risks are introduced to the payments market. (Alternatively, new rules need to be introduced to bring the innovations fully to fruition.)	Lower cash usage leads to the risk that fewer merchants/shops are willing to accept cash and banks offer fewer Automated Teller Machines (ATMs). In the end, vulnerable consumers who cannot operate a smartphone for payments cannot use cash either.
(iv)	Regulators and legislators respond to these new risks (or facilitate these new possibilities) via new rules.	The legislator requires that cash can continue to be used and obtained, obliging merchants to accept cash and banks to maintain a sufficient coverage of ATMs.

New risks or newly perceived risks emerge outside of new technological possibilities as well. For example, a major overarching risk that has recently come to the fore is geopolitical risk. The COVID-19 pandemic, as well as the sanctions against Russia, triggered an acute awareness that companies based in other countries cannot always be relied on for vital services or products. Under pressure from their national governments they may be forced to refuse to offer services (sanctions) or their limited supplies may be funnelled towards domestic markets instead of international markets. Within the payments market this has led to concerns about the overreliance on non-EU payment infrastructure (ie VISA and MasterCard).[2] In particular, the sanctions against Russia and the subsequent unavailability of VISA and MasterCard in Russia has made EU (policymakers) realise how dependent the EU is on these non-EU players for the smooth functioning of its payments market. Earlier, the US sanctions on Iran prevented EU banks from handling payments to Iran even though the EU did not join these sanctions, which led to specific EU measures targeted at nullifying the effects of these US sanctions.[3]

[2] The ECB has tried to nudge EU players towards an EU card scheme as an alternative to VISA and MasterCard, but so far unsuccessfully. Available at: www.ecb.europa.eu/press/intro/mip-online/2019/html/1904_card_payments_europe.en.html.

[3] Delegated Regulation (EU) 2018/1100 of 6 June 2018 amending the Annex to Council Regulation (EC) No 2271/96 protecting against the effects of extra-territorial application of legislation adopted by a third country, and actions based thereon or resulting therefrom [2018] OJ L199I.

This chapter first describes the main trends in the payments markets and how they translate into new (or newly perceived) risks. It then describes how these risks are addressed by the EU legislator and/or EU supervisors. The risks are to some extent described in the EU retail payments strategy and most of the legislative projects discussed below flow from this strategy document.[4] We will see that many of the legislative measures will require private sector entities to invest in capabilities they would not invest in on their own accord. Also, I will discuss initiatives that are meant to facilitate the digital transformation in payments (and bring the new innovations fully to fruition). These are – at least by most – perceived as pro-business initiatives. In the last section I will critically evaluate these regulatory and legislative strategies by indicating to what extent they are market led or government led, who pays for these mandatory capabilities (government or private sector) and to what extent the law requires private sector entities to cooperate in order to accomplish the public goals set forth by the EU legislator. I will analyse to what extent these far-reaching requirements on business fit the economic ordering principles of the EU.

2. Trends and Risks

Here I will discuss the five trends affecting the payments market and the risks that come along with them.

2.1. Declining Use of Cash

The use of cash as a means of payment has been declining. The European Central Bank (ECB) undertakes research into the use of cash across the eurozone. Some key conclusions drawn by the ECB in December 2022 were:[5]

- Cash was the most frequently used payment method at the point of sale (POS) in the eurozone and was used in 59 per cent of transactions, though down from 79 per cent in 2016 and 72 per cent in 2019.
- In terms of value of payments, cards (46 per cent) accounted for a higher share of POS transactions than cash (42 per cent).[6] This contrasts with 2016 and 2019, when the share of cash transactions was higher than the share of card

[4] Commission, 'Retail Payments Strategy for the EU' (Communication) COM (2020) 592 final. See also ECB, 'The Eurosystem's Retail Payments Strategy' (2021). Available at: www.ecb.europa.eu/paym/integration/retail/retail_payments_strategy/html/index.en.html, which sets out similar initiatives as the ones discussed below.

[5] ECB, 'Study on the Payment Attitudes of Consumers in the Euro Area' (December 2022) 4. Available at: www.ecb.europa.eu/stats/ecb_surveys/space/shared/pdf/ecb.spacereport202212~783ffdf46e.en.pdf.

[6] Cards are credit cards and debit cards. Card payments also include payments where no physical card is present, but which are based on card networks, such as GooglePay and ApplePay.

transactions (54 per cent cash and 39 per cent card in 2016; and 47 per cent cash and 43 per cent cards in 2019).

- Cash was the dominant means of payment in person-to-person (P2P) transactions in the eurozone. However, its share in the total number of payments declined from 86 per cent in 2019 to 73 per cent in 2022, and from 65 per cent to 59 per cent in terms of value. The main alternative is account-to-account (A2A) payments. Many banks offer the possibility for payees to send a link to their friends via social media, such as WhatsApp, which enables the friend to easily send a payment from their bank account to that of the payee.
- Cash was accepted in 95 per cent of physical payment locations throughout the eurozone, down from 98 per cent in 2019.

Looking at these results we see that cash is not yet obsolete as a means of payment, but its use is declining across the board. However, these eurozone-wide numbers do not tell the whole story. For some markets the decline of cash has progressed much further.[7] For example, the percentage of POS transactions in which cash is used is only 21 per cent in the Netherlands and 19 per cent in Finland. Also, for Belgium, France, Latvia, Estonia and Luxemburg, cash is used in fewer than 50 per cent of transactions. Importantly, it is typically the less educated, less affluent or older consumer who uses cash, whereas digital payment means are typically used by younger, better educated or more affluent consumers.[8]

2.2. Digitisation: Fewer Bank Offices and Digital First Services

The number of bank offices across Europe is declining. As part of its EU structural financial indicators, the ECB collects detailed data on the number of bank offices across the EU and across the eurozone.[9] The number of offices shows a clear downward trend (Table 9.2). For example, for the eurozone as a whole the number came down from 170,847 in 2002 to 108,772 in 2022, even though new Member States have joined the eurozone.

Table 9.2 Number of bank offices across Europe 2002–2022

Year	2022	2017	2012	2007	2002
Number of bank offices	108,772	143,165	171,813	183,673	170,847

[7] ECB, 'Study on the Payment Attitudes of Consumers in the Euro Area' (December 2022) 19. Available at: www.ecb.europa.eu/stats/ecb_surveys/space/shared/pdf/ecb.spacereport202212~783ffdf46e.en.pdf.

[8] ibid 22.

[9] ECB, 'EU Structural Financial Indicators'. Available at: https://data.ecb.europa.eu/publications/financial-corporations/3030658.

But, just as with the use of cash, the numbers differ significantly across EU Member States. Whereas in Germany the number of bank offices 'only' came down from 50,868 to 20,432, in the Netherlands the number declined from 4,269 to only 729. A related trend, which cannot really be expressed in numbers, is that bank services have become primarily digital. Simultaneously with the closure of bank offices, clients are now enticed to use digital communications, such as internet banking and banking apps, instead of cheques and written and telephonic bank transfer orders.

2.3. Payment Fraud

Simultaneously with the digitalisation of payments there has been an increasing prevalence and awareness of payment fraud. Whereas payment fraud originally was confined to stealing someone's bank credentials – eg copying a bank card in a shop (*skimming*) – new payment fraud has as its hallmark social engineering.[10] Examples of relatively novel forms of fraud are sending WhatsApp message pretending to be someone's child in urgent need of money,[11] or calling pretending to be the bank itself requesting the money to be transferred immediately by the client to a safekeeping account (*spoofing*).[12] The faster and more seamless payments are, the more common these new types of fraud become.[13] In the old days (when a client still had to submit a written payment order on paper and WhatsApp did not exist), these fraud scenarios were not possible. The new fraud scenarios are highly scalable, and a whole new criminal industry providing tools for cybercriminals has emerged. Apart from the fact that payment fraud is considered sad for the victim, it may also lead to problems for the economy at large if not dealt with sufficiently. If victims are not compensated, some consumers may lose faith in modern payment methods and may continue to use methods that they consider safer but which may be less efficient for society a whole

2.4. BigTech in Payments

The fourth concern relates to the increasing presence of BigTech in the payments value chain. With BigTech I especially refer to Apple and Google and their dominant

[10] See, for fraud numbers, EBA and ECB, *Report on Payment Fraud* (2024). Commission, 'Proposal for a Regulation of the European Parliament and of the Council on payment services in the internal market' COM (2023) 367 final 2023/0210(COD) (PSR) Recital 79.

[11] 'Friends and Family WhatsApp and Text Scams – How to Spot the Signs' (18 January 2023). Available at: www.co-operativebank.co.uk/content-hub/articles-and-advice/WhatsApp-Scams/.

[12] See Europol 'Cyber Scams Infographics' (6 December 2021). Available at: www.europol.europa.eu/sites/default/files/documents/1_spoofed_bank_websites.pdf.

[13] PSR, Recital 79.

hold over smartphones.[14] As more and more people pay with their phone, instead of a physical card, control over phones becomes increasingly important in the payments markets.[15] Next to that are the platforms who also offer payments services, such as Uber, Booking and Amazon,[16] but so far (at least in Europe) these payments services all have a strong connection with the transactions executed via their platforms. In that sense Europe is different from, for example, China, where Alipay and WeChat Pay have grown to be the largest and second-largest mobile payment platforms, also executing transactions that do not originate from their platforms.[17]

2.5. Geopolitical Tensions

The fifth trend is that payments have gained geopolitical relevance. Without a smooth functioning payment system, the European economy would come to a grinding halt. As explained above, the COVID-19 epidemic and the use by the US of the financial system for geopolitical ends (sanctions against Iran and Russia) have made the European Commission acutely aware of its dependence on US players, such as VISA, MasterCard and SWIFT. Chinese means of payments are not really prevalent in the EU payments markets – at least for payments not involving Chinese payers or payees – and the Commission wants to keep it that way. A clear sign that the Commission wants to defend EU interests in the international arena was given in the speech by President-elect Von der Leyen in the European Parliament Plenary, on the occasion of the presentation of her College of Commissioners and their programme.[18] Here she coined the term 'Geopolitical Commission'.

The challenges resulting from these developments have given rise to various initiatives to address them.

3. Targeted Measures to Improve the Positions of the Vulnerable Consumer in the Digital Transition

In this section, I will address measures that have as their purpose remedying the disadvantages and/or mitigating the risk to which vulnerable consumers are

[14] See EBA, *Report on the Use of Digital Platforms in the EU Banking and Payments Sector* (EBA/REP/2021/26, September 2021) 25.

[15] See, eg, Commission, 'Antitrust: Commission sends Statement of Objections to Apple over practices regarding Apple Pay' press release (2 May 2022). Available at: https://ec.europa.eu/commission/presscorner/detail/en/ip_22_2764.

[16] See EBA, *Report on the Use of Digital Platforms in the EU Banking and Payments Sector* (EBA/REP/2021/26, September 2021) 22.

[17] DNB, 'Changing Landscape, Changing Supervision: Developments in the Relationship Between BigTech and Financial Institutions' (2021) 9. Available at: www.dnb.nl/media/32apiuom/dnb-big-tech-supervision-changing-landscape-changing-supervision.pdf.

[18] 'Speech by President-elect von der Leyen in the European Parliament Plenary on the Occasion of the Presentation of Her College of Commissioners and Their Programme' (Strasbourg, 27 November 2019). Available at: https://ec.europa.eu/commission/presscorner/detail/en/speech_19_6408.

subject because of the digitalisation of payments.[19] Put differently, new technology leads to new ways of services being delivered, requiring additional measures to protect or assist consumers less digitally savvy or for other reasons unable to operate digital means of payment, who may otherwise get lost in the digital world.

3.1. The EU Accessibility Directive and Accessibility Requirements in the Draft Payment Services Regulation

The first EU measure to assist vulnerable consumers in the digital payments world is the Accessibility Directive.[20] This directive is part of a generic EU strategy to create an environment where products and services are more accessible, allowing for a more inclusive society and facilitating independent living for persons with disabilities.[21] It forms the EU's 'implementation' of the United Nations Convention on the Rights of Persons with Disabilities. Although it concerns all kinds of products and services, specific attention is devoted towards financial services, especially payments.[22] The Accessibility Directive sets forth specific rules for the accessibility of payment terminals and ATMs.[23] Payment terminals are the devices in shops enabling a client to authorise payments using their (contactless) payment card. ATMs are machines where clients can obtain cash from their bank account. These payment terminals and ATMs should be accessible for people with disabilities.[24] Besides rules specifically targeting payment terminals and ATMs, the Accessibility Directive requires that the entire payments service, for example the online internet environment and banking, be designed in such a way that it is also accessible for people with disabilities.[25]

Similar requirements are set forth in the proposal for the Payment Services Regulation (PSR). Under the Second Payment Services Directive (PSD2) the legal concept of strong customer authentication (SCA) was introduced.[26] SCA is used to establish that it is the client themself who authorised a payment transaction. An example of SCA is a client authorising a transaction at a shop counter by tapping their card against the card reader and then entering the personal identification number (PIN). For some people, remembering the PIN and making sure their bank card does not get lost is a challenge. For other people, just remembering the PIN itself may be

[19] See also, about vulnerability in the payments market, Maria Cecilia Paglietti and Maddalena Rabitti, 'A Matter of Time. Digital-Financial Consumers Vulnerability in the Retail Payments Market' (2022) 33(4) *European Business Law Review* 581.

[20] Directive (EU) 2019/882 of the European Parliament and of the Council of 17 April 2019 on the accessibility requirements for products and services (Accessibility Directive) [2019] OJ L151.

[21] Accessibility Directive, Recital 2.

[22] ibid Recital 39.

[23] ibid art 2 (1) (b).

[24] ibid, Annex 1, s I (2)(o)(i) for the exact requirements.

[25] ibid, art 3 (28). These obligations apply to so-called consumer banking services. Consumer banking services include loans to consumers and investment services provided to consumers, as well as payment services. See, for the exact requirements, Accessibility Directive, Annex 1, s III and Annex 1, s IV(e).

[26] Directive (EU) 2015/2366 of the European Parliament and of the Council of 25 November 2015 on payment services in the internal market (PSD2) [2015] OJ L337, art 4 (30).

easy but typing it in and reading the card reader may be complex because of visibility problems. Currently, new methods of SCA are being introduced that can be even more challenging, for example scanning a QR code or typing a specific code in an app on a smartphone connected to a bank account when engaging in online shopping. For that reason, PSR provides, with explicit reference to the Accessibility Directive, that payment service providers (PSPs) shall ensure that all their clients, including persons with disabilities, older persons, persons with low digital skills and those who do not have access to digital channels or payment instruments, have at their disposal at least a means, adapted to their specific situation, that enables them to perform SCA.[27]

3.2. PSR Fraud Fighting

As indicated in section 2.3, combatting payment fraud is considered of increasing importance in EU policymaking.[28] In essence, PSR introduces six new ways of alleviating the problem of payment fraud for potential victims:[29]

1 Conditional reversal of liability for authorised push payment (APP) fraud.
2 Confirmation of payee services extension of International Bank Account Number (IBAN) verification to all credit transfers.
3 Improvements to the application of SCA.
4 Improved fraud monitoring.
5 A legal basis for exchange of information on fraud.
6 Measures to increase the availability and acceptance of cash.

3.2.1. Conditional Reversal of Liability for APP Fraud

PSD2 included rules making PSPs liable only for unauthorised payment transactions.[30] An unauthorised payment transaction is one that has not been authorised by the client. A typical example is where a bank card has been used,

[27] PSR, art 88 and Recital 110.

[28] Relevant prior work about payment fraud: MC Paglietti, 'Restitution and Liability in the Multilevel Regulatory Framework of Unauthorized Digital Payment Transactions' (2022) 1 *European Review of Private Law* 155; EJ van Praag, *PSD2: naar open banking en bankieren in een ecosysteem (Preadvies voor de Vereniging voor Financieel Recht 2020)*, Serie Van der Heijden Instituut nr 169 (Wolters Kluwer 2020) 137 and EJ van Praag, 'Fighting Payment Fraud: Some Key Considerations for the EU Legislator' (*Oxford Business Law Blog*, 9 September 2024); J Braithwaite, '"Authorized Push Payment" Bank Fraud: What Does an Effective Regulatory Response Look Like?' (2004) *Journal of Financial Regulation* 1; M Eidsand Kjørven, *Who Pays When Things go Wrong? Online Financial Fraud and Consumer Protection in Scandinavia and Europe* (EBLR 2020) 88; MR Guimares and R Steennot, 'Allocation of Liability in Case of Payment Fraud: Who Bears the Risk of Innovation? A Comparison of Belgian and Portuguese Law in the Context of PSD2' (2022) *European Review of Private Law* 29.

[29] A critical evaluation of the measures taken so far can be found in European Court of Auditors, *Digital Payments in the EU: Progress Towards Making Them Safer, Faster, and Less Expensive, Despite Remaining Gaps* (2025) 36.

[30] PSD2, art 73.

and the PIN entered, but not by the client (because the bank card has been stolen and the PIN uncovered by the fraudster). In that case the PSP must reimburse the client with the amounts stolen, unless the client acted fraudulently or with gross negligence.[31] A typical example of negligence is keeping your bank card with a Post-it with the PIN on it in your purse or in the cabinet.

However, as explained in section 2.3, a new type of payment fraud is coming to the fore involving social engineering. In these cases, the client actually submits and authorises the payment order but on false grounds, hence the name 'authorised push payment'. These clients as it stands now are not compensated by their PSP, as the payment transaction was authorised. The EU legislator intends to change this to some extent. In case of bank impersonation fraud – where a consumer has been manipulated by a third party pretending to be an employee of the consumer's PSP, using the name, email address or telephone number of that PSP unlawfully, and that manipulation gave rise to subsequent fraudulent authorised payment transactions – the PSP will refund the client.[32] The only exceptions are fraud and gross negligence by the client. In the EU Parliament it was suggested that PSPs should be liable in all cases of APP fraud, regardless of whom the fraudster was impersonating.[33] Such a wider liability for APP has been introduced in the UK.[34]

Interestingly, besides PSPs, electronic communications services providers are also enlisted in the fight against APP fraud. Where informed by a PSP of the occurrence of this type of fraud, electronic communications services providers shall cooperate closely with PSPs and act swiftly to ensure that appropriate organisational and technical measures are in place to safeguard the security and confidentiality of communications, including with regard to calling line identification and electronic mail address.[35]

3.2.2. Confirmation of Payee Services: Extension of IBAN Verification to All Credit Transfers

PSD2 provides that a PSP may rely on the unique identifier supplied by its clients.[36] The unique identifier is the payee's IBAN. Often PSPs offer the opportunity to include the name of the payee in the payment order, but this name was not traditionally used by the PSP when executing the payment order and this was also not required.[37] This meant that a payer could intend to pay party A but would, in fact, be paying another party who tricked the client into using its bank account number

[31] ibid art 74.
[32] PSR, art 59.
[33] See PSR, art 59(1), Decision by Parliament, first reading voted upon 23 April 2024, T9-0298/2024. Available at: www.europarl.europa.eu/doceo/document/TA-9-2024-0298_EN.html.
[34] PSR, 'APP Scams'. Available at: www.psr.org.uk/our-work/app-scams/.
[35] PSR, art 59 and Recital 81.
[36] PSD2, art 88.
[37] Case C–245/18 Tecnoservice Int. Srl in liquidation v Poste Italiane SpA [2019] ECLI:EU:C:2019:242, para 28.

(eg by sending a false invoice). In the Netherlands, a private initiative, the so-called IBAN Name Check, has been introduced. This name and number check, also called a confirmation of payee service, informs the client whether the name of the payee entered matches the bank account number of the payee. In the Instant Payments Regulation it has been mandatory for all credit transfers.[38] In case of failure of the PSP of the payer to notify the payer of a detected discrepancy between the unique identifier and the name of the payee provided by the payer, the payer shall be reimbursed.[39] In the Instant Payments Regulation it is made explicit that the payee's PSP shall verify whether the payment account identifier and the name of the payee provided by the payer match, wholly or partially. This information will then need to be forwarded to the PSP of the payer who will inform the payer accordingly. The exact modus of cooperation, however, needs to be worked out by the market.[40] One such initiative is the Verification of Payee scheme of the European Payments Council.[41] A scheme is, in essence, a multilateral contract between parties in a specific industry. Because such a multilateral contract has thousands of participants, a scheme like this has a governance structure with representatives developing and maintaining the scheme rules. There are also private schemes, for example by VISA and MasterCard, where the schemes rules are developed and maintained by a private organisation with no or limited stakeholder representation.

3.2.3. Improvements to the Application of SCA

The PSR dedicates much attention to SCA. In setting the rules for the requirement to use SCA, a balance needs to be set between fighting fraud on the one hand and ease of use on the other. Every application of SCA leads to friction in the payment process, which is annoying for users, leads to longer queues at the counter and may cause clients to drop off in the purchasing process. On the other hand, the requirement to use SCA leads to less fraud. In PSR the pendulum swings towards safety, requiring SCA in more situations.[42]

3.2.4. Improved Fraud Monitoring

In the recital of the PSR it is considered that payment fraud often targets the most vulnerable consumer.[43] PSR therefore considers the timely detection of fraudulent

[38] Regulation (EU) 2024/886 of the European Parliament and of the Council of 13 March 2024 amending Regulations (EU) No 260/2012 and (EU) 2021/1230 and Directives 98/26/EC and (EU) 2015/2366 as regards instant credit transfers in euro (Instant Payments Regulation) [2024] OJ L2024/886, art 5c.

[39] PSR, art 57.

[40] Instant Payments Regulation, Recital 23.

[41] European Payments Council, 'Verification Of Payee'. Available at: www.europeanpaymentscouncil.eu/what-we-do/other-schemes/verification-payee#:~:text=The%20Verification%20Of%20Payee%20(VOP,PSU)%2Dto%2DPSP%20space.

[42] PSR, art 85.

[43] ibid Recital 100.

payment transactions essential and considers that transaction monitoring plays an import role in that detection. PSPs must therefore have in place transaction-monitoring mechanisms.[44] This transaction monitoring will also need to take into account environmental and behavioural characteristics related to the payment habits of the payment service user. Also, PSPs are called upon to use artificial intelligence to keep on par with the fraudsters.[45]

3.2.5. *A Legal Basis for Exchange of Information on Fraud*

It is also considered in the PSR that PSPs often do not have the full picture about all elements that could lead to timely fraud detection.[46] Fraud detection, according to the PSR, can be made more effective with a greater amount of information on potentially fraudulent activity stemming from other PSPs. For that reason, the PSR provides that PSPs may exchange the unique identifier (bank account) of a payee with other PSPs, when the PSP has sufficient evidence to assume that there was a fraudulent payment transaction.[47] This sharing needs to take place in the context of so-called information sharing arrangements.[48]

3.2.6. *Measures to Increase the Availability and Acceptance of Cash*

As indicated in section 2.1, the availability of cash is declining. The Commission is proposing two targeted measures; a Regulation on the legal tender of euro banknotes and coins,[49] namely to maintain the availability of availability of cash (via ATMs) and to require the mandatory acceptance of cash in shops and government services. In the recitals, the European legislator pays specific attention to the importance of cash for those excluded from the financial system, such as the unbanked, asylum seekers and migrants, who may not be able or willing to use a means of payment supplied by the private sector and therefore rely on cash as a payment method.[50] It is considered that vulnerable groups are more at risk of losing their access to a method of payment if their access to cash deteriorates. According to research by the Dutch Central Bank, out of the total Dutch population of 18 million, approximately 2.6 million individuals aged over 18 struggle with digital payments and other banking affairs.[51]

[44] ibid art 83(1) and (2).
[45] ibid Recital 103.
[46] ibid.
[47] ibid art 83(3).
[48] ibid art 83(4).
[49] Commission, 'Proposal for a Regulation of the European Parliament and of the Council on the legal tender of euro banknotes and coins' COM (2023) 368 final (Regulation on the legal tender of euro banknotes and coins).
[50] Regulation on the legal tender of euro banknotes and coins, Recital 14.
[51] DNB, 'Digital Banking is a Struggle for Many' (30 January 2023). Available at: www.dnb.nl/en/general-news/news-2023/digital-banking-is-a-struggle-for-many/.

Therefore, the Regulation sets out to preserve financial inclusion of vulnerable groups with a dependency on cash payments by ensuring that everyone in the euro area is free to choose their preferred payment method and has access to basic cash services.

The Regulation stipulates two concrete measures. Firstly, it requires that Member States ensure that cash is sufficiently available for these vulnerable groups throughout the territory of each Member State (in all their different regions, including urban and non-urban areas) and that they intervene if this availability is threatened.[52] The Netherlands is leading the way in digital payments and thus the use of cash has declined. That is why the Netherlands is not waiting for this Regulation. The Dutch Minister of Finance has proposed to lay down in law (i) that the three major banks must keep sufficient ATMs and sufficient places to deposit cash available, (ii) that all banks must offer cash services to their clients and (iii) rules that constrain the possibility for banks to charge for these cash services.[53]

Secondly, the draft Regulation on the legal tender of euro banknotes and coins also prescribes the mandatory acceptance of cash.[54] The proposal requires anyone to accept cash as a means of discharging, at full face value, an obligation. Payees may not charge for accepting cash. Only in exceptional cases may cash be refused. Just like with the availability of cash, the extent to which cash is accepted by payees must also be monitored and reported upon to the Commission.[55] If a Member State considers that the level of acceptance of payments in cash in their territory or parts thereof undermines mandatory acceptance of euro banknotes and coins, it must take measures and inform the Commission accordingly.

4. The Digital Euro

A key proposal addressing some of the risks discussed in section 2 is the (draft) Regulation on the establishment of the digital euro (the draft Digital Euro Regulation), introducing the digital euro, also referred to as a central bank digital currency (CBDC).[56] A CBDC is a digital as opposed to physical (notes and coins) means of payment, issued not by a commercial bank but by the central bank. The digital euro is introduced as an alternative to cash (banknotes and coins). In essence, it is comparable to banknotes and coins, because it represents a claim on the ECB rather than on a commercial bank or other PSP.[57] This means that, even though banks and other PSPs have a role in distributing the digital euro (as will

[52] Regulation on the legal tender of euro banknotes and coins, art 8.
[53] See draft Wet chartaal betalingsverkeer, www.internetconsultatie.nl/chartaal/b1.
[54] Regulation on the legal tender of euro banknotes and coins, art 4.
[55] ibid art 7.
[56] Commission, 'Proposal for a Regulation of the European Parliament and of the Council on the establishment of the digital euro' COM (2023) 369 final (Digital Euro Regulation).
[57] Digital Euro Regulation, art 4 (2).

be discussed in sections 4.4 and 4.5 below), an insolvency of one of these financial institutions does not impact the digital euro holder. The reason for this is that the digital euro holder has a claim not on the financial institution but on the ECB. Naturally the ECB cannot become insolvent, which makes the digital euro 100 per cent safe. The digital euro will also be a means of payment/payment scheme, with a set of rules laid down in a rulebook, which is under development. In that sense it is comparable to, for example, VISA or MasterCard or national equivalents of those.

In this section I discuss the digital euro initiative. I first discuss the rationale behind the digital euro (section 4.1). Next, I discuss how the digital euro works (section 4.2), explain its mandatory acceptance (section 4.3), and then focus on the roles of the diverse stakeholders (who are the major retail banks and other PSPs) (section 4.4), the remuneration model for these stakeholders (section 4.5) and the role of the ECB (section 4.6). Lastly, I focus on some targeted measures to improve the accessibility of the digital euro for vulnerable consumers (section 4.7).

4.1. The Three Reasons for the Digital Euro

The Commission noted that banknotes and coins are on the decline in the digital economy (see section 2.1). In the view of the Commission, the demise of cash leads to three problems/vulnerabilities.[58]

4.1.1. Loss of a Monetary Anchor

The Commission reiterates at various places its concern that the decline of cash – because of the digitalisation of the economy – will cause the loss of the monetary anchor for the euro currency. The idea is that there is a desirable balance between central bank money and private digital means of payment. Declining use of cash would tilt this balance towards private digital means of payment, such as bank accounts, credit cards and electronic money. By introducing a digital euro that is also attractive in the modern economy and would therefore be widely used, the use of central bank money would increase again, thus restoring the desired balance. This balance is needed since euro-denominated deposits with banks and other private actors are only trusted because these deposits can be withdrawn and converted into cash (notes and coins) issued by the central bank. If this withdrawal possibility is, in fact, not effective because these notes and coins cannot be spent, this trust would be lost. It is hard to evaluate the veracity of this monetary anchor argument. There are various authors who question this.[59] These authors also contend that the digital euro could only function as a monetary anchor if

[58] ibid 1.

[59] See eg P Bofinger and T Haas, 'The Digital Euro (CBDC) as a Monetary Anchor of the Financial System' (European Money and Finance Forum 2023). Available at: www.suerf.org/publications/suerf-policy-notes-and-briefs/the-digital-euro-cbdc-as-a-monetary-anchor-of-the-financial-system/.

consumers were able to convert substantial amounts of their private money into the digital euro (when ecessary); this is, however, not possible, as the digital euro would be subject to a relatively low holding limit (see section 4.4).

4.1.2. Vulnerability Towards Third Country CBDCs and Private Stablecoins

The Commission is also worried about the potential uptake within the EU of a third-country CBDC and/or stablecoin. This could be the case if these CBDCs and stablecoins are really convenient to use and become widely accepted across the EU.

The archetypical stablecoin was the Libra/Diem project.[60] This project was driven by Facebook (Meta) and was joined by various other major internet companies, such as Uber and Spotify, along with financial institutions such as VISA. In the end it failed, possibly because of the major backlash from regulators which led to the withdrawal of all financial institutions who initially joined the project. The main concern was that Diem, together with all major internet players supporting it, could become successful and be used as a general means of payment by the public in the EU. In that case the ECB would no longer have control over the EU currency. This is comparable to the phenomenon of dollarisation, where in (typically smaller) countries the national currency is driven out because of the public's preference for the US dollar. The main difference is that the dollar is at least a state-backed currency controlled by an independent central bank, whereas for a stablecoin these safeguards do not apply.

The main CBDC that could be of concern to the Commission is the Chinese digital Yuan. The Commission worries that, if the Chinese CBDC became really successful, in the end people in Europe would also prefer to pay with the digital Yuan rather than euro coins or notes or European digital payment solutions. The reason why such foreign payment systems may become successful is that they are easy to use and come to dominate the market. In Europe this risk is exacerbated by the fact that no homegrown EU payment system exists that is accepted across the EU.

In two-sided markets – like payments – a means of payment becomes successful if many people accept it and if many people want to pay with it. A merchant will want to invest in the technical infrastructure to accept a means of payment if many clients want to use this means of payment. Clients want to adopt a means of payment if it is widely accepted. In practice, this leads to a winner-takes-all economy where, once a means of payment has a substantial adoption either at the client or the merchant side, others must join in so as not to miss out on business opportunities. To mitigate this risk, the EU wants to introduce a strong pan-European payment scheme with significant acceptance by merchants and uptake

[60] See 'Diem (digital currency)' Wikipedia, The Free Encyclopedia, Wikimedia Foundation, 6 May 2025. Available at: https://en.wikipedia.org/wiki/Diem_(digital_currency).

by consumers across the whole EU. Given that the winner takes all, this should mitigate the risk that other payment schemes would take such a position.

4.1.3. Back Up for Other Payment Systems

Lastly the digital euro is meant to act as a backup for other payment schemes. Currently the idea is that if a certain payment scheme does not work (eg because of an IT malfunction with an issuing bank, a disruption in telephone connections or a deliberate cyber-attack),[61] cash would be available as a backup payment scheme. As, however, indicated in section 2.1, cash is on the demise and is therefore less able to perform this backup function in times of need. Also, given the decreasing number of ATMs and bank branches (see section 2.2), the possibility to quickly distribute cash within the general public is limited.

4.2. How will the Digital Euro Work?

According to the ECB in its stocktake report, the digital euro will have several features enabling it to have the best of both worlds of cash and digital payments.[62] These features will be discussed in the following sections. An important feature that we will not discuss in this chapter is the high level of privacy aimed for when using the digital euro.[63]

The digital euro will have two variants: an online variant, which is highly comparable to a bank account, and an offline variant, which is meant to mimic cash.[64] The online variant is a bookkeeping entry in an administration of a financial institution. This cannot be stressed enough. Users have no direct contractual relationship with the ECB; only with their PSPs.[65] In order to spend this online digital euro, a live connection needs to be established with the financial institution where the digital euro is held. The offline variant will be a digital representation of value stored in, for example, a user's smartphone. No online connection is needed to transfer this digital euro. Naturally, because there is no internet connection, the

[61] See, eg, 'Remarks by Executive Vice-President Dombrovskis and Commissioners Gentiloni and McGuinness on the Digital Euro and the Legal Tender of Euro Banknotes and Coins' (28 June 2023). Available at: https://ec.europa.eu/commission/presscorner/detail/%20en/speech_23_3576: 'A digital euro would enhance the integrity and safety of European payment systems at a time when growing geopolitical tensions make us more vulnerable to attacks on our critical infrastructure'.

[62] See ECB, *A Stocktake on the Digital Euro, Summary Report on the Investigation Phase and Outlook on the Next Phase* (18 October 2023) 3. Available at: www.ecb.europa.eu/euro/digital_euro/progress/shared/pdf/ecb.dedocs231018.en.pdf (ECB Stocktake).

[63] See A Chomczyk Penedo, M Van den Poel, and P Trigo Kramcsak, 'The European Commission's Proposal for a Digital Euro: A Preliminary Personal Data Protection and Privacy Analysis' (2023) Brussels Privacy Hub Working Paper 9(2).

[64] Digital Euro Regulation, art 23(q) and ECB Stocktake 13.

[65] ibid, art 13 (4) and ECB Stocktake 12.

transfer of offline digital euro can only be effected in face-to-face situations where the telephones can connect via a near-distance electronic connection.

With these characteristics, the digital euro can be used in the following cases according to the ECB:[66]

- Person-to-person (P2P) payments
  Individuals could transfer offline digital euro to each other via the NFC chip in their telephones. Alternatively, the payee could present the payer with a QR code, which would then trigger an online digital euro payment, or the payee could provide its phone number, which would then be linked as an alias to the digital euro account. In this context, the ECB has conveyed its concerns to the Commission that the proposed commitments by Apple will not be enough to allow the digital euro wallet to function on the iPhone, which also ties into the risk mentioned in section 2.4 about the potential dominance of BigTech in payments.[67]
- Point-of-sale payments
  POS payment would work the same as P2P payment. Additionally, the common chip in a card system is being considered as a means to authenticate and initiate a digital euro payment.
- E-commerce payments
  Individuals could transfer online digital euro to a shop via a QR code or link, which would then trigger a digital euro payment. Alternatively, the payer could be invited to provide their phone number that is linked back to the digital euro account. The payer would then receive a notification on the phone enabling the authorisation of the payment. Naturally, in an online environment only, the online version of the digital euro could be used.
- Payments to and from government (G2X, X2G)
  These would work similarly to P2P payments and/or e-commerce payments but then having the government as payer or payee.

4.3. Mandatory Acceptance by Businesses, Individuals and Government

For the use cases to work, the draft Digital Euro Regulation provides for mandatory acceptance.[68] This means anyone must accept digital euro as a means of payment

[66] See ECB Stocktake 16.

[67] European Central Bank, 'Feedback on Commitments Offered by Apple over Access Restrictions to Near-Field Communication Technology' (19 April 2024). Available at: www.ecb.europa.eu/pub/pdf/other/ecb.letter240419_Vestager~8f8210db09.en.pdf.

[68] Digital Euro Regulation, art 7. See ECB Stocktake 11.

at full face value. Also, the payee may not charge for acceptance of the digital euro. A general exception applies to natural persons acting in the course of a purely personal or household activity and a more limited exemption applies to SMEs and charities that also do not accept comparable digital means of payments.[69] Once an SME or charity accepts bank payments, it must also accept digital euro payments. Apart from these exceptions, digital euro payments may only be refused on an exceptional basis.

4.4. The Role of the PSPs and Especially Retail Banks

The ECB points out that private parties (ie PSPs) would have a significant role in distributing the digital euro:[70]

> People would open and manage digital euro accounts with PSPs (like for other digital payments or for accounts from which cash can be withdrawn), but the digital euro they hold would be a liability of the central bank (like cash). PSPs would distribute digital euro and be responsible for relationships with end users.

In practice this would mean that PSPs must do various things, per the draft Digital Euro Regulation. Out of all PSPs, the retail banks (credit institutions) would have most obligations.

- PSPs must enable their clients to fund and defund their digital euro accounts.[71] In practice this means that all PSPs must create a connection with the digital euro system in order to be able to send and receive digital euro payments.
- PSPs providing account servicing payment services will need to enable the so-called waterfall functionality.[72] It is envisaged that the digital euro will come with a limit that any natural person or business can hold; in case of an overflow on a digital euro account because of an incoming payment, the remainder will need to be swept automatically into a non-digital euro payment account.[73] Also, in case of a shortage on the digital euro account because of an outgoing payment above the limit, the deficit will automatically be swept from the connected payment account into the digital euro account. In practice this is an obligation that will mainly rest on credit institutions, as they usually hold payment accounts for clients.[74]

[69] ibid, art 9.
[70] ECB Stocktake 18.
[71] Digital Euro Regulation, art 13(2) and (3).
[72] ibid art 13(2) and (3). ECB Stocktake 14.
[73] Digital Euro Regulation, art 16. See, for the amounts, www.ecb.europa.eu/press/financial-stability-publications/fsr/focus/2023/html/ecb.fsrbox202311_04~5f8d06f0d2.en.html and for the rationale ECB Stocktake 33.
[74] See, for the definitions, PSD2, art 4(12) and (17).

- Credit institutions, when offering payment accounts to natural persons, will be obliged to also offer digital euro accounts to these clients with all basic digital euro services.[75]

On top of these obligations, PSPs would have many implicit obligations in order to operate a digital euro account, such as onboarding users, KYC and AML checks, the issuance of payment instruments and authentication of payment orders.[76]

4.5. Remuneration and Business Models of the Retail Banks

The remuneration model for retail banks for digital euro services is significantly constrained.[77] Banks may not charge natural persons for basic digital euro payment services.[78] Banks may charge a so-called interchange fee.[79] An interchange fee is paid by the acquirer to the issuer of a payment instrument. In practice this means that the bank of a natural person is remunerated by the PSP of the merchant for enabling the client to pay for a transaction.[80] Of course, the PSP of the merchant will recover this interchange fee as part of the merchant fee. However, this amount shall be limited to the lowest of:[81]

- the relevant costs incurred by PSPs for the provision of digital euro payments, including a reasonable margin of profit; or
- fees or charges requested for comparable digital means of payment.

The same principles apply to the merchant fee charged by the acquiring PSP to the merchant.

4.6. The Role of the ECB

For the digital euro to function, the ECB will have to make available certain technical facilities.

- Most importantly the ECB will arrange for the settlement of digital euro transactions between PSPs and even users. Each user will be administrated in the books of the ECB, be it on pseudonymised basis.[82]

[75] Digital Euro Regulation, art 14(1).
[76] ECB Stocktake 18.
[77] ibid 31.
[78] Digital Euro Regulation, art 17.
[79] See, about interchange fees extensively, Regulation (EU) 2015/751 of the European Parliament and of the Council of 29 April 2015 on interchange fees for card-based payment transactions [2015] OJ L123.
[80] A critical evaluation of this kind of price regulation at the payments market can be found in European Court of Auditors, *Digital Payments in the EU: Progress Towards Making Them Safer, Faster, and Less Expensive, Despite Remaining Gaps* (2025) 16.
[81] Digital Euro Regulation, art 17(2).
[82] ECB Stocktake 27.

- The ECB will develop a scheme for the digital euro.[83]
- PSPs may make available their own front-end services, but those PSPs that do not want to can make use of the front-end services that will be offered by the ECB.[84]
- The ECB may facilitate the fraud detection and prevention tasks that PSPs shall perform under PSD2 by establishing a general fraud detection and prevention mechanism for online digital euro transactions.[85]

4.7. Targeted Measures to Assist the Vulnerable Consumer

As the digital euro should have cash-like features, it is considered important that is also accessible for vulnerable consumers.[86] For that reason it is mandated that post office giro institutions of Member States, or their regional or local authorities (when not acting in their capacity as public authorities), provide basic digital payment services and digital inclusion support that is face-to-face in physical proximity.[87] These parties, as well as normal credit institutions, shall provide digital inclusion support to persons with disabilities, functional limitations or limited digital skills, and elderly persons. Digital inclusion support shall comprise dedicated assistance for onboarding to a digital euro account and using all basic digital euro services.[88] Also, the digital euro shall: (a) have usage and service features that are simple and easy to handle, including for persons with disabilities, functional limitations or limited digital skills, and older persons; and (b) be accessible for persons with disabilities by complying with the accessibility requirements laid down in the Accessibility Directive.[89]

5. Alternative Payment Rails

Besides the digital euro, various other new payment rails are proposed. They have in common that they are meant to break the traditional hold of US-owned card networks MasterCard and VISA over point-of-interaction payments. Point-of-interaction payments are payments that need to be guaranteed immediately because of their economic role. For example, when ordering a pizza online, for the pizza to be sent over immediately, the restaurant must have an immediate confirmation that the payment is guaranteed. Likewise, when eating pizza in a restaurant abroad, immediate payment is paramount. The regular SEPA payments

[83] ibid 28.
[84] Digital Euro Regulation, art 17(2). ECB Stocktake 29.
[85] ibid art 32 and ibid 29.
[86] ECB Stocktake 35.
[87] Digital Euro Regulation, art 14(3).
[88] ibid art 14(4).
[89] ibid art 22(1).

(push bank transfers) are not a viable solution in these cases as the money may take a full business day to arrive.[90] Except for certain national alternative payment methods, which only have national coverage (such as iDEAL in the Netherlands), the main payment methods providing the required immediate guarantee are MasterCard and VISA (or cash in the case of face-to-face payment). MasterCard or VISA are the only payment networks with international (and so Europe-wide) coverage that can facilitate payment at the point of interaction. Several alternatives have been proposed.

5.1. Instant Payments

In March 2024, the new Instant Payments Regulation was published in the *Official Journal* of the EU. The Instant Payments Regulation has two main goals.[91] The first is protecting the interest of the consumer. As explained in the introduction to this chapter, VISA and MasterCard are the dominant payments routes in Europe, especially when it concerns cross-border point-of-interaction payments across EU Member States. Instant payments are meant to introduce a cross-border alternative. Instant payments are required to arrive within 10 seconds.[92] It is envisaged that competition in the market increases by introducing such an alternative to VISA and MasterCard, leading to better and cheaper services for the payment services users. Also, by setting such an EU alternative to VISA and MasterCard, the reliance on these US-owned companies decreases, which is meant to mitigate the geopolitical risk elaborated upon in section 2.5.

The implementation of the Instant Payments Regulation requires a substantial investment from PSPs across the EU. All PSPs that currently offer the payment service of sending and receiving credit transfers must be able to receive instant credit transfers 24 hours per day on any calendar day.[93] Naturally this is a significant IT change as compared to the current situation where payments can take a business day to arrive. Additionally, PSPs should treat instant payments the same as non-instant payments in terms of available payment initiation channels[94] and charges.[95]

5.2. European Payments Initiative (EPI)

Even though instant payments may help to create point-of-interaction solutions for EU cross-border payments, it may by itself be insufficient. Imagine that, when

[90] PSD2, art 83 lid 1.
[91] Instant Payments Regulation, Recitals 2 and 7.
[92] ibid art 5a 4 (c).
[93] ibid art 5a 1.
[94] ibid art 5a 4 (a).
[95] ibid art 5b.

ordering a pizza, one has to manually copy the bank details of the restaurant into one's banking app; this would seriously hinder the efficient ordering of a pizza. Also, on the side of the restaurant itself, significant impediments would remain if the restaurant needed to match the incoming payment with the relevant order before starting baking. More is required. This is where the EPI comes into play. The EPI is an initiative from 14 major retail banks from Germany, France, Belgium and the Netherlands and two major acquirers.[96] It will facilitate (cross-)border payments by adding a layer on top of (instant) SEPA payments. This could be a QR code, for example, which, when scanned, automatically triggers the payment in the usual bank environment of the payer (to be authenticated in the usual way), then followed by an automatic confirmation from the bank of the payer that the payment has been initiated or even a guarantee that the payment order will be executed.[97]

5.3. Open Banking and SEPA Payment Account Access Scheme

Another legislative initiative to arrange for additional payment rails is Open Banking. Open Banking was introduced in PSD2 in 2018,[98] also referred to – to the extent it relates to the actual execution of payments as opposed to the mere accessing of data – as a payment initiation service (PIS). A PIS is defined as 'a service to initiate a payment order at the request of the payment service user with respect to a payment account held at another payment service provider'.[99] Already, then, the PIS was seen as a more cost-efficient alternative to credit cards. Firstly, the PIS was envisaged to form a software bridge between the website of the merchant and the online banking platform of the payer's account servicing PSP (ASPSP).[100] Secondly, a PIS enables the payment initiation service provider (PISP) to provide confirmation to a payee that payment has been initiated, in order to provide an incentive to the payee to release the goods or to deliver the service without delay.[101] PSD2 required ASPSPs to enable PISPs to access bank accounts in order to initiate these payments (of course after client authorisation).

Unfortunately, this regulatory goal has only been achieved to a limited extent.[102] Firstly, consumers were already familiar with other means of payments.

[96] ABN AMRO, Belfius, Credit Mutuel, BNP Paribas, Groupe PBCE, Credit Argricole, Deutsche Bank, Sparkasse, DZBank, ING, KBC, La Banque Postale, NEXI, Rabobank, Societe General and Wordline.

[97] See the EPI website www.epicompany.eu/members/.

[98] PSD2, art 115.

[99] ibid art 4 (15).

[100] ibid Recital 27.

[101] ibid Recital 29.

[102] See also European Court of Auditors, *Digital Payments in the EU: Progress Towards Making Them Safer, Faster, and Less Expensive, Despite Remaining Gaps* (2025) 23.

For example, when offered the opportunity to choose between their familiar credit card or a novel means of payment presented to them by an unknown financial institution (namely the PISP), they prefer the credit card. Especially in the Netherlands with iDEAL established as the dominant alternative payment method next to credit cards, there was not much room for PISPs. Secondly, it was believed that the APIs offered by ASPSPs did not work that well, as they only confirmed that payment had been initiated; this was, however, no guarantee that payment would also be successful, as it could be blocked for other reasons.[103]

To increase the usability of Open Banking, market parties have agreed on a specific scheme with agreements that go beyond PSD2: the SPAA scheme. Leveraging existing investments in PSD2-compliant APIs, PSPs can offer premium data and transaction services on top of what PSD2 currently mandates them to provide for free. For those premium services, the ASPSP will receive a default remuneration from the PSP accessing the SPAA API. Notably, the SPAA scheme arranges for a confirmation that the payment will indeed go through, confirming that sufficient funds are available and the payment will not be blocked because of alleged fraud.[104] A similar requirement has been included in PSR.[105] Also, the SPAA scheme has laid down in more detail what kind of information a PISP would need to provide to the ASPSP and provides for additional use cases, such as variable recurring payments, for example for subscriptions to services such as Netflix or telephone providers where the monthly payments vary.

6. Evaluation of the Initiatives

Looking at the initiatives we can discern various methods to address the new risks and trends set out under section 2. What all the methods have in common is that the private sector is enlisted to solve common societal and geopolitical problems.

Traditionally, financial services regulation is concerned with regulating the externalities caused by the services offered. For example, banks need to hold capital because their services entail the risk that they become insolvent, leading to a government bail-out or losses with depositors. Regulatory capital requirements are meant to mitigate these risks, which are caused by the activities that banks undertake of their own volition but may not sufficiently manage of their own volition. In the same vein, the conduct-of-business supervision of PSPs (such as information requirements) is meant to address the risk that, in engaging in their activities, the interests of clients are not sufficiently taken into account. Once more, these are

[103] PSD2, art 46.

[104] See SEPA Payment Account Access (SPAA) Scheme Rulebook EPC012-22 (version 1.0, 30 November 2022) 23, effective from 30 November 2023.

[105] PSR, art 36 (5).

externalities potentially caused by the service provision that need to be managed. In the rules set out above, however, a different logic is at play.

- Some of the rules require that PSPs adjust their services so they are also accessible for vulnerable consumers. This concerns the Accessibility Directive (see section 3.1) and the additional efforts that need to be made when distributing the digital euro (see section 4.7). In these cases the rules are not meant to cure negative externalities, but rather PSPs need to adjust their services for the attainment of a higher public good, namely the full participation of people with disabilities. Even though traditionally not part of financial services regulation, this is quite common in general law. However, with the requirement to make cash available (see section 3.4), PSPs and merchants need to implement entire services rather than arrange for accessibility of their services. This is normally not required by anti-discrimination law[106] or by the Accessibility Directive.[107]
- Some rules lead to risk sharing between vulnerable customers (see sections 3.2.1 and 3.2.5) and other customers. When a liability is shifted from consumers to all PSPs, the expected result is that prices of the PSPs' services will increase. Naturally it may also have another effect, namely that PSPs improve their fraud monitoring systems and that consumers may have more faith in digital banking, leading to a higher uptake of digital banking services. Still, at the start it will be risk sharing via PSP with the customers less susceptible to fraud, insuring the more susceptible customers.
- Various rules require PSPs to invest in products and services they would not invest in of their own volition. An example is that all PSPs will be required by law to distribute the digital euro for limited compensation (see sections 4.4 and 4.5) and to arrange for the receipt and sending of instant payments (see section 5.1). The key reason for this is to mitigate the geopolitical risk of a foreign stablecoin or CBDC obtaining a dominant position in the EU market and to limit the market power of existing payment such as MasterCard and VISA. Demanding such significant investments in products and services from private companies to achieve a public good is unheard of.[108] Also, these requirements infringe in two ways the freedom to conduct a business as laid down in Article 16 of the Charter of Fundamental Rights of the European Union. Firstly, it requires PSPs to make significant investments in products they would not offer of their own volition. The freedom to conduct a business includes, inter alia, the right for any business to be able to freely use, within

[106] Commission, 'Proposal for a Council Directive on implementing the principle of equal treatment between persons irrespective of religion or belief, disability, age or sexual orientation' COM (2008) 0426 final, art 4.

[107] Accessibility Directive, art 14.

[108] For example, with respect to achieving strategic autonomy in the energy markets, energy companies are not forced into producing or obtaining energy differently. See L Hancher and A De Hauteclocque, 'Strategic Autonomy, REpowerEU and the Internal, Energy Market: Untying The Gordian Knot' (2024) 61(1) *Common Market Law Review* 55.

the limits of its liability for its own acts, the economic, technical and financial resources available to it.[109] Secondly, the digital euro project in particular may have a fundamental impact on the competitive position of banks, as depositors may prefer the digital euro.[110] Infringements of the freedom to conduct a business under article 16 can be acceptable only if sufficiently justified.[111]

- The digital euro is really a breach of the general idea that the payments markets should be a competitive market where the best payment solution should win. Normally, different payment solutions vie for the attention of merchants and customers and the payment solution that, because of its attractiveness, gets high adoption rates on both sides wins the market. Now, however, the digital euro is forced on the merchant side of the market. Even if it is not such a desirable product because of its features, it may still get high adoption rates. Because it will have high (mandatory) acceptance rates with merchants it will become desirable for the customer side as well and may become even more desirable than a superior product that does not have the benefit of mandatory acceptance. This is also at odds with the freedom to conduct a business.
- For society as a whole, requirements are imposed in order to mitigate the geopolitical risk, namely the mandatory acceptance of the digital euro by payees without charging for this (see section 4.3). Payees also must accept cash without charging for this, as this mandatory acceptance of cash is in the interest of vulnerable consumers (see section 3.2.6).
- PSPs are nudged into working together in order to achieve political goals. They are nudged to develop standards to facilitate the confirmation of payee services mandated to protect vulnerable consumers from fraud. Also, the EPI and the SEPA scheme (see sections 5.2 and 5.3), which both require deep cooperation and standard setting, are really applauded by the Commission and ECB in the interests of strategic autonomy, even though, ostensibly, they are voluntarily entered into by the founding financial institutions.

The key conclusion is therefore that the new risks and trends lead to significant requirements being imposed on financial institutions to solve societal problems that are caused by neither them nor their services. Although there probably are good reasons for this, it is in any case a watershed from traditional financial regulation and a breach of the general idea that business should be able to freely use, within the limits of its liability for its own acts, the economic, technical and financial resources available to it.

[109] Case C–314/12 UPC Telekabel Wien GmbH v Constantin Film Verleih GmbH and Wega Filmproduktionsgesellschaft mbH [2014] ECLI:EU:C:2014:192, para 49.

[110] See S Grünewald, C Zellweger-Gutknecht, and B Geva, Digital Euro and ECB Powers (2021) 58(4) *Common Market Law Review* 1045 and L Kriese, *Central Bank Digital Currency A Technical, Legal and Economic Analysis* (Springer 2023) 165.

[111] Charter of Fundamental Rights of the European Union, art 52.

10

Regulatory Strategies to Introduce Smart Technologies in Positive Energy Districts

MAX BAUMGART AND JASPER VAN DEN BOOM*

1. Introduction

Both the EU and the Netherlands have the ambition to achieve a CO_2 emissions-neutral society by 2050.[1] A team of experts, appointed by the government of the Netherlands, has issued a report outlining a vision for 2050, with the overarching goal of achieving socially integrated, green, quiet and predominantly energy-neutral neighbourhoods.[2] Buildings will be well insulated (reducing the energy requirement by 50–70 per cent), and energy will be produced through solar panels on roofs and heat from the ground, surface water and residual underground streams.[3] High levels of system integration allow for the efficient use of heat that is otherwise wasted, while coherent and mutually reinforcing sustainability interventions are utilised to maximise the energy efficiency of neighbourhoods and districts.[4] Besides the long-term objectives of the energy transition, there are objectives to be achieved in the short term, including a 55 per cent reduction in emissions by 2030 as compared to 1990.[5]

* With this chapter, the author Max Baumgart contributes to his Starter Grant project 'Transformation Processes in European and National Economic Law: Energy Law as Law of Socio-Technical Change', for which he was awarded funds by Tilburg University.

[1] European Commission, 'The European Green Deal' (Communication) COM (2019) 640 final; Regulation (EU) 2021/1119 establishing the framework for achieving climate neutrality ('European Climate Law') [2021] OJ L243/1, in particular art 2; Rijksoverheid, Klimaatakkoord [Climate agreement] (2019).

[2] B Ter Haar and others, 'Energie door perspectief: rechtvaardig, robuust en duurzaam naar 2050' ['Energy through Perspective: Just, Robust, and Sustainable to 2050'], *Report for the RVO* (2023) 66–68.

[3] ibid; B Krishna Saha, B Chakraborty, and R Dutta, 'Estimation of Waste Heat and Its Recovery Potential from Energy-Intensive Industries' (2020) 22 *Clean Technologies & Environmental Policy* 1.

[4] ibid.

[5] These goals were set in the Paris Agreement; see more recently European Commission, '"Fit for 55": Delivering the EU's 2030 Climate Target on the Way to Climate Neutrality' (Communication) COM (2021) 550 final.

The creation of positive energy districts (PEDs), and the transformation of living areas, forms part of the plans to achieve the 2030 and 2050 objectives. Following the EU's 'Strategic energy Technology Plan' (SeT Plan), 100 neighbourhoods are to be transformed into so-called PEDs by 2025.[6] PEDs should become adopted relatively quickly and, over time, become the norm in urbanised energy strategies to achieve the EU's 2050 sustainability goals.[7] The European Commission's SeT Plan defines PEDs as '(local) districts with annual net zero energy import and net zero CO_2 emissions working towards an annual local surplus production of renewable energy'.[8] PED participants (ie energy pro-/consumer within the PED) both contribute to the decarbonisation of the energy system and aim to provide additional energy that can be fed back into the grid. The notion of 'positive' thus is twofold: 'positive' relates both to the production of clean energy and to a surplus in generated energy. The creation of PEDs is a complex task: it requires interactions and integration between buildings, users, and local (or regional) energy, mobility and Information and Communication Technology (ICT) systems and grids.[9] Achieving this integration requires a holistic approach that includes technological, spatial, regulatory, financial, legal, social and economic perspectives.[10]

In practice, the transition towards PEDs is happening slowly in the Netherlands. This is partly a result of technical restraints and also in part due to legal obstacles that exist either because legislation is not (yet) updated to implement the latest EU Directives or because there is a mismatch between the legislative frameworks and practical needs.[11] In some instances, the lagging regulatory framework may limit or block the adoption of smart technologies and associated solutions.[12]

Smart technologies can play a crucial role for developing PEDs as they can help to overcome technical and legal challenges. Smart technologies enhance efficiency,

[6] SeT Plan Action 3.2, *Implementation Plan – Europe to Become a Global Role Model in Integrated, Innovative Solutions for the Planning, Deployment, and Replication of Positive Energy Districts* (2018) 6.

[7] C Gollner, 'PEDs for Sustainable Urbanization' (*JPI Urban Europe*, 22 February 2019); European Commission, 'REPowerEU Plan' (Communication) COM (2022) 230 final.

[8] SeT Plan *Implementation Plan* (n 7).

[9] Ter Haar and others 'Energie door perspectief' (n 3) 6; Gollner 'PEDs for Sustainable Urbanization'; JPI Urban Europe, *White Paper on PED Reference Framework for Positive Energy Districts and Neighbourhoods* (2020). Available at: https://jpi-urbaneurope.eu/wp-content/uploads/2020/04/White-Paper-PED-Framework-Definition-2020323-final.pdf.

[10] Ter Haar and others ibid 6; Gollner ibid; JPI Urban Europe ibid.

[11] DG Tempelman, *De rol van het recht in de energietransitie, Rede voor het Lectoraat Juridische en economische vraagstukken binnen de energietransitie* (2023) 19; see also Rijksoverheid, 'Nieuwe Energiewet wordt fundament van de energietransitie' (2024); J van den Boom, 'Experimenting with Co-Ownership of Energy Storage Facilities: A Case Study of the Netherlands' (2023) 24(4) *Competition and Regulation in Network Industries* 1–25; on legal obstacles for the energy transition related to the delay in transposing EU law through the Energiewet see also S Lavrijssen, L Reins, and T Ten Caten, 'Realizing Peer-to-Peer Trading in the Electricity Market in the EU and Its Member States' in *Handbook of Energy Law in the Low-Carbon Transition* (De Gruyter 2023).

[12] Prosumers with smart meters, solar panels and smart batteries could, for instance, engage in peer-to-peer trading or offer services as energy aggregators. Peer-to-peer trading and aggregation, as well as the creation of energy communities, are arranged in the Energiewet, but were not yet possible under the Electriciteits- and Gaswet. See also Lavrijssen, Reins, and Ten Caten 'Realizing Peer-to-Peer Trading' (n 12); ACM, *Verkenning naar belemmeringen voor de rol van aggregator* (2019).

reduce regulatory complexities and align energy practices with existing law.[13] They can help by optimising energy generation, distribution and consumption. Through advanced data analytics and automation, smart technologies facilitate the balancing of local energy production and demand, reducing waste and emissions. They enable real-time monitoring and management of energy flows, integrating renewable energy sources and enhancing energy efficiency.[14] Additionally, smart technologies promote the active participation of residents and stakeholders.[15] Smart batteries allow users to more actively manage their own consumption as they can choose if they want to use the stored energy themselves or sell it to the grid. Smart meters and technologies also allow new business models to emerge, such as peer-to-peer trade or energy aggregators.[16] The law can either facilitate and promote or hinder the implementation and use of smart technologies in the described way. In this chapter, we discuss how the regulator may ensure that legal frameworks facilitate and stimulate the deployment of smart technologies for creating PEDs.[17] In the context of this chapter, we understand smart technologies as technical solutions that collect, communicate, visualise and/or use data, with the primary goal of improving economic and/or regulatory efficiency.[18]

We discuss the possibilities of using command-and-control regulation, principles-based regulation, design solutions, direct action, incentive-based regulation, market-harnessing control regulation, and regulatory sandboxes to introducing smart technologies in PEDs.[19] The discussion of regulatory strategies should provide regulators with a clear overview of the pros and cons of interventions with respect to PEDs and the energy transition broadly. Lessons are predominantly drawn from experiences in the Netherlands but generalised for application across jurisdictions. Whether the same problems and opportunities

[13] For instance, smart technologies may facilitate the decentralisation of the energy system, thereby preventing overinvestment in a central energy grid, see A Razmjoo and others, 'Development of Smart Energy Systems for Communities: Technologies, Policies and Applications' (2022) 248 *Energy* 123540. Alternatively, smart systems may help to meet the legal standards for energy efficiency in buildings, see European Commission, 'Smart Readiness Indicator'. Available at: https://energy.ec.europa.eu/topics/energy-efficiency/energy-efficient-buildings/smart-readiness-indicator_en.

[14] See M Baumgart and B Espinosa Apráez, 'On the Implementation of Smart Meters in the European Union: Legal Considerations Regarding Privacy and Personal Data Protection in Times of the Twin Transitions' in R Leal-Arcas (ed), *Research Handbook on EU Energy Law and Policy* (Edward Elgar Publishing2nd edn, 2024) 500.

[15] ibid.

[16] SS Sachinkumar, HC Cherukuri, and NM Pindoriya, 'Peer-to-Peer Energy Trading in Smart Grid: Frameworks, Implementation Methodologies, and Demonstration Projects' (2023) 214/A *Electric Power Systems Research* 108907.

[17] See in the case of sustainable hydrogen M Baumgart and S Lavrijssen, 'Exploring Regulatory Strategies for Accelerating the Development of Sustainable Hydrogen Markets in the European Union' (2023) 42(2) *Journal of Energy & Natural Resources Law 137*.

[18] For a more in-depth discussion of the definition of smart technologies see M Hildebrandt, 'Smart Technologies' (2020) 9(4) *Internet Policy Review 1*. Available at: https://doi.org/10.14763/2020.4.1531.

[19] For an overview of these regulatory strategies: see Baumgart and Lavrijssen 'Exploring Regulatory Strategies' (n 18); R Baldwin and others, *Understanding Regulation: Theory, Strategy, and Practice* (Oxford Scholarship Online 2011) 121; B Morgan and K Yeung, *An Introduction to Law and Regulation: Text and Materials* (Cambridge University Press 2012) 87.

arise depends on the national socio-legal context. This chapter proposes a three-step assessment for regulators to launch adequate regulatory strategies for introducing smart technologies in PEDs: (1) an assessment of the technical and legal landscape; (2) the definition of clear goals and objectives for specific timeframes; and (3) a set of principles of good regulation that should be incorporated in the strategies used.

2. Positive Energy Districts: Definition, Challenges and Experiences

2.1. Defining Positive Energy Districts

Following the EU SeT Plan on Positive Energy Districts, the European Commission aims to realise 100 PEDs across Europe in 2025.[20] The focus of the ongoing strategy is on PED neighbourhoods, focusing specifically on urban areas and cities.[21] However, PEDs can be understood more broadly. As PEDs are a novel concept, defining and identifying them is still open to interpretation.[22] The SeT plans requires that there is a connection between at least three buildings with zero energy import and zero CO_2 emissions, which have been or are working towards creating a surplus of energy, to be considered a PED.[23] This means that any connected rural community or industrial hub could qualify as a PED, not just urban areas. JPI Urban Europe – a knowledge hub for urban transitions towards sustainability – provides a more elaborate definition than the European Commission, explaining that PEDs should be understood conceptually as

> energy-efficient and energy-flexible urban areas or groups of connected buildings which produce net zero greenhouse gas emissions and actively manage an annual local or regional surplus production of renewable energy. They require integration of different systems and infrastructures and interaction between buildings, the users and the regional energy, mobility and ICT systems, while securing the energy supply and a good life for all in line with social, economic and environmental sustainability.[24]

These definitions are, notwithstanding any debate on what actually constitutes near zero, net zero or positive energy.[25]

[20] SeT Plan (n 7) 1.

[21] ibid.

[22] SG Krangsås and others, 'Positive Energy Districts: Identifying Challenges and Interdependencies' (2021) 13(19) *Sustainability* 13; X Zhang and others, 'Characterizing Positive Energy District (PED) through a Preliminary Review of 60 Existing Projects in Europe' (2021) 11 *Buildings* 318.

[23] ibid 3.

[24] JPI Urban Europe (n 10) 7; for more information on JPI Urban Europe see their official website: https://jpi-urbaneurope.eu/.

[25] L-N Sassenou, L Olivieri, and F Olivieri, 'Challenges for Positive Energy Districts Deployment: A Systematic Review' (2024) 191 *Renewable and Sustainable Energy Reviews* 114152.

Creating a PED requires an integrative approach, meaning that technological, spatial, regulatory, financial, legal, environmental, social and economic perspectives are taken into account in developing it. The development also requires cooperation between several actors, including public authorities representing the city, industry, investors, and research and citizen organisations.[26]

An example of how certain demographic characteristics (eg a neighbourhood versus an industrial area) shape the purpose of a PED can be found in the European Commission's SeT Plan, where, with reference to neighbourhoods specifically, the objectives of the European Commission go beyond the quantitative criteria (eg zero CO_2 emissions and/or a surplus of green energy produced). While creating an energy surplus and climate neutrality are two of the pursued objectives, the Commission also aims to (i) promote quality of life, by creating liveable, attractive and healthy urban environments; (ii) foster inclusiveness, through a special focus on reducing energy poverty and by creating economic opportunities (jobs in green industries, local economic growth); and (iii) promote a resilient and secure energy supply within the locality of the PED, by ensuring a healthy energy mix and by minimising the risk of disruptions.[27] For PEDs in industrial areas, objectives related to liveability and the reduction of energy poverty are likely to be ancillary, especially when compared to urban areas. Taking these objectives into account as well, the notion of 'positive' in PEDs goes beyond even the twofold definition mentioned earlier.

There are, however, a number of common pillars that support any type of PED project, irrespective of the involved parties or local peculiarities. With their systematic review, Sassenou and others found that each PED is characterised by the pursuit of three main functions: energy efficiency, energy flexibility and energy production.[28] These three main functions will be explained in more detail in the next sections, along with discussion of how these objectives interconnect and can be pursued in a symbiotic manner.

2.1.1. *Energy Efficiency*

Energy efficiency describes the ratio between energy consumption and the level of performance.[29] Thus, as a pursuit with a legal meaning in relation to PEDs, it aims at the optimal reduction of energy consumption while maintaining the same level of performance. Energy efficiency can be achieved in a multitude of ways, including energy saving technologies, sustainable construction, insulation

[26] SeT Plan (n 7) 1; JPI Urban Europe (n 10) 4.

[27] See JPI Urban Europe (n 10) 7.

[28] Sassenou and others 'Challenges for Positive Energy Districts Deployment' (n 26) 3.

[29] See Directive 2023/1791 of the European Parliament and of the Council of on energy efficiency (Energy Efficiency Directive), art 2(8); D Winkler, M Baumgart, and T Ackermann, *Europäisches Energierecht* [European Energy Law] (Nomos 2021) pt II, mn 77.

and restoration, and preventing the waste of energy.[30] According to the World Economic Forum, increasing energy efficiency could reduce global energy consumption by up to 31 per cent without reducing economic output, saving over €2 trillion in energy costs.[31]

Reducing energy waste is ensured by storing, sharing or reusing excess heat. Energy storage may happen in batteries, molecules (ie hydrogen) or heat.[32] Reusing energy may include the voluntary sharing of excess energy through energy communities, through peer-to-peer sales of energy, or by selling excess energy to aggregators.[33]

The reuse of excess heat is exceptionally important in reducing energy waste. Industrial energy use forms a significant share of total energy use, and the majority of this energy is consumed to generate heat.[34] Therefore, proper channels to reuse heat, within the firm, through inter-firm cooperation and through public-private partnerships, will help to increase energy efficiency. According to a study by JPI Urban Europe, recovering heat from industrial plants may help to power cities by as much as 25 per cent.[35] The importance of public-private partnerships should not be underestimated.

2.1.2. Energy Flexibility

Preventing energy waste through storage, sharing or reuse is also strongly linked to energy flexibility. This refers to the ability of an energy grid to deal with peaks and troughs in the production and demand for energy.[36] Energy flexibility is of particular relevance in energy grids that are driven by renewable energy, as renewables are often characterised by intermittent production and unpredictable fluctuations in total energy produced at any given time.[37]

Energy storage helps to increase flexibility as it allows for energy that is produced at one point in time to be consumed at a later point in time. Excess energy that is produced during production peaks can be stored and consumed

[30] See Energy Efficiency Directive, particularly Recitals 1–16.

[31] RE Moritz, 'This Overlooked Solution Can Unlock Abundant and Affordable Clean Energy' (World Economic Forum 2024). Available at: www.weforum.org/stories/2024/01/energy-efficiency-abundant-affordable-clean-energy/.

[32] Van den Boom (n 12); see also Rijksoverheid, *Routekaart Energieopslag [Roadmap Energy Storage]: Final Report* (2023).

[33] This is facilitated in Directive 2018/2001 on the promotion of the use of energy from renewable sources [2018] OJ L328, arts 2(18), 17, 22 and 23.

[34] A Aydemir and C Rhode, 'What About Heat Integration? Quantifying Energy Saving Potentials for Germany' (2018) *ECEEE Industrial Summer Study Proceedings 1*.

[35] JPI Urban Europe (n 10).

[36] See Van den Boom 'Experimenting with Co-Ownership of Energy Storage Facilities' (n 12) 200, in reference to the definition provided in Commission, 'Proposal for a Regulation of the European Parliament and of the Council, amending Regulations (EU) 2019/943 and (EU) 2019/942 as well as Directives (EU) 2018/2001 and (EU) 2019/944 to improve the Union's electricity market design' COM (2023) 148 final, Recital 80.

[37] ibid.

during production lows (or peaks in demand).[38] Where there is insufficient capacity to store excess energy to meet demand at any given time, these gaps have to be filled by using energy from non-renewable sources.[39] In PEDs, grey energy can be used via a life cycle approach, where it is used in the short term as part of a strategy to achieve net zero quicker in the longer term.[40] However, this does mean that any use of non-renewable resources should be in the context of a larger strategy, where the use of fossil fuels is phased out. To meet the criterion of zero CO_2 emissions, PEDs will ultimately need the flexibility to meet all demand through production from renewable sources.[41]

To achieve the goal of 100 per cent renewable energy consumption, sector coupling,[42] demand-side management, and storage are crucial.[43] However, while storage is a necessity to meet lulls in production, maximising energy efficiency helps to save significant amounts of energy and reduces the need for additional investment on the supply side by creating reductions on the demand side, thus also benefitting energy efficiency.[44] For this, the use of smart technologies are crucial to promote the efficient sharing of energy at different points in time and to coordinate demand-side management.[45]

2.1.3. Energy Production

Energy production simply refers to the fact that, to be considered a PED, a district must produce a surplus of renewable energy, thereby ensuring that its reduction of carbon emissions is equal to or greater than its produced emissions.[46]

2.2. Enablers, Challenges and Experiences

JPI Urban Europe has found that there are several enablers and challenges for the development of PEDs. Enablers are (a) the political vision and governance

[38] Van den Boom (n 12).

[39] ibid.

[40] Life Cycle Initiative, 'Life Cycle Management: How Business Uses It to Decrease Footprint, Create Opportunities and Make Value Chains More Sustainable' (2009).

[41] JPI Urban Europe (n 10) 8.

[42] Sector coupling 'refers to the idea of interconnecting (integrating) the energy consuming sectors – buildings (heating and cooling), transport, and industry – with the power producing sector', K Appunn, 'Sector coupling: Shaping an Integrated Renewable Energy System' (*Clean Energy Wire*, 25 April 2018).

[43] See M-J Zondag and others, 'Analysis to Support the Implementation of the Energy Efficiency First Principle in Decision-Making', *Final Report* (2021); Energy Efficiency Directive, Recital 18, to fully decarbonise a holistic and integrative approach is considered a necessity.

[44] Zondag and others ibid.

[45] JPI Urban Europe (n 10) 8.

[46] In the Paris Agreement, nations agreed to ensure that emissions 'fall to net zero by around 2050'. At its core, net zero means that the removal of carbon emissions is equal to or greater than the amount of carbon emitted. For an elaborate conceptualisation of what net zero means, see S Fankhauser and others, 'The Meaning of Net Zero and How to Get It Right' (2022) 12 *Nature Climate Change* 15. Available at: https://doi.org/10.1038/s41558-021-01245-w.

framework; (b) the active involvement of problem owners and citizens; (c) the integration of energy and urban planning; and (d) the ICT and data management.[47] Challenges exist in several areas. First, JPI Urban Europe has observed that PEDs are developed mostly in newly constructed neighbourhoods and hardly at all in existing building stock.[48] This is problematic as the latter entails the largest share of buildings.[49] Second, it has proven difficult to ensure zero-emissions local mobility, which forms a fair percentage of local CO_2 emissions.[50] Third, the pursuit of building PEDs may clash with the affordability of housing and building: building sustainably is expensive, as is conducting renovations of existing buildings.[51]

The presence of enablers may help to overcome challenges: a clear political vision and governance framework can set rules, steer subsidies and investments, and ensure coherent approaches in making the existing building stock more sustainable while keeping it affordable, and ICT management and data (as a result of using smart devices) can help reduce inefficiencies and costs.[52] Practice has shown that a top-down approach to sustainability efforts (ie imposing sustainability rules) produces backlash and limited effects, whereas stimulating active citizen groups in developing energy communities, building trust and adopting innovative solutions are drivers that help to create support for the energy transition.[53] Ultimately, any transition consists of a number of frontrunners that pave the way for a broader adoption of new technologies. Experience with PED projects will help to develop guiding principles for integrated urban and energy planning.

Gohari Krangsås and others (2021) have taken a more generalised approach to identifying enablers and challengers, and find that the two categories are often interrelated.[54] Their study identifies seven categories of factors that impact the success or failure of PED implementation: governance, incentives, social, process, market, technology and context.[55] The findings of the Gohari Krangsås study indicate that all seven factors jointly determine the success of implementing the PED.[56] However, political vision and governance are considered to have the greatest impact on the success or failure of implementing PEDs.[57] This approach to identifying drivers and challenges is sensible: besides practical challenges in the form of problem areas (local mobility, existing building stock), it should be recognised

[47] JPI Urban Europe (n 10) 8.
[48] ibid 7–8.
[49] ibid 15–18.
[50] ibid.
[51] ibid.
[52] ibid 18.
[53] Mehmet Efe Biresselioglu, Berfu Solak, and Zehra Funda Savas, 'Unveiling Resistance and Opposition Against Low-Carbon Energy Transitions: A Comprehensive Review' (2024) 107 *Energy Research & Social Science* 103354.
[54] Krangsås and others 'Positive Energy Districts' (n 23).
[55] ibid 3, 4, 13–16.
[56] ibid 13.
[57] ibid.

that a lack of enablers (or the wrong enablers) in themselves are likely to constitute challenges or limitations.

Besides theorisation on what drives and limits the emergence of PEDs, there is ample data to draw lessons from practice. There are already numerous PED projects, and there has been significant progress towards the goal set out in the 2018 SeT Plan. With significant funding and subsidisation at the European level, PED projects have been initiated in various EU Member States under a variety of conditions. A study by Bossi and others, published in 2020, already identified 61 PED and so-called 'Towards PED' (TO-PED) projects in 19 countries: 18 EU Member States and Turkey.[58] TO-PED projects are those that are working towards zero emissions but have not yet achieved zero emissions. These include renovations of existing building stock.[59] The highest numbers of projects were found in Norway (9), Italy (8), Finland (7), Sweden (6) and the Netherlands (6).[60] On the contrary, only two projects were located in Eastern and Southeastern Europe.[61]

The Bossi study allowed PED projects at varying stages of implementation to be included; choices ranged from planned (24 per cent) and implementation stage (69 per cent) to realised (3 per cent) and in operation (3 per cent).[62] For TO-PED projects, the percentage of projects in operation was already much higher (31 per cent).[63] There was also a mixture in the types of neighbourhoods where PED projects were initiated: newly built (28 per cent), developed from existing neighbourhoods (7 per cent) or mixed (66 per cent). For TO-PED, a significant number of existing neighbourhoods were being used (41 per cent).[64] This shows that there is still much work to be done to have 100 fully emissions-free PEDs in 2030, in accordance with the European Commission's SeT Plan, and that the adaptation of legal frameworks and promotion of smart technologies should remain a priority so as to achieve these goals. The Bossi study has shown that solar energy and district heating are the most prominently used tools to achieve zero emissions.[65] However, the majority of PEDs included a mix of energy sources to work towards zero emissions.[66] Out of the studied projects, 60 per cent used two or three energy sources simultaneously and 30 per cent

[58] S Bossi, C Gollner, and S Theierling, 'Towards 100 Positive Energy Districts in Europe: Preliminary Data Analysis of 61 European Cases' (2020) 13(22) *Energies* 6083.

[59] ibid 2–3.

[60] ibid.

[61] JPI Urban Europe, 'Europe Towards Positive Energy Districts' (2020). Available at: https://jpi-urbaneurope.eu/wp-content/uploads/2020/06/PED-Booklet-Update-Feb-2020_2.pdf.

[62] Bossi and others 'Towards 100 Positive Energy Districts in Europe' (n 59) 4.

[63] ibid 7.

[64] ibid 5.

[65] ibid 7.

[66] ibid. The research also categorised the energy typology of the different neighbourhoods, looking at a mix of 'solar thermal energy', 'geothermal energy', 'district heating/local heating', 'heat pump system', 'industrial waste heat', 'photovoltaic', or 'other' energy. Most of the projects include district or local heating (75 per cent). Furthermore, PED projects often rely on solar energy generated through PV (71 per cent), half of PED projects rely on thermal energy, and around 25 per cent of PED projects relied on the use of industrial waste heat.

used four or five.[67] The number of projects that attempted to reach net zero with a single source of energy is low (7 per cent), as is the number of projects that try to mix more than five sources of energy (3 per cent).[68]

As these numbers reflect the status in 2020, they are subject to change.[69] However, the Bossi study and subsequent studies do allow a number of preliminary conclusions to be drawn. First, PEDs will probably entail a mix of several renewable energy sources, including at least electricity and heat (be it thermal energy or rest heat). Second, the boundaries of what constitutes a PED are subject to discussion, yet the pillars and enablers return throughout a number of studies.[70] Third, the use of smart technologies such as meters and smart management systems is a crucial component in coordinating supply and demand in PEDs.[71] Fourth, governance and regulatory frameworks are seen as one of the most vital, or the most vital, drivers of success or causes of failure in setting up PEDs.[72]

2.3. Smart Technologies for Developing PEDs

The SeT Plan proposes the assessment and integration of technologies for PEDs. Smart meters, and other smart technologies, are considered vital for producing the bottom-up approach, where stakeholders and citizens can actively monitor and participate in the pursuit of zero emissions. These provide users and stakeholders with the information that they need to assess their energy needs and consumption, thereby laying the foundation for active involvement and conscious choices towards more energy-efficient behaviour.[73] Insights derived from the collected data in turn help to create economic or regulatory efficiencies.

Besides smart meters, there are numerous possibilities for deploying smart ICT and data management solutions that help to reduce emissions. These include the following:[74]

Smart management systems are technology-driven solutions that efficiently monitor, control and optimise the use of energy within a building, home or

[67] ibid 7.
[68] ibid.
[69] Currently, projects are ongoing to establish a database of PED projects in Europe. However, the PED-EU-NET Database is not accessible online at the time of writing. A recently published conference paper on the establishment of the database remarks that it is hard to determine the number of valid PED projects due to differences in methodological approaches and how they are defined in different jurisdictions, see European Commission, 'Positive Energy Districts European Network, *PED-EU-NET*' (2022). Available at: https://build-up.ec.europa.eu/en/resources-and-tools/links/positive-energy-districts-european-network-ped-eu-net.
[70] Bossi and others (n 59); S Shnapp, D Paci, and P Bertoldi, *Enabling Positive Energy Districts Across Europe: Energy Efficiency Couples Renewable Energy* (JRC Technical Report 2020); Sassenou and others (n 26).
[71] JPI Urban Europe 'Europe Towards Positive Energy Districts' (n 62).
[72] Krangsås and others (n 23).
[73] See Baumgart and Espinosa Apráez (n 15) 500.
[74] SeT Plan (n 7) 62.

energy grid.[75] Such a system should integrate data analytics, automation and communication to enhance efficiencies and reduce costs. Smart meters are an essential part of smart management systems, yet would only produce limited efficiencies without having a smart management system in place.[76] The regulator can also use reactive compensation schemes, rewarding users for improving their consumption behaviour, based on the collected data.[77]

Interoperability in ICT for urban services refers to the seamless connection of different systems, devices, platforms and networks. There should be interoperability in terms of real-time data sharing and access, and interoperability in the sense of system compatibility and standardisation. As PEDs mostly seem to use mixed sources of energy, the availability and use of each type of source should be analysed and prioritised depending on waste and availability.[78]

Controller algorithms in grid-balancing allow for the emergence of local (micro) grids. Balancing energy needs is a complex task, especially for smaller energy communities. Algorithmic steering helps to prevent the over- or underproduction and consumption of energy.[79] Algorithms can also help to coordinate peer-to-peer energy sales or local aggregation platforms.[80] These platforms can facilitate local exchanges by aggregating and selling energy on the behalf of users, making it easier to redistribute overproductions of energy.[81]

The use of *cloud platforms related to the building sector* for the purpose of combining aggregated and open data to support energy efficiency measures (including investments and real-time control) does not have direct applicability to managing grids but has proven useful in developing more energy-efficient buildings.[82] The use of virtual reality, IoT data, augmented reality and Big Data analytics significantly impacts the sustainable design of new buildings.[83]

Finally, *vehicle-to-grid integration* ensures that the infrastructure is able in terms of capacity and technology to both charge electric vehicles from the grid and send energy back from the vehicles to support grid management.[84] This is not

[75] See A Tomar and A Pattnaik, 'Smart Energy Management in Renewable Energy Systems' in M Rizwan and M Jamil (eds), *Smart Energy Management Systems and Renewable Energy Resources* (AIP Publishing 2021).

[76] ibid.

[77] ACM, *Evaluatie ACM: Meer ruimte op het elektriciteitsnetwerk mogelijk door congestiemanagement* (2023).

[78] Tomar and Pattnaik (n 76).

[79] F Bano and others, 'Intelligent Control Algorithms for Enhanced Frequency Stability in Single and Interconnected Power Systems' (2024) 13(21) *Electronics* 4219.

[80] S Kerscher and P Arboleya, 'The Key Role of Aggregators in the Energy Transition under the Latest European Regulatory Framework' (2022) 134 *International Journal of Electrical Power & Energy Systems* 107361.

[81] ibid.

[82] See CA Balaras and others, 'Intelligent Services for Building Information Modeling: Assessing Variable Input Weather Data for Building Simulations' (2013) 2013(7) *The Open Construction and Building Technology Journal 138.*

[83] SA Bello and others, 'Cloud Computing in the Construction Industry: Use Cases, Benefits and Challenges' (2021) 122 *Automation in Construction* 103441.

[84] P Kumar and others, 'A Comprehensive Review of Vehicle-To-Grid Integration in Electric Vehicles: Powering The Future' 2025) 25 *Energy Conversion and Management* 100864.

only an effective use of the batteries of stationary cars but also a cost-efficient way to stimulate the electrification of urban mobility.[85]

The development of PEDs requires a mix of smart solutions. Smart meters should be viewed as a starting point, as it allows for the collection of data. However, absent further means to efficiently process and analyse data, introduce policies to adjust user behaviour, or stimulate efficiencies through technological enhancements or interoperability solutions, the collection of data is insufficient to work towards energy-neutral areas.[86]

3. The Regulatory Toolbox

While smart technologies provide the tools and infrastructure to enable energy-efficient and sustainable solutions within PEDs, their successful implementation relies heavily on a supportive regulatory framework. To ensure these technologies can be effectively deployed and scaled, regulatory interventions must address existing challenges and pave the way for innovation.[87] PEDs, currently, are not being developed at a large scale. Regulators must make the effort to support pilots to identify technological and regulatory innovations to support the creation of PEDs going forward.

The regulator has a toolbox of different regulatory strategies at hand to implement smart technologies. These range from principle-based regulation to command-and-control regulation. Experimental approaches help identify effective regulatory strategies before they are applied on a wider scale. There are several types of regulation that could be used by the legislator to enable PEDs (Figure 10.1).[88]

Figure 10.1 Three steps to introducing smart technologies in positive energy districts (own illustration)

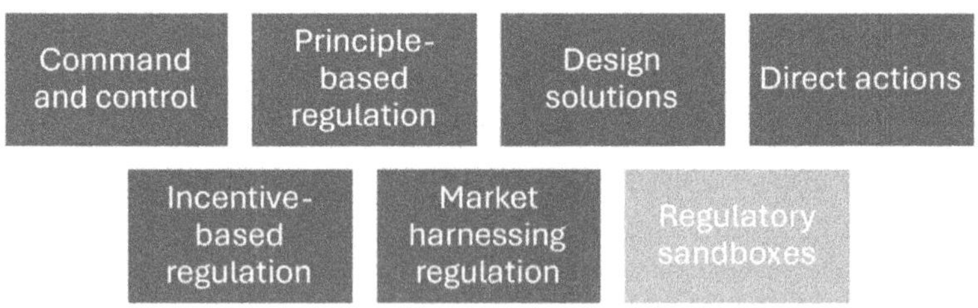

[85] Rijksoverheid (n 33).

[86] Many of these systems are already used in water management, see Tomar and Pattnaik (n 76); see Bossi and others (n 59); Rijksoverheid (n 33).

[87] New regulatory intervention is needed if new technologies and socio-technical change create issues that cannot be addressed with existing tools, cf R Leenes, 'Regulating New Technologies in Times of Change' in Leonie Reins (ed), *Regulating New Technologies in Uncertain Times* (Springer 2019) 11–15.

[88] For an overview of these regulatory strategies: cf Baumgart and Lavrijssen (n 18); Baldwin and others *Understanding Regulation* (n 20) 121; Morgan and Yeung *An Introduction to Law and Regulation* (n 20) 87.

The traditional form of *command-and-control* regulation involves setting specific rules and standards that market participants must follow, and includes prescriptive laws and regulations that enforce compliance through monitoring and penalties for non-compliance.[89] Command-and-control frameworks for PEDs could, eg, prohibit the use of non-renewables, or at least the use of non-renewables without a lifecycle approach, in order to be considered a PED legally.[90] Moreover, legal frameworks should prohibit certain behaviours by consumers if these are detrimental to the emergence of PEDs, for instance by setting minimum standards for energy efficiency in buildings or even setting limits to consumption for certain parties (if this cannot be arranged privately). There should also be obligations for the operators of centralised grids to facilitate the export of energy between PEDs, to ensure that surplus energy is not wasted. In terms of smart technologies and tools, an example for command-and-control regulation can be found in Article 19(2) and Annex II(1) of Directive (EU) 2019/944, which requires Member States to mandate the installation of smart meters in households.[91]

Instead of setting rigid rules, *principle-based regulation* focuses on broader principles that guide the behaviour of market participants and provides flexibility for companies to achieve regulatory objectives in ways that best suit their operations.[92] Principle-based regulation can aid in the development of PEDs by offering legal flexibility, allowing tailored approaches to local conditions and promoting innovation. This regulatory approach encourages creativity in energy solutions, fostering the development of new technologies and systems. It provides an adaptive framework that evolves with advancements in energy and urban technologies. Principle-based regulation also incentivises long-term sustainability by focusing on broader goals like energy independence and community well-being. However, the flexibility that principle-based regulation offers can create opportunities for exploitation and regulatory arbitrage, while also posing challenges for enforcement and accountability. Additionally, without specific rules, different stakeholders may approach similar issues in diverse ways, potentially leading to uneven standards and unpredictable results.

Design solutions involve embedding regulatory objectives directly into the design of a system: regulators can organise the system in such a way that an undesired behaviour just cannot happen, eg because the infrastructure just does not allow it.[93] One could also think of markets being designed in a way that compliance with certain regulatory objectives is immanent to the market. By integrating renewable energy generation, smart grid technologies and energy-efficient buildings at the design stage, PEDs can achieve a surplus of locally produced energy.

[89] Baumgart and Lavrijssen (n 18) 150; Morgan and Yeung (n 20) 221, 80ff; Baldwin and others (n 20) 119 and references therein.

[90] Life Cycle Initiative (n 41).

[91] See Baumgart and Espinosa Apráez 'Smart Meters in the European Union' (n 15) 500, 509.

[92] Baumgart and Lavrijssen (n 18) 150–51; Baldwin and others (n 20) 119; J Black, 'Forms and Paradoxes of Principles-Based Regulation' (2008) LSE Legal Studies Working Paper 13, 9–10.

[93] See Baldwin and others (n 20) 122.

This proactive approach ensures that regulatory objectives like carbon reduction and resource efficiency are met naturally through the district's operation. By embedding monitoring and compliance systems within the infrastructure, design solutions can facilitate seamless collaboration between energy producers, consumers and regulators. Additionally, designing for flexibility allows districts to adapt to future energy demands and regulatory changes. The inclusion of sustainable technologies and standards in building new homes is therefore vital to enhance energy efficiency and move towards net zero emissions as the norm for urban areas. In the Netherlands, the national climate agreement determines that, by 2050, seven million homes must be carbon neutral.[94] This means that a large number of residences must be renovated, and that new buildings should be designed with zero emissions in mind. New homes in the Netherlands are no longer connected to the gas infrastructure and there is a legal obligation to ensure that they are well insulated.[95]

Regulators take *direct action*, which means using their resources to stimulate the development of a market.[96] Direct action includes government-funded projects or the creation of public-private partnerships,[97] for example to kick-start market activities, provide the infrastructure for a market, or show the viability of a project. Governments can also create public-private partnerships to share costs and expertise, encouraging innovation and accelerating PED deployment. Direct involvement in knowledge-sharing platforms and community engagement can ensure that best practices are widely adopted. Direct action strategies can stimulate the development of PEDs by initiating government-funded pilot projects that demonstrate the feasibility of PEDs and set a benchmark for future developments. Public investment in smart grid infrastructure, renewable energy installations, and energy storage systems such as batteries within these districts can reduce the initial risk for private investors. Targeted subsidies move users to purchase certain technological solutions or to reduce their energy consumption (for instance through insulation). Also, funding research on PEDs can be considered direct action.

[94] Rijksoverheid, Klimaatakkoord [Climate agreement] (n 2).

[95] Article 10(7) of the Gaswet contains an exemption from the obligation to connect households to the gas grid; this amendment is also known as the Wet Voortgang Energietransitie (Wet VET). Since 1 July 2018, new houses will no longer be connected to the gas infrastructure as per the Dutch building code (Bouwbesluit). This policy will be continued under the new Energy Act (energiewet), Environmental Act (Omgevingswet) and the updated building codes (Wet BBL); see also TNO, *Accelerating Towards a Climate-Neutral Built Environment*. Available at: www.tno.nl/en/sustainable/energy-built-environment/accelerating-towards-climate-neutral/.

[96] Baldwin and others (n 20) 121–22.

[97] From the perspective of hydrogen markets see Baumgart and Lavrijssen (n 18) 151; S Lavrijssen and B Vitéz, 'Make Hydrogen Whilst the Sun Shines: How to Turn the Current Momentum into a Well-Functioning Hydrogen Market?' (2020) *Carbon & Climate Law Review* 266, 268, 266, 276.

Incentive-based regulation uses economic incentives to encourage desired behaviours in the market, eg tax incentives.[98] Pricing schemes may be used to incentivise users to consume more or less energy depending on its production. Additionally, regulators can offer financial incentives, such as low-interest loans, to support the implementation of energy-efficient technologies in buildings. Providing incentives to start or participate in peer-to-peer trading or selling to aggregators, or providing performance-based compensation, may be desirable to effect behavioural changes in regard to the use of smart technologies. Regulatory frameworks for PEDs must facilitate behaviour that serves the creation of PEDs. In some instances, a lack of recognition in laws and regulation blocks the employment of certain technologies. In the Netherlands, the emergence of energy communities has long been hindered by delays in the implementation of Directive 2018/2001, as there was no legal basis to set up such energy communities in the law. Under Article 2.4 of the new Dutch Energy Act, energy communities are recognised by law, making it easier to set up an energy community through the adoption of voluntary statutes. This means that, when the new Energy Act enters into force on 1 January 2026, parties that want to start an energy community will no longer have to register as a foundation and the adoption and signing articles of association will be sufficient.

Regulation may also hinder other developments that are desirable from the perspective of managing utilities but need to be balanced with other fundamental rights. For instance, the availability of data may be limited in light of data protection laws. Here, specialised regulatory frameworks may help to strike a balance between conflicting interests to find a desirable level of data use.[99]

Market-harnessing regulation seeks to use market mechanisms to achieve regulatory goals.[100] It assumes that the market contains forces that will achieve regulatory goals, such as low product prices for consumers or a higher product quality.[101] Instead of direct interventions, regulators create conditions for market forces to drive the desired outcomes, such as creating competitive markets.[102] Market-harnessing regulation can aim to resolve market failures, allowing missing markets to emerge, or correct undesirable market results.[103] Competition law is the horizontally applicable market-harnessing regime, as it resolves general

[98] See Baumgart and Lavrijssen (n 18); Morgan and Yeung (n 20); Baldwin and others (n 20).

[99] See also B Espinosa Apráez, 'The Challenges of Sharing Data at the Intersection of EU Data Protection and Electricity Market Legislation: Lessons from the Netherlands' (2023) 41(4) *Journal of Energy & Natural Resources Law 403*.

[100] K Biedenkopff and J Wettestad, 'Harnessing the Market' in A Jordan and others (eds), *Governing Climate Change: Polycentricity in Action?* (Cambridge University Press 2018).

[101] J den Hertog, *Review of Economic Theories of Regulation* (Tjalling C Koopmans Research Institute Discussion Paper Series 10–18, 2010) 12–17.

[102] ibid.

[103] ibid.

competition issues. However, market-harnessing regulation may also be sector-specific or contain non-economic elements.

These regulatory strategies can be tested out through another type of regulation approach: within *regulatory sandboxes*. A regulatory sandbox is 'a scheme that enables undertakings to test … innovative technologies in a controlled real-world environment, under a specific plan, developed and monitored by a competent authority'[104] (for more details on the implementation of regulatory sandboxes see Chapter 11). These sandboxes provide temporary regimes, often with sunset clauses.[105] They create space for regulatory innovation, enabling experimentation with regulatory strategy mixes and principles of good regulation while maintaining compliance with overarching EU law.[106] By fostering regulatory learning and dialogue, sandboxes reduce uncertainty (if they are well designed), enhance market development and promote innovation.[107] They are particularly valuable in rapidly evolving technical, societal and economic contexts.[108] The Council of European Energy Regulators (CEER) has specifically referred to the need to set up regulatory sandboxes as a means to allow Distribution System Operators as drivers of innovation, to help national regulatory authorities facilitate innovation without compromising effectiveness or incentives for efficient operation, and to find ways forward that do not necessarily require allowing additional revenues or remuneration.[109]

In the context of PEDs, regulatory sandboxes can enable practical experimentation with new energy coordination models and technologies, helping regulators identify optimal frameworks. Regulatory sandboxes are particularly suitable for the development of PEDs, which can differ vastly in terms of participating stakeholders, energy mixes, local contexts and other peculiarities. The development of PEDs is at this stage inherently experimental as PEDs bring together new technologies and social constructs to transform the urban area. It is only sensible to have a regulatory framework that learns from experimentation while providing the necessary safeguards without unduly restricting possible ways forward or hindering competition. Regulatory sandboxes may eventually result in defined principles and guidelines for regulatory frameworks that include command-and-control regulation or design choices, as lessons from specific contexts become generalised.

[104] Regulation (EU) 2024/1735, art 3(22); see Baumgart and Lavrijssen (n 18) 17 with references therein; cf European Commission '"Better Regulation" Toolbox' (July 2023).

[105] Baumgart and Lavrijssen (n 18) 17–18 with references therein.

[106] ibid.

[107] ibid.

[108] ibid 18.

[109] CEER, 'Regulatory Sandboxes in Incentive Regulation', Distribution Systems Working Group (2022) 12.

4. Three Steps to Introducing Smart Technologies in Positive Energy Districts

For regulators to develop effective regulatory strategies for introducing smart technologies in PEDs, in this chapter the authors propose a three-step assessment framework (see Figure 10.2; see also Chapter 11 which explores guidelines for designing a regulatory sandbox). It should be noted that this framework precedes taking implementing decisions and evaluating these choices. An assessment of legal possibilities and viable technologies can take place at the national, regional or local level.

Figure 10.2 Three steps to introducing smart technologies in positive energy districts (own illustration)

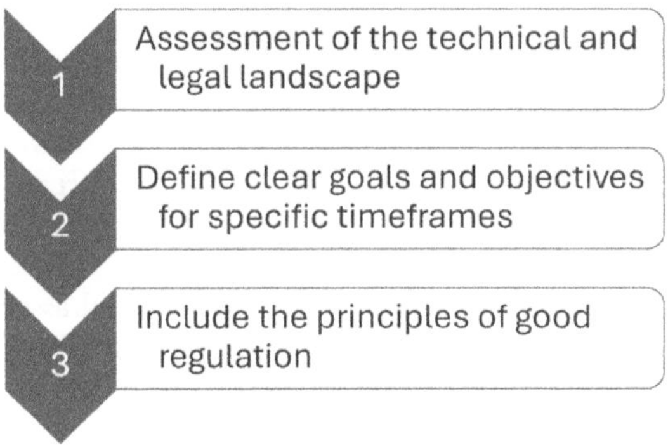

4.1. Assessment of the Technical and Legal Landscape

Regulators must first thoroughly evaluate the current technical capabilities and legal frameworks that impact smart technology integration in PEDs. This involves assessing the readiness of energy infrastructure, the maturity of smart technologies, and ensuring compliance with existing regulations. Identifying legal barriers, gaps or areas needing updates is essential to creating a supportive environment for innovation. The operation of the smart grid must be technologically feasible. This means that the required meters, sensors, connections and interventions are available. Some desirable forms of energy management, such as the creation of vehicle-to-grid connections, green hydrogen production, or the transportation of electricity, are often subject to technological limitations or capacity restraints governing the energy grid.[110]

[110] See Rijksoverheid (n 33).

4.1.1. Coordinating Energy Use: Establishing a Hierarchy in Multi-Energy Districts

Effective energy coordination is crucial to ensure the seamless integration of local production with broader energy grids. Assessing the technical and legal landscape must include an understanding of how these coordination mechanisms operate, as they are vital to the successful implementation of PEDs.

Modern energy systems are characterised by their scale and centralised operation. Electricity was originally a distributed network, with each user producing electricity on its premises. Thomas Edison built the first integrated and centralised energy system, producing electricity in one location and transporting it to a large number of users connected to the grid. Over the following decades, scale efficiencies and complementarities would be maximised by creating a universal energy grid that serviced industry and households across large geographic areas (distribution systems) and countries (transmission systems).[111] In essence, PEDs are a partial return to a distributed network, where local grids emerge and where energy is locally produced and consumed. The return is partial as PEDs are a hybrid between local and central energy grids: while they have a local self-sustaining function, they must be integrated into a more expansive energy grid to export their surplus energy to other localities. This movement towards decentralisation is happening across a wide range of industries as a result of the digitisation and platformisation of the economy, which allows for the coordination of distributed assets through smart management.[112] Energy grids are no exception: while centralisation allows for the maximisation of scale and network externalities, it also creates inefficiencies in the form of bottlenecks, losses of energy due to long transport ranges, and a lack of adaptability to local situations. PEDs harness both the benefits of scale and network externalities by connecting to a single grid, while also resolving these inefficiencies by optimising production for local demand.[113] This is, however, only possible if the coordination of supply and demand happens both locally (within the PED) and regionally (for the grids and areas to which the PED is connected). This type of coordination requires smart grids, in which information can be managed despite the increasingly complex and fragmented energy system.[114]

The use of smart technologies to manage energy grids becomes even more pressing in light of integrated energy systems. Energy systems historically consisted of two or three complementary grids: gas, electricity and heat networks. Gas and electricity networks are often regional, spanning the entire geographical range of a country. Heat networks are local, or supralocal, and often relate to block heating or the reuse of heat sources generated upstream in a downstream locality (ie using the

[111] J Montero and M Finger, 'Towards a Smart and Sustainable Single European Transport Area: An Assessment of the Past 10 Years of EU Regulation' (2022) *Florence School of Regulation* 1, 177–79.

[112] ibid 180–92.

[113] ibid.

[114] ibid 190.

rest heat of industrial areas or natural heat sources to supply households at lower temperatures). In PEDs, gas networks could generally be replaced by hydrogen infrastructure.[115] However, the direct use of hydrogen is likely to play a larger role in industrial processes than in heating homes, as hydrogen is scarce and it is costly to create (safe) residential hydrogen networks. It may therefore be an attractive alternative to use hydrogen indirectly by reusing the excess heat of hydrogen-based industrial processes to heat households.[116]

The coordination of these different forms and carriers of energy requires real-time, high-level, reliable coordination. PEDs are both self-sustaining and part of a larger central network to which they can export energy. Thus, the coordinator (in this case probably an algorithmic coordinator) of the energy grid will have to make choices in how it prioritises different forms of energy and different production. The visualisation in Figure 10.3 helps to clarify the process of decision-making that a coordinator could follow to optimise the use of energy in the PED and beyond.

Figure 10.3 Hierarchy of energy use in PEDs (own illustration)

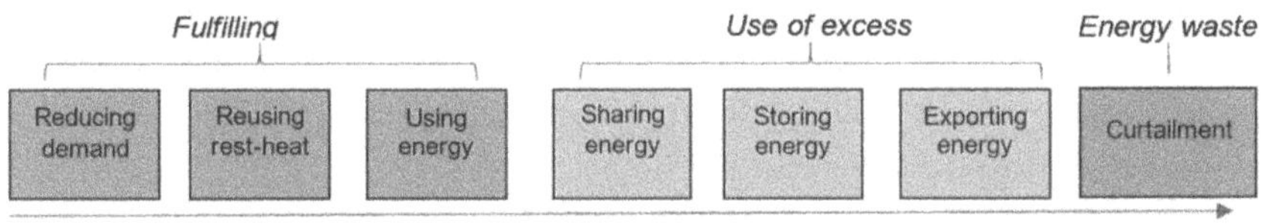

The hierarchy starts with reducing demand: the less energy that is consumed, the easier it will be to meet the demand locally. Even if energy production stays the same, the ability to export surplus energy will be greater. Reusing heat should be the first priority in generating energy, especially if it cannot be stored. Using rest heat is more efficient than using energy in the form of produced electricity or hydrogen, as rest heat implies that it is produced as a byproduct and would be wasted if not utilised. After the *reuse* of heat follows the *use* of other types of produced energy, which may include electricity, hydrogen, geothermal energy or stored energy of any of these types. Use, in this case, implies use within the firm, household or entity that generated the energy.

Any excess energy that is produced should first be shared internally in the PED as heat and electricity use within a limited geographic area minimises losses associated with travel. Sharing requires less investment than storage and should therefore be prioritised if it helps to meet energy demand through renewables. Any energy that is not needed directly to meet demand should be stored, especially

[115] See, 'ACM Gives Green Light to Pilot Project Involving Distribution of Hydrogen To Homes'(1 November 2022) for the first projects in the Netherlands to supply private households with hydrogen'. Available at: www.acm.nl/en/publications/acm-gives-green-light-pilot-project-involving-distribution-hydrogen-homes; Rijksoverheid (n 33).

[116] Rijksoverheid ibid.

with the purpose of using it during lulls in production. Here, a mix of short-, medium- and long-term storage provides high levels of security and resilience for the PED. Any energy that is not needed to meet demand and cannot be effectively or efficiently stored should be exported outside the PED to support the central grid. Any energy that is produced and cannot be used, stored or exported will be wasted, thus hurting the energy efficiency of the PED.

The hierarchy provided shows one route to maximising energy efficiency. Algorithms could be programmed to prioritise the use of one type of energy, or use of energy, over another, thereby maximising efficiencies. However, there are several technological challenges to managing energy grids, and especially managing multi-energy districts, discussed briefly hereunder.

4.1.2. Technological Challenges Around Energy Grids and Energy Integration

The first step towards creating smart grids is the introduction of measurement tools; after all, digital coordination cannot take place if the information related to production and consumption is not digitised and available. In gas and electricity grids, measurement by both the grid operator and energy users is facilitated through the introduction of smart meters.[117] The availability of information on the production and consumption of energy makes it possible to intervene on either the supply or the demand side.[118] An overproduction of energy can be regulated through curtailment, stopping the production from certain sources of energy, to match the production with (low) demand. In PEDs, matching energy demand and supply is crucial to ensure efficiency, prevent overinvestment and manage grid congestion. This is particularly important for electricity, where mismatches can compromise grid security. Properly balancing generation and consumption avoids the pitfalls of overcapacity, which can lead to unnecessary expense, especially in areas like battery storage. On the other hand, underinvestment can leave communities vulnerable to rising energy demands. A holistic approach is essential: by considering not just energy generation but also strategies like heat reuse and demand reduction, we can avoid costly overinvestment while ensuring a reliable, efficient energy system. As shown in Figure 10.3, curtailment is the least desirable form of managing oversupply in the production of renewable energy as it requires energy waste.[119]

Excess demand can be governed by manually or automatically reducing energy consumption. This can happen voluntarily (eg by requesting users in certain geographic areas not to engage in activities with high energy consumption between

[117] See Baumgart and Espinosa Apráez (n 15) 500.
[118] ibid.
[119] See Van den Boom (n 12).

certain hours), be incentivised (eg charging higher prices at certain hours or offering compensation to those that lower their energy consumption), be mandatory (eg rationing energy or making excess use of energy subject to sanctions) or happen automatically (eg rolling blackouts, appliances that switch off automatically). In this regard, many different regulatory strategies can be applied, ranging from a flexible principle-based approach to a very strict command-and-control regime, also including nudging mechanisms.

Smart grids can automise the management of energy grids to a certain extent as they can detect errors automatically, interfering to stop certain consumption or generation units or to route electricity flows elsewhere, be it into sharing, storage or the export of energy. This increases the resilience of the energy grid and promotes security of supply.[120]

While technologies to manage the independent energy grids (electricity, gas, heat) are available and well-studied, a new challenge lies in the coordination (and regulation) of integrated smart energy grids required for PEDs.[121] A study by Martínez Ceseña and Mancarella highlights that modelling the efficient use of energy and efficient energy mixes is a complicated endeavour, which makes it difficult to optimise the design of PEDs, especially those that use multiple energy sources.[122] This provides not only theoretical challenges but also practical challenges in terms of designing the energy mix of PEDs and designing regulatory frameworks that lead to desirable outcomes. Consequently, the emergence of PEDs will probably (at least in the short term) result in second-best outcomes (as compared to a theoretical perfect energy mix) and suboptimal regulatory frameworks.

As a result of the definitional unclarities as to what constitutes a PED, their geographic and other peculiarities, and the complicated assessment of a healthy energy mix in PEDs, it is hard if not impossible to set out a clear legislative agenda. As a result, we argue in favour of using a mix of regulatory tools that are used for experimentation, in particular within a regulatory sandbox. Lessons learned through sandboxes can inform revisions of regulatory regimes to ensure they remain flexible and responsive to future challenges. By using a mix of different regulatory tools, putting in place methods for reporting and analysis, and by ensuring the responsiveness of a regulatory framework to a wide range of needs, regulation can facilitate and incentivise the emergence of PEDs while minimising the risk of hindering specific PED projects.

[120] Montero and Finger 'Towards a Smart and Sustainable Single European Transport Area' (n 113).

[121] E-A Martínez Ceseña and P Mancarella, 'Energy Systems Integration in Smart Districts: Robust Optimisation of Multi-Energy Flows in Integrated Electricity, Heat and Gas Networks' (2019) 10(1) *IEEE Transactions on Smart Grid* 1122–31.

[122] ibid.

4.2. Definition of Clear Goals and Objectives for Specific Timeframes

Once the technical and legal groundwork is understood, regulators need to establish a selection of clear, measurable goals for implementing smart technologies within PEDs. These objectives should be tied to specific timeframes, ensuring a structured rollout that aligns with broader energy, sustainability and urban-development policies. The selected goals must be justifiable in terms of the procedure by which they have been selected, their balancing and hierarchy, and their impact in practice.[123]

Further, these goals should align with the goals of energy regulation, which are usually summarised as the energy triangle or energy dilemma: availability, affordability and sustainability.[124] Since the liberalisation of the energy markets,[125] another goal of energy regulation is addressing market failures.[126] As PEDs also attempt to achieve several ancillary goals, a fifth goal of energy regulation becomes particularly import: the concept of energy justice.[127] Energy justice is commonly recognised as 'establishing a more equitable, just and sustainable energy sector', serving as a concept that can guide decision makers in shaping energy law and policy for the sake of a more integrated and just approach.[128] The use cases of the technology must be embedded in regulatory frameworks that adhere to goals of good energy governance. While energy regulation in general aims at availability, affordability and sustainability, scholars discuss more and more the aim of energy justice as a goal of energy regulation.[129] Taking into account the purpose of PEDs, they are a good example of why energy justice can be considered a goal of energy regulation, as they also aim to promote quality of living and to minimise risks of energy poverty or inequality.[130] Political vision and regulatory frameworks are essential in the creation and functioning of PEDs in a number of areas, as they have the capacity to shape, directly and indirectly, the number and form of PEDs that emerge.

4.3. Set of Principles of Good Regulation

In a third and final step, regulatory strategies should incorporate principles of good regulation. By embedding these principles, regulators can create a dynamic and resilient regulatory environment that supports the sustainable growth of PEDs

[123] M Groenleer and others, 'Sturen op brede welvaart en rechtvaardigheid: Naar een afwegingskader voor keuzes richting een klimaatneutraal energiesysteem in 2050' (Tilburg University 2024).
[124] See, for an overview of these goals, Baumgart and Lavrijssen (n 18) 145–46.
[125] See Winkler and others *Europäisches Energierecht* (n 30).
[126] Baumgart and Lavrijssen (n 18).
[127] ibid.
[128] L Kaschny, 'Energy Justice & the Principles of Article 194(1) TFEU Governing EU Energy Policy' (2023) 12(2) *Transnational Environmental Law* 270.
[129] Baumgart and Lavrijssen (n 18); Kaschny ibid.
[130] See SeT Plan (n 7); JPI Urban Europe (n 62).

through smart technologies. The principles of good regulation, embedded in the EU liberalisation packages, proved suitable for regulating and creating competitive energy markets in the past and therefore can be guiding principles for regulation to come.[131] We here set out the principles discussed in the literature,[132] providing short explanations for these concepts. It should be noted that while some principles can be pursued in a manner that is mutually reinforcing, there may be frictions in pursuing multiple goals at once. If tensions between different objectives arise, it is the duty of the decision maker to explore these tensions ex-ante and to develop procedures and mechanisms for balancing different interests.[133]

Figure 10.4 Principles of good regulation (own illustration)

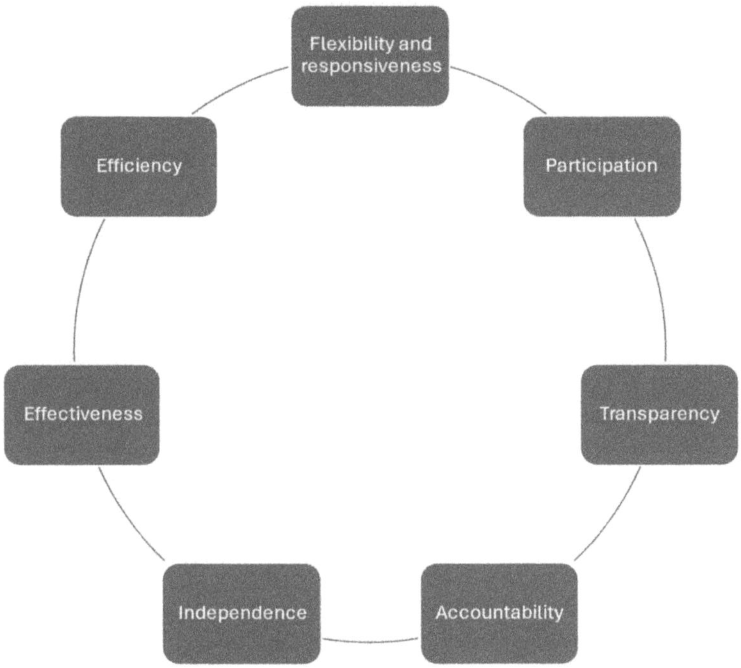

A regulatory regime needs to be *flexible* and *responsive* to adapt to technical, societal and economic changes, ensuring that the law stays relevant and aligned with its original objectives.[134] Regulations should be designed to accommodate the rapidly evolving nature of energy technologies and market conditions. This could be achieved through mechanisms like regulatory sandboxes (see section 3). Flexibility

[131] Baumgart and Lavrijssen (n 18) 147 and 165.
[132] ibid.
[133] Groenleer and others 'Sturen op brede welvaart en rechtvaardigheid' (n 125).
[134] ibid 147 with references therein. Please note that legal flexibility is a distinct concept from flexibility within an energy grid; for the latter see Van den Boom (n 12).

could also mean setting broad goals rather than rigid rules, allowing PEDs to adapt to local conditions and emerging technologies. To be able to include the results of a periodical assessment, the law should be *adaptive* enough to still reflect the evolutions of the market and check if the law is still fit for purpose. Adaptiveness goes beyond flexibility (see also Chapter 11). It forms part of a *responsive* framework: if the law can adapt to evolutions of the market, it can respond to new challenges. Where the law is not flexible enough to answer to the needs of evolving PEDs, it must be possible to change it.

The *participation* principle aims to include an ongoing process that involves openness to external input, including ideas, financial resources and local ownership, as this can enhance the legitimacy and acceptance of regulatory decisions, especially in the energy market and with citizen energy initiatives.[135] Regulations should promote active participation from a wide range of stakeholders, including local communities, energy producers and consumers. This can be done by encouraging energy communities, by supporting local decision-making processes and by ensuring that regulations allow for peer-to-peer energy trading, co-ownership of energy resources, and public consultations during the planning and implementation of PEDs.

The *transparency* principle aims for regulators and market participants to openly share information about their goals and activities.[136] Regulations must ensure that all processes related to PED development, including energy management and distribution, are transparent. This includes clear rules for how energy data is collected, used and shared, as well as transparent reporting requirements for PED projects. Transparency builds trust among stakeholders and helps ensure that PEDs operate fairly and efficiently.

The *accountability* principle involves justifying actions, providing a basis for evaluating them, and facing consequences for poor decisions.[137] Regulatory frameworks should establish clear lines of accountability for all actors involved in PEDs, from energy providers to regulators themselves. This could involve setting performance benchmarks, regular audits and reporting obligations. There should be consequences for non-compliance with regulations, ensuring that all parties are held responsible for their roles in achieving PED goals. PEDs should probably also depend on private governance mechanisms, which hold parties accountable within the PED. The balancing of supply and demand is essential for the continued

[135] Baumgart and Lavrijssen (n 18) 147–48; M Wahlund and J Palm, 'The Role of Energy Democracy and Energy Citizenship for Participatory Energy Transitions: A Comprehensive Review' (2022) 87 *Energy Research & Social Science* 102482; Lavrijssen and Vitéz 'Make Hydrogen Whilst the Sun Shines'(n 99); A Alemanno, 'Unpacking the Principle of Openness in EU Law – Transparency, Participation and Democracy' (2014) 39(1) *European Law Review* 72, 82 and references therein.

[136] Baumgart and Lavrijssen (n 18); Lavrijssen and Vitéz (n 99).

[137] ibid; ibid; OECD, *The Governance of Regulators*, OECD Best Practice Principles for Regulatory Policy (2014) 84–5; Morgan and Yeung (n 20) 221; D Curtin and A Nollkaemper, 'Conceptualizing Accountability in International and European Law' (2007) 36 *Netherlands Yearbook of International Law* 3, 7ff and references therein; L Hancher and others, 'Principles of Good Market Governance' (2003) 4(4) *Journal of Network Industries* 339, 369.

operation of electricity grids. A mismatch in supply and demand can cause damage to the system and/or can lead to blackouts. As such, there must be a party responsible for balancing and parties must adhere to their agreed upon use. Here, again, smart technologies may help parties to balance the grid and automatically enforce agreements through usage caps or warnings.

The *independence* principle emphasises that regulators and markets should operate free from undue political influence, and greater regulatory independence typically enhances trust in their decisions, though this can be a contentious issue.[138] The regulatory bodies overseeing PEDs should operate independently of political or commercial pressures to ensure unbiased decision-making. This can be implemented through independent regulatory agencies that have the authority to enforce rules, oversee market activities, and ensure fair competition within the energy sector (see also Chapter 11).

The *effectiveness* principle involves making decisions at the right level and ensuring actions are appropriate, are constrained by proportionality and can be measured by whether markets achieve their long-term objectives.[139] Regulatory schemes must be periodically assessed and updated to see if they still reflect the evolutions of the market and if they are still fit for purpose. The integrative approach required to develop PEDs demands that governments assure the relevant frameworks, not only to guide the production and flows of energy but also to steer financial flows towards desirable technological solutions. According to the pillars and principles underlying PEDs, and the identified hierarchy of energy use, incentive schemes should not result in energy waste. As such, if there is an oversupply of solar energy, financial incentives should be aimed at stimulating the sharing or storing of excess energy. Regulations should be outcome-oriented, focused on achieving key goals such as energy efficiency, sustainability and grid resilience. This involves regularly reviewing and updating regulations to ensure they are meeting their intended objectives and adjusting them based on feedback from stakeholders and performance data from PED projects.

The *efficiency* principle involves organising the market in a way that actions are taken by the most suitable actors using the most appropriate tools.[140] Regulatory frameworks must ensure that the rules governing PEDs promote the efficient use of resources and avoid unnecessary bureaucratic burdens. This includes minimising administrative costs, streamlining permitting processes and encouraging innovations that reduce energy waste. Regulations should also prevent overinvestment in certain technologies by promoting a balanced approach to energy generation, storage and reuse.

[138] Baumgart and Lavrijssen (n 18) 149; Lavrijssen and Vitéz (n 99) 266, 273; OECD *The Governance of Regulators* (n 139) 47–48.

[139] ibid; ibid 266, 274; OECD, 'Recommendation of the Council on Regulatory Policy and Governance' (2012).

[140] ibid; ibid.

After this inventory of the technical and legal realities, objectives and principles, the legislator or regulator can make informed decisions about adaptations to the legal framework governing PEDs, the use of the regulatory toolbox or the amendment of policy. Of course, the introduction of new policy requires periodic evaluations to determine whether the assessment has missed potentially desirable solutions or if it has created unintended side effects. This creates a cyclical approach to regulation, experimentation and evaluation: the principles of good regulation shape practice, and practice again feeds back into the development of the principles of good regulation.

5. Conclusion

5.1. Bringing the Principles of Good Regulation into Practice: Towards a Market for PEDs

The previous subsection has discussed a great number of principles of good regulation: flexibility, responsiveness, adaptivity, participation, transparency, accountability, independence, effectiveness and efficiency. We have also identified several regulatory strategies: command-and-control, design solutions, direct action, incentive schemes and market-harnessing regulation. How can a regulator then ensure to apply the right mix of regulatory strategies in a way that is in line with the identified regulatory principles?

The concept of market-harnessing has been used in relation to the emergence of carbon markets. Carbon markets, in principle, do not exist. They are a legal fiction that is introduced through carbon emission schemes. By introducing emissions schemes, firms are able to internalise externalities (in this case CO_2 emissions) and barter in the reduction of emissions.[141] For PEDs, regulation may serve a similar purpose of directing market forces towards an issue where the market cannot emerge by itself. After all, unless emissions are internalised through regulation, it is often more cost efficient to build in a less sustainable manner.[142]

To develop a PED requires the creation of a complex ecosystem, where different actors communicate and coordinate to fulfil their respective roles. This may have to do with the production (and the produced amount) of energy, the consumption of energy, the balancing of production and consumption, and development of a shared vision and coherent strategy towards decarbonisation through a 'just'

[141] Biedenkopff and Wettenstadt 'Harnessing the Market' (n 102).

[142] See Den Hertog *Review of Economic Theories of Regulation* (n 103) 15; here it is described why unregulated market competition may lead to undesirable outcomes in light of externalities: 'Externalities are cost or utility effects for third parties outside the market interactions where these external effects develop … Because the private costs for the discharging manufacturer differ from the social costs, production will be increased further than would be desirable from the point of view of efficient allocation of resources.'

transition.[143] Each PED is different in terms of size, demographic makeup, access to resources, energy mix and a number of different factors. Consequently, it is extremely difficult, if not impossible, to fully legislate the procedure towards the design and functioning of PEDs. At least not efficiently and not without stifling innovation.[144]

The regulator should therefore rely on a mix of regulatory strategies to stimulate efficient outcomes, while allowing problem holders and stakeholders to find desirable solutions. Different types of regulatory tools may help to shape practical outcomes in a number of ways. Our proposed three-step assessment helps to ensure a targeted implementation of tools and measures: by conducting a comprehensive assessment of legal and technological realities, the regulator can adjust course and stimulate or disincentivise certain types of behaviour based on existing needs. Uncertainties in the readiness of the legal and technological realities could be addressed through experimentation such as in regulatory sandboxes. Outdated compensation schemes may actually hinder the emergence of new technologies that accelerate the emergence of PEDs. In the Netherlands, a delay in the removal of the metering arrangement is viewed as a strong contributor to the lack of adoption in energy storage solutions.[145] At the same time, the continued existence of this arrangement is leading to an oversupply in solar energy produced by households.[146] The metering arrangement has become counter-productive to achieving a healthy energy mix. Allowing outdated subsidy schemes to continue is a general risk for inefficient use of resources. An update on the technological realities also helps to ensure that stimulus is aimed at the latest and most efficient technologies, without mandating the use of such technologies for PEDs that have unique or different needs. A (re)assessment of the legal realities helps to determine whether the law is still suitable to facilitate enablers and mitigate challenges and helps to identify how the law and its enforcement can be future-proofed.

The outcomes of the initial assessment of the technical and legal landscape must weigh what is feasible now against the pursued objectives: a reduction in emissions and the achievement of net zero is an overarching goal, but the regulator may pay extra attention to ensure that this happens in a way that adheres to the idea of 'energy justice', moving beyond a purely quantifiable objective.

[143] See WRR, *Rechtvaardigheid in klimaatbeleid Over de verdeling van klimaatkosten* [*Justice in Climate Policy: On the Division of Costs of Climate Change*] (2023); this report discusses how policy related to decarbonisation should always be framed in the context of a just energy transition, and it gives practical guidance on how to achieve this.

[144] See P Aghion, W Carlin and M Schaffer, 'Competition, Innovation and Growth in Transition: Exploring the Interactions Between Policies' (2002) William Davidson Institute Working Papers Series 501, University of Michigan, on the relationship between competition, regulation and innovation. The idea that competition is a driver of efficient investment and innovation is a fundamental principle underlying the free market economy.

[145] J-W Zwang, *Handboek Verdienmodellen Batterijopslag* [Manual Business Models Battery Storage] (Stratergy 2022) 36ff.

[146] See Van den Boom (n 12).

To effectively create a market for PEDs, the regulator should rely on a mix of regulatory strategies that are aligned to the needs of consumers and market participants. It is not possible to effectively and efficiently regulate the energy transition strictly via top-down rules. Regulation must be flexible and adaptive, harnessing and promoting stakeholder- and problem holder-driven solutions and participation by these groups. Stakeholders and problem holders should be subjected to transparent and non-discriminatory rules that establish accountability for participants in different roles, allowing them to cooperate to achieve legitimate objectives. This process of competition and cooperation should happen under the supervision of an independent authority, to ensure that the harnessed market continues to function absent political influence, so that a coherent long-term vision and governance structure can be developed.[147]

The creation of a market for PEDs, with a strong governance and regulatory framework is, in itself, a driver for new technological advancements including smart technologies. Once the externalities of a new market have been internalised, it is possible to allocate and reap the benefits of competition in this area. This, in turn, creates an innovative environment for the suppliers of technology that specialise in PEDs. With complex challenges such as climate change and the reduction of CO_2 emissions, regulation can be a driver of innovation by addressing market failures and creating markets that otherwise cannot or will not emerge (or that remain externalised).[148] By creating a market for PEDs and harnessing the efficiencies of the market, regulatory interventions can steer and promote innovation targeted at greener technologies that may not emerge otherwise. There is thus a bidirectional relationship between smart technologies and regulation: smart technologies are needed to achieve the objectives pursued by the regulator, yet regulation is also needed to steer innovation towards such technologies.[149]

5.2. In Summary

The concept of 'positive' in (PEDs) reflects multiple dimensions, such as achieving climate neutrality, generating surplus energy and fostering sustainable urban environments. Implementing PEDs is a complex regulatory challenge that requires an interdisciplinary approach, balancing technological, legal, environmental and social perspectives. Smart technologies are essential for the successful implementation of PEDs as they enable real-time energy management, integration of renewable sources and the optimisation of energy use. To effectively introduce these technologies, regulators must follow a three-step approach. This chapter

[147] Den Hertog (n 103) 35 describes that independent regulatory oversight in itself may be a driver of innovation.
[148] ibid 15–16.
[149] See N Droste and others, 'Steering Innovations Towards a Green Economy: Understanding Government Intervention' (2016) 135(1) *Journal of Cleaner Production* 426.

proposes a three-step assessment for regulators to launch adequate regulatory strategies for introducing smart technologies in PEDs: (1) an assessment of the technical and legal landscape; (2) the definition of clear goals and objectives for specific timeframes; and (3) a set of principles of good regulation that should be incorporated in the strategies used. Moreover, regulatory strategies should include experimental tools like regulatory sandboxes to test innovative solutions. This also entails giving the relevant authorities and enforcers sufficient space to experiment with new technologies and settings for the development of new laws. The law, much like the used technologies, should be based on a holistic and integrative approach that makes sure that legislation works as a driver of the energy transition and not a limiting factor. This can be done by periodically engaging in an assessment of the legal and technological realities, to hold this assessment against the goals that are pursued through the energy transition, and to transform the law based on sound regulatory principles as proposed in this chapter. Ultimately, with well-designed regulatory frameworks that allow for the integration of new technologies, PEDs can play a pivotal role in the energy transition towards a sustainable and resilient (urban) future.

11

Fuelling Innovation

Regulatory Sandboxes for the Hydrogen Sector in the Netherlands

RENSKE VAN 'T VEER, MAX BAUMGART AND SASKIA LAVRIJSSEN*

1. Introduction

New solutions for the transition to a clean, sustainable and affordable energy system have resulted in the promotion of innovations in the energy sector as a key target in the EU.[1] In the decarbonisation of the energy system, hydrogen energy has gained attention around the world.[2] The potential of green hydrogen in sustainable development is increasingly recognised,[3] as this particular hydrogen is produced through the electrolysis of water using renewable energy sources and consequently does not emit greenhouse gases during its production.[4] However, in recent years, the development of the hydrogen market has encountered regulatory barriers,[5] such as the lack of a harmonised legal framework related to the hydrogen

* With this chapter, the author Max Baumgart contributes to his Starter Grant project 'Transformation Processes in European and National Economic Law: Energy Law as Law of Socio-Technical Change', for which he was awarded funds by Tilburg University. This chapter was completed before the final adoption of the Dutch Energy Act. The Energy Act will enter into force on 1 January 2026.

[1] K Sunila and A Ekroos, 'Regulating Radical Innovations in the EU Electricity Markets: Time for a Robust Sandbox' (2023) 41(1) *Journal of Energy & Natural Resources Law* 5, 5.

[2] L Pingkuo and H Xue, 'Comparative Analysis on Similarities and Differences of Hydrogen Energy Development in the World's Top 4 Largest Economies: A Novel Framework' (2022) 47(16) *International Journal of Hydrogen Energy* 9485, 9495.

[3] M Yue and others, 'Hydrogen Energy Systems: A Critical Review of Technologies, Applications, Trends and Challenges' (2021) 146(1) *Renewable and Sustainable Energy Reviews* 111180, 1.

[4] SO Bade and others, 'Economic, Social, and Regulatory Challenges of Green Hydrogen Production and Utilization in the US: A Review' (2023) 49(2024) *International Journal of Hydrogen Energy* 314, 318.

[5] C Smith and others, 'Towards a 100% Hydrogen Domestic Gas Network: Regulatory and Commercial Barriers to the First Demonstrator Project in the United Kingdom' (2022) 47(55) *International Journal of Hydrogen Energy* 23071, 23074.

market in the EU[6] or the unsuitability of the existing regulatory framework to handle the various new solutions brought by the energy transition.[7]

For the acceleration of the energy transition, the challenge is the integration of innovation and allowing new services, entrants, and ways of meeting energy needs without losing values such as fairness, public acceptability and the promotion of economic efficiency, from the current energy policy and regulatory framework.[8] However, the current legal and regulatory frameworks are unable to keep up with the rapid scientific and technological developments, resulting in legal uncertainty and social conflict.[9] This is also apparent in the energy market where the traditional harmonised regulation is lacking or is substantially different from the regulation of the emerging, less traditional markets,[10] such as that of green hydrogen. The hydrogen sector in general is subject to rapid changes, given that the technologies involved in the production of green hydrogen are still in the development stage and the market is expected to scale up over time.[11] Regulatory barriers encountered are, for instance, the need to adapt regulations to enable the deployment of hydrogen into the energy system[12] or issues with the permitting process being too restrictive for the creation of geographically bounded areas that combine several hydrogen applications into an integrated hydrogen ecosystem.[13]

When innovations do not fit into the current legal framework, there is a chance of ending up in the legal 'valley of death',[14] whereby firms are still exploiting their innovations but investors do not feel enough certainty to finance the project.[15] Authors therefore call for regulatory approaches to green hydrogen that differ from the conventional approach, for instance a more dynamic approach[16] or more flexibility in the regulatory framework to be responsive to technological, societal and economic changes to ensure the law does not fall behind the market needs.[17] One of

[6] M Baumgart and S Lavrijssen, 'Exploring Regulatory Strategies for Accelerating the Development of Sustainable Hydrogen Markets in the European Union' (2023) 42(2) *Journal of Energy & Natural Resources Law* 1, 2.

[7] European Commission, 'Regulatory Learning in the EU. Guidance on Regulatory Sandboxes, Testbeds, and Living Labs in the EU, with a Focus Section on Energy' (2023) SWD 277/2 final, 44.

[8] R Carlson and A Nciri, 'Enter the Sandbox: Developing Innovation Sandboxes for the Energy Sector' (2020) *Quest* 8.

[9] A Veseli and others, 'Practical Necessity and Legal Options for Introducing Energy Regulatory Sandboxes in Austria' (2021) 73 *Utilities Policy* 101296, 1; S Lee and Y Seo, 'Exploring How Interest Groups Affect Regulation and Innovation Based on the Two-Level Games: The Case of Regulatory Sandboxes in Korea' (2022) 183 *Technological Forecasting and Social Change* 121880, 1.

[10] S Lavrijssen and B Vitéz, 'Make Hydrogen Whilst the Sun Shines' (2020) 14(4) *Carbon & Climate Law Review* 266, 267.

[11] G Mete and L Reins, 'Governing New Technologies in the Energy Transition – The Hydrogen Strategy to the Rescue?' (2020) 14(3) *Carbon and Climate Law Review* 210, 230.

[12] Smith and others 'Towards a 100% Hydrogen Domestic Gas Network' (n 5).

[13] U Weichenhain and others, *Hydrogen Valleys: Insights into the Emerging Hydrogen Economies Around the World* (Publications Office of the European Union 2021) 7.

[14] Sunila and Ekroos 'Regulating Radical Innovations in the EU Electricity Markets' (n 1) 6.

[15] M Granieri and A Renda, *Innovation Law and Policy in the European Union: Towards Horizon 2020* (Springer Science & Business Media 2012) 31.

[16] Mete and Reins 'Governing New Technologies in the Energy Transition' (n 11) 230.

[17] Baumgart and Lavrijssen 'Exploring Regulatory Strategies' (n 6) 11, 30.

these alternative approaches is the implementation of regulatory sandboxes, which are experimental spaces where innovations can be tested in a real-world environment subject to regulatory safeguards and support.[18] The implementation of regulatory sandboxes can be useful for innovative products, services or business models that differ from those in traditional markets and the existing regulatory framework;[19] they not only enable participants to test their product in a scaled-down, time-limited, real-world environment but also enable regulators to gain insight into potential changes needed in regulation or legislation (see also Chapter 10).[20]

The concept of regulatory sandboxes has been gaining interest in academic literature with most research focused on their application in the fintech sector.[21] Alternative regulatory approaches, including regulatory sandboxes, in the energy sector have been increasingly studied: an analysis of the potential of, and need for, an EU regulatory sandbox for the EU electricity market;[22] the examination of the outcomes of approved sandbox projects in the European energy sector and the resulting areas of innovation and regulatory learning;[23] a case study analysis of sandboxes in the energy sector;[24] and the comparison of regulatory sandboxes in the energy sector in the three pioneering countries, the Netherlands, Great Britain and Italy.[25] In terms of alternative approaches in the Dutch energy sector, studies analysed lessons learned from the Dutch Experimentation Decree for experiments with decentralised renewable electricity generation[26] and the resulting new roles and power division changes in the energy sector.[27] An in-depth analysis of the existing regulatory sandboxes, their potential design, and legislative basis in the context of the sustainable hydrogen value chain or market has, to the authors' knowledge, not been performed. Additionally, in the analysis of regulatory sandboxes, no research yet has connected their design with established principles for the development of good regulation.

[18] European Commission, *'Better Regulation' Toolbox* (2023) 178. Available at: https://commission.europa.eu/law/law-making-process/better-regulation/better-regulation-guidelines-and-toolbox_en.

[19] A Attrey, M Lesher, and C Lomax, *The Role of Sandboxes in Promoting Flexibility and Innovation in the Digital Age* (OECD Going Digital Toolkit Notes, No. 2, OECD Publishing 2020) 4.

[20] S Ranchordás, 'Experimental Regulations and Regulatory Sandboxes – Law Without Order?' (2021) 2021 *Law and Method* 8.

[21] Lee and Seo 'Exploring How Interest Groups Affect Regulation and Innovation' (n 9) 3; D Ahern, 'Regulators Nurturing Fintech Innovation: Global Evolution of the Regulatory Sandbox as Opportunity-Based Regulation' (2019) 15(2) *Indian J L & Tech* 345, 5; DA Zetzsche and others, 'Regulating a Revolution: From Regulatory Sandboxes to Smart Regulation' (2017) 23 *Fordham J Corp & Fin L* 31; CY Tsang, 'From Industry Sandbox to Supervisory Control Box: Rethinking the Role of Regulators in the Era of FinTech' (2019) 2019(2) *Journal Of Law, Technology & Policy* 355.

[22] Sunila and Ekroos (n 1).

[23] E Beckstedde and others, 'Regulatory Sandboxes: Do They Speed Up Innovation in Energy?' (2023) 180 *Energy Policy* 113656.

[24] K Kubeczko and others, *Regulation as an Instrument of Innovation Policy–Two Case Studies* (Joanneum Research Forschunsgesellschaft Report, 2023).

[25] T Schittekatte and others, 'Regulatory Experimentation in Energy: Three Pioneer Countries and Lessons for the Green Transition' (2021) 156 *Energy Policy* 112382.

[26] I Lammers and L Diestelmeier, 'Experimenting with Law and Governance for Decentralized Electricity Systems: Adjusting Regulation to Reality?' (2017) 9(2) *Sustainability* 212.

[27] EC van der Waal, AM Das, and T van der Schoor, 'Participatory Experimentation with Energy Law: Digging in a "Regulatory Sandbox" for Local Energy Initiatives in the Netherlands' (2020) 13(2) *Energies* 458.

This chapter seeks to address how good regulation principles can be used to design regulatory sandboxes that can provide the needed flexibility and temporality for the emerging green hydrogen market and a learning opportunity for regulators. It answers the question of how regulatory sandboxes for the emerging hydrogen market in the Netherlands should be designed and to what extent the design guidelines address the principles of good regulation (flexibility and responsiveness, participation, transparency, effectiveness, independence, efficiency and accountability). First, a definition of regulatory sandboxes is provided through a review of academic and legal documents as well as previously implemented regulatory sandboxes. Afterwards, section 3 discusses regulatory sandboxes in the context of the emerging hydrogen market. Further, in section 4, principles of good regulation are used to assess the design guidelines for regulatory sandboxes to identify the suitability and potential pitfalls of regulatory sandboxes in the emerging hydrogen market. The fifth section addresses the legislative room to implement regulatory sandboxes for hydrogen activities in the Netherlands. We focus on the Netherlands since the country is one of the biggest hydrogen consumers in the EU, attributes a significant role to sustainable hydrogen in its strategies for decreasing greenhouse gas emissions and has the potential to play an important role in the supply of sustainable hydrogen to other European countries, such as Germany and Belgium.[28] Additionally, the country's regulator has introduced a tolerance policy for hydrogen pilots in the built environment,[29] indicating an interest in alternative regulatory approaches for hydrogen. The final conclusion assesses what can be learned from the analysis of regulatory sandboxes in the context of the Dutch hydrogen market accompanied by recommendations for further research and policy-making on the integration of sustainable hydrogen in the Netherlands.

2. What are Regulatory Sandboxes?

In the European Economic Area, as of October 2023, 14 regulatory sandboxes for fintech exist in 12 countries.[30] The approach of regulatory sandboxes was first introduced by the Financial Conduct Authority (FCA) of the UK in November 2015, allowing fintech companies to try their products on a limited set of customers in a controlled testing environment.[31] In subsequent years, regulatory sandboxes have

[28] Nationaal Waterstof Programma, *Routekaart Waterstof* (2022) 23.

[29] ACM, *Tijdelijk kader voor waterstofpilots: gedoogbeleid voor betrokkenheid van netbeheerders bij pilots met waterstof in de gebouwde omgeving* (2022) 1. Available at: www.acm.nl/system/files/documents/tijdelijk-kader-waterstofpilots.pdf.

[30] ESA, 'Update on the Functioning of Innovation Facilitators – Innovation Hubs and Regulatory Sandboxes' (2023) 3. Available at: www.eiopa.europa.eu/publications/joint-esas-report-innovation-facilitators-innovation-hubs-and-regulatory-sandboxes_en.

[31] G Cornelli and others, 'Regulatory Sandboxes and Fintech Funding: Evidence from the UK' (2024) 28(1) *Review of Finance* 203, 204.

emerged in other regulated sectors[32] and countries.[33] The concept of regulatory sandboxes has emerged with two kinds of innovation dynamics: those where technological progress is very rapid and it is unclear which legal changes – including introducing new legal norms, amending existing norms or abolishing overly restrictive norms – are consequently needed; and those innovation dynamics where there is a need for solutions to major societal challenges, such as decarbonisation of the energy, mobility and industrial sectors.[34] Both dynamics can be found in the emerging hydrogen market, making regulatory sandboxes an interesting approach to stimulate those dynamics.

The implementation and characteristics of regulatory sandboxes differ across sectors and countries.[35] Recently the EU introduced and defined regulatory sandboxes in several legislative documents, such as the Artificial Intelligence Act, Net Zero Industry Act and the Interoperable Europe Act (Box A).

Box A: Definition of regulatory sandboxes in EU documents

'AI regulatory sandboxes means a controlled framework set up by a competent authority which offers providers or prospective providers of AI systems the possibility to develop, train, validate and test, where appropriate in real-world conditions, an innovative AI system, pursuant to a sandbox plan for a limited time under regulatory supervision.'[36]

'Net-zero regulatory sandbox' 'a scheme that enables undertakings to test innovative net-zero technologies and other innovative technologies in a controlled real-world environment, under a specific plan, developed and monitored by a competent authority'.[37]

'"Interoperability regulatory sandbox" means a controlled environment set up by a Union entity or a public sector body for the development, training, testing and validation of innovative interoperability solutions, where appropriate in real world conditions, supporting the cross-border interoperability of trans-European digital public services for a limited period of time under regulatory supervision.'[38]

[32] Ranchordás 'Experimental Regulations and Regulatory Sandboxes' (n 20) 6.
[33] Cornelli and others 'Regulatory Sandboxes and Fintech Funding' (n 31) 2.
[34] K Kubeczko and A Wang (2019) cited in A Veseli and others 'Practical Necessity' (n 9) 2.
[35] Attrey, Lesher, and Lomax *The Role of Sandboxes in Promoting Flexibility and Innovation in the Digital Age* (n 19) 27.
[36] T Madiega and L Van De Pol, 'Artificial Intelligence Act and Regulatory Sandboxes' (European Parliamentary Research Service 2022). Available at: www.europarl.europa.eu/RegData/etudes/BRIE/2022/733544/EPRS_BRI(2022)733544_EN.pdf, 3; EU Artificial Intelligence Act (2024) https://artificialintelligenceact.eu/article/3/, art 3(55).
[37] Council Regulation (EU) 2024/1735 of 13 June 2024 on establishing a framework of measures for strengthening Europe's net-zero technology manufacturing ecosystem and amending Regulation (EU) 2018/1724, OJ L2024/1735, art 3(22).
[38] Council Regulation (EU) 2024/903 of 13 March 2024 laying down measures for a high level of public sector interoperability across the Union OJ L2024/903 (Interoperable Europe Act), art 2(14).

In its *'Better Regulation' Toolbox*, the European Commission defines regulatory sandboxes as 'schemes that enable firms to test innovations in a controlled real-world environment, under a specific plan developed and monitored by a competent authority'.[39] In line with this, and the definitions in these EU legislative acts, elements present in most regulatory sandboxes are the focus on the advancement of innovation and entrepreneurialism through regulatory relief, the definition of specific entry rules, a limited extent of regulatory relief and the determination of sandbox rules beforehand.[40] Synonyms that are used to refer to regulatory sandboxes are 'safe space',[41] 'test bed'[42] or 'safe playground'.[43] Common characteristics in the current regulatory sandboxes are shown in Figure 11.1.[44]

Figure 11.1 Regulatory sandbox characteristics (own illustration)

As the characteristics listed above indicate, regulatory sandboxes need to have boundaries in time and scope. This also includes clarification of the legislation and sectors the sandbox covers, as well as the duration and exit conditions. This might already be grounded in law (experimentation clauses), but it ensures legal predictability and facilitates measuring and evaluation of sandbox outcomes.[45] Thus, participation in a regulatory sandbox is governed by entry and exit requirements.[46] Certain requirements are set by the regulator, which determine whether a firm can

[39] European Commission (n 18) 599.
[40] Ranchordás (n 20) 6.
[41] Financial Conduct Authority, *Regulatory Sandbox – November 2015* (2015) 1; Lee and Seo (n 9) 3.
[42] Ahern 'Regulators Nurturing Fintech Innovation' (n 21) 356.
[43] JG Jiménez and M Hagan, *A Regulatory Sandbox for the Industry of Law* (Thomson Reuters 2019) 2. Available at: https://law.stanford.edu/wp-content/uploads/2019/04/Regulatory-Sandbox-for-the-Industry-of-Law.pdf; Wolf-Georg Ringe and Christopher Ruof, 'A Regulatory Sandbox for Robo Advice' (2018) Institute of Law and Economics Working Paper Series No 14, University of Hamburg, 30.
[44] Attrey, Lesher, and Lomax (n 19) 7–11.
[45] Ringe and Ruof 'A Regulatory Sandbox for Robo Advice' (n 43) 30; Attrey, Lesher, and Lomax (n 19) 7–11.
[46] Ranchordás (n 20) 6.

participate in the sandbox.[47] In terms of genuine innovation, a new use of an existing regulation also qualifies and the expected benefits achieved can, for instance, be meeting social needs or contributing to policy objectives.[48] Looking at previously implemented regulatory sandboxes, the entry criteria vary depending on the regulator that established the sandbox. Important aspects for regulators in granting firms access to a sandbox are: an innovation test has been undertaken, its effect on market stability has been shown, there is an individual need for participation and there are safety requirements that participants should meet. In most sandboxes, participants are also required to provide an exit strategy in their application. This minimises the potential detriment to participating consumers and it gives specific grounds for regulators to withdraw the firm from the sandbox.[49]

Since regulatory sandboxes are a form of testing, they have a limited timeframe for participating firms to test their product, service or business model. The timeframe typically ranges from six to 24 months,[50] but the duration can also be determined on a case-by-case basis.[51] For instance, in the UK, regulatory sandboxes were valid for periods of six to 12 months, in France they were valid up to two years and in the Netherlands 10 years. A short period for the derogation limits the potential of market distortion that the experiment can cause and it can allow for quick learning and potential adaptation of the regulation. A long duration can give security for innovators, who sometimes have to invest a significant amount of capital and need guarantees that their project will be able to run for multiple years.[52]

The exact extent of regulatory leeway provided within a regulatory sandbox differs from sandbox to sandbox.[53] Most regulatory sandboxes applied thus far have the common aim of reducing unnecessary authorisation requirements and other regulatory burdens.[54] In most cases, they involve a specific derogation (waiver or exception) from standard regulations, subject to conditions imposed by the regulator.[55] Ahern identified four types of regulatory relief offered in regulatory sandboxes implemented in fintech.[56] These range from no relaxation of applicable rules in sandboxes, but participants receive guidance, to tailor-made sandboxes that are based on the relaxation of specific rules on a case-by-case basis to create an individualised sandbox for each participant.

The regulation of sandboxes takes place at national level and, usually, a competent, sector-specific authority is entitled to supervise them. This authority can

[47] Ringe and Ruof (n 43) 32.
[48] ibid 30; Attrey, Lesher, and Lomax (n 19) 7–11.
[49] Ringe and Ruof (n 43) 35.
[50] Attrey, Lesher, and Lomax (n 19) 10.
[51] Ringe and Ruof (n 43) 34.
[52] Schittekatte and others 'Regulatory Experimentation in Energy'(n 25) 4.
[53] Ahern (n 21) 371.
[54] Ringe and Ruof (n 43) 4.
[55] CEER, 'CEER Paper on Regulatory Sandboxes in Incentive Regulation' (2022) Distribution Systems Working Group, 16.
[56] Ahern (n 21) 372–76.

accept projects in the sandbox and grant deviations from the applicable law.[57] Regulatory sandboxes are a form of experimental legal regime and are required to be based on clear legislative mandates;[58] this legal basis normally contains rules regarding the conditions, scope of application, expected outcomes and evaluation criteria.[59] The regulatory leeway provided in regulatory sandboxes is based on experimentation clauses or other instruments to deliver flexibility,[60] for instance no enforcement action letters, waivers or modifications, alternative interpretation of rules, individual guidance or restricted licences for unregulated firms.[61] Secondary legislation can provide additional guidance, for instance in the Netherlands this is done through the Dutch Guidelines for Regulation.[62] However, Member States of the EU are limited in their options for waiving regulatory requirements when elements of their legal framework are based on EU-level legislation.[63]

2.1. Strengths and Weaknesses

Regulatory sandboxes allow for a two-way regulatory dialogue between an innovative business and a regulator, which enables the innovation of regulation and the development of new sociotechnical arrangements.[64] This means that, on the one hand, regulatory sandboxes provide room for participating firms to test their products or services in a scaled-down, time-limited, real-world environment where they are not subject to the full regulatory framework. Hence, they are at less risk of being penalised for not adhering to regulations.[65] On the other hand, sandboxes enable regulators to obtain experience and knowledge regarding the applicability of the existing set of rules or potential alternatives before going through the process of creating new rules. This includes assessing if the product can be developed in compliance with general rules and whether the rules exempted in the sandbox are truly necessary to protect the consumer.[66]

Together with the mutual learning in a relatively unknown field, the improved communication between firms and regulators facilitated by a sandbox[67] can help in decreasing regulatory uncertainty for all market participants.[68] Regulatory

[57] Sunila and Ekroos (n 1) 20; Ranchordás (n 20) 6.
[58] Sofia Ranchordás (2014) cited in Ranchordás (n 20) 3.
[59] R Van Gestel and G Van Dijck, 'Better Regulation through Experimental Legislation' (2011) 17(3) *European Public Law* 541.
[60] BMWi, *Making Space for Innovation: The Handbook for Regulatory Sandboxes* (Federal Ministry for Economic Affairs and Energy 2019) 7.
[61] Ringe and Ruof (n 43) 34.
[62] Ranchordás (n 20) 5.
[63] Sunila and Ekroos (n 1) 15.
[64] Van der Waal, Das, and Van der Schoor 'Participatory Experimentation with Energy Law' (n 27) 1.
[65] Zetzsche and others 'Regulating a Revolution' (n 21) 45.
[66] Jiménez and Hagan *A Regulatory Sandbox for the Industry of Law* (n 43) 2; Ranchordás (n 20) 3; Ahern (n 21) 351.
[67] Ranchordás (n 20) 8.
[68] Ringe and Ruof (n 43) 3.

uncertainty can cause investors to be hesitant to invest in a firm that has to operate within the boundaries of the unclear regulatory framework. The implementation of a regulatory sandbox can enable regulators to collect information on new products, identify new risks, and adapt existing regulations or introduce new ones throughout the process,[69] while participating businesses receive support in navigating through the procedures in the regulatory framework, enabling them to better understand the supervisory expectations.[70] The reduction of regulatory uncertainty, improved communication, reduced regulatory burdens and the promotion of expedited regulatory decisions, while simultaneously safeguarding consumer protection, can fuel the development of business practices[71] and assist in achieving an optimal level of openness for innovation, thereby stimulating competition.[72] Other beneficial potential effects of regulatory sandboxes are shortening the time to market for products and services,[73] improving financing opportunities for new entrants[74] and signalling to market participants the supervisor's support for innovation, potentially spurring an innovation boost in the respective market.[75] Sandboxes can also function as an intermediate step towards changing the regulatory framework.[76] Regulatory learning about the risks and opportunities of emerging technologies and innovations, and the gaps in the applicable regulatory frameworks, provides authorities with a better understanding of possible changes or new interpretations of existing legislation,[77] which can contribute to facilitating an adequate policy response.[78] Especially with innovative products or businesses, their early-stage, rapid changes and the inability to assess risks with certainty makes conventional regulatory processes for altering the regulatory framework ill-suited. In a regulatory sandbox, the risks of the product on the market can be assessed without the long process of law-making. This avoids making rushed, inappropriate, and poorly designed adjustments to the legislation.[79]

Despite the various benefits regulatory sandboxes can provide, the regulatory approach also has some potential drawbacks. One weakness is related to the validity of the regulatory approach. Despite the increased interest in and adoption of regulatory sandboxes, systematic empirical evidence on their effectiveness is

[69] Cornelli and others (n 31) 10.

[70] R Parenti, 'Regulatory Sandboxes and Innovation Hubs for Fintech: Impact on Innovation, Financial Stability and Supervisory Convergence' (European Parliament 2020) 22. Available at: www.europarl.europa.eu/RegData/etudes/STUD/2020/652752/IPOL_STU(2020)652752_EN.pdf.

[71] Ringe and Ruof (n 43) 3; Ranchordás (n 20) 8.

[72] Zetzsche and others (n 21) 78.

[73] Ringe and Ruof (n 43) 3; AFM and DNB, 'More Room for Innovation in the Financial Sector: Discussion Document' (2016) 15, www.dnb.nl/media/xqhnsc2k/more-room-for-innovation-in-the-financial-sector.pdf.

[74] Parenti 'Regulatory Sandboxes and Innovation Hubs for Fintech' (n 70) 23.

[75] ibid 22.

[76] Ringe and Ruof (n 43) 30.

[77] European Commission 'Regulatory Learning in the EU' (n 7) 6.

[78] Parenti (n 70) 9.

[79] Ringe and Ruof (n 43) 42.

limited[80] and the legal, methodological and ethical challenges of these regulatory frameworks have been understudied.[81] Resulting adverse effects can be of limited internal validity since it is unclear if the verified results stem directly from the experimental intervention or other circumstances. Additionally, validation can also be impeded by the limited potential of the scaling-up of sandbox results in the testing environment to the wider market, since sandboxes are often locally implemented.[82] Besides limited validity of results, a poor design and implementation of experimental legislation[83] can also have methodological and legal implications.[84] Legal principles requiring experimental regulations to follow objective, transparent and predictable standards can, for instance, be violated due to methodological deficiencies,[85] or regulators may prioritise innovation over establishing adequate safeguards. The latter case might occur as a result of the economic benefits a sector might provide for a jurisdiction, resulting in a 'race-to-the-bottom' to attract start-ups and investors. This could, however, be at the expense of consumer protection and financial stability, especially if the design of the sandbox allowed for leniency on substantial regulatory standards and safeguards.[86] Consequently, market participants could be discouraged from entering into business with sandbox firms, thereby slowing down the growth of the business or sector.[87] Additionally, the temporary approval might not always encourage the development and testing of innovations, because the sandboxes cannot guarantee the adoption of the legislative relief or changes implemented in the sandbox after it has taken place.[88]

Given that the innovativeness of an applicant's product, service or business model is an important requirement for entering the regulatory sandbox and the regulator decides which firms can participate, it indirectly influences the market viability propositions and thereby also the market outcomes. Moreover, the competitive selection process results in a small group of participants having a considerable competitive advantage over those outside of the sandbox in terms of testing, negotiating routes to the market and navigating regulatory compliance. The reduced regulatory uncertainty with sandboxes enables participants to focus on their technical performance and business model of the product. This special treatment of participants therefore removes the level playing field for market entry.[89] These drawbacks of regulatory sandboxes raise the question of how the process can be designed in a non-discriminatory way. Additionally,

[80] Cornelli and others (n 31) 2.
[81] Ranchordás (n 20) 87.
[82] European Commission *'Better Regulation' Toolbox* (n 18) 602.
[83] Regulatory sandboxes are a form of experimental legislation. See Sofia Ranchordás (2014) cited in Ranchordás (n 20) 2.
[84] Ranchordás (n 20) 11.
[85] ibid 1.
[86] Parenti (n 70) 24.
[87] Zetzsche and others (n 21) 79.
[88] Sunila and Ekroos (n 1) 16.
[89] Ahern (n 21) 360.

standardisation and cost reduction functions of law are not captured in sandboxes, making the activity unfit for cross-border provision of services.[90] Moreover, creating and executing a sandbox may be resource-intensive and, thus, costly, which might be a problem for jurisdictions that have no well-equipped and financially strong regulators.[91] Having insufficient resources brings the risk of suboptimal selection of participants, harming the regulator's reputation.[92] Other risks relate to the supervisor becoming too sympathetic towards firms or herding behaviour by consumers and investors based on the participation in a sandbox and the label they have.[93]

2.2. Regulatory Sandboxes in Practice

Since the first application of a regulatory sandbox to the UK's fintech sector (Box B), the scope of regulatory sandboxes has expanded from the financial area to various other industries, such as healthcare and the energy sector.[94]

Box B: UK fintech regulatory sandbox[95]

The FCA introduced the first regulatory sandbox in 2015 with the main goal being to facilitate fintech's access to financing at early stages of development, consequently fostering innovation. At the same time, regulators could learn about new financial technologies and emerging trends and identify risks before the launch of the products for the mass market. The sandbox consisted of 118 accepted firms between 2016 and 2019. The firms in the sandbox were start-ups and small or medium enterprises in retail banking, wholesale markets, retail and wholesale investment, and lending or insurance propositions. These firms offered a wide array of new products or services.

The sandbox did not entail stricter regulation for non-sandbox firms nor did it provide protection for customers of sandbox firms for risks associated with the use of the firms' products. The FCA selected firms based on whether the firm offered a genuine innovation benefitting UK consumers, where the innovation had to be an improvement over existing products and services, thereby promoting competition. Moreover, the FCA input had to be deemed useful for the firm. Each application was reviewed by the FCA's sandbox unit and assessed which, if any, applicable regulations could be relaxed. A dedicated

[90] Zetzsche and others (n 21) 80.
[91] Ringe and Ruof (n 43) 43.
[92] Parenti (n 70) 26.
[93] ibid 26.
[94] Lee and Seo (n 9) 15.
[95] Cornelli and others (n 31) 2, 8–11; Ahern (n 21) 352.

case officer was assigned to firms to help in designing the test set-up, to provide guidance to complete the necessary paperwork for authorisation and to help in navigating through the regulatory environment throughout the process.

During the testing step, firms could test their products in a limited market environment. Firms had to familiarise themselves with the regulation with the help of the case officer. A final testing report was submitted after six months and firms exited the sandbox. Upon completion they could apply for permanent authorisation.

The growing interest in alternative regulatory approaches for innovations across the EU is also evident from the wide establishment of innovation hubs in nearly all EU and EFTA jurisdictions. Innovation hubs differ from regulatory sandboxes in the level of facilitation they provide: regulatory sandboxes usually involve some form of leniency or supervisory discretion on the applicable regulatory framework for the innovation; innovation hubs are more geared towards a platform for knowledge exchange and informal guidance. Although different from sandboxes, innovation hubs are often a first step in developing the regulatory framework for innovations because they can be set up under existing supervisory mandates, thereby not requiring changes in legislation or regulations, making them easier to establish. Still, regulatory sandboxes have garnered increasing interest[96] and several sandboxes have been introduced in recent years. In the context of the energy transition, Germany has made attempts in establishing a regulatory sandbox (Box C).

Box C: Regulatory sandbox in the energy sector in Germany: Smart Energy Showcases – Digital Agenda for the Energy Transition (SINTEG)

The SINTEG funding programme was developed to support real experiments on the energy transition. Consisting of five demonstration projects, the programme focused on challenges and solutions for new applications in the energy sector, in particular digital applications. Initially, regulatory experimentation was not in the scope of the programme, but the SINTEG-V ordinance in 2017 enabled projects to deviate from specific regulatory requirements, thereby creating a legal basis for the SINTEG projects.[97]

The evaluation of the programme showed that it facilitated a framework for the interaction of new actors from different industries and stages of the value chain, which enabled the development of new approaches and ideas.

[96] Parenti (n 70) 20.

[97] Beckstedde and others 'Regulatory Sandboxes' (n 23) 2; G Brunekreeft, M Buchmann, and J Kusznir, 'Regulatory Experiments and Incentive Regulation: Experiences with the SINTEG-Regulation' (2022) Paperseries Bremen Energy Working Paper No 38, 3–4.

The SINTEG-V ordinance particularly stimulated those project partners who would otherwise not have participated to be involved in the programme.[98] However, the SINTEG programme did not result in sandbox projects and the SINTEG-V ordinance expired. The implementation of the sandboxes encountered barriers related to the limited scope of the application, lack of participant incentives and the administrative burden. Regarding the latter obstacle, an extensive procedure for the reconciliation of evidence that had to be carried out by participants and the required certification by the auditor might have disproportionately burdened smaller players. On the regulatory authority side, the ordinance lacked a learning mechanism for authorities to learn from the processes and adapt SINTEG-V accordingly.[99]

The Netherlands is regarded as one of the pioneers in implementing regulatory sandboxes.[100] The first regulatory sandbox was introduced in 2015 and directed at projects on decentralised generation of electricity.[101] This was enabled under the Electricity Act 1998. Network operators and energy communities were allowed to apply for temporary exemptions in the decentralised generation of renewable electricity.[102] The sandbox resulted in 18 experiments, of which 14 received an exemption from specific articles within the Electricity Act. The experiments could last for a maximum of 10 years.[103] Among the experiments in the sandbox were the creation of an energy-neutral apartment complex in the Hague and an energy trading project using blockchain and a smart grid.[104] The sandbox is further explained in Box D.

In the evaluation of the regulatory sandbox, it was concluded that only five projects of the 14 exemptions had been started. It was concluded that the experiments did not result in noteworthy innovative breakthroughs or benefits in costs, nor did the experiment result in regulatory learning by providing evidence on whether regulation should be changed.[105] Potential reasons for the low number of applications were the overly restrictive format, the non-existent collaboration mechanisms present in the sandbox, and the limited support for potential applications. Evaluation among participants indicated that

[98] Brunekreeft, Buchmann, and Kusznir 'Regulatory Experiments and Incentive Regulation' (n 97) 7.
[99] Beckstedde and others (n 23) 2; Brunekreeft, Buchmann, and Kusznir (n 97) 8–9.
[100] Beckstedde and others (n 23) 2.
[101] IEA-ISGAN, 'Innovative Regulatory Approaches with Focus on Experimental Sandboxes 2.0: Casebook' (2021) 47. Available at: www.iea-isgan.org/wp-content/uploads/2021/10/Regulatory-Sandbox-2.0_For-Publication.pdf.
[102] Veseli and others (n 9) 2.
[103] IEA-ISGAN (n 101) 48; Brunekreeft, Buchmann, and Kusznir (n 97) 3–4.
[104] Carlson and Nciri 'Enter the Sandbox' (n 8) 15.
[105] Min EZK, 'Evaluatie experimenten decentrale duurzame elektriciteitsopwekking' (2021). Available at: https://open.overheid.nl/documenten/ronl-f7ac8015-060c-4c6a-aec0-f79df3613f2e/pdf.

actors eligible to participate had limited resources and it was challenging for them to meet all the criteria of demonstrating the necessary organisational, financial and technical expertise for fulfilling all the goals of an experiment.[106] As a follow-up to the Experimentation Decree under the Electricity Act 1998, a regulatory sandbox was initiated, called the Experimentation Regulation Electricity and Gas Act 1998. However, due to encountered limitations in the preceding sandbox and following the consultation of the new Energy Law this regulatory sandbox finished at the end of 2020.[107]

Box D: Executive order Decentral Sustainable Electricity Production Experiments (EDSEP)

Article 7a, sub 1 of the Electricity Act 1998 states that derogation of the Act is possible by means of an experiment through executive order and in accordance with EU legislation. This is aimed at relatively small-scale, localised renewable energy experiments for which, under specific conditions for a particular target group, the regulated separation between commercial activities production and supply and the publicly managed distribution side of the energy system can be relaxed.[108]

The derogation was laid down in executive order Decentral, Sustainable Electricity Production Experiments (EDSEP), also referred to as the Experimentation Decree, and entered into force on 1 April 2015.[109] This decree pre-defined from which articles of the Electricity Act projects in the sandbox could be exempted. These related to the right to own and operate the grid, grid tariff discounts, DSO (distribution system operator) metering, obligations and exemptions from supplier licences, certain specific rules regarding the transparency and liquidity of the energy market and obligations related to invoicing and data management.[110]

In terms of regulatory learning, the Dutch government intended with the experiment to gain more insight into grid stabilisation by prosumers and the identification of barriers in the existing regulations. The goal of the Experimentation Decree was to stimulate renewable energy use at the local level, more efficient use of the existing infrastructure and the increase of energy consumer involvement with their own energy supply.[111]

[106] Carlson and Nciri (n 8) 31, 34.
[107] Beckstedde and others (n 23) 2; Min EZK, 'Besluit experimenten Elektriciteitswet 1998 en Gaswet' (2020). Available at: https://open.overheid.nl/documenten/ronl-5bf09608-1863-48be-8edb-3883964974d3/pdf; RVO, 'Experimenten Elektriciteitswet en Gaswet' (25 January 2021) www.rvo.nl/subsidies-financiering/experimenten-elektriciteitswet-en-gaswet.
[108] Van der Waal, Das, and Van der Schoor (n 27) 3.
[109] ibid; Lammers and Diestelmeier 'Experimenting with Law and Governance' (n 26) 2.
[110] Van der Waal, Das, and Van der Schoor (n 27) 10–11.
[111] ibid 3.

This Experimentation Decree allowed experiments with the following purposes:[112]

(1) increased utilisation of renewable energy or combined heat and power at local level
(2) more efficient use of available energy infrastructure
(3) increased involvement of energy-users in their own energy provision

Two types of projects were distinguished in the Experimentation Decree: project grids with a maximum of 500 connected users plus one connection of the project grid with the national grid; and large grid projects with a maximum of 10,000 connected users, where the regional DSO continued to exercise its legal tasks and purposes. Project promotors that were eligible to apply for derogations with the sandbox were limited to homeowner associations and energy communities, which must be entirely controlled by their members.[113] This meant that members decided on the organisation, progress and distribution of costs of a project whereas DSOs and energy suppliers were not allowed to exercise any control.[114]

The sandbox programme was organised by the government agency and the regulator ACM took up the advisory and monitoring role.[115]

In June 2016 the Dutch National Bank (DNB) and Authority for Financial Markets (AFM) introduced the innovation hub dedicated to the financial sector. This InnovationHub is currently still operational and supports firms with questions about supervision and regulations related to innovative financial products and services.[116] In December 2016, six months after the introduction of the InnovationHub, the regulatory sandbox was added. This sandbox offers a solution to parties with unnecessarily restrictive supervisory rules or policies applicable to their innovative concepts. The DNB and/or AFM help determine how these obstacles can be overcome, taking into account the scope for interpretation of legislation, but derogations do not happen since laws and regulations remain fully applicable.[117] After the withdrawal of the UK from the

[112] Lammers and Diestelmeier (n 26) 5.
[113] Schittekatte and others (n 25) 4.
[114] Lammers and Diestelmeier (n 26) 6.
[115] Beckstedde and others (n 23) 6.
[116] Baker McKenzie, *A Guide to Regulatory Fintech Sandboxes Internationally* (2020) 30. Available at: www.bakermckenzie.com/-/media/files/insight/publications/2020/05/a_guide_to_regulatory_fintech_sandboxes_internationally_8734.pdf?la=en; AFM and DNB 'More Room for Innovation' (n 73) 3.
[117] DNB, 'Continuing Dialogue: InnovationHub and Regulatory Sandbox: Lessons Learned After Three Years' (2019) 4. Available at: www.afm.nl/%7E/profmedia/files/rapporten/2019/innovationhub-rapport-nl.pdf?la=nl-NL?.

EU, this sandbox is one of the longest-running in the EU.[118] Box E describes its content and structure.

Box E: AFM & DNB financial sector sandbox – the Netherlands

The InnovationHub (in Dutch, *Maatwerk voor Innovatie*) allows for more room for firms in the financial sector to bring their products, services or business models on the market without unnecessary barriers.[119] The sandbox has a principles-based approach, where the regulator offers a firm a bespoke solution conditional on the innovation satisfying the underlying purposes of the respective policies, rules and regulations.[120] Other options offered by the authorities are partial authorisation, opt-in authorisation or authorisation with requirements. The supervisors have more room to enforce changes to their own established policies, rules or regulations. If the required changes relate to policies not set by the supervisor, the supervisors may urge a change in rules at the national or European level.[121]

Enterprises can gain access to the Dutch regulatory sandbox if the enterprise is unable reasonably to meet the standard applicable rules, regulations and guidelines due to the innovative concept. Other criteria are that the innovative concept achieves the purpose of the rules in some way and the existing rules leave room for interpretation and customisation. Lastly, the innovative concept contributes to the solidity of the enterprise and does not jeopardise the stability of the financial system. An application from an enterprise to join the sandbox entails at least a detailed proposal for the innovative financial concept, a process proposal and an analysis of the rules and regulations forming an obstacle. After application, the regulators will consider how an appropriate bespoke arrangement can be provided, which conditions will apply and how the sandbox will be terminated. The duration of the sandbox varies per enterprise, which will monitored with re-evaluations. The supervisor is at any time able to partially or wholly end, change or constrain the sandbox. After the sandbox or partial authorisation ends, enterprises can introduce their innovation to a broader market if it can meet all legal and regulatory requirements.[122]

Thus, the regulatory sandboxes have various potential strengths and weaknesses. One of the strengths is the learning potential, both for regulators and market entities, before bringing the respective innovation fully into the market. Regulatory

[118] Parenti (n 70) 35.
[119] DNB Continuing Dialogue' (n 117) 4.
[120] Ringe and Ruof (n 43) 51.
[121] Baker McKenzie *A Guide to Regulatory Fintech Sandboxes Internationally* (n 116) 30.
[122] ibid 30–31.

sandboxes are an adaptive approach that can ensure appropriate safeguards and at the same time provide the needed flexibility to facilitate the energy transition. The effectiveness of this adaptive approach is, however, strongly influenced by their design. Poorly designed regulatory sandboxes can result in various adverse effects, such as the lack of a level playing field and consumer risks. This also became clear from the analysis of sandboxes that have already taken place where overly strict entry conditions, administrative tasks, or limited resources and collaboration opportunities for participants played a role in their limited success. Regulatory sandboxes should be seen not as the ultimate approach or solution but rather as a complementary tool to the existing regulatory structure.[123] This highlights the importance of a legislative framework that facilitates the implementation of regulatory sandboxes.

3. Regulatory Sandboxes for the Emerging Hydrogen Sector

In the energy transition, regulatory sandboxes are regarded as essential tools to foster innovation and regulatory learning.[124] Since regulatory sandboxes are not a means to change regulation permanently,[125] they can be useful for innovative products, services or business models that differ from those in traditional markets and sometimes the existing regulatory framework.[126] The implementation of sandboxes provides evidence for understanding whether the regulatory framework should be changed permanently[127] and thereby achieve long-term changes to the energy system to enable an innovation that benefits all consumers.[128]

The transformation of the energy system can, according to the Council of European Energy Regulators (CEER), result in the need for national regulatory authorities (NRAs) to build temporary spaces that allow for testing and demonstrating solutions for technical, economic and regulatory challenges related to the energy transition on a small scale. This can be done through pilot projects and regulatory sandboxes. NRAs may also need to ensure regulation is not a barrier in the larger-scale rollout of innovative practices, after these have been tested and proven to be successful.[129] Areas within the energy sector that may necessitate the implementation of regulatory sandboxes are those of electricity and gas. This is due to their network-boundedness, making them extensively regulated compared

[123] A Schneiders, *Regulatory Sandboxes in the Energy Sector: Are They Key to the Transition to a Net Zero Future?* (UCL Energy Institute 2021) 11. Available at: https://discovery.ucl.ac.uk/id/eprint/10161899/1/BIEE21_ASchneiders.pdf.

[124] Beckstedde and others (n 23) 8.

[125] Ofgem, 'What is a Regulatory Sandbox?' (September 2018) 1. Available at: www.ofgem.gov.uk/sites/default/files/docs/2018/09/what_is_a_regulatory_sandbox.pdf.

[126] Attrey, Lesher, and Lomax (n 19) 4.

[127] Ofgem (n 125) 1.

[128] Carlson and Nciri (n 8) 12.

[129] CEER (n 55) 8.

to other energy carriers that are not bound to a network.[130] In the context of the electricity sector, the concept of an EU regulatory sandbox framework that can provide the (currently lacking) robust legal basis for national sandboxes in Member States has, for instance, been suggested by Sunila and Ekroos.[131] Alternatively, gas regulation has also been identified as a suitable area for implementing regulatory sandboxes, because of the expected prominent role of gases such as hydrogen, synthetic methane or biogas in the future energy system and the increasing importance of storage due to fluctuating generation. In the case of Austria, two identified potential topics for regulatory sandboxes are (1) the potential adjustments of standards for increasing the hydrogen or biogas share in the gas network while ensuring safety and energy quality and (2) the degree of adaptation possible in standards to allow for the direct feed-in of hydrogen or biogas to the gas grid.[132]

The emerging hydrogen sector, in particular that of green hydrogen, can potentially benefit from the implementation of regulatory sandboxes. The green hydrogen market needs tailored support because – unlike the costs of solar and wind energy, which are driven by capital expenditure – green hydrogen production is driven by operational costs that, for a larger market share, depend on the electricity price.[133] However, green hydrogen is relatively new within the energy sector, as its large-scale production is still in an early stage. This deployment of hydrogen on a larger scale is, however, hindered by high production costs, the lack of a market, and investment risks due to regulatory uncertainties.[134] South Korea is the first nation to establish a legal framework for governmental efforts to develop hydrogen as a fuel source. The Hydrogen Economy Promotion and Hydrogen Safety Management Law also includes the subsidies that are provided to industry by the government. However, legislation for the enforcement of ordinances and rules is still needed.[135] Establishing a regulatory sandbox in an unregulated field can contribute to learning and identifying whether regulation is possible and desirable.[136] For instance, in the local production and use of hydrogen, pilot projects can offer the opportunity to directly explore and test the small-scale production facilities without having to comply with the legal and tax frameworks for the production of a fuel that currently large producers, traders and providers can handle.[137] Regulatory sandboxes can thus, for emerging hydrogen economies, be a suitable tool for the identification and demonstration of necessary regulatory requirements for the revision or implementation of new regulations.[138]

[130] Veseli and others (n 9) 5.
[131] Sunila and Ekroos (n 1) 24.
[132] Veseli and others (n 9) 5.
[133] S Van Renssen, 'The Hydrogen Solution?' (2020) 10 *Nature Climate Change* 799, 801.
[134] Bade and others 'Economic, Social, and Regulatory Challenges of Green Hydrogen Production' (n 4) 316.
[135] T Stangarone, 'South Korean Efforts to Transition to a Hydrogen Economy' (2021) 23 *Clean Technologies and Environmental Policy* 509, 513.
[136] European Commission (n 7) 37.
[137] B Nastasi, 'Hydrogen Policy, Market, and R&D Projects' (2019) *Solar Hydrogen Production* 31, 38.
[138] PA Ashari, H Oh, and C Koch, 'Pathways to the Hydrogen Economy: A Multidimensional Analysis of the Technological Innovation Systems of Germany and South Korea' (2024) 49 *International Journal of Hydrogen Energy* 405, 417.

Within the development of a hydrogen market, the regulatory environment is recognised as a hampering force and could potentially benefit from the introduction of a regulatory sandbox. In terms of cross-boundary hydrogen-related activities, the lack of a harmonised definition of green hydrogen has been identified as a barrier, making the inclusion of hydrogen in energy policies and international trade more difficult.[139] Permitting hydrogen projects has also been identified as having a hampering effect.[140] For instance in the development of a hydrogen economy within the Dutch port area in Rotterdam, pilots for green hydrogen production through electrolysis are needed for knowledge building and the preparation for future scale-up. For these pilots, experimental space should be created where a more flexible approach to the permitting and inspection regime is established.[141]

Despite their perceived potential, to date and to the authors' knowledge, no regulatory sandboxes have been introduced on (green) hydrogen in the Netherlands, or at least have not been acknowledged as such. Experimentation in the context of hydrogen activities has been initiated using pilots in the Netherlands, partially driven by a lack of regulation regarding hydrogen. Regional network operators initiated four pilots on the use of hydrogen for heating houses. For the pilots to take place, the Dutch regulator ACM has set up generic and specific guidelines to ensure the safety of hydrogen.[142] For the network operators to participate in these pilots, the ACM has developed a tolerance policy,[143] because legislation on the supply of hydrogen to the consumer in the built environment does not yet exist in the Netherlands and, consequently, network operators do not have a legal basis for activities related to hydrogen.[144] When these plots were first established in 2022, the Dutch Gas Act defined the tasks and responsibilities of a network operator; according to Article 2, a network operator is a company that is attributed the task of operating one or more gas transport networks, but the definition of gas in this Act means network operators do not have a legal basis for activities related to hydrogen.[145] Gas is defined in Article 1.1.b of the Act as a substance that consists mainly of methane or another substance that is, due to its properties, equal to methane and that can be safely transported in line with the provisions

[139] S Griffiths and others, 'Industrial Decarbonization via Hydrogen: A Critical and Systematic Review of Developments, Socio-Technical Systems and Policy Options' (2021) 80 *Energy Research & Social Science* 102208, 33.

[140] Weichenhain and others *Hydrogen Valleys* (n 13) 44.

[141] N Rijk and J van Dinther, *Rotterdam Hydrogen Hub* (SmartPort 2019) 16–17. Available at: https://smartport.nl/wp-content/uploads/2019/09/SmartPort-Position-paper-Rotterdam-Hydrogen-Hub-1.pdf.

[142] RVO, 'Generiek richtsnoer waterstofveiligheid, eerste versie' (2022) 2. Available at: www.rvo.nl/sites/default/files/2022-10/Generiek%20richtsnoer%20Waterstofveiligheid%20%28eerste%20vastgestelde%20versie%2C%205%20oktober%202022%29.pdf; RVO, 'Aanvullend richtsnoer waterstof pilots in de gebouwde omgeving, eerste versie' (2022) 2. Available at: www.rvo.nl/sites/default/files/2022-10/Aanvullend%20veiligheidsrichtsnoer%20voor%20vier%20waterstofpilots%20in%20de%20gebouwde%20omgeving%20%28eerste%20vastgestelde%20versie%2C%205%20oktober%202022%29.pdf.

[143] ACM (n 29) 1.

[144] ACM, 'Signaal 2021' (2021) ACM/INT/421329, 1. Available at: www.acm.nl/sites/default/files/documents/acm-signaal-2021.pdf.

[145] Koninklijke VENMW, 'Position Paper Waterstof' (2020) 4. Available at: www.tweedekamer.nl/kamerstukken/detail?id=2020Z08148&did=2020D17364.

stated in the Gas Act. This means that the provisions in the Gas Act do not apply to green hydrogen,[146] thereby prohibiting network operators from participating in the hydrogen pilots in the built environment. However, the ACM believes it is important for network operators to gain experience with the distribution of hydrogen and has therefore introduced its tolerance policy, under which, if the pilots adhere to certain requirements, network operators are allowed to participate in hydrogen distribution in these pilots.[147]

In their tolerance policy document, the ACM has established general requirements for participation, entry and exit conditions, and requirements for consumer protection and safety. The tolerance policy is only directed at the application of hydrogen for heat in the built environment and the duration is limited to five years from the public communication of the tolerance policy. Central to the requirements on consumer protection is that the supply of hydrogen should be subject to the same measures (at least) as the supply of gas under the Gas Act. For the safety requirements, the pilots need to comply with the temporary policy framework of the Ministry of Economic Affairs and Climate on hydrogen safety. The regulator ACM monitors the execution of the pilots and can require participants to share information regarding the pilot.[148] Looking at the definition of regulatory sandboxes in section 2, the tolerance policy resembles a regulatory sandbox, despite not having been acknowledged as such. Drawing from the common characteristics: (1) the introduction of hydrogen for heating can be identified as a genuine innovation, (2) hydrogen is expected to bring benefits to society, (3) the innovation can be tested in a controlled environment and the legislative barrier had been identified before the regulatory sandbox, and (4) boundaries in time and scope have been set. The fifth characteristic regarding appropriate safeguards to preserve policy objectives and legal requirements being in place can be contested; in the communication about the tolerance policy, there is no legislative mandate on which the tolerance policy is based. The policy in itself does not provide a ground for allowing experiments that derogate from existing regulations and it does not provide the needed legal certainty.[149]

Thus, in the context of hydrogen, the experiences thus far with regulatory approaches to innovations in the emerging hydrogen market come from pilot projects. Both pilots and regulatory sandboxes are forms of experimental legislation, but they differ in their objectives. Pilots are designed to obtain the data needed for the continuation of a business, taking place once or a few times, with the underlying assumption that the technology central to the pilot will be adopted in the market without having to address policy or regulatory barriers.[150] Regulatory sandboxes are directed at enhancing communication between regulators and

[146] Bart van Oorschot and Veii Jacobs, 'Opschalen van Groene Waterstof' (2021) *Nederlands Tijdschrift Voor Energierecht* 73.
[147] ACM (n 29) 1.
[148] ibid 2–3.
[149] Van Oorschot and Jacobs 'Opschalen van Groene Waterstof' (n 146) 77.
[150] Carlson and Nciri (n 8) 11.

innovative firms, allow for testing of products or services, providing guidance and enabling elevation in the regulation.[151] There is an inherent connection between both approaches as a regulatory sandbox can be seen as an overarching area that contains a test or pilot.[152] In that view, the hydrogen pilots that are currently, or were historically, taking place can be seen as frontrunners for regulatory sandboxes. The latter in turn function as a stepping stone towards full introduction to the market while ensuring appropriate safeguards for consumers and the market and the knowledge-gathering for regulators about the appropriate regulatory environment.

In conclusion, the hydrogen market is still under development, including in the Netherlands. The lack of regulation has a hampering effect on the transition to hydrogen. At both the national and the European level, the regulatory framework for hydrogen is in development and expected to come into force in the near future. Even though this addresses the lack of a regulatory framework, flexibility and adaptability within this framework is recommended to allow for new developments in the hydrogen sector or related sectors. Given the various changes taking place in the hydrogen sector (such as in its technologies) and in the energy system itself, overly stringent regulation might not be the best regulatory route. Consequently, a regulatory framework that sets the scene, including sufficient safeguards, and incorporates sufficient flexibility and adaptability would enable regulators to move along with potential future developments that cannot be foreseen at this moment in time. Secondly, flexibility in the regulatory framework in the form of regulatory sandboxes has the potential to provide the needed regulatory learning for the materialisation of the hydrogen value chain, which is complex due to the interdependency between the value chain nodes. Application of a regulatory sandbox in this view can provide the needed regulatory learning about the specific parts of the value chain, at the same time allowing stakeholders to have a stepping stone into the market and to learn from this. At the same time, anticipation of the fast-changing environment of hydrogen and regulations is facilitated with a regulatory sandbox, thereby avoiding the time loss currently experienced with hydrogen projects. Especially given the safety risks of hydrogen use, the option to establish a regulatory sandbox where safety guidelines are present can be perceived as a suitable middle ground between the no-regulation, laissez-faire approach and a strict, set-in-stone regulatory approach.

4. Designing a Hydrogen Regulatory Sandbox

The application of regulatory sandboxes has the potential to benefit emerging sectors, such as green hydrogen or hydrogen in general. To achieve this potential, well-designed sandboxes are imperative, as it determines the project's functioning

[151] Ranchordás (n 20) 5.
[152] Zetzsche and others (n 21) 85.

and successful implementation.[153] As section 2 has outlined, the poor design of sandboxes can result in non-compliance with legal principles, unjust practices by regulators or participants, or risks for consumers and the system; they can even block innovation by increasing uncertainty for innovators.[154] Careful design is therefore important, including suitable safeguards, to avoid issues with non-discrimination.[155] This section therefore addresses the design of regulatory sandboxes as advised in the preceding literature.

For the assessment of the design guidelines, the principles of good regulation as defined in the preceding legal literature[156] are used. These principles (flexibility and responsiveness, participation, transparency, effectiveness, independence, efficiency and accountability) provide a good basis for designing and evaluating regulatory frameworks (see also Chapter 10). The principles aim to enhance the quality of regulation and ensure the goals of the regulation are realised. Their effectiveness has been shown in previous energy regulation and they have contributed to the regulation of markets in energy and other network sectors.[157] The design guidelines for regulatory sandboxes can be seen as the implementation of the principles of good regulation. An assessment of the guidelines using the principles can indicate whether the guidelines are sufficient in ensuring good-quality regulatory sandboxes. The seven principles of good regulation and their definition used to guide the analysis are shown in Figure 11.2.

Figure 11.2 Principles of good regulation (own illustration)

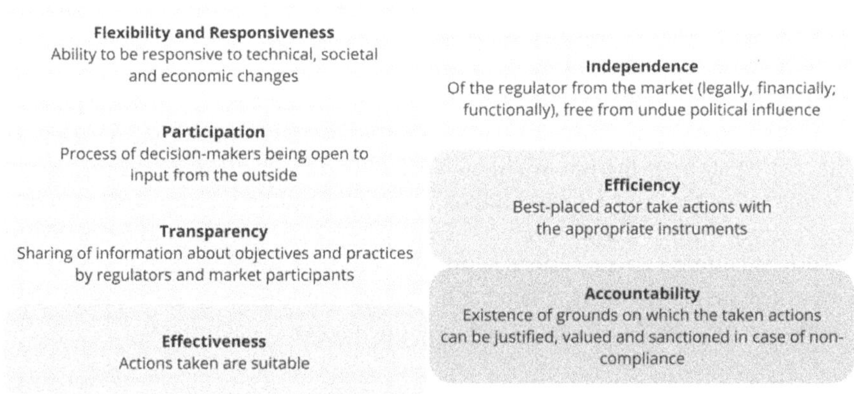

[153] European Commission (n 7) 63.
[154] ibid.
[155] Sunila and Ekroos (n 1) 16.
[156] Baumgart and Lavrijssen (n 6) 11–13; Lavrijssen and Vitéz, 'Make Hydrogen Whilst the Sun Shines' (n 10) 272–75.
[157] ibid 8.

The design of a regulatory sandbox should begin with a thorough feasibility assessment to identify the required resources, the alignment of internal and external stakeholders, regulatory programmes that are complementary, and other potential constraints. The design should reflect the local conditions, including the legal framework that determines with which mandates the sandbox must align, the market conditions that determine the application and testing volumes, and the resources that are available for the sandbox to take place.[158] To achieve this design, several authors have discussed guidelines or recommendations. A general legal and methodological framework for the design of experimental legal regimes is proposed by Ranchordás[159] to ensure that experimental legal regimes can be evidence-based instruments and their transparency, effectiveness assessment, rationality and objectivity can be increased. The framework discusses the design, treatment group and evaluation of experimental legal regimes. Guidelines or recommendations specifically addressing the design of regulatory sandboxes have been established by the German Federal Ministry of Economic Affairs and Energy (BMWi).[160] The Consultative Group to Assist the Poor (CGAP) of the World Bank has shared design elements of regulatory sandboxes,[161] as has the European Commission in its staff working document on regulatory learning in the EU.[162] Established guidelines and elements for the design of regulatory sandboxes, or experimental legislation, in the literature are listed in Table 11.1.

Table 11.1 Design guidelines for regulatory sandboxes[163]

Objective & scope	• Determine goals and develop indicators beforehand • Determine the limits of the sandbox in terms of scope, scale and/or conduct • Ensure sandbox design can be revised and improved
Monitoring/ governance	• Define the coordination of the sandbox, including the roles, responsibilities and key operational processes • Identify and use established networks to facilitate the sandbox's development and implementation

(continued)

[158] I Jeník and S Duff, 'How to Build a Regulatory Sandbox: A Practical Guide for Policy Makers' (CGAP Technical guide, 2020) 12–14.

[159] Ranchordás (n 20) 16–18.

[160] BMWi (n 60) 19–59.

[161] Jeník and Duff 'How to Build a Regulatory Sandbox' (n 158) 12.

[162] European Commission (n 7) 66–83.

[163] Combination of guidelines as stated by Ranchordás (n 20) 16–18; BMWi (n 60) 19–59; Jeník and Duff (n 158) 12; European Commission (n 7) 66–83.

Table 11.1 ***(Continued)***

Stakeholders	• Determine stakeholder roles and interests • Ensure stakeholders are informed about what is tested and how • Determine who can participate and communicate this clearly • The selected groups should be representative of the population or sector • The design should encompass the definition of comparable groups
Time span	• Establish the duration of the sandbox admission and of the testing • Tailor the duration of the sandbox proportionately to the characteristics of the sector and to the complexity of the experiment
Admission	• Have a controlled system of self-selection and voluntary participation in place for admission
Evaluation	• The evaluation protocol of the sandbox should be determined • Determine and clarify who has the responsibility for evaluation • Determine who will receive the findings and how
Legal aspects	• There should be a legal mandate (principle of legality) • Identify legal obstacles and potential exemptions • Observe state aid rules

The guidelines for designing a regulatory sandbox as discussed in the preceding literature have been allocated to seven categories, based on their content. The first category addresses the objective and scope of the regulatory sandbox that needs to be addressed in the design. When designing a regulatory sandbox, the objectives, indicators and scope of the sandbox need to be defined. Clear and transparent objectives help manage the expectations of participants and provide a basis for an internal review of the effectiveness,[164] thereby addressing the good regulation principle of transparency.

In terms of the governance of a sandbox, the design should provide for clarity on the internal operating structure, roles and responsibilities.[165] This also accounts for a clear definition and moderation of the cooperation of the participating stakeholders.[166] This relates to the good regulation principle of accountability, which ensures it is clear who is responsible for which actions and the consequences

[164] Parenti (n 70) 9.
[165] Jeník and Duff (n 158) 12.
[166] BMWi (n 60) 29.

if market players do not adhere to this.[167] The principle of transparency, referring to unambiguity in the rules and decisions stakeholders have access to and understand, is also addressed. Lastly, the use of established networks can decrease the search for sandbox participants,[168] aligning with the principle of efficiency: the ratio of investments (time, financial, personal etc) to the outcome and aiming at saving economic resources.[169]

In the design of a sandbox, several guidelines have been established regarding the stakeholders involved. Potential stakeholders and their roles should be identified, for instance using stakeholder analysis, and the stakeholders should be informed about what is tested in the sandbox.[170] This reflects the principles of efficiency and effectiveness, as the sandbox can be made specific for the respective stakeholders, thereby strengthening the sandbox's execution. The guideline on informing stakeholders about what is tested reflects the principles of transparency and participation. The latter refers to the extent to which market players can provide input to decisions and developments that can have a beneficial effect on the legitimacy and acceptance of regulatory outcomes.[171] Additionally, the target group should be representative of the sector and comparable to justify the differentiated treatment for the purpose of the sandbox and thereby the external validity of the sandbox.[172] Once again, effectiveness is represented with this guideline, because it reflects that the actions taken are suitable to the participants and the market.[173]

In terms of the time frame of regulatory sandboxes, the guidelines state that both the duration of the admission period and the testing itself should be established in the design.[174] Proportionality of the timeframe to the characteristics of the sector, potential participants and complexity of the sandbox is advised.[175] These guidelines ensure actions taken are suitable and at the appropriate level (effectiveness) and with the most appropriate instruments in terms of time invested being proportional to the outcomes (efficiency). The guidelines state that, in the admission of participants, the sandbox should be designed to facilitate self-selection and voluntary participation,[176] representing the principle of participation. To avoid regulatory arbitrage and to maintain a level playing field, Parenti[177] addresses the need for clearly defined and transparent eligibility criteria and the development of a robust framework to ensure that those eligibility criteria are applied consistently.

[167] Baumgart and Lavrijssen (n 6) 12.
[168] BMWi (n 60) 29.
[169] Baumgart and Lavrijssen (n 6) 13.
[170] Ranchordás (n 20) p.16.
[171] Baumgart and Lavrijssen (n 6) 12.
[172] Ranchordás (n 20) 17.
[173] Baumgart and Lavrijssen (n 6) 13.
[174] Jeník and Duff (n 158) 12.
[175] Ranchordás (n 20) 16.
[176] ibid 17.
[177] Parenti (n 70) 9.

This recommendation could be added to the design guidelines of regulatory sandboxes, which would represent the principles of transparency and accountability.

An evaluation protocol should be included in the design, detailing the criteria for evaluation, type of evaluation, moment of evaluation, data gathering methods and how to evaluate the data.[178] Transparency is represented with these guidelines as the stakeholders are informed about the evaluation protocol and potentially the outcomes. In case the outcomes of the evaluation are shared, participating and non-participating actors can benefit from the outcomes of the sandbox, thereby positively impacting the effectiveness and information asymmetries.[179]

Lastly, in the design of a sandbox a legal mandate should be present and identified.[180] Among key legal requirements for the design of experimental legal regimes, to which regulatory sandboxes belong, are the principles of legality and legal certainty.[181] Also the legal obstacles, potential exemptions and state aid rules should be identified in the design of the sandbox.[182] These guidelines all represent the principle of effectiveness, as it requires the decisions to be taken at the most appropriate level.[183] The principle of accountability can also be represented with the guideline, as the presence of a legal mandate would ensure the existence of ground on which the actions taken can be justified, valued and sanctioned in case of non-compliance.[184]

Bringing together the guidelines for designing a regulatory sandbox as stated in the preceding literature and the principle of good regulation sheds light on the quality of the design framework and potential points of attention. The analysis has shown that the principles of effectiveness, efficiency, participation, transparency and accountability are well-represented in the guidelines. The remaining two principles (independence; flexibility and responsiveness) are not specifically addressed in the sandbox guidelines. The principle of independence refers to that of regulators and the market. Their independence has a positive influence on trust in the actions taken.[185] Since regulatory sandboxes provide an experimental space for participants to test their products in the real-world market, there is the risk of the unequal distribution of benefits (see section 3) as some market players may not be granted entry or be eligible to participate in the regulatory sandbox. Additionally, a potential weakness of regulatory sandboxes if poorly designed is the risk of political interference. This political interference can also negatively impact the level playing field, by favouring certain market players for admission. The entity that establishes, monitors and evaluates the sandbox needs to be independent from the government. This is needed to avoid political interference. It can therefore be

[178] Ranchordás (n 20) 18; BMWi (n 60) 29, 53.
[179] Lavrijssen and Vitéz (n 10) 273.
[180] European Commission (n 7) 72.
[181] Sunila and Ekroos (n 1) 18.
[182] BMWi (n 60) 36–48.
[183] Baumgart and Lavrijssen (n 6) 13.
[184] ibid 12.
[185] ibid 13.

relevant to extend the design framework with a guideline that requires a certain extent of independence for the entity that establishes, monitors and evaluates the sandbox (see also Chapter 10).

The remaining principle of good regulation that is not clearly represented in the design guidelines is that of flexibility and responsiveness, referring to the ability to be responsive to technical, societal and economic changes. Only the guidelines regarding the time frame of the sandbox design reflect to a certain extent this principle, as a limited time frame enables the sandbox to be responsive to changes. A certain extent of flexibility is needed to adapt regulation to ensure the law does not fall behind the market needs. With the uncertainty on how new markets in the energy sectors will and should develop, the ability to adapt helps avoid unsuitable regulatory choices and the hampering of innovation.[186] Especially in the case of the emerging hydrogen market, flexibility and responsiveness are essential. The European Commission argues in its staff working document that a sandbox should be flexible by design and be able to benefit from learning during its implementation.[187] When perceived as a tool within existing regulation, the establishment and execution of regulatory sandboxes is a way of creating flexibility and responsiveness of regulation. Given that sandboxes create temporary, experimental space to derogate from the existing legislative framework, regulatory sandboxes create a way for regulation to be responsive to technical, societal and economic changes. As argued in Chapter 10, adaptiveness goes beyond flexibility. However, the guidelines for the design of the sandbox itself do not reflect this. Following the European Commission, the design guidelines for regulatory sandboxes could be extended. An extension could ensure that adaptation of the sandbox itself is possible when changes to the societal, technological or economic system occur.

5. Dutch Hydrogen Regulatory Sandboxes

As stated by Sunila and Ekroos,[188] in terms of regulatory sandbox design, there is no need to reinvent the wheel as models for regulatory sandboxes already exist. At the same time, every sector has its particularities, objectives and structure of competencies, which all affect the design of a sandbox regime. However, experimental legislation, including regulatory sandboxes, requires a legislative mandate to be based upon.[189] The structure of this legal regime for experimentation is thus important in enabling radical or disruptive innovations, such as that of hydrogen, to take place.[190] This section aims to build further on the design principles for

[186] Baumgart and Lavrijssen (n 6) 11.
[187] European Commission (n 7) 79.
[188] Sunila and Ekroos (n 1) 18.
[189] Ranchordás (2014) in Ranchordás (n 20) 3.
[190] M Heldeweg, 'Legal Regimes for Experimenting with Cleaner Production – Especially in Sustainable Energy' (2017) 169 *Journal of Cleaner Production* 48, 49.

regulatory sandboxes in general towards the design of hydrogen regulatory sandboxes in the Netherlands. This is done by analysing the extent to which existing and forthcoming legislation enables regulatory sandboxes to be set up and take place. Since the Netherlands is a Member State of the EU, the first section discusses the legal basis for regulatory sandboxes for hydrogen in the Netherlands followed by a discussion of the overarching structure at the EU level.

5.1. The Netherlands

Experience in the past with experimental legislation in the Netherlands is evident from the regulatory sandbox for decentral renewable energy experiments (Box D). The development and execution of this sandbox were enabled by the experimental legislation provision included in the Electricity Act 1998. This provision (Article 7) still exists, but applies to the transport and supply of decentralised produced sustainable electricity or electricity produced from cogeneration,[191] making it less applicable as a legal basis for establishing hydrogen regulatory sandboxes in the Netherlands.

The Gas Act 2000 contains an experimentation clause (Article 1i(1)) and instruments for derogation (Articles 10b; 10d). However, as discussed in section 3, the definition of 'gas' in the Act makes most provisions not applicable to green hydrogen. The space for experimentation of the Act's Article 1i(1) is similar to the experimentation clause in the Electricity Act 1998 with the condition that the experiment contributes to developments on decentralised production, transport and supply of decentralised produced gas from installations that exclusively use renewable energy sources. The Act and thereby the experimentation clause could be made applicable to green hydrogen using Article 1(2) of the Gas Act. The instruments for derogation allow for assigning different duties to network operators than normally regulated using an executive order, conditional on a set of requirements (Article 10b) and allowing other activities for a network company for a predetermined period (Article 10d). However, the Dutch minister has decided not to make use of the experimentation clause or the instruments, stating that first a legal ground for hydrogen needs to be established before (temporary) duties are assigned through an executive order.[192] Additionally, the experimentation by means of an executive order under the Gas Act applies to derogation of existing law, but not to admitting network companies or activities that current legislation does not (yet) cover. Therefore, the derogation using an experiment is not an option since alternative energy carriers are not (yet) covered with existing legislation.[193]

[191] Elektriciteitswet 1998, art 7. Available at: https://wetten.overheid.nl/BWBR0009755/2024-01-01.
[192] Van Oorschot and Jacobs (n 146) 74–76.
[193] ACM, 'Leidraad Netwerkbedrijven en alternatieve energiedragers: Toegestane activiteiten onder huidig wettelijk kader' (2020) ACM/UIT/555471, 8. Available at: www.acm.nl/system/files/documents/leidraad-netwerkbedrijven-en-alternatieve-energiedragers.pdf.

Hydrogen and related activities are expected to be regulated with the adoption of the Energy Act, which will replace the Electricity and Gas Acts. The Energy Act has been under development since December 2020 and on 4 June 2024 an agreement was reached in the Dutch Parliament,[194] but it still needs to come into effect. It will establish a more up-to-date legislative framework for the energy system, create more synergy between rules for gas and electricity and ensure that rules are more aligned with the anticipated future energy system.[195] In the proposed Energy Act, legislative experiments are only discussed in the context of the existing experiments that commenced under the Electricity Act or Gas Act (Article 7.47), stating that these experiments can continue until the planned end date of the experiment is reached.[196] Alternatively, the proposed Energy Act allows for certain derogations potentially related to hydrogen: Article 3.20 allows an infrastructure company to conduct other activities related to energy infrastructure through an executive order that contains a timeframe for the derogation, with a maximum of 10 years, if the activities are not related to the production, supply or trade of energy carriers.[197] However, an explicit clause providing the regulatory authority ACM with space for experimentation, as was included in the Gas and Electricity Acts, is not included in the new Energy Act. According to the Minister of Climate and Energy, the reasons for this are (1) ACM's competencies as granted by EU legislation already provide for sufficient experimentation on certain subjects in the energy transition, (2) derogating from certain provisions that translate binding EU regulation is not possible thereby decreasing the experimental space and (3) an experimental space in the Energy Act has limited added value considering the Environment and Planning Act.[198]

One Dutch law that was recognised as enabling regulatory sandboxes to be set up and take place is the Crisis and Recovery Act.[199] This Act allowed for exemptions from a list of legislative acts, among which are the Electricity Act, Gas Act, Environmental Act and Environmental Management Act. However, as of 1 January 2024, the Act has been integrated into the Environment and Planning Act.[200] The respective experimental clause can now be found in Article 23.3 of the Environment and Planning Act, which allows for the derogation of a smaller list of legislative acts through an executive order if the experiment is expected to contribute to the procedures to follow, the decision-making, or achieving and maintaining

[194] L Diestelmeier and J Swens, 'Energy Communities in the Netherlands: Learning from Local Energy Initiatives' in Martha M Roggenkamp and Catherine Banet (eds) *European Energy Law Report* (Cambridge University Press) 256.

[195] Rijksoverheid, 'Brede steun voor nieuwe energiewet' (4 June 2024). Available at: www.rijksoverheid.nl/actueel/nieuws/2024/06/04/brede-steun-voor-nieuwe-energiewet.

[196] E Kamer der Staten-Generaal, 'Energiewet: Gewijzigd voorstel van wet' (4 June 2024) 123. Available at: www.eerstekamer.nl/behandeling/20240604/gewijzigd_voorstel_van_wet_5/document3/f=/vme0g1k12yyv.pdf.

[197] ibid 43.

[198] Kamerstukken *II* 2023/2024, 36378 nr 10 (Regels over energiemarkten en energiesystemen (Energiewet)) 155–57.

[199] European Commission (n 7) 54.

[200] Informatiepunt Leefomgeving, 'Crisis- en herstelwet' (2024). Available at: https://iplo.nl/regelgeving/omgevingswet/overgangsrecht/overgangsrecht-per-wet/crisis-herstelwet/.

a safe and healthy physical living environment. The Electricity Act and Gas Act are among the listed legislative acts for which an experiment can be introduced. Requirements for what should be included in the executive order for the experiment are given (Article 23.2, clause 3), ultimately determining the design of the experiment. Among these are the experiment's goal, the regulatory body that monitors the experiments, the timeframe of the experiment, which rules are derogated from, and how the experiment will be evaluated. Interestingly, clause 8 of the Article states that if the evaluation of the experiment gives reason for changes to the regulation, the Minister of Internal Affairs can derogate from the timeframe stated in the executive order and extend the experiment by a maximum of five years with the aim of adopting this change in the regulation.[201] In this way, the experimentation clause seems to enable the creation and implementation of a regulatory sandbox. The clause will be adapted to cover the Energy Act instead of the Gas and Electricity Acts with the adoption of the Energy Act,[202] which will potentially create legislative space for regulatory sandboxes dedicated to hydrogen developments.

A visualisation of relevant legislation and its scope at both the Dutch and the EU level for establishing hydrogen regulatory sandboxes is given in Figure 11.3.

Figure 11.3 Relevant legislation and its scope at the EU (blue) and Dutch (orange) level for establishing hydrogen regulatory sandboxes in the Netherlands

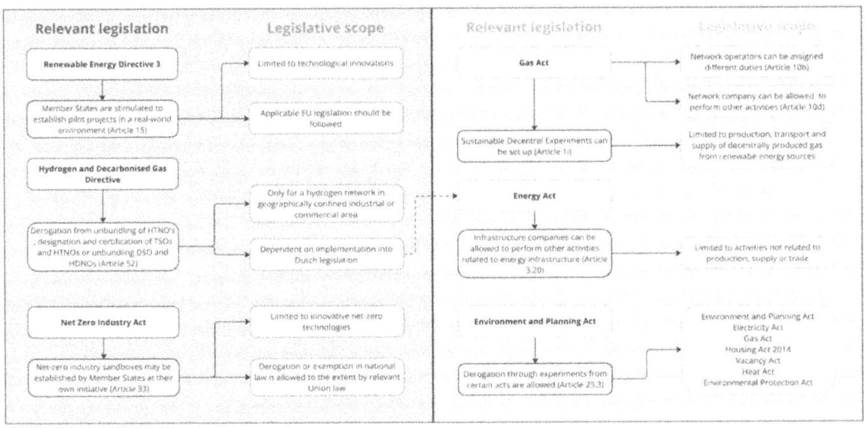

5.2. European Union

At the EU level, regulatory sandboxes have gained interest and are recognised as an important tool for developing dynamic regulation.[203] This is shown by the

[201] Omgevingswet, art 23.3. Available at: https://iplo.nl/regelgeving/omgevingswet/overgangsrecht/overgangsrecht-per-wet/crisis-herstelwet/.
[202] Kamerstukken *II* 2023/2024 (n 198) 88.
[203] Beckstedde and others (n 23) 1.

various documents that communicate about, provide guidance on or present tools for regulatory sandboxes. Among these are regulations and directives which influence the Dutch regulatory framework. This section therefore analyses to what extent hydrogen regulatory sandboxes are addressed at the EU level and what this entails for their implementation in the Netherlands.

In its REPowerEU package of May 2022, the EU advocated for establishing a regulatory sandbox for energy.[204] Also in its accompanying recommendation on speeding up permit-granting procedures and facilitating Power Purchase Agreements, the Commission encouraged Member States to put in place regulatory sandboxes for granting targeted exemptions from the legislative framework at national, regional or local levels for innovative technologies, products, services or approaches.[205] Despite stimulating sandboxes to be implemented in the energy sector, these documents do not provide a legal ground for their establishment.

The Hydrogen and Decarbonised Gas Package (hereafter Package), which entered into force on 13 June 2024, is expected to create a regulatory framework for hydrogen in the EU. It is expected that the provisions of the Package in the Directive will be implemented at the Dutch level with an amendment to the Energy Act.[206] With the revision of the Gas Regulation and Gas Directive,[207] the Package establishes rules for the organisation of the natural gas market as well as for the development of the future hydrogen market.[208] However, neither the Directive[209] nor the Regulation[210] addresses experiments or regulatory sandboxes. It is limited to derogations from specific articles, as the Directive (Article 52) allows Member States to derogate from the Directive's Articles 68 and 71 – on the unbundling of hydrogen transmission network operators (HTNO) and the designation and certification of TSOs and HTNOs, respectively – or from Article 46 – on the unbundling of DSOs and hydrogen distribution network operators. These derogations are, however, limited to hydrogen networks that transport hydrogen and are located within a geographically confined industrial or commercial area.[211]

[204] Sunila and Ekroos (n 1) 17.
[205] European Commission (n 7) 8.
[206] Kamerstukken *II* 2023/2024 (n 198) 19.
[207] L Tanase and I Herrera Anchustegui, 'EU Hydrogen and the Decarbonized Gas Market Package: Unbundling, Third-Party Access, Tariffs and Discounts Rules at the Core of Transport of Hydrogen' (2023) 3. Available at: https://papers.ssrn.com/sol3/papers.cfm?abstract_id=4431113.
[208] European Council, 'Fit for 55: Council Signs Off on Gas and Hydrogen Market Package' (21 May 2024). Available at: www.consilium.europa.eu/en/press/press-releases/2024/05/21/fit-for-55-council-signs-off-on-gas-and-hydrogen-market-package/.
[209] Council Directive (EU) 2024/1788 of 13 June 2024 on common rules for the internal markets of renewable gas, natural gas and hydrogen, amending Directive (EU) 2023/1791 and repealing Directive 2009/73/EC (2024) OJ L2024/1788.
[210] Council Regulation (EU) 2024/1789 of 13 June 2024 on the internal markets for renewable gas, natural gas and hydrogen, amending Regulations (EU) No 1227/2011, (EU) 2017/1938, (EU) 2019/942 and (EU) 2022/869 and Decision (EU) 2017/684 and repealing Regulation (EC) No 715/2009 (recast) (2024) OJ L2024/1789.
[211] Council Directive (EU) (n 209) 60.

Another relevant regulatory document is the amended Renewable Energy Directive (RED 3). Article 15, paragraph 2a states:

> Member States shall promote the testing of innovative renewable energy technology for producing, sharing and storing of renewable energy through pilot projects in a real-world environment, for a limited period, in accordance with the applicable Union law and accompanied by appropriate safeguards to ensure the secure operation of the energy system and avoid disproportionate impact on the functioning of the internal market, under the supervision of a competent authority.[212]

With this Article, the European Commission obligates Member States to promote the testing of new renewable energy technologies through pilot projects in a real-world environment.[213] The term 'regulatory sandbox' is not explicitly named in the Directive or in the accompanying Delegated Acts.[214] As noted by Sunila and Ekroos on the proposed Directive,[215] the promotion of regulatory sandboxes in the RED 3 is a good step forward but seems to be insufficient in addressing the challenges related to the innovations that are radical in the EU context. The scope of the regulatory sandbox in the Directive is limited to technological innovations, thereby excluding systemic and social innovations, and remains ambiguous. The Directive states that applicable EU legislation should be followed in setting up the sandbox. This means that the Directive stimulates the establishment of national sandboxes but with limited legal space for manoeuvre.

A third legislative document that relates to the emerging hydrogen sector is the Net Zero Industry Act that entered into force on 13 June 2024. This regulation is directed at establishing a framework for ensuring the Union's access to a secure and sustainable supply of net-zero technologies.[216] The Act introduces 'net-zero regulatory sandboxes' that Member States can establish together with local authorities, regional authorities and other Member States. A company, organisation or consortium developing innovative net-zero technologies that fulfils eligibility and selection criteria can request the establishment of a net-zero regulatory sandbox by the respective Member State.[217] The definition in section 2 (Box A) shows that the regulatory sandboxes are limited to innovative net-zero technologies[218] and other

[212] Council Directive (EU) 2023/2413 of 18 October 2023 amending Directive (EU) 2018/2001, Regulation (EU) 2018/1999 and Directive 98/70/EC as regards the promotion of energy from renewable sources, and repealing Council Directive (EU) 2015/652, OJ L2023/2413, 30.

[213] European Commission (n 7) 17.

[214] Council Delegated Regulation (EU) 2023/1184 of 10 February 2023 supplementing Directive (EU) 2018/2001 of the European Parliament and of the Council by establishing a Union methodology setting out detailed rules for the production of renewable liquid and gaseous transport fuels of non-biological origin, OJ L157/11; Council Delegated Regulation (EU) 2023/1185 of 10 February 2023 supplementing Directive (EU) 2018/2001 of the European Parliament and of the Council by establishing a minimum threshold for greenhouse gas emissions savings of recycled carbon fuels and by specifying a methodology for assessing greenhouse gas emissions savings from renewable liquid and gaseous transport fuels of non-biological origin and from recycled carbon fuels, OJ L157/20.

[215] Sunila and Ekroos (n 1) 17–18.

[216] Council Regulation (EU) 2024/1735 of 13 June 2024 (n 37) art 1(1).

[217] ibid art 33.

[218] European Commission (n 7) 47.

innovative technologies that are genuine innovations, currently not available on the (Union) market and advanced enough to be tested in a controlled environment.[219] The Act allows for derogations or exemptions in national law by the competent authorities in the net-zero regulatory sandboxes to the extent allowed by relevant Union law. And it should be ensured that the sandbox plan respects the requirements of Union law as well as the key objectives and essential requirements of national law.[220] However, the Act does not provide details on the modalities and conditions for the operation of these sandboxes but will be established through implementing acts at the EU level.[221]

In their discussion of the draft version of the Hydrogen and Decarbonised Gas Package[222] and the draft Net Zero Industry Act,[223] Baumgart and Lavrijssen[224] questioned whether sandbox approaches can be applied in the context of hydrogen transport and distribution through pure hydrogen grids. This is because the draft Net Zero Industry Act only allowed for derogation or exemption from relevant EU or national law (Article 26(4), sentence 1)[225] while the draft EU Package did not provide for exemptions other than in the geographically confined areas. Since then, both the Net Zero Industry Act and the Package have reached a final version. The final Net Zero Industry Act allows for exemptions and derogations in national law to the extent allowed by relevant Union law (Article 33(5), sentence 1),[226] instead of to the extent allowed by relevant EU or national law stated in the Draft Act. This means that the implementation of a net-zero regulatory sandbox for a hydrogen technology that is genuinely innovative and not yet on the market can derogate from regulations at the national level if that is allowed by Union law. However, the final Package does not seem to provide for more exemptions than its draft version. It is therefore still questionable whether hydrogen regulatory sandboxes can be implemented, as the legal space at the EU level is limited to '(net-zero) innovative technologies' and the limited space for derogation in the Package.

The Dutch Energy Act will replace the Dutch Electricity Act and Gas Act, both of which contain a legal basis for experiments in certain circumstances. However, such legal space will not be included in the Energy Act. Alternatively, the Environment and Planning Act provides the legislative space for experiments

[219] See Article 3(12) for the full definition of innovative net-zero technologies and Article (13) for the definition of other innovative technologies Council Regulation (EU) (n 37).

[220] ibid art 33(5).

[221] European Commission (n 7) 36.

[222] European Commission, 'Proposal for a Directive of the European Parliament and of the Council on Common Rules for the Internal Markets in Renewable and Natural Gases and in Hydrogen' COM (2021) 803 final; European Commission, 'Proposal For a Regulation of the European Parliament and of the Council on the Internal Markets for Renewable and Natural Gases and for Hydrogen' COM (2021) 804 final.

[223] European Commission, 'Proposal for a regulation of the European Parliament and of the Council on establishing a framework of measures for strengthening Europe's net-zero technology products manufacturing ecosystem (Net Zero Industry Act)' COM(2023) 161 final.

[224] Baumgart and Lavrijssen (n 6) 28.

[225] European Commission, Net Zero Industry Act (n 223) art 26(4).

[226] Council Regulation (EU) (n 37) art 33(5).

for certain legislative acts. This means that the legislative space for setting up regulatory sandboxes for hydrogen in the Netherlands could therefore be found in the Environment and Planning Act, once the Energy Act has been adopted. At the European level, with the introduction of net-zero regulatory sandboxes, the Act allows for derogations from national law to the extent allowed by relevant Union law. This legal space is, however, limited to '(net-zero) innovative technologies'. This can be a limiting factor for the establishment of hydrogen regulatory sandboxes as certain hydrogen technologies might already be in the making, thereby excluding them from the sandbox even though their participation would have beneficial effects for the emerging hydrogen market. Additionally, the sandboxes can be established to the extent allowed by relevant Union law, which is the Hydrogen and Decarbonised Gas Package. However, the legislative space for experimentation is in this Package limited to derogations from certain articles in the Directive, resulting in a restricted space for establishing these net-zero regulatory sandboxes.

6. Conclusion

Hydrogen, especially hydrogen produced from renewable energy sources, is perceived to play a role in the decarbonisation of the energy system. Given the energy carrier's versatility in production methods and transportation and its potential end-use applications, a significant increase in governmental efforts to materialise a hydrogen sector has taken place. However, regulatory barriers are encountered. These barriers relate to the regulatory framework being unclear, incomplete, or not fit for keeping up with the innovations and developments brought with the emerging hydrogen market. Regulatory sandboxes can be the potential pathway for nations to circumvent the regulatory barriers currently impeding the hydrogen transition. This chapter aimed to shed light on the concept of regulatory sandboxes and their potential for the emerging hydrogen market in the Netherlands.

As time-limited and geographically dedicated safe spaces that contain appropriate consumer protection safeguards, regulatory sandboxes provide a way for testing products, services or businesses that do not align with the existing regulatory structure. Starting in fintech, the implementation of regulatory sandboxes has progressed towards other sectors, including the energy system. Sandboxes are a form of experimental legislation and can be especially suited to the emerging hydrogen market because it allows both regulators and market players to gain insight into the market and regulatory framework for hydrogen. Market players can gather preliminary insights on the potential of their product, service or business in the market, which might otherwise be too costly or not (yet) possible. Regulators can gather insight into the role of the regulatory framework and potentially the required alterations to the framework to allow for the emerging hydrogen market to materialise.

The analysis of the concept of regulatory sandboxes, and their strengths and weaknesses, has indicated their added value for hydrogen activities. Sectors in transition, such as the hydrogen sector, can benefit from the implementation of regulatory sandboxes as they appear to provide enough realistic conditions to gain insight into the innovations' market viability while at the same time providing the safeguards needed to avoid market failure of the product. The analysis has also shown that the design of a sandbox is pivotal in avoiding the potential adverse effects of regulatory sandboxes. Preceding literature has established guidelines for the design of regulatory sandboxes, which can be seen as the implementation of principles of good regulation. These principles have been used for the assessment of the quality of design guidelines for regulatory sandboxes.

This research is novel in using the principles of good regulation to assess the design guidelines of regulatory sandboxes, indicating that the principles of flexibility and responsiveness and of independence are present in existing guidelines. Given that the hydrogen market is emerging, thus not yet established, attention should be given to ensuring that the implementation of regulatory sandboxes does not negatively affect the developments. It is therefore recommended to extend the design guidelines to ensure the independence of the entity that establishes, monitors and evaluates the sandbox from political interference and ensure that sandboxes are adaptable to changes in technology, society or economy. Additionally, given the novelty of regulatory sandboxes as a tool in regulations, the design guidelines themselves should also be subject to evaluation. If regulatory sandboxes are increasingly established for the hydrogen sector – or in general, which is also subject to change – evaluation of the guidelines is important in ensuring the quality and suitability of the guidelines.

In the design of regulatory sandboxes, the presence of a legal mandate is required. This chapter therefore analysed whether regulatory sandboxes can in reality be implemented for hydrogen activities in the Netherlands. We provided an assessment of the legislative framework for regulatory sandboxes directed at hydrogen in the Netherlands. The assessment shows that several regulatory documents could potentially enable the development and implementation of regulatory sandboxes. At the European level the implementation of sandboxes is limited to (net-zero) innovative technologies and geographically confined areas. At the national Dutch level, the implementation of regulatory sandboxes for hydrogen depends on the alteration of both the Environment and Planning Act and the Energy Act. Despite several regulatory documents supporting and introducing regulatory sandboxes, both at the EU and the Dutch level, the legal space for implementing these regulatory instruments for the emerging hydrogen market remains limited and ambiguous. This could potentially hamper the beneficial effects that the implementation of regulatory sandboxes could have on the emerging hydrogen market.

Future research is recommended to assess the implementation of regulatory sandboxes in different sectors and nations, which can provide valuable insights about the dos and don'ts for regulatory sandboxes. As it is likely that (green) hydrogen will not be the last disruptive development in the energy system and beyond, more knowledge about the potential and design of anticipatory regulatory approaches is needed and should be given attention in future research.

12

Regulatory Strategies to Promote Digitalisation in the Finnish Electricity Sector

KANERVA SUNILA

1. Background

Digitalisation of the energy sector can be described as one of the cornerstones of the clean energy transition. The 'smartness' of energy systems is often seen as one of the main characteristics of a clean energy system, enabling more efficient use of energy and infrastructure, sector integration and clean energy integration. This 'smartness' is, in practice, based on digitalised solutions. Unsurprisingly, the digitalisation of the energy sector has become a priority in energy policies: the EU Commission has adopted an action plan for the digitalisation of energy systems in the EU,[1] and the International Energy Agency tracks digitalisation as part of its clean energy progress assessment.[2]

In the EU, the energy sector is highly regulated. The electricity sector, which is the focus of this chapter, provides an ultimate example. The electricity market legislation focuses on the electricity system operators that are the gate keepers to the electricity grid and natural monopolies, which affects the level of detail and adopted regulatory strategies.[3] When considering digitalisation of the electricity sector, it is no surprise that digitalisation has found its place on the legislators' desks. While digitalisation can be driven by the markets, the markets do not necessarily encourage a single market participant or system operators to carry out investments that could be beneficial from the system perspective. The urgency of

[1] Commission, 'Digitalising the Energy System: EU Action Plan' (Communication) COM (2022) 552 final.

[2] International Energy Agency, *Digitalisation*. Available at: www.iea.org/energy-system/decarbonisation-enablers/digitalisation#tracking.

[3] K Sunila, 'Regulating the Change in the EU Electricity Markets – Finding the Balance Between Tomorrow and Yesterday' (Doctoral thesis, Aalto University 2023) 14–16, 33 and the references therein. Available at: https://urn.fi/URN:ISBN:978-952-64-1253-5.

the clean energy transition and the objective of 'empowerment' of small customers have also affected the willingness of legislators to promote new digital solutions enabling their market activity.[4] Thus, legal and regulatory interventions have been seen to promote digitalisation in the energy sector.

This chapter focuses on regulatory strategies to promote digitalisation in the Finnish electricity market. While the definition of digitalisation often remains unclear both in policy and academic contexts, data and the use of it can unarguably be considered as the building blocks of digitalisation. Therefore, to bring the abstract and overarching question to a more concrete level, the chapter studies how the *availability of and access to data*, as well as *the use of data by digital technologies*, have been promoted in Finnish legislation. The focus of the chapter being in the electricity sector, refers, in particular, to electricity metering and consumption data.

It is evident that privacy and cyber security are of the utmost importance when considering access to and use of data. It could also be argued that promoting data privacy and cyber security could advance the safe use of data. However, it may also, for understandable reasons, sometimes hinder the use of data. Given the limited extent of this chapter, the questions of privacy and cyber security are not discussed in this context.[5]

The following sections study the Finnish electricity market legislation and regulation from the past 15 years and discuss what kind of regulatory strategies have been applied to promote digitalisation in the sector. The examples under the loupe have been selected to provide the reader with an understanding of the main regulatory strategies adopted in Finland. However, the chapter is not meant to be exhaustive. The last section looks forward and discusses the measures we may see in future.

2. Finland as a Forerunner in the Rollout of First-Generation Smart Electricity Meters

When taking the *availability of data* as the starting point in assessing digitalisation of the electricity sector in Finland, one cannot ignore 'smart meters'. In the EU, the Electricity Market Directive (EU) 2019/944 nowadays lays down the definition of a smart metering system and sets out the requirements for the functionalities of the meters. These smart meters stipulated by the EU law can be described as 'second-generation' smart meters as they are more advanced than the early smart meters used in the first rollouts. Before the Electricity Market Directive (EU)

[4] See eg, Directive (EU) 2019/944 of the European Parliament and of the Council of on common rules for the internal market for electricity and amending Directive 2012/27/EU (recast) [2019] OJ L158 (the Fourth Electricity Market Directive) Recitals 10, 23, 24 and 37.

[5] For legal questions regarding privacy and smart metering, see eg, K Huhta 'Smartening Up While Keeping Safe? Advances in Smart Metering and Data Protection Under EU Law' (2019) 38(1) *Journal of Energy & Natural Resources Law* 5. Available at: https://doi.org/10.1080/02646811.2019.1622244.

2019/944, the (first-generation) smart meters were only loosely regulated at EU level. The rollout of smart meters has basically been dependent on the Member States' economic assessments. Even in the case of positive rollout, a transition until 2020 was applied.[6] However, despite the discretion left to Member States, the first-generation smart meter rollout has taken place in many European countries.[7]

One of the first countries in Europe to do so, Finland conducted its rollout of first-generation smart meters in the early 2010s.[8] This early rollout also provides an interesting example when considering regulatory strategies to promote digitalisation in the electricity sector.

In 2009, a legal obligation for hourly metering was placed on electricity system operators.[9] Previously, the customers had had a right to use their own electricity meters capable of hourly metering but, after the revision of the legislation, the electricity system operators became solely responsible for the hourly metering.[10] According to the provisions, the metering as well as the imbalance settlement should be based on hourly metering, with some exemptions. The legislation contained transition periods, because the switch to hourly metering was considered to be a burdensome transformation, even though some of the network operators had already started to apply it.[11] The full rollout was thus to take place after a five-year transition period, by the end of 2013. After 2013, distribution system operators (DSOs) could still be exempt from the obligation in 20 per cent of the supply points in their distribution systems in the case of smaller supply points.[12]

In addition to the obligation to transfer to hourly metering, the *minimum requirements* for the meters themselves were laid down, although at quite a general level. As mentioned, the meter should be capable of hourly metering and of registering electricity consumption and production. The registered data should be remotely readable, and the meter should also be able to, eg, register de-energised periods of over three minutes and to forward load control commands.[13]

[6] Directive 2009/72/EC of the European Parliament and of the Council concerning common rules for the internal market in electricity and repealing Directive 2003/54/EC [2009] OJ L211 (the Third Electricity Market Directive) annex I, point 2; Directive 2012/27/EU of the European Parliament and of the Council on energy efficiency, amending Directives 2009/125/EC and 2010/30/EU and repealing Directives 2004/8/EC and 2006/32/EC [2012] OJ L315, arts 2 and 9. It can be noted, also, that in the Fourth Electricity Market Directive (EU), annex II, the mandatory rollout is subject to a cost–benefit analysis.

[7] C Alaton and F Tounquet, *Benchmarking Smart Metering Deployment in the EU-28 – Final Report* (European Commission: Directorate-General for Energy, Publications Office 2020) 62. Available at: https://data.europa.eu/doi/10.2833/492070.

[8] ibid.

[9] Government Decree on the Settlement and Metering of the Electricity Supplies (66/2009) ch 6, ss 1–4.

[10] For detailed reasonings of ch 6, s 4, see työ- ja elinkeinoministeriö, *Ehdotus valtioneuvoston asetukseksi sähköntoimitusten selvityksestä ja mittauksesta* (29 January 2009) 8–9.

[11] ibid 8–9, 13.

[12] Government Decree (66/2009) ch 6, s 4; ch 8, s 3.

[13] ibid ch 6, s 8.

When analysing the regulatory strategies adopted to promote first-generation smart meters in Finland, the rollout itself was based on a traditional *command-and-control* measure, setting out an obligation to electricity system operators. This is a logical solution given that the tasks of the system operators as natural monopolies are, and were already back then, highly regulated, and hourly metering was considered a necessary part of these tasks in future. Further, the main objectives behind the revision of the legislation were to promote – through ensuring the availability of the hourly metering data – a demand response, particularly during the peak consumption hours, and to contribute to the indicative energy saving objectives under the EU energy efficiency legislation.[14] Thus, the main reasons for the revised legislation were the anticipated benefits at the electricity *system level*, although individual network operators had already identified the benefits of using remotely readable meters and the transformation had already started before the legislation entered into force. The legislator thus had objectives that were anticipated to be possible to achieve through a concrete and relatively easily definable task.

Even though the legal obligation was clear, the technical specifications for the first-generation smart meters were rather loosely defined, which gave the electricity system operators some room for manoeuvre. The legislation set out the specifications as *minimum* requirements, thus the legislation was not to completely harmonise the functionalities. Prosumers throughout Finland experienced varied treatment as the meters of DSOs registered electricity consumption and production differently.[15] The situation was later solved by the provisions on the netting of measurements within an imbalance settlement period.[16] Even though the selected regulatory approach led to some differences in the markets, this also ensured that, in principle, the specifications were not locked by the legislator and innovation and new solutions could also be implemented.

In addition to the obligation to install new meters, the DSOs also had an obligation to *plan* the transition to the hourly metering.[17] This was to be submitted to the Finnish Energy Authority, which allowed the authority to monitor the DSOs' progress in implementing first-generation smart meters. Thus, this obligation was

[14] Työ- ja elinkeinoministeriö, *Ehdotus valtioneuvoston asetukseksi sähköntoimitusten selvityksestä ja mittauksesta* (29 January 2009) 1. The indicative energy-saving objective was laid down in Directive 2006/32/EC of the European Parliament and of the Council on energy end-use efficiency and energy services and repealing Council Directive 93/76/EEC [2006] OJ L114, art 4.

[15] One part of the metering system netted the consumption and production measurements of the three phases, whereas another part did not. See Työ- ja elinkeinoministeriö, *Pienimuotoisen energiatuotannon edistämisen työryhmän loppuraportti* (julkaisuja 55/2014, 2014). Available at: https://tem.fi/documents/1410877/2859687/Pienimuotoisen+energiatuotannon+edist%C3%A4misty%C3%B6ryhm%C3%A4n+loppuraportti+16122014.pdf; K Auvinen, 'Mittauksessa ongelma – aurinkosähkö ei usein päädykään pientuottajan hyödyksi' (*Finsolar*, March 2019). Available at: https://finsolar.net/mittauksessa-ongelma-aurinkosahko-ei-usein-paadykaan-pientuottajan-hyodyksi/.

[16] Government Decree on the amendment of the Decree on the Settlement and Metering of Electricity Supplies (1133/2020).

[17] Government Decree 66/2009, ch 6, s 4.

most likely to encourage the DSOs to prepare the transition in a timely manner, as well as to some extent already enable the *control* of the compliance of the command before the legislation became applicable.[18]

After the amendment of the legislation, the new meters were updated to be part of the economic regulation model, which basically allowed the DSOs to get a return for their metering investments.[19] In addition, a separate incentive for the implementation of the smart meters was laid down in the economic regulation of the DSOs.[20] While 'the reasonable rate of return' referring to the acceptable profit of the network operators was calculated based on the CAPEX,[21] the Energy Authority, which is responsible for drafting and approving the economic regulation model in Finland, recognised that the switch to the first-generation smart meters could increase the OPEX of the DSOs during the transition period. A separate incentive taking into account this potential increase of OPEX was thus included in the methodology for the regulatory period of the years 2012–2015.[22] The command-and-control measure was thus further backed by an *economic incentive* to the DSOs.

Even though the DSOs were entitled to exemption from the hourly metering obligation in 20 per cent of the supply points, almost a full rollout of first-generation smart meters could be seen in 2014. The uptake of the meters was already around 97 per cent of all the supply points in distribution systems.[23] Currently, the rollout is almost 100 per cent.[24] Although it is difficult to assess the exact impact of the separate economic incentive and how swiftly the DSOs would have otherwise implemented the first-generation smart meters, it is clear that the full rollout took place relatively quickly. Thus, the chosen regulatory measures can be considered successful in relation to the underlying objective: fast rollout of the first-generation smart meters. The energy savings were also reported to be 1–3 per cent.[25] However, whether the rollout could have been done without the specific

[18] This note is speculative, as the reasoning memorandum of the Government Decree does not elaborate on the background of the planning obligation.

[19] Energiamarkkinavirasto, *Liite 1 Valvontamenetelmät sähkön jakeluverkkotoiminnan ja suurjännitteisen jakeluverkkotoiminnan hinnoittelun kohtuullisuuden arvioimiseksi 1.1.2012 alkavalla ja 31.12.2015 päättyvällä kolmannella valvontajaksolla* (23 November 2011) 77. In Finland, the Finnish Energy Authority, as the national regulatory authority, drafts and approves the economic regulation model of the electricity system operators. The model is a rate-of-return-based model. The first-generation smart meters were included in the regulated unit prices, which affects the calculation of the reasonable of return.

[20] Energiamarkkinavirasto, *Liite 1 Valvontamenetelmät sähkön jakeluverkkotoiminnan ja suurjännitteisen jakeluverkkotoiminnan hinnoittelun kohtuullisuuden arvioimiseksi 1.1.2012 alkavalla ja 31.12.2015 päättyvällä kolmannella valvontajaksolla* (23 November 2011) 57–58.

[21] This is a simplified description of the model.

[22] Energiamarkkinavirasto, *Liite 1 Valvontamenetelmät sähkön jakeluverkkotoiminnan ja suurjännitteisen jakeluverkkotoiminnan hinnoittelun kohtuullisuuden arvioimiseksi 1.1.2012 alkavalla ja 31.12.2015 päättyvällä kolmannella valvontajaksolla* (23 November 2011) 57–58.

[23] Government Proposal 182/2014, 8.

[24] Government Proposal 144/2018, 40.

[25] Commission, 'Benchmarking Smart Metering Deployment in the EU-27 with a Focus on Electricity' COM (2014) 356 final, 6.

economic incentive and with less cost to the electricity customers is difficult to analyse. As stated, the electricity sector was already shifting to the remotely readable smart meters because of their benefits.[26] Therefore, it could be said that the command-and-control measure was, at least to some extent, a reconnection to the real world, not the (only) driver of the change.[27]

3. Rollout of the Second-Generation Smart Meters

As mentioned above, the Electricity Market Directive (EU) 2019/944 stipulates in more detail the functional requirements for the smart meters. These requirements are, nevertheless, not harmonising meters across the EU. While the obligation to rollout is still subject to an economic assessment by each Member State, all Member States shall ensure that every final customer is entitled, upon request and at their own expense, to a smart meter.[28] After the latest amendment of the EU electricity market legislation, the final customer shall also be entitled to use a 'dedicated measurement device' for the purposes of settlement of demand responses and flexibility services, if the meter of the customer does not deliver the necessary data.[29]

Focusing on the Finnish development regarding second-generation smart meters, the new requirements for these were adopted in 2021.[30] The new legislation implemented the requirements set out at EU level and took into account national circumstances. As was the case before the adoption of the legislation in 2009, experts and stakeholders were engaged in its preparation. The minimum functionalities had already been discussed and prepared by the Finnish Smart

[26] See also Commission Staff Working Document, 'Cost–Benefit Analyses & State of Play of Smart Metering Deployment in the EU-27 Accompanying the Document Report from the Commission Benchmarking Smart Metering Deployment in the EU-27 with a Focus on Electricity' SWD (2014) 189 final, 21.

[27] On regulatory disconnection and law as a driver, see eg K Sunila, 'Regulating the Change in the EU Electricity Markets – Finding the Balance Between Tomorrow and Yesterday' (Doctoral thesis, Aalto University 2023). Available at: https://urn.fi/URN:ISBN:978-952-64-1253-5, 29–31; A Butenko, 'User-centered Innovation in EU Energy Law: Market Access for Electricity Prosumers in the Proposed Electricity Directive' (2018) 16(1) *OGEL Energy Law Journal* 1; N Soininen and others 'Brake or Accelerator? The Role of Law in Sustainability Transitions' (2022) 41 *Environmental Innovation and Societal Transitions* 71; K Huhta 'The Contribution of Energy Law to the Energy Transition and Energy Research' (2022) 73 *Global Environmental Change* 2.

[28] Directive (EU) 2019/944 of the European Parliament and of the Council of on common rules for the internal market for electricity and amending Directive 2012/27/EU (recast) [2019] OJ L158, art 21.

[29] Regulation (EU) 2024/1747 of the European Parliament and of the Council amending Regulations (EU) 2019/942 and (EU) 2019/943 as regards improving the Union's electricity market design [2024] OJ L1747.

[30] Government Decree on the Settlement and Metering of the Electricity Supplies (767/2021). It should be disclosed that the author of this chapter has been responsible for drafting the said Government Decree.

Grids Working Group, which gave its final report in 2018.[31] Further, a national expert group was consulted when the legislation was drafted.[32]

When comparing the regulatory strategies adopted in 2009 and 2021, the main principle remained the same: the legislation laid down the minimum criteria for the smart meters and the transition to quarter-hour metering. Also, longer transition periods for the 15 minutes' metering and meters were applied to ensure that the rollout could be made cost-efficiently. Again, electricity system operators were also obliged to draw up a plan on how the transformation to the quarter-hour metering would be carried out.

What deviated from the earlier meter rollout was that there was no separate economic incentive for implementing the changes.[33] As mentioned above, the earlier economic incentive was to speed up the rollout of first-generation meters. Concerning the second-generation smart meters, the legislative preparatory work emphasised the cost-efficient transition.[34] Another difference compared to the 2009 legislation is that the technical requirements set out for the second-generation smart meters were more detailed and advanced than previously.[35]

As regards the first-generation smart meters, a command-and-control measure was possible because the obligation was rather easy to define.[36] What remains to be seen is whether the specifications of the second-generation smart meters are future-proof enough, given the long transition periods provided to achieve a cost-efficient rollout. These kinds of technical requirements in general provide a good example of the balancing between too detailed specifications interfering with the technological development and clear enough rules providing certainty

[31] T Pahkala, H Uimonen, and V Väre, *Flexible and Customer-Centred Electricity System: Final Report of the Smart Grid Working Group* (Työ- ja elinkeinoministeriön julkaisuja 39/2018, 2018). Available at: https://julkaisut.valtioneuvosto.fi/handle/10024/161147.

[32] Työ- ja elinkeinoministeriö, *Ehdotus valtioneuvoston asetukseksi sähköntoimitusten selvityksestä ja mittauksesta* (Muistio 2021) 2.

[33] The unit prices have been updated for the second-generation smart meters in the regulation model but no separate incentive for installation has been adopted. See Energiavirasto, *Valvontamenetelmät kuudennella 1.1.2024–31.12.2027 ja seitsemännellä 1.1.2028–31.12.2031 valvontajaksolla* (2023) Dnro 3171/040300/2023, 119–20. Available at: https://energiavirasto.fi/documents/11120570/12766832/S%C3%A4hk%C3%B6n+jakelu+-+Menetelm%C3%A4liite.pdf/bc07b3d7-9b1b-e970-9be9-f46f1c1dfc94/S%C3%A4hk%C3%B6n+jakelu+-+Menetelm%C3%A4liite.pdf?t=1703848648980.

[34] See Työ- ja elinkeinoministeriö, *Ehdotus valtioneuvoston asetukseksi sähköntoimitusten selvityksestä ja mittauksesta* (Muistio 2021).

[35] For example, pursuant to the 2021 legislation, a one-way customer interface was enacted to be a basic functionality of the second-generation smart meter, and detailed specifications with which the interface should comply were set out. In 2009, the electricity system operator was obliged to provide its customers with an hourly readable meter with a standardised interface in real time on the customer's request.

[36] However, from the point of view of drafting the technical requirements for the second-generation smart meters at the level of binding legislation, the exercise was not straightforward. It must also be noted that the legislation is rather complex due to the multiple different transition periods. The latter is mainly because the amendments concerning 15 minutes' imbalance settlement and metering requirements were adopted simultaneously.

for the investors and final customers.[37] In particular, when the investments are remarkable, as is the case for the second-generation smart meters, the electricity sector and the final customers should have visibility of both the requirements to be complied with and the costs and possibilities brought about by compliance with the requirements in the (near) future.[38] In this legislative project, one concrete way to try to avoid the regulatory disconnection was to set a requirement that the second-generation smart meters should be (partly) remotely updatable to mitigate future costs.[39]

4. Facilitating the Data Exchange

The data 'produced' by the smart meters is seldom useful if it cannot be moved forward from the meter. While electricity meters could previously be read on site, the increased metering data and more frequent readings have required a transfer to the digitalised systems and remote reading. To ensure that the metering and consumption data can be used in billing and as the basis for the imbalance settlement, the data should also be shared between different market participants. This *data exchange* should preferably be carried out efficiently. Many European countries have implemented datahubs, which enable a centralised information exchange instead of dozens of actors in the market having their own systems to communicate with each other.[40]

In Finland, the information exchange of the electricity retail market and DSOs was moved to the national datahub in 2022.[41] Previously, the metering information exchange was, in principle, carried out by the DSOs and electricity retailers by bilateral arrangements. However, the practice was not completely decentralised, as there were a few service providers who mediated the data exchange.[42] The legislation facilitated the data exchange by way of laying down obligations to take care of the required data exchange and to follow certain protocols and timeframes.[43] The legislation remained on a rather general level and it was therefore supplemented

[37] On the balancing in the electricity sector, see K Sunila, 'Regulating the Change in the EU Electricity Markets – Finding the Balance Between Tomorrow and Yesterday' (Doctoral thesis, Aalto University 2023) 31–33 and the references therein.

[38] On visibility and predictability see eg K Huhta, 'Anchoring the Energy Transition with Legal Certainty in EU Law' (2020) 27(4) *Maastricht Journal of European and Comparative Law* 425, 442, 427. A Boute, 'The Quest for Regulatory Stability in the EU Energy Market: An Analysis through the Prism of Legal Certainty' (2012) 37 *European Law Review* 675.

[39] Työ- ja elinkeinoministeriö, *Ehdotus valtioneuvoston asetukseksi sähköntoimitusten selvityksestä ja mittauksesta* (Muistio 2021) 12.

[40] For some examples see Government Proposal 144/2018, 14–16.

[41] Government Decree on the Implementation of the Services of Centralised Datahub (1073/2019).

[42] Government Proposal 144/2018, 4.

[43] Government Decree (66/2009); Decree of the Ministry of Economic Affairs and Employment on the data exchange to be followed in the electricity trade and imbalance settlement of electricity supplies (273/2016).

by the industry's own recommendations.[44] This was found to be an inadequate solution to ensure effective compliance.[45] The decentralised system was also considered to be too slow and inefficient, and it did not serve well, eg, the electricity service providers' access to their customers' data.[46]

The Finnish Electricity Market Act (588/2013) had already in 2013 laid down a task to the Finnish main grid operator with systems responsibility, Fingrid Oyj, to *develop* the data exchange in the electricity markets.[47] Following this mandate, the main grid operator proposed that a centralised information exchange for the distribution systems and electricity retail markets be implemented. After getting a political green light for the project, the main grid operator engaged stakeholders in the development of the datahub through different working groups, which produced several reports on different topics.[48] It could be said that the concept of and procedures for the datahub had already been prepared before the legislation was drafted. In 2019, the amendment of the legislation created a regulated-monopoly, centralised information-exchange 'datahub', for which the main grid operator with systems responsibility would be responsible.[49] The legislation entered into force in the same year, but a transition period was applied to the commissioning of the centralised information-exchange services. Pursuant to the Government Proposal, the centralised information exchange-services were to be commissioned in 2021, but the process was delayed and the final implementation took place a year later.[50] In accordance with the requirements of the Electricity Market Act, the main grid operator has organised the tasks of the datahub in a wholly owned subsidiary.[51]

The legislator, as usual, relied on a command-and-control measure by obligating the main grid operator to develop and implement the services of centralised data exchange for distribution systems and electricity retail markets.[52] The DSOs and electricity retailers were also obligated to use the services of the centralised data exchange, and they needed to adequately prepare for that. This time, the preparation was not only an obligation to draw up a plan but also a registration obligation with a hard deadline: those who could not reach the technical requirements and register within the set deadlines would risk their business. In ultimate cases, all the supply agreements of a retailer could be dissolved, and a DSO could lose its network licence, which is a requirement for acting as a DSO in Finland.[53]

[44] E.g. Energiateollisuus, *Sähkön vähittäismarkkinoiden menettelytapa- ja sanomaliikenneohje* (2016, updated 2019).

[45] Government Proposal 144/2018, 16–17.

[46] ibid 17.

[47] Electricity Market Act (588/2013) s 49.

[48] Government Proposal 144/2018, 29.

[49] Act on amending the Electricity Market Act (108/2019).

[50] Government Proposal 144/2018, 1; Government Decree 1073/2019.

[51] Electricity Market Act, s 8. This is to increase transparency (Government Proposal 144/2018, 32).

[52] Electricity Market Act (588/2013) s 49 a.

[53] Act on certain measures relating to the commissioning of the services of the centralised data exchange (892/2021). It should be disclosed that the author of this chapter was involved in drafting the said legislation.

These extreme provisions were to ensure that the electricity markets were ready for the implementation of the datahub and that the system worked without disruption.

The introduction of datahub is another example of the command-and-control approach in a case where a 'concrete' (albeit software-based) building block of a smart electricity system is to be implemented. The legislator assessed that there was a need for a centralised information exchange and simply obligated the relevant parties to develop it, prepare for it and use it. However, as can be read from above, the industry was extensively involved in the process of developing the content of these obligations. In addition, the legislation defined the services to be provided by the datahub but did not specify how the datahub should organise these services.

In this context, an interesting question is the balancing between the binding legislation and non-binding self-regulation of the industry. In the decentralised data exchange model, the general level legislation and non-binding recommendations did not provide a sufficient level of harmonisation and control. The precise enough legislation is hard to draft when it comes to the technical specifications and data traffic protocols. In addition, overly detailed specifications could hamper the development of market practice, and the regulatory disconnection becomes an evident risk.[54] However, non-binding self-regulation, which may fit in some cases, could be ignored without consequence – and it has not passed a democratic procedure.

After the implementation of the datahub, some general level provisions regarding the data exchange format are still set out at the level of binding legislation. In addition, the market participants using the services of the datahub are responsible for ensuring that they comply with the data traffic requirements set out in the *service agreement* entered into with the datahub.[55] The terms and conditions of the service agreement are drafted by the datahub, and the Energy Authority needs to approve them ex-ante.[56] The service agreement itself sets out a contractual obligation to a market participant to comply with the guidance issued by the datahub, and if the market participant essentially breaches the guidance, the datahub ultimately has a contractual right to block the market participant from the datahub services. Pursuant to the agreement, the guidance documents are prepared together with the stakeholders.[57]

Thus, when it comes to the technical specifications relating to the data exchange between the DSOs, electricity retailers and the datahub, the attempt to harmonise market practices (not only by the legislator but by the industry) relies on several different 'regulatory measures', all the way from binding law to

[54] See K Sunila, 'Regulating the Change in the EU Electricity Markets – Finding the Balance Between Tomorrow and Yesterday' (Doctoral thesis, Aalto University 2023) 31–33, 44.

[55] Decree of the Ministry of Economic Affairs and Employment on the data exchange to be followed in the electricity trade and imbalance settlement of electricity supplies (839/2021) ch 4. It should be disclosed that the author of the chapter has been responsible for drafting the said Decree.

[56] Act on the Surveillance of Electricity and Natural Gas Markets (590/2013) s 10.

[57] Service Agreement on the Centralised Information Exchange of Electricity Transactions. Available at: https://palvelut.datahub.fi/en/dokumentaatio/laskutus-ja-palvelusopimukset.

contractual obligations and self-regulation by the industry. The legislation sets out general level rules and obligations, the more precise terms and conditions are drafted by a regulated monopoly actor and approved by the national regulatory authority, the service agreement sets out the contractual obligations between the regulated monopoly and market actors, and the guidance documents referred to in the service agreement are prepared by the regulated monopoly together with stakeholders.

The system is arguably complex from the legal point of view and does not necessarily provide the highest level of certainty to the market participants. However, the flexibility to develop the data exchange is needed as, in practice, it would be impossible to amend the legislation at the same speed. The technical nature of the rules can also be seen to support the structure partly based on the self-regulation. It remains to be seen how well the system serves for the efficiency of the data exchange, 'regulatory connection', the certainty to the market participants, and transparency.

The next big development process of the datahub will relate to the demand response interface and it is to be enforced by binding law. In this case, the main grid operator with systems responsibility was mandated to propose the way forward, this time to implement a demand response interface. The main grid operator ordered a consultancy report to assess the feasibility of different solutions; based on this, it suggested that the datahub extends its services to cover the new interface.[58] In November 2024, the Finnish Government submitted the proposal for amending the Electricity Market Act to Parliament. The demand response interface is to promote market-based demand response by facilitating the data traffic that enables the DSOs to implement the demand response commands of end customers through the relay, which is to be included in the second-generation smart meters.[59]

5. Right of the Customers to the Metering and Consumption Data

As stated above, the electricity metering and consumption data is practically useless if it cannot be sent forward from the meter. Therefore, the reading of the meter and data exchange is crucial. However, from the customer point of view, this is not enough. First, the customers should get *access* to the data regarding their own electricity use and production. Second, the customers should be able to *use*

[58] Government Proposal 197/2024, 9; Loppuraportti, *Kuormanohjausrajapinnan määrittely* (Afry 2024) (consultancy report). Available at: www.fingrid.fi/globalassets/dokumentit/fi/sahkomarkkinat/kysyntajousto/kuormanohjausrajapinnan-maarittely---loppuraportti.pdf.

[59] See Draft Government Proposal to amend the Electricity Market Act and the Act on the Comparison Tool for Electricity Supply Agreements, s 49 a.

that data. Thus, the customers' right to access the data in a timely manner is critical to ensure that the expectations set out for the smart meters can be met both from the customer side and from the electricity system perspective.

When the hourly metering requirement was adopted in 2009, customers' rights to their own electricity consumption data was also ensured by the legislation.[60] Although the legislation set out the customers' *rights*, in practice this provision laid an obligation on the electricity system operators to provide their customers with the consumption data free of charge. Nowadays, the provision is set out in the Electricity Market Act, which enacts a clear obligation for the electricity system operators to provide the customer, or another party the customer has nominated (eg an aggregator), with the information. The information that should be given also covers the historical data to enable the comparison to the earlier consumption.[61] When second-generation smart meters are installed, the customers should also be able to get nearly real-time data directly from the meter through a consumer interface.[62]

As the electricity consumption data can constitute personal data or business secrets, it is important that the data is not distributed without the consent of the customer. The legislation from 2009 was already based on this principle. However, certain exemptions to the main rule are needed to enable the use of data in, eg, the billing and imbalance settlement. The cases are specified in the Electricity Market Act, in particular to address the restrictions stemming from the General Data Protection Regulation (EU) 2016/679.[63]

6. Facilitating the Use of Data

The earlier sections have described obligations that enable, facilitate and restrict the availability of data and data exchange. The Finnish electricity market legislation also includes provisions encouraging the *use* of data. Evident examples are the requirement that the end customer is billed on the basis of the metering[64] and that the imbalance settlement is based on the electricity metering.[65] However, the Finnish electricity market legislation also applies provisions that indirectly promote the use of data.

The first example of such provisions is the end customers' right to participate in the organised marketplaces by offering demand response, either independently or through an aggregator.[66] The provision does not explicitly refer to the data, but the electricity consumption data provides the basis for the demand response. (As

[60] Government Decree (66/2009) ch 6, s 8.
[61] Electricity Market Act (588/2013) s 75 e.
[62] Government Decree (767/2021) ch 6, s 5.
[63] Electricity Market Act, s 75 f. Government Proposal 144/2018, detailed reasonings for s 75 f. The business secrets are addressed in the Electricity Market Act, s 76.
[64] Electricity Market Act (588/2013) s 105 g, which applies to electricity retailers and DSOs.
[65] Government Decree (767/2021) ch 4, s 1.
[66] Electricity Market Act (588/2013, as amended) s 65 a.

mentioned, the demand response and electricity savings were key drivers when implementing first-generation smart meters in Finland.) The customers' right to participate in the markets is backed by an equivalent obligation to the marketplace operators: they shall not set out terms and conditions that unfoundedly discriminate the demand response services provided by the customers compared to the electricity production.[67] As mentioned, the demand response will be further encouraged or facilitated by an interface which is to be included in the services of the datahub.[68]

Another example of provisions that may indirectly promote new solutions and services, based on the use of data, concerns the DSOs. After the national transposition of the Electricity Market Directive (EU) 2019/944, the DSOs shall consider alternative measures for increasing the distribution capacity in their network development plans. These alternative measures include the use of demand response, energy storages and increasing energy efficiency.[69] In addition, the DSOs shall procure, where possible, flexibility services on market-based terms to increase the efficiency of the use and development of their distribution systems.[70] For example, the local DSO in Helsinki and the main grid operator are together launching a new market platform for demand response which will be built on a new IT system.[71]

The third example also relates to electricity system operators. Pursuant to the Electricity Market Act, the electricity system operators shall plan and build their electricity systems in such a way that the quality requirements set out in the legislation can be met. These requirements are set out differently for the main grid, high-voltage distribution systems and other distribution systems.[72] When it comes to the DSOs, the legislation also defines standard compensation to which a DSO's customers are entitled to if the network service has ceased for certain periods of time and the DSO cannot prove that this was beyond its control and due care.[73] These requirements may encourage the electricity system operators to apply new digital technologies to monitor and control their electricity systems. There are currently several service providers offering digital solutions for the Finnish electricity system operators to improve the efficiency and reliability of their electricity systems.

7. Relying on Market Signals

Another regulatory strategy is not to regulate. The Finnish electricity markets had already been opened for competition in the 1990s. The electricity suppliers have

[67] ibid.

[68] See section 4 of this chapter above.

[69] Electricity Market Act (588/2013, as amended) s 52.

[70] ibid s 52 a.

[71] Fingrid Oyj, 'Siirtojenhallinnan markkinapaikan pilottihankkeen kauppapaikan toimittajaksi valittu NODES AS' (17 December 2024). Available at: www.fingrid.fi/ajankohtaista/tiedotteet/2024/siirtojenhallinnan-markkinapaikan-pilottihankkeen-kauppapaikan-toimittajaksi-valittu-nodes-as/.

[72] Electricity Market Act (588/2013) ss 40, 50 and 51.

[73] ibid s 100.

been free to determine the price at which they sell electricity and customers have been able to choose their supplier.[74] After the market opening, the legislator has not intervened in electricity price formation; this has been left to the markets.

Digitalisation in the electricity sector has also been encouraged through market signals. The electricity producers and industrial customers utilise different kinds of digital solutions to gather data from their processes. The optimisation of the processes and electricity sales is obviously a necessity in competitive markets and many energy companies and industrial electricity users are nowadays using artificial intelligence (AI) for their optimisation. For example, virtual power plants gathering demand response on the consumption side have become increasingly common and different kinds of energy service providers are entering into the markets.[75]

While the legislator has not actively regulated this development, it should be noted that basic market rules need to facilitate it. For example, meter-based billing and balance responsibility enable the market participants to benefit from optimisation. Due to the specific nature of electricity, even the basic functioning of the market requires certain rules to be laid down in legislation.[76] The *laissez-faire* approach in the electricity markets very seldom means that the markets are not to some extent regulated.[77]

8. Summarising the Finnish Regulatory Strategies

Although this chapter has not provided an exhaustive description of the measures taken to promote digitalisation in Finland, some conclusions on the regulatory strategies can be drawn. The chapter has focused on the measures adopted by the legislator, whereas, for example, public information campaigns to promote the use of metering data and energy savings have not been studied. This naturally affects the conclusions.

In Finland, the basic building blocks necessary for digitalisation of the electricity system have been laid down by using a command-and-control approach. The installation of smart meters and the implementation of the datahub have been rather clearly definable tasks. The subject of the legislation in these cases has been the electricity system operators, who are, as natural monopolies, also otherwise heavily regulated.

Even though the legislation has set out clear obligations, room for manoeuvre has been left for the implementation: the specifications for the smart meters have

[74] Electricity Market Act (386/1995); see Government Proposal 138/1994 and Government Proposal 227/1997.

[75] For example, mobile operator Elisa Oyj uses its reserve batteries as a virtual power plant; see E Oyj, 'Virtual Power Plant'. Available at: https://elisa.com/corporate/sustainability/virtual-power-plant/.

[76] Balance responsibility and third-party access to electricity systems are maybe the most evident examples on this.

[77] K Sunila, 'Regulating the Change in the EU Electricity Markets – Finding the Balance Between Tomorrow and Yesterday' (Doctoral thesis, Aalto University 2023) 33.

been enacted as minimum requirements, and the legislation does not elaborate in detail how the datahub should organise its services. It could be said that an output-based approach is combined with the command-and-control measures.[78]

Sometimes the selected regulatory approach has been based on a combination of different measures. As mentioned, the technical specifications for the data exchange and the enforcement of them have been built on a complex set of different measures, from binding law to self-regulation. The rollout of the first smart meters was backed by a legal obligation and incentivised in the economic regulation model. In some cases, the legislator has decided not to regulate.

What is characteristic in the Finnish legislation is that the wider legislative projects for digitalising the electricity system have been prepared in conjunction with the stakeholders. This can be argued to be necessary as the legislator does not normally hold the best understanding of the technological possibilities. This is particularly true when it comes to innovative solutions.[79] However, as has been noted earlier in the literature, the legislator is responsible for ensuring that the binding law also takes into account other interests than those represented in the preparation of the law and that the end result implements efficiently the underlying political objectives.[80] This is typically ensured through public consultations on the draft legislation, and sometimes organising consultations on the preparatory reports. The later the consultations are conducted, the harder it is, however, to impact the end result.

EU legislation has impacted regulatory approaches in the national electricity market legislation. The Finnish legislation has traditionally focused on the regulation of system operators by defining their tasks and obligations towards other market participants. An output-based approach can also be identified. Usually, the legislator has not adopted detailed rules on how the electricity system operators should carry out their tasks. This is left to the system operators themselves to decide, although the applicable economic regulation obviously directs their decisions.[81] The competitive activities are, by contrast, to a large extent left to the market powers, although the legislator has set out certain rules to ensure that the system functions and to guarantee a level playing field. In addition, basic contractual rights of the consumers, in particular, have been guaranteed by the law.

The EU legislation, by contrast, adopts a more 'intervening' approach. The Electricity Market Directive (EU) 2019/944 pushes, for example, towards

[78] About output-based approach in the context of smart electricity systems; see L Diestelmeier, 'Unlocking Flexibility with Law: Developing a Legal Framework for Smart Electricity Systems' (Doctoral thesis, University of Groningen 2019) 123.

[79] L Bennett Moses, 'Agents of Change: How the Law "Copes" with Technological Change' (2011) 20 *Griffith L Rev* 763, 787.

[80] S Lavrijssen and B Vitéz, 'Good Governance and the Regulation of the District Heating Market' in MPC Weijnen and others (eds), *Shaping an Inclusive Energy Transition* (Springer Nature 2021). Available at: https://doi.org/10.1007/978-3-030-74586-8_9; L Hancher, P Larouche, and S Lavrijssen, 'Principles of Good Market Governance' (2004) XLIX(2) *Journal of Network Industries* 339.

[81] See eg K Sunila, P Järventausta, and A Ekroos, 'Legal and Regulatory Challenges in the Development of "Smart Electricity System" in Finland' (2016) 7(3) *Renewable Energy Law and Policy Review* 21.

empowering customers and smarter grids, by requiring Member States to guarantee the rights of active customers and energy communities and to ensure that electricity system operators consider alternative solutions for capacity increases when developing electricity systems. Instead of setting only the objectives, the EU legislation also hints towards the measures. The obvious risk with this approach is that the measures are later proved to be inefficient, or that the detailed legislation starts to lag behind the real world.[82] However, the interventions may sometimes be needed to speed up the development towards cleaner energy systems.

The impact of EU law has been growing over recent years and the legislative culture has already affected the national electricity market legislation. When considering digitalisation and the use of data, this can specifically be seen in the provisions encouraging indirectly the use of data (see section 6 above). The development from output-based regulation and rather general obligations towards more detailed and specifically targeted rules can be seen.

9. Facilitating Radical Innovations?

How about truly innovative solutions? They have not particularly been addressed in the Finnish electricity market legislation. However, according to the recently updated Finnish *National Energy and Climate Plan*, research, innovation and competitiveness in the energy sector will be supported by various measures. Not only is state aid to be granted to innovative projects but also experiments are to be promoted.[83] The plan states that:

> Test platforms provide an opportunity to conduct experiments and pilots, and to implement research and development projects in the programme focus areas. These include smart networks, renewable energy, energy efficiency, sustainable and smart energy solutions and systems, their related products and services, and resources-wise solutions based on user needs. Instead of developing an individual technology, the intention is to develop ecosystems and integrate technology into a smart system. The aim is to create several test platforms in Finland that are internationally attractive and will also bring investments to Finland.[84]

The described focus areas refer almost directly to the experiments applying new digital solutions in the electricity sector. The plan does not specify what is meant by the test platforms, but the earlier policy papers may provide some clarification. In the Finnish *Climate and Energy Strategy* adopted by the Government of then Prime Minister Sanna Marin, it was stated that the test environments for

[82] See K Sunila, 'Regulating the Change in the EU Electricity Markets – Finding the Balance Between Tomorrow and Yesterday' (Doctoral thesis, Aalto University 2023) 30, 31, 44 and the references therein.

[83] Ministry of Economic Affairs and Employment, *Finland's Integrated National Energy and Climate Plan* (Publication 2024:30, 2024) 162–67. Available at: http://urn.fi/URN:ISBN:978-952-327-527-0.

[84] ibid 163.

innovative solutions through legislative measures would be studied. In this context, the test environments were understood as a solution to test innovations that were not necessarily compliant with the current legislation.[85] It could be understood that 'regulatory sandboxes' were suggested to be studied.[86]

The recently adopted EU legislation also promotes regulatory sandboxes. The AI Act sets out rules regarding regulatory sandboxes,[87] and the Net-Zero Industry Act (NZIA) introduces 'net-zero regulatory sandboxes'.[88] As well it might, the first one aims to establish a real-world testbed for artificial intelligent systems.[89] The second one focuses on innovative net-zero technologies and other innovative technologies.[90] Net-zero technologies under the NZIA include, eg, technologies to digitalise the electricity grid.[91]

Both regulatory sandboxes will be subject to more specific rules to be laid down by implementing acts at the EU level.[92] These criteria will be crucial to define the functioning of the sandboxes. For example, the eligibility criteria and selection procedure for participation in the sandboxes are to be laid down by implementing acts.[93] At the time of writing, the AI Act and NZIA have not been nationally implemented (to the extent needed), and no regulatory sandboxes have yet been established. However, it can already be said that the digitalisation of the electricity sector is most likely within the scope of these sandboxes.

Regulatory sandboxes could bring a completely new approach to the promotion of digitalisation and other innovative solutions in Finland. As has been stated above, the electricity sector has been strongly involved in the development of legislation concerning digitalisation of the energy sector. Regulatory sandboxes may, however, promote dialogue between the law and the real world in a new way.[94] The idea of the regulatory sandboxes is quite often seen as giving room for development

[85] Työ- ja elinkeinoministeriö, *Hiilineutraali Suomi 2035 – kansallinen ilmasto- ja energiastrategia* (julkaisuja 2022:53, 2022) http://urn.fi/URN:ISBN:978-952-327-811-0. It should be disclosed that the author of the chapter has been involved in preparing the said strategy.

[86] For the concept of regulatory sandboxes, see the following footnotes and eg K Sunila and A Ekroos 'Regulating Radical Innovations in the EU Electricity Markets: Time for a Robust Sandbox' (2022) 41(1) *Journal of Energy & Natural Resources Law* 5 and the references therein.

[87] Regulation (EU) 2024/1689 of the European Parliament and of the Council laying down harmonised rules on artificial intelligence and amending Regulations (EC) No 300/2008, (EU) No 167/2013, (EU) No 168/2013, (EU) 2018/858, (EU) 2018/1139 and (EU) 2019/2144 and Directives 2014/90/EU, (EU) 2016/797 and (EU) 2020/1828 [2024] OJ L1689 (Artificial Intelligence Act) art 2, 57.

[88] Regulation (EU) 2024/1735 of the European Parliament and of the Council on establishing a framework of measures for strengthening Europe's net-zero technology manufacturing ecosystem and amending Regulation (EU) 2018/1724 [2024] OJ L1735 (NZIA) art 2, 33.

[89] AI Act, arts 57, 58.

[90] NZIA, art 33.

[91] ibid arts 3, 4.

[92] ibid art 33(3); AI Act, art 58. At the time of writing this chapter, the implementing acts have not been adopted.

[93] ibid.

[94] T Schittekatte and others, 'Regulatory Experimentation in Energy: Three Pioneer Countries and Lessons for the Green Transition' (2021) 156 *Energy Policy* 112382; K Sunila, 'Regulating the Change in the EU Electricity Markets – Finding the Balance Between Tomorrow and Yesterday' (Doctoral thesis, Aalto University 2023) 43.

of 'radical innovations', thus they specifically address innovative solutions.[95] In this context, 'radical innovations' refers to those innovations that are not fully compliant with the current legislation. This may bring new stakeholders (like new service providers) into the projects, which may later affect the legislation.

However, in the context of the new EU Regulations, the promotion of radical innovations through regulatory sandboxes seems to remain limited. In general, Member States cannot deviate from binding EU law – unless EU law itself empowers Member States to do so. For example, the NZIA states that 'the competent authorities shall consider whether to grant *derogations or exemptions in national law to the extent allowed by relevant Union law*'.[96] As the national electricity market law is increasingly European, the scope of derogations and exemptions will be restricted.[97]

It seems that regulatory sandboxes will first and foremost promote innovations that are compliant with the current legislation or that enter into an unregulated field where the legislation does not exist, yet. In neither of these cases are regulatory sandboxes interesting to all innovations or projects, due to the characteristics of the concept. For example, the regulatory sandboxes always provide a real-life testbed for a certain period of time; this most likely excludes innovative solutions requiring extensive investments.

It remains to be seen how Finland implements regulatory sandboxes and whether this will affect the regulatory strategies more generally.

10. Concluding Remarks

This chapter discusses the regulatory strategies to promote digitalisation in the Finnish electricity sector during the past 15 years in Finland. The focus has been on legislative measures. It can be concluded that Finland has applied several different measures and also combined them to obligate, facilitate and encourage digitalisation in the electricity sector. The Finnish legislator has often relied on command-and-control measures, when the obligation has been easy to define. However, in many cases, the command-and-control strategy has been combined with an output-based model leaving the exact implementation to the market parties. When wider legislative amendments have been implemented, stakeholders have often been engaged from the very beginning. Given the technical nature

[95] See eg K Sunila and A Ekroos, 'Regulating Radical Innovations in the EU Electricity Markets: Time for a Robust Sandbox' (2023) 41(1) *Journal of Energy and Natural Resources Law* 1. Available at: https://doi.org/10.1080/02646811.2022.2088175.

[96] NZIA, art 33(5).

[97] For more about the regulation of radical innovations in the electricity sector, see K Sunila and A Ekroos, 'Regulating Radical Innovations in the EU Electricity Markets: Time for a Robust Sandbox' (2023) 41(1) *Journal of Energy and Natural Resources Law* 1. Available at: https://doi.org/10.1080/02646811.2022.2088175.

of the electricity market legislation, this approach balances the risk of regulatory disconnection associated with overly detailed rules and the lack of investment security associated with rules that are too vague and so open to interpretation.

The impact of EU legislation can already be seen in the Finnish electricity market legislation, and this development is likely to continue. The recent EU electricity market legislation has adopted a more 'intervening' approach than traditionally has been applied in Finland. In some cases, this approach may prove to be successful in advancing specific objectives but, in the rapidly changing electricity markets, the risk of regulatory disconnection looms in the background.

Until now, the Finnish electricity market legislation has not particularly addressed innovative solutions. A completely new kind of a measure may be seen in the future, as the Finnish policy papers and the recently adopted EU legislation point towards regulatory sandboxes. As can be read from above, the 'dialogue' between the legislator and the stakeholders is not a new concept in Finland. However, the scope of this dialogue may expand to more innovative areas after the introduction of regulatory sandboxes. Given the limitations of the regulatory sandboxes described above, this effect may be most evident in the unregulated sectors where new legislation is being considered.

13

Conclusion

OLGA HRYNKIV, SHANYA RUHELA AND SASKIA LAVRIJSSEN

1. Charting New Frontiers of Energy and Finance: An Introduction

As digitalisation accelerates across critical sectors, the vulnerabilities it introduces have elevated systemic risk, cybersecurity, and infrastructural resilience to the forefront of regulatory concern. The massive and unexpected power outage that struck Spain, Portugal, and parts of France on 28 April 2025 is a stark reminder of this reality.[1] The blackout, which plunged millions into darkness and disrupted essential services, including metro systems, air traffic and communications, has amplified fears about the growing exposure of critical infrastructure to both natural disturbances and technological vulnerabilities.[2] Spain, long regarded as a frontrunner in the shift toward renewable energy, now faces renewed scrutiny over whether its power grid can withstand the pressures of increasing demand and the fluctuating nature of green energy supply.[3] Much like the GameStop saga introduced at the beginning of this edited volume, this incident raised urgent questions: Could the disruption have been foreseen or prevented? Were regulatory mechanisms equipped to assess and mitigate the risks of such technological failures? And, once again, whose interests were protected, and who were left behind? These recurring challenges underline the pressing need for regulatory frameworks to keep pace with the speed, scale and complexity of green and digital transitions.

Various case studies in this edited volume have demonstrated that the regulatory landscapes of both energy and finance share certain fundamental similarities in their evolution, challenges, and adaptation to technological disruptions. As both sectors undergo parallel transformations driven by digitalisation and

[1] E Pinedo and others, 'Power Begins to Return after Huge Outage Hits Spain and Portugal' *Reuters* (29 April 2025). Available at: www.reuters.com/world/europe/large-parts-spain-portugal-hit-by-power-outage-2025-04-28/.

[2] ibid.

[3] D Sharrock and I Johnston, 'Spain's Electricity Grid Operator Rules out Cyber Attack as Cause of Blackout' *Financial Times* (29 April 2025). Available at: www.ft.com/content/1363127b-014e-4f30-ab5d-38f76d640274.

decarbonisation, they confront *common regulatory challenges*. The 2021 ransomware attack on Colonial Pipeline in the US, which resulted in fuel shortages across the East Coast, illustrates the immediate economic and public safety repercussions that can occur when cyber intrusions compromise energy infrastructure. Similarly, the 2022 cyberattack on KP Snacks in the UK, which disrupted supply chains for weeks, highlights how digital breaches in seemingly peripheral sectors can have a contagion effect on broader economic systems. The systemic nature of cyber risks in finance mirrors the complex interdependencies in energy systems. Eyup Kun's analysis of systemic cyber risk, exemplified by the 2023 ION Group ransomware attack, shows how failures in one node can ripple through entire financial markets, much like cascading failures in energy infrastructure. These examples, among others, demonstrate how innovation rapidly outpaces governance structures, and systemic risks emerge from increased interconnectivity and technological complexity.

The energy and financial sectors operate within complex, multi-level regulatory frameworks where *balancing* innovation, competition and consumer protection is of utmost importance. As Emanuel van Praag demonstrates in the context of EU payment markets, digitalisation is not only reshaping the way services are delivered but also the very role of regulation. Shanya Ruhela further highlights in her research that the UK financial regulator embracing digital transformation through RegTech and SupTech has become central to regulatory innovation in finance. Legal interventions are no longer merely reactive tools for managing risk but are instrumental for achieving broader societal goals such as financial inclusion, strategic autonomy and digital sovereignty. This development mirrors a similar trajectory in the energy sector, where regulation is increasingly used as a tool to strengthen infrastructural resilience and safeguard strategic autonomy.

Shirley Kempeneer and Magdalena Brewczyńska further illustrate that the sectors of energy and finance face similar challenges in balancing innovation with stakeholder protection. These challenges are not new or novel but rather reflect long-standing societal conflicts, such as power struggles between individuals and the state or between consumers and service providers. However, in today's era of digitalisation, these challenges often revolve around the control, access, and processing of information, making *data governance* a central concern in regulatory discussions.

At times, digital transformation amplifies pre-existing tensions between *regulatory flexibility* and *legal certainty*. For example, Renske van't Veer, Max Baumgart, and Saskia Lavrijssen assert that the current state of the energy sector and legal and regulatory frameworks are inadequate when it comes to keeping pace with rapid scientific and technological developments. This results in legal uncertainty and social conflict, particularly in the energy market, where traditional harmonised regulation is either absent or significantly diverges from the frameworks needed to govern emerging, less conventional sub-sectors such as green hydrogen. Kanerva Sunila's contribution to this debate is particularly instructive. She notes that the technical nature of electricity market legislation often requires a careful balance between the risk of regulatory disconnection arising from overly detailed rules and the lack of investment security associated with vague legal provisions that leave too much room for interpretation. This insight reflects a tension that is echoed across both energy and financial regulation, where the need for precise rules must be balanced with market flexibility to preserve innovation and investor confidence.

Cross-sectoral insights indicate that regulatory solutions in one sector can serve as valuable reference points for the other. Just as regulatory sandboxes and experimental approaches have gained traction in the financial sector in response to digital innovation, the energy sector must also embrace flexible and adaptive regulatory models. Renske van't Veer, Max Baumgart, and Saskia Lavrijssen underscore the value of regulatory sandboxes as mechanisms for iterative learning, enabling a two-way dialogue between innovative businesses and regulators. This process of dialogue fosters not only regulatory innovation but also the emergence of new sociotechnical arrangements tailored to evolving market conditions. The mutual learning process helps to reduce legal uncertainty, builds trust, and supports more transparent and effective communication among stakeholders. The emphasis on trust-building, transparent communication and regulatory responsiveness speaks directly to the broader themes of cross-sectoral coordination and governance that run throughout this edited volume.

Furthermore, the contributions in this edited volume reaffirm that effective governance in the digital age cannot be confined to formal legal rules alone. As infrastructures and markets become more interconnected and dynamic, regulatory success increasingly depends on multi-level coordination, organisational learning and flexible implementation strategies. *Governance beyond the law*, rooted in collaboration, adaptability and institutional trust, emerges as a vital complement to traditional regulatory tools in addressing the complex challenges of digitalisation across energy and finance. In this context, Wendy van der Valk argues that governance necessitates the application of sound governance principles at different levels and, increasingly, across multiple sectors to ensure resilience and adaptability. This makes governance models as important as regulatory strategies while tackling emerging challenges in energy and finance.

Finally, the examples and insights discussed throughout this edited volume push regulators and policymakers, innovators, private and public sector actors and decision-makers to effectively work towards a new dawn, one where they do not merely respond to emerging challenges but also proactively shape *a sustainable and adaptable regulatory future* for both energy and finance. The following sections explore how the discussed examples and insights can bridge theory and practice, helping to craft more anticipatory and forward-looking regulatory approaches.

2. Regulatory Experimentation and Adaptive Governance in the Digital Age

Regulatory experimentation is one of the powerful tools for navigating the complexity and intricacies brought by digital transformation. From positive energy district pilots to EU-level initiatives like the Digital Euro, experimental law-making and sandbox approaches provide a unique space for regulators to test new paradigms, gather evidence, and iterate policy in collaboration with market actors. When such models are grounded in core regulatory principles and are implemented with transparency and foresight, they not only support innovation but strengthen institutional legitimacy, consumer protection and cross-sectoral coherence across Europe's evolving regulatory landscape. While different countries often prioritise distinct goals, a comparative examination of diverse case studies in this edited volume reveals converging design principles and governance mechanisms that demonstrate effective experimentation.

The contribution by Renske van't Veer, Max Baumgart, and Saskia Lavrijssen highlights that sandbox approaches allow regulators to develop the domain-specific expertise necessary to mediate between competing objectives, ensuring regulatory compliance while encouraging innovation. This reflects a shift in the energy sector toward regulatory strategies that are not only rules-based but also *responsive and future-orientated*. Learnings from Max Baumgart and Jasper van den Boom on positive energy districts and smart regulatory strategies also reinforce the broader argument that regulations must evolve in tandem with technological advancements. Just as energy markets require regulatory experimentation to accommodate decentralised energy production and digital grid management, financial markets must develop more responsive regulatory frameworks to manage digital risks and promote sustainable innovation.

In the Finnish context, Kanerva Sunila provides a rich example of regulatory foresight supporting technical and market transitions. She observes that the concept and procedures for Finland's centralised datahub were developed even before the corresponding legislation was drafted, reflecting a proactive alignment between regulatory ambition and infrastructural readiness. This forward-looking approach underscores the importance of synchronising institutional vision with technological capability. Importantly, while the legislation clearly defined the services the datahub was to provide, it did not dictate how these services should be operationalised, leaving room for flexibility and innovation by market actors. This *deliberate regulatory ambiguity* highlights a valuable model for experimentation: legislation can guide outcomes without prescribing means, thus promoting efficiency and adaptability. Renske van't Veer, Max Baumgart, and Saskia Lavrijssen add that adaptive governance models must be capable of adjusting to the evolving realities of emerging markets. Without flexibility, regulators risk implementing static frameworks that fail to reflect market shifts or technological progress and ultimately hinder innovation rather than enable it.

Kanerva Sunila rightly cautions that, from a legal standpoint, embracing flexible and responsive regulatory models does not always provide *optimal certainty* to market participants. This observation is also instructive for financial markets, particularly when grappling with cross-border regulatory inconsistencies and platform-based market architectures. Striking the right balance between the necessity of flexibility and the risks of legal uncertainty remains a central challenge for effective regulatory design.

Liebrich Hiemstra's chapter makes an assertive argument for future research on balancing the need for legal clarity with regulatory adaptability. She warns against overly complex regulatory frameworks that discourage compliance and advocates for clear, simple and *principles-based legislation* that can evolve with technological innovation and digital transformation. Further, she suggests that legislators must reflect on the role of regulation itself and whether to act as a barrier or a bridge in guiding sustainable finance towards its public mission. This insight supports broader calls in the edited volume for adaptive, responsive regulation that can accommodate change without compromising oversight or public trust.

Liebrich Hiemstra also proposes that regulatory sandboxes and RegTech solutions offer mutually beneficial tools for both supervisors and market actors. Regulatory sandboxes, in particular, allow supervisors to gain deeper market insights while providing innovators with legal clarity. Her chapter aligns with other contributions in calling for *proactive supervision*. Proactive supervision refers to a type of supervision whereby the regulators act not only as enforcers but also as collaborators in shaping sustainable markets. She argues for the need for formal and informal supervisory tools to be used together and in parallel to each other; while public consultations and industry roundtables build trust and transparency, regular reviews and digital monitoring are essential to detect market abuse.

Testing innovations in regulatory sandboxes involves risks, but these can be acceptable if they lead to valuable regulatory insights, especially when balanced by strong safeguards. Inge Graef and Din Buljević suggest that a *risk* and *proportionality-based approach* ensures that higher-risk experiments are only permitted when the innovation offers significant public interest benefits, such as in public health. Tailoring the sandbox implementation to the complexity and technical needs of the innovation, the market players and the associated risks can help minimise harm while promoting learning. According to Graef and Buljević, this often means stricter controls and narrower regulatory exemptions for riskier innovations, with sandboxes being limited in time to what is necessary.

Additionally, Wendy van der Valk argues that effective policies must *balance private sector efficiency with public values* such as sustainability, accessibility and affordability. Inge Graef and Din Buljević also highlight the importance of aligning eligibility criteria for participation in regulatory sandboxes with the overarching objectives of the policy and regulation and ensuring that experiments generate broader insights. Max Baumgart and Jasper van den Boom further argue that market harnessing regulation, which leverages competitive forces to drive policy objectives, can play a key role in both energy and finance. In positive energy districts, for example, market-based mechanisms such as P2P energy trading and dynamic pricing incentives have been proposed to optimise energy consumption. Similarly, in finance, regulatory frameworks that encourage data-sharing and interoperability have been instrumental in fostering innovation while maintaining regulatory oversight.

Emanuel van Praag's discussion of the Digital Euro and Instant Payments Regulation in the EU demonstrates how legal measures mandate infrastructure development and accessibility not merely for market efficiency but to serve strategic objectives such as ensuring access for vulnerable consumers and reducing dependency on foreign payment systems. These legal developments, often *requiring private entities to take on public responsibilities*, highlight how experimental law-making can shift traditional notions of private-sector autonomy. The interplay between public policy goals and private sector duties reflects a broader regulatory transformation. He argues that payment service providers are increasingly expected to implement costly changes such as distributing the Digital Euro or enabling cross-border instant payments, not because of direct market failure but to fulfil wider social or geopolitical mandates. This raises questions about the boundaries of regulatory experimentation and business autonomy.

Finally, Renske van't Veer, Max Baumgart, and Saskia Lavrijssen argue that *core principles of good governance* (such as transparency, participation, accountability, efficiency, effectiveness and independence) offer a valuable foundation for developing responsive, context-sensitive sandboxes that meet both policy and innovation goals.

As digitalisation reshapes critical infrastructure, regulatory frameworks must evolve not only through experimental design but also through *institutional coordination* and *shared understanding*. Liebrich Hiemstra's analysis of how European authorities and national regulators navigate overlapping mandates reinforces the need for enhanced institutional coordination to enable regulatory reform in the face of digital transformation. Similarly, Shanya Ruhela argues that the human element or accountability remains essential in the era when regulators are increasingly deploying digital and AI tools to keep up with the demands of a digitalised society.

Wendy van der Valk additionally argues that regulations in the sectors of energy and finance cannot exclusively rely on top-down rules or models but must *adapt to modern organisational structures*. This calls for a fundamental rethinking and a subsequent overhaul of oversight mechanisms whereby we move away from hierarchical enforcement toward governance frameworks that accommodate networked and loosely connected actors, who may not be legally bound to one another through formal contracts.

Wendy van der Valk also emphasises that regulatory frameworks should go beyond imposing rules to actively create incentives for compliance and innovation. This requires integrating market-based instruments (such as subsidies and carbon pricing) with governance mechanisms (such as government-led mission strategies) to drive coordinated action. Moreover, policies should harmonise formal contracts with relational governance, ensuring that both legal frameworks and trust-based mechanisms contribute to compliance and operational efficiency in dyadic and network-based collaborations.

In this context, David Wodak and Tom AE Aben argue that regulatory challenges within critical infrastructures cannot be effectively addressed by individual managers or organisations operating in isolation. Instead, they advocate for *robust collaboration among organisations within the same sector and with governmental institutions*. This collaborative approach is a structural necessity for overhauling outdated regulatory models and crafting adaptive frameworks that meet the demands of digital transformation.

Wodak and Aben, through their case study, also assert the need for more *effective collaboration between managers and lawyers*. Accordingly, this collaboration must be grounded in recognition of the distinction between perceived and actual legal barriers, particularly in multi-stakeholder and inter-organisational settings. They demonstrate that even strong initial cooperation can be undermined by perceived legal risks, which can lead to communication breakdowns, a lack of trust and hesitation to commit to necessary actions. Addressing these concerns requires proactive engagement, legal clarity, and a shared understanding of the regulatory environment.

To cultivate more effective interdisciplinary collaboration, Wodak and Aben advocate for the *creation of safe spaces* where organisations can experiment, test regulatory assumptions, and launch pilot projects without jeopardising ongoing operations. Their argument reinforces the idea that regulatory innovation is not just a legal process but also a managerial and cultural process that needs to become established in an organisation's ethos. By building trust, fostering legal literacy and encouraging openness, organisations can better navigate regulatory complexity while driving innovation and resilience in critical infrastructure management.

Thus, by fostering cross-sectoral dialogue and regulatory experimentation, policymakers can develop more resilient and adaptive governance structures capable of responding to emerging challenges in both energy and finance.

3. The Road Ahead: Mapping Future Research Directions

As this edited volume has demonstrated, the impact of digitalisation on regulation in energy and finance presents not only a challenge but also an opportunity. If the first wave of digital transformation exposed regulatory shortcomings, the next must focus on designing frameworks that are future-proof, legally sound and responsive. The insights offered by the contributions in this edited volume highlight important questions that future research must address in order to achieve this goal.

Inge Graef and Din Buljević argue that the intricate nature of European data spaces encompasses multiple interests and is governed by a diverse set of regulatory bodies, which may pose a significant challenge in developing guidelines for regulatory sandboxes. They note that certain EU Member States are already ahead of the curve in managing cross-sectoral regulatory sandboxes, largely due to a comprehensive national strategy supporting regulatory experimentation across industries. An important question for future research is how regulatory sandboxes can be effectively designed and implemented across EU Member States to develop governance frameworks that align with European values in the rapidly evolving sectors.

Kanerva Sunila adds that while the EU legislation does promote the use of regulatory sandboxes, their transformative potential has yet to be realised in many EU Member States. She notes that regulatory sandboxes could bring a completely new approach to the promotion of digitalisation and other innovative solutions, particularly by fostering experimentation in sectors that have traditionally lacked such engagement. At the same time, Sunila underscores that EU Member States cannot unilaterally deviate from binding EU law unless they are explicitly empowered to do so. This limitation imposes a legal ceiling on the extent of sandbox experimentation, which serves as an important reminder that innovation must operate within clearly defined legal boundaries. Accordingly, a research and policy challenge that remains is to design regulatory sandboxes that maximise flexibility while complying with the constraints of EU legal frameworks.

Emanuel van Praag raises similar concerns by showing how the regulatory design of the Digital Euro and mandatory acceptance rules may restrict the freedom to conduct business under Article 16 of the Charter of Fundamental Rights of the EU. This tension between legal obligations and market autonomy presents a fertile ground for future research into how far regulators can and should go in enlisting private actors to achieve public ends. Shanya Ruhela's analysis of the FCA's use of digital and AI tools reiterates these concerns.

Shirley Kempeneer and Magdalena Brewczyńska further urge the regulators to carefully balance the benefits of digitalisation of finance with the need to protect privacy, data security and fairness for all stakeholders. They assert that the European-level initiatives like the EU's Digital Finance Strategy and the European Financial Data Space aim to enhance transparency, encourage competition and foster data-sharing while safeguarding fundamental rights. Transparency, too, emerges as a significant challenge across sectors. As Shanya Ruhela states, without transparency, it becomes difficult to justify regulatory action or defend it through due process. However, the extent to which these initiatives succeed in ensuring fairness remains uncertain.

In response to national fragmentation, several experts have proposed the creation of an EU-wide or cross-border regulatory sandbox. Such a framework could enhance flexibility by temporarily waiving or adapting specific EU-level rules, providing a safe and harmonised environment for experimentation. Shanya Ruhela notes that operationalising such frameworks is not only a question of legal design but also of organisational capacity. There exists a need to examine institutional incentives, resource disparities, and the public sector's capacity to compete for technical talent. This represents an important area for future research.

Furthermore, a significant governance challenge in energy and finance is the clarification of decision-making authority within collaborative networks. Without clearly defined roles, regulatory coordination falters, reinforcing power asymmetries and undermining policy effectiveness. To facilitate meaningful collaboration between public and private actors, regulations must provide structure while also enabling flexibility, thereby fostering innovation, preserving legal certainty and safeguarding public interests.

Finally, as Renske van't Veer, Max Baumgart, and Saskia Lavrijssen caution, despite numerous regulatory initiatives supporting regulatory sandboxes in theory, the legal foundation for applying such tools in practice, especially in emerging sectors, remains limited and unclear. This gap between regulatory ambition and the limits of regulatory and legal architecture points to the need for future research to address the structural barriers that hinder the effective implementation of experimental instruments. This concern is highly relevant for both energy and finance, where similar mismatches exist between innovative policy narratives and the underlying regulatory frameworks.

As we look ahead, the above considerations underscore the need for both creative solutions and a cautious approach. Legal experimentation must be built on a solid foundation of institutional scaffolding, not rhetorical ambition. Thus, future research must further explore how to reconcile flexibility with legal certainty, innovation with legitimacy and private-sector collaboration with public accountability.

4. Concluding Remarks

This edited volume has mapped the evolving limits of regulation in the digital era, offering a cross-sectoral examination of how energy and financial sectors are being transformed, and has studied how law and policy must evolve in parallel. By examining case studies, regulatory tools and governance approaches, it has highlighted the tensions, opportunities and innovations that define the current moment of institutional change set by technology and innovation.

This volume has outlined a set of evolving principles that underpin effective regulatory experimentation and adaptive governance in the context of digital transformation. Regulation must be adaptive, foster institutional coordination and shared understanding, and be grounded in core public values. Successful experimentation involves proportionality in design, tailoring regulatory sandboxes and pilots to the nature of innovations and associated risks, while also fostering flexibility in legal frameworks to allow for iterative, evidence-based policymaking. Collaboration emerges as a structural necessity, both across institutions and between public and private actors, with regulators increasingly adopting proactive, supervisory roles that blend formal oversight with informal engagement. Legal clarity, institutional foresight, and the strategic use of ambiguity further enable innovation without sacrificing legitimacy or consumer protection. Importantly, regulation shall no longer be viewed merely as a constraint but as an enabler of regulatory transformation and one that must balance private-sector efficiency with public values such as inclusion, sustainability, and resilience.

The various sections and case studies in this volume have presented a compelling argument that the future of regulation in energy and finance is neither purely legal nor solely technological. Instead, it is collaborative, adaptive and experimental. As the twin transitions of digitalisation and decarbonisation accelerate, the regulatory landscape must evolve accordingly, grounded in public values but responsive to market realities. This vision of forward-looking, mission-driven governance depends on a critical prerequisite: *clear legal direction*. Where the law fails to offer direction, fear and hesitation often fill the void. The challenge now is not just to predict this direction but to build it – deliberately, collectively and with purpose.

INDEX

www.ingramcontent.com/pod-product-compliance
Ingram Content Group UK Ltd.
Pitfield, Milton Keynes, MK11 3LW, UK
UKHW020239290926
15470UKWH00002B/633

9 781509 987481